P9-ANY-543

WAYWARD
REPORTER

WAYWARD REPORTER

the life of
A. J. Liebling

by Raymond Sokolov

Donald S. Ellis, Publisher, San Francisco

Creative Arts Book Company
1984

For Michael and Joseph

WAYWARD REPORTER: THE LIFE OF A. J. LIEBLING. Copyright © 1980 by Raymond
Sokolov. All rights reserved. Printed in the United States of America. No part of this
book may be used or reproduced in any manner whatsoever without written permission
except in the case of brief quotations embodied in critical articles and reviews. For
information contact: Donald S. Ellis, Creative Arts Book Company, 833 Bancroft Way,
Berkeley, California 94710.

This is the first paperback edition of the book published originally in hardcover by
Harper and Row, New York.

Library of Congress Catalog Card No. 83-45026
ISBN 0-916870-63-4

Contents

Acknowledgments

Biography can never be written without help. This one could not have been done at all without the trust, support and courage of Jean Stafford Liebling. She opened her home, her records, her memories and herself to me, treated me as a friend and, more importantly, as a colleague. Her fatal illness finally exacted its tragic toll just as I was completing the job she had so generously fostered. Selfishly, I regret in particular that her death kept her from reading this book in manuscript and telling me how to improve it.

Mrs. Liebling made many doors open for me. The most crucial one was that of Joseph Mitchell's office at *The New Yorker*. Mr. Mitchell and his wife, Therese, knew Joe Liebling better than anyone else, understood him profoundly, and were gracious enough to allow me access to their collection of his letters.

Susan Spectorsky sought me out in the early stages of the project and continued to offer help, information, documents and friendly encouragement right along.

Philip Hamburger lent me his collection of bound volumes of *The New Yorker* so that I could have convenient access to Liebling's uncollected articles and cheaply. My debt to him is concrete but in another sense unmeasurable.

My editor, Frances McCullough, suggested that I write this book. Her enthusiasm for it never wavered; her good taste saved me from a mawkish false start. Simon Michael Bessie and Amy Bonoff contributed valuable editorial help. My agent, Lynn Nesbit, provided steadying good advice throughout. My family gave so much so willingly for these four years that I can never properly thank them.

During that time, I have followed Liebling to Normandy and Nevada, to Far Rockaway and London, to *The New Yorker* and the *East Hampton Star*. Notebooks have piled up with the memories of Lieblings' colleagues and friends. I have been able to trace his moods and movements through letters and passport stamps, in a newsreel and on a tape of a lecture he gave at Vassar. The major record he left behind, however, was his work: millions of words.

With virtually any other important writer, the published work would contribute only secondarily to the composition of the man's "life." The biographer of Shakespeare or Hemingway or Faulkner can assume that his readers will already know at least the major texts and can easily locate the rest in bookstores and libraries. In Liebling's case, the books are either difficult to find or out of print. And it is a virtual certainty that no one will ever be able to locate everything Liebling published.

Almost nothing that Liebling wrote in the Providence *Evening Bulletin* and *Journal* between 1926 and 1930 carried a byline. By combining Liebling's later allusions to stories he worked on then with card references in the enormously valuable Rhode Island Index (and an associated index of the Providence papers) in the Providence Public Library, I have been able to find a small but crucial number of those articles.

Liebling worked briefly for the New York *World*, starting in the fall of 1930 and continuing until that great newspaper stopped publication early in 1931. Presumably all of those pieces were signed, and so I have been able to find them all. Unfortunately, this bibliographical certainty evaporates when we come to the *World-Telegram* period. The morgue for that paper, which employed Liebling from March of 1931 to May of 1935, was donated to the journalism school at the University of Missouri. Since this donation did not include funds for cataloguing, the morgue sits in an isolated, unelectrified building on a Missouri highway. Some future researcher may wish to hire a crew to move and burrow through those sadly abandoned file cabinets. But he will still have no assurance that somewhere in that mass of material he will find the byline file of A. J. Liebling. Barring that unlikely discovery, we must content ourselves with the more than three hundred signed articles that can be found by cranking through microfilms of the paper. Liebling claimed that during his four years at the *World-Telegram* he "wrote between seven hundred and fifty and one thousand features ... nearly all under my own byline." This claim does not stand up to a careful day-by-day reading of the relevant period of the *World-Telegram*. Perhaps Liebling underestimated the number of mandatorially unsigned "second or third stories" he wrote "on days when I had more than one in the paper." At any rate, it is fair to guess that several hundred articles have been lost, probably forever.

For most of his career at *The New Yorker*, from his breakthrough profile of Father Divine until his last, posthumous review, of Camus's *Notebooks*, Liebling's articles can all be easily found in the meticulous scrapbooks and files kept in the magazine's own library. With the gracious permission of William Shawn, editor of *The New Yorker*, I was privileged to work in that collection for several weeks in the fall of 1975. The postwar files also contain a complete record of authors of "Notes and Comment" (the first article in each "Talk of the Town" section), so that it has been possible to pinpoint a great many of those written by Liebling.

There remain a small but not insignificant number of articles from other magazines, notably book reviews in *Esquire* for every month from November 1946 to February 1948.

It has been possible, then, to construct a working bibliography for Liebling's *disjecta membra*. But since it is improbable in the extreme that any reader will approach this book with even a sketchy knowledge of these scattered treasures, or that anyone reading outside a major library will be able to refer to the full range of Liebling's work (insofar as that can be established), it has been essential for me to quote extensively from Liebling's published writing.

This is an opportunity as well as an obligation. It gives me the chance to revive the currency of Liebling's vigorous, funny, strong but uncollected writing. It would, moreover, have been foolish to attempt to portray the life of so prolific a writer, who spent so much of his time at the typewriter, without setting out many examples of his work within the overall narrative frame.

Liebling left another kind of legacy, a personal record in scattered documents and, most of all, in the memories of friends and colleagues. Many of them talked to me. Other people helped in other crucial ways. If there were not so many of them, I would explain in detail how each of the following gave me indispensable assistance:

Roger Angell, Michael Arlen, Emily Aronson, David Astor, Mortimer E. Bader, Richard A. Bader, Christina Barnes, Frederick Berlinger, Max Bird, Irene Borger, Gardner Botsford, Mary Breasted, James Oliver Brown, Margaret Charoux, Walter Clemons, Alexander Cockburn, William Cole, the Columbia University Graduate School of Journalism, the Columbia University Library, Ann Corio, the Cornell University Library, Ralph Crowley, Dartmouth College, Michael Davie, Far Rockaway High School, Pamela Fiori, Elsa First, Janet Flanner, Cynthia Fontayne, Robert Giroux, Michel Gordey, Eleanor Gould, Milton Greenstein, Charlotte Guedenet, Pierre Guedenet, Sheward Hagerty, Emily Hahn, Johanna Hecht, Eleanor Hempstead, Hendrick Hertzberg, Alger Hiss, Anthony Hiss, Edith Iglauer, Arthur Jacobs, Ruth Jacobs, William R. Johnson, Jack Kroll, Daniel Lang, Irene Le Cornec, Solomon Levine, the Library of Congress, Andy Logan, Herbert Lottman, J. Anthony Lukas, Harland Manchester, Ann Mandelbaum, Ada Jo Mann, Thomas O. Mann, Thomas Meehan, Ved Mehta, Yvonne Michel, Suzette Namin, Edwin Newhouse, the New York Public Library, the New Yorker Magazine Library, Joe Nichols, Helen Paniguian, Mary Paniguian, Mollie Panter-Downes, S. J. Perelman, Pat Perry, Richard Pollak, the Providence, R.I., Library, James Quitslund, Everett Rattray, James Reid, Jean Riboud, H. K. Rigg, Pat Riley, Ken Robbins, Maria Robbins, John Rockwell, Dorothy Rodgers, Waverley Root, Harold Rosenwald, Berton Roueché, Kay Roueché, Nora Sayre, Harriet Schwed, Peter Schwed, William Shawn, Eugene Jay Sheffer, the Hon. Charles Sifton, Claire Sifton, Elisabeth Sifton, Louis J. Soffer, Erica Spellman, Helen Stark, Saul Steinberg, Leo Stone, Arthur Stonehill, John Stonehill, Norma Stonehill, the Surrogate's Court of New York County, Alan Ternes, Ed Taylor, Allen Weinstein, Katharine S. White, Don Whitehead, the Widener Library of Harvard University, Roy Wilder, Jr., Joan Winterkorn, Henry Wittenberg, Burton Wolf, William Yankauer.

WAYWARD
REPORTER

"What Is a Liebling?"

Green and full of feisty ambitions, the editors of *More, The New York Journalism Review*, decided to celebrate their first year of publication with a great gathering of the working press in New York. They billed this meeting of American reporters as a counter-convention, invoking the already faded spirit of sixties protest and calling ironic attention to the traditional annual conclave of newspaper publishers that would take place during that same week in the spring of 1972. Casting about for a lustrous and suitably subversive name for their own meeting, the *More* editors chose to call it the Liebling Convention.

A. J. Liebling must have seemed like the perfect emblem. Already a legendary figure among journalists less than a decade after his death, Liebling had invented modern press criticism in his "Wayward Press" columns in *The New Yorker*. He was the pioneer and the epitome of the art *More* intended to practice. Beyond that, Liebling may well have been the greatest reporter of his time. Liebling buffs haunted secondhand bookstores hoping to find a copy of

1

one of his many out-of-print collections of articles. And so it was with authentic surprise that Richard Pollak and his staff at *More* opened their mail and discovered that the man they had picked as the first saint of American journalism was not a household god, not even a known name to many reporters around the country.

"What is a Liebling?" asked one letter.

For an answer to this unsettling question, *More* might have turned to Liebling's press columns, quoting judiciously to show him at his vigorous best attacking the press lords and their monopoly control of news and newsmen. They might, for instance, have cited his remarks published in May 1960, just after that year's American Newspaper Publishers' Association meeting:

> American cities with competing newspapers will soon be as rare as those with two telephone systems. I had occasion to regret this not long ago during a visit to New Orleans, where the Times-Picayune Company now owns the only morning and the only evening newspaper, having bought out the *Item*, sole channel of occasionally dissenting opinion. The resulting daily complacency is hard to take. The recent annual convention of the American Newspaper Publishers' Association brought the trend even more poignantly to mind. The convention reaches here at the same season as the Ringling Brothers and Barnum and Bailey Circus. (Circuses were hit by mergers even earlier than newspapers.) Like the Big Show, the convention always bears a certain resemblance to its predecessors. The New York publishers, through their editorial-page hirelings, welcome their country cousins, usually referred to as "the newspaper clan" or "the press family," and acclaim them as uniformly astute fellows, with their ears to the grass roots beneath every paved street from San Diego, California, to Bangor, Maine, and their fingers on the pulse of the nation. Reporters then go out and ask the fingermen what the pulse says, and the publishers predict a year of unexampled prosperity, accompanied by high costs that preclude a rise in wages. If a national election is coming up, they say that the Republicans will win, and after denouncing the current Administration (of no matter which party) for withholding information from the press they go off to a series of closed meetings and later dole out releases to reporters, who wait respectfully in the hall between the door and the men's room.

That excerpt captures Liebling's basic method, the flood of irony and metaphor, the incredible exuberance of a man with a flock of ramifying secondary thoughts pulled together into the service of his main point: the oppressive, self-serving power of publishers to manage their own image in their own papers with the enslaved help of their own reporters. "Freedom of the press," he said, "belongs to those who own one."

Which brings us to Liebling's wit: "Inconsiderate to the last," he wrote on March 28, 1953, "Josef Stalin, a man who never had to meet a deadline, had the bad taste to die in installments." Stalin's death caused obituary writers trouble, but it gave Liebling a fine opportunity to compare the various follies of the nation's newspapers as they dealt with the problem of Stalin's death:

> Within a week after Stalin's announced demise, the American public knew that he had died of natural causes or been murdered subtly, either on the date named by *Pravda* or several weeks earlier; that the people of Moscow had demonstrated grief but (a *Journal-American* scoop) the demonstration had been a carefully organized fake; that his death portended either a hardening or a softening of policy toward the West, which, in turn, would lessen or increase the chances of open war; and that his death would either precipitate an immediate struggle for power among the surviving leaders or impel them to stand together until they got things running smoothly. It was freely predicted that, in the event there was a struggle, Malenkov would destroy his associates or his associates would destroy him. The subject permitted a rare blend of invective and speculation—both Hearst papers, as I recall, ran cartoons of Stalin being rebuffed at the gates of Heaven, where Hearst has no correspondents—and I have seldom enjoyed a week of newspaper reading more.

Surely, a young reporter planning to leave Dubuque or Detroit to forgather with his colleagues under the benign auspices of Joe Liebling ought to have known that his portly hero had landed at Normandy on D-day, under fire. Shortly afterward, Liebling described how his landing craft offloaded its casualties in wire baskets, "like Indian papooses" onto a transport ship in the Channel called the *Dorothea Dix*. Liebling, who had covered the entire war in Europe since the winter of 1939, and covered it closely, cabling *The New Yorker* diamond-hard dispatches full of the small, revealing, all-important details that the wire services and other battle reporters left out, on this supreme occasion also kept his eye on what was in front of him:

> A couple of Negroes on the upper deck of the *Dix* dropped a line which our men made fast to the top of one basket after another. Then the man would be jerked up in the air by the Negroes as if he were going to heaven. Now that we carried no passengers and were lighter, the sea seemed rough. We bobbed under the towering transport and the wounded men swung wildly on the end of the line, a few times almost striking against the ship. A Coastguardsman reached up for the bottom of one basket so that he could steady it on its way up. At least a quart of blood ran down on him, covering his tin hat, his upturned face, and his blue overalls. He stood motionless for an instant, as if he didn't know what had happened, seeing the world through a film of red, because he wore eyeglasses and blood had covered the lenses.

Liebling did not explain until many years later, when this passage was reprinted, that the "Coastguardsman" had been a cover name for himself. "It seemed more reserved at the time to do it this way," he wrote in a footnote. "A news story in which the writer said *he* was bathed in blood would have made me distrust it, if I had been a reader."

Such reticence over the first person did not normally inhibit Liebling. Indeed, personal reactions and anecdotes cropped up throughout his work at *The New Yorker*, even before the war. The Coastguardsman pose is an example of artistic judgment, not an instance of sanctimonious journalistic high principle. Later in 1944, just after the liberation of Paris from the Nazi occupation, he cabled home jubilantly:

> For the first time in my life and probably the last, I have lived for a week in a great city where everybody is happy. Moreover, since this city is Paris, everybody makes this euphoria manifest. To drive along the boulevards in a jeep is like walking into some as yet unmade

René Clair film, with hundreds of bicyclists coming toward you in a stream that divides before the jeep just when you feel sure that a collision is imminent. Among the bicyclists there are pretty girls, their hair dressed high on their heads in what seems to be the current mode here. These girls show legs of a length and slimness and firmness and brownness never associated with French womanhood.

This Liebling in a jeep, happily reporting on the victory celebration in his favorite foreign city, is the same Liebling who would later write with equal zest of his Gargantuan eating experiences in France in *Between Meals*, which won him an enthusiastic special readership among gastronomes. Liebling speculated that Proust would have written an even better book than *Remembrance of Things Past* if he had had a "heartier appetite" and had been frequently in the mood for the sort of repast that, by implication, often passed down Liebling's epic gullet: "a dozen Gardiners Island oysters, a bowl of clam chowder, a peck of steamers, some bay scallops, three sautéed soft-shelled crabs, a few ears of fresh-picked corn, a thin swordfish steak of generous area, a pair of lobsters, and a Long Island duck."

Although Liebling often wrote with absorption and technical verve on culinary matters, he was never a pure food writer any more than he had ever been a conventional battle correspondent. His mind ranged outward from food to take in France and the French culture he knew from broad experience and from study. *Between Meals* is subtitled "An Appetite for Paris." The same appetite had come over him in 1944 as he delighted at the sight of those leggy cyclists from his jeep. And this physical lust for the street life of a great city was the same passion that infused his "lowlife" reportage for the New York *World-Telegram* and for *The New Yorker*. When he specified, in 1944, that for the first time in his life he was in "a great city" where everybody was happy, the astute reader of earlier Liebling pieces knew that the apparently inconspicuous phrase mattered. It came from the pen of the same Liebling who wrote, consciously, in the tradition of great urban observers, of Dickens and of Stephen Crane. The man in the jeep crawling through Paris was also the man who had chronicled Lower East Side pinochle games and who immortalized sleazy Broadway promoters in the glossy pages of *The New Yorker*. Did many people remember at the Liebling Convention that the foe of Hearst and Pegler had frequently descended, without a wince or backward glance, into the lower depths of Gotham to visit Izzy Yereshevsky's I. & Y. Cigar Store, an all-night emporium that supplied smokes to nightclubs and refuge to a special clientele?

> Most of [Izzy's] evening guests—their purchases are so infrequent that it would be misleading to call them customers—wear white felt hats and overcoats of a style known to them as English Drape. Short men peer up from between the wide-flung shoulders of these coats as if they had been lowered into the garments on a rope and were now trying to climb out. To Izzy his guests are the people of Broadway. They are the big talkers and, on rare occasions when they have cash in their pockets, the big spenders. In truth, the boys in the white felt hats and the English Drapes do not love money for its own sake. Each fosters a little personal legend of lost affluence; fifty grand dropped on the races in one day, twenty grand blown on a doll in a brief sojourn at Atlantic City. Never to have been in the chips marks one as a punk or a smalltimer. It precludes conversation in big figures. Continuous prosperity to the boys, however, hints of avarice and is discreditable.

Liebling loved these spirited loungers, these con men. He loved their rant, and their raffish style. Years later, he devoted an entire book, a kind of nonfiction novel, to that pluperfect Broadway type, Colonel John R. Stingo, the sportswriter-deadbeat, alias James A. Macdonald. And he would find a southern version of Stingo's Broadway madness in Louisiana, in the lunacy of Earl Long. As Liebling saw it, Broadway stretched its white way down to the Mississippi delta and led him to electoral politics. His world was a seamy, antic whole. The same men in white felt hats whom he met at the I. & Y. turned up at the track and at ringside, where Colonel Stingo held court and where Joe Liebling steeped himself in those prototypically urban sports, racing and boxing. Eventually he turned his interest in the fights to account and became the most important boxing writer in a century. Not since Pierce Egan, a pre-

Dickensian chronicler of the London fight scene, had anyone written so well about the "Sweet Science." Egan, who was Liebling's model sports journalist, wrote in a richly colloquial style and anticipated *The Pickwick Papers* with his sketches of racy, gin-besotted London life in the early nineteenth century. Liebling's approach to the world of boxing was similar to Egan's but even more direct and visceral. Liebling had boxed himself, and in his introduction to his collected boxing pieces he asserts that he traced his "rapport with the historic past" through the "laying on of hands":

> Jack O'Brien, the *Arbiter Elegantiarum Philadelphiae* . . . hit me, for pedagogical example, and he had been hit by the great Bob Fitzsimmons, from whom he won the light-heavyweight title in 1906. Jack had a scar to show for it. Fitzsimmons had been hit by Corbett, Corbett by John L. Sullivan, he by Paddy Ryan, with the bare knuckles, and Ryan by Joe Goss, his predecessor, who as a young man had felt the fist of the great Jem Mace. It is a great thrill to feel that all that separates you from the early Victorians is a series of punches on the nose. I wonder if Professor Toynbee is as intimately attuned to his sources. The Sweet Science is joined onto the past like a man's arm to his shoulder.

Liebling had sharpened his eye for violence during a hundred afternoons at Stillman's gymnasium, the "University of Eighth Avenue," where fighters trained. This eye was the same one that had looked through a lens of blood at Normandy and remembered the sight with a clinician's composure. And he applied this skill with memorable effect to dozens of prize fights. Liebling rose to an especial eloquence, for instance, in recounting the events of the third round of a bout between the venerable Archie Moore and the young, bull-necked Rocky Marciano:

> Both came out for the third very gay, as Egan would have said. Marciano had been hit and cut, so he felt acclimated, and Moore was so mad at himself for not having knocked Marciano out that he almost displayed animosity toward him. He may have thought that perhaps he had not hit Marciano *just* right; the true artist is always prone to self-reproach. He would try again. A minute's attention from his squires had raised his spirits and slaked down his hair. At this point,

Marciano set about him. He waddled in, hurling his fists with a sublime disregard of probabilities, content to hit an elbow, a biceps, a
shoulder, the top of a head—the last supposed to be the least profit-
able target in the business, since, as every beginner learns, "the head
is the hardest part of the human body," and a boxer will only break
his hands on it. Many boxers make the systematic presentation of the
cranium part of their defensive scheme. The crowd, basically anti-in-
tellectual, screamed encouragement. There was Moore, riding
punches, picking them off, slipping them, rolling with them, ducking
them, coming gracefully out of his defensive efforts with sharp, pat-
terned blows—and just about holding this parody even on points. His
face, emerging at instants from under the storm of arms—his own
and Rocky's—looked like that of a swimming walrus. When the
round ended, I could see that he was thinking deeply. Marciano
came back to his corner at a kind of suppressed dogtrot. He didn't
have a worry in the world.

In Moore, Liebling saw an intellectual and an artist at work in a
field mostly populated with crude Marcianos. In Moore, he also detected a side of himself, for Liebling, too, was a shrewd walrus
swimming in subtle patterns few people perceived. He was a writer
of major skills and a "true artist" in the same sense as Moore. Liebling possessed a first-rate literary sensibility and worked intricately
in genres the world dismisses as second rate.

Liebling was as much an artist in prose as any novelist of his day.
But he had committed himself to what writers at *The New Yorker*
like to call "the literature of fact." Liebling, proud and never prone
to excuse himself, insisted that fiction was a lesser form. When people would ask him why he didn't write a novel, he retorted: "What?
And make things up?"

This was not a candid reply. He had indeed tried his hand at fiction, with great zeal and modest results, early in life, but he had
found himself as a writer only in later years, through reporting.
Liebling the man is the common factor that connects the press criticism and the pugilistic chronicles and the book reviews and the
frontline dispatches from France. Liebling's sly and raffish personality, his easy learning, his flaunted sensuality and worldliness, his bold
metaphors, give order to an outwardly disuniform body of writing.

At the Rome Olympics, at Madison Square Garden, on board a tanker crossing the Atlantic during World War II, covering British elections or damning Chicago with loud brays of New York chauvinism, Joe Liebling was always there on the page, a vivid presence. He insisted on the personal note, on the importance and relevance of his, the reporter's, reactions to the event he was covering.

This stance is now a commonplace. A whole generation of reporters active since Liebling's death have written themselves into their pieces and claimed they were inventing something new, something they called the New Journalism. Tom Wolfe, the leading evangelist for this group, thought of Liebling as his master. Liebling, however, was not the father of a movement. Or at least, he would have bridled at the tag, even though he hated the anonymous, depersonalized, "objective" brand of news reporting so dear to newspaper publishers: he is the leading example in our time of a journalist who insisted on the autobiographical note. And a great deal of what we know about him now he salted subversively into articles he had officially produced as a reporter of news events.

Yet Liebling did not think he was blazing a trail. He saw himself in a long tradition of writer-journalists and writer-essayists, a tradition that went back to Defoe and even further to that sublimely autobiographical poet-journalist Villon. With Liebling, there were always forebears, models who transcended simple categories of fact and fiction, prose and poetry. He saw a logic and a format—a category cut to his own personal requirements—in the group that included Hazlitt and Egan, Dickens and Stendhal, William Cobbett and George Borrow, the British literary adventurer, Bible salesman and honorary Gypsy.

Liebling wrote in this tradition for almost forty years, producing a flood tide of articles that number in the hundreds. His fertility, like everything else about him, came out of an earlier, heroic time. The sheer quantity of his work (even without counting the thousand or so lost, unsigned newspaper articles) recalls the graphomania of Defoe and Hazlitt and Cobbett. Liebling's boast was that he could "write better than anyone who could write faster, and faster than anyone who could write better."

Liebling posed and faked and feinted, but he kept quiet about his

tricks. With him, the occasional flash of bragging or self-advertise-
ment that glints in a "Wayward Press" piece or a "Letter from
France" is a revealing lapse but only that. He would never have unmasked his full intent, as Mailer did when he announced in *Esquire*
that he would write a complete novel, *An American Dream*, on
deadline, as Dickens had written *Pickwick*. Liebling habitually took
on the past masters of prose, mimicked them and went them one
better, but he rarely let on. He was covert and deep; his stunts were
unproclaimed. His personal life was almost completely private, until
his last few years. And even then, as a campus lecturer and occasional television pundit, he never came close to the blatant show-
boating of Mailer and Hemingway.

Liebling's shyness in public and slyness in print may have helped
to keep him from the large public that sanctified Mailer and Hemingway in their lifetimes. But there was also a second obstacle in
Liebling's way. He wrote in short takes. He was, until the end, a
nominal journalist, a *New Yorker* writer. And almost all his books
were, at bottom, collections of *New Yorker* pieces stitched together
into volumes that, however unified in spirit and conception, never
found the big market Liebling deserved.

Why this should be is a question for metaphysicians of the *Zeit-
geist*, those "boys at the literary quarterlies" whom Liebling loved
to laugh at. But even lacking a theory—and it is a contemporary tic
to be shy about large, all-encompassing explanations—we cannot
help noticing that we live in a time of confused genres, where energies focus at the no man's land between fact and fiction.

We live, in short, in Liebling country.

It is a puzzling place, like Liebling himself. Indeed, anyone who
knew or read him seriously could understand that it was not entirely
naïve to ask "What is a Liebling?" On numerous occasions, for example, Saul Steinberg, Liebling's *New Yorker* colleague, good
friend and summer neighbor in East Hampton, would sit with Joe
and ponder the question with him. Steinberg says:

> He was fascinated with con men. It was like Thomas Mann's seeing
> artists as crooks and crooks as artists. That, combined with the old
> New York tradition of liking someone who gets away with short cuts.

Liebling showed us that newspapers were offering us smoke, that they were in the business of fraud. As a historian, he was interested in the relation of facts to fantasy, for example, in war propaganda. His connection with horses was part of a search for what he called "sporting man" who was part crook. He felt the same interest in other people of dubious ethics: prostitutes, telephone booth Indians. His involvement with the press was the same thing. He would have loved being an underworld figure. You could see it when he went to North Africa as a correspondent in a dubious time. He had a rare quality for an American. He understood the mentality of the native, which was the same as the mentality of the crook. Essentially, he practiced the trade of the novelist as Mann saw it. Just as the con man's stock in trade is a thorough knowledge of man's lowest impulses, so is the novelist's. The novelist must be able to put himself in the greatest number of shoes. Liebling finally became his own sort of hero. Even his love of food and wine was part of the world he admired, and was slightly sinful and forbidden for a Jewish American man. He had a whole system of such masks, as bon vivant, journalist, man of the world. He was out of an eighteenth-century world of elegance based on artificiality, and he had prepared a sort of personality for himself.

It was crucial to this complex pose, says Steinberg, that Liebling should have hidden his novelist's sensibility inside the confining and less "artistic" or "elegant" role of the reporter:

> He was like a ballerina who chooses to walk or a VIP who visits a building site wearing a hard hat.

Liebling's con game was a tease that played with the two great mysteries that surround all writing: what makes it art (and not simply craft) and who is the writer (how does the artist infuse himself into his work)? Liebling's conceit—his con man's self-dare—was to play this classic game at the margins of literature. By slumming in journalism, he could commit art on the q.t., sneak up on the reader, who only expected truth, but suddenly found he was getting beauty into the bargain. Journalism also gave Liebling an ideal disguise. The reporter's supposed anonymity was his beard, which he would don and doff as it pleased him, and as it suited the unfolding drama of his work. "Now you see me, now you don't" is the unwritten refrain close readers will detect between the lines of Liebling's literary shell game.

The difference between Liebling and a real con man is that Liebling wants to be found out. He wants to have it both ways: to fool the reader into believing, first, that his work is merely journalism, but then to let him into the secret that it is also something more, and that he, Liebling, is someone much more skillful and interesting than he appeared at first.

His subjects, too, involved him in a kind of slumming with themes and people too humble for official literature. Taken together, Liebling's pugs and lowlifes and dogfaces amount to a metaphor of his enterprise. He stooped to conquer. This condescension was itself a gambit, a ploy which implied that he had begun from an elevation sufficiently high to necessitate stooping. This bending down of Liebling's to his material was, however, not snobbish. It was a trick of perspective that did not diminish Liebling's subjects but did serve to enlarge and exalt Liebling. This Liebling, who was an artist of universal sympathies, so confident of his powers that he could work unashamedly with mud and be sure he would come away clean, this master of cosmopolitan prose was the last person you would think had been a clumsy prodigy from a mundane suburb or a scapegrace tainted with petty, willful failure. But that was how he started out.

one

Back Where He Came From

People I know in New York are incessantly on the point of going back to where they came from to write a book, or of staying on and writing a book about back where they came from. Back where they came from, I gather, is the American scene (New York, of course, just isn't America). It is all pretty hard on me because I have no place to go back to. I was born in an apartment house at Ninety-third Street and Lexington Avenue, about three miles from where I now live. Friends often tell me of their excitement when the train on which they are riding passes from Indiana into Illinois, or back again. I am ashamed to admit that when the Jerome Avenue express rolls into Eighty-sixth Street station I have absolutely no reaction.

—"APOLOGY FOR BREATHING," 1939

Abbott Joseph Liebling was born into comfortable circumstances on the Upper East Side of Manhattan on October 18, 1904. His parents' red-brick building, with its arched stone doorway topped by a wrought-iron balcony, was not chic, but it was solid and respectable.

13

It was also definitely a step up in the world for Liebling's father. Joseph Liebling had arrived in New York without a penny in the 1880s, seven years old, a Jewish immigrant from Austria. He had gone to work as a furrier's apprentice on the Lower East Side at ten, had risen rapidly, started his own wholesale fur business, married Anna Slone, a Jewish woman of some means and education from San Francisco, and had moved uptown with her shortly before the birth of their first and only son.

The Lieblings had German servants to do the housework and look after Abbott. Joseph and Anna subscribed to the fashionable Monday night series at the Metropolitan Opera. And they made frequent trips to Europe, with Abbott in tow as he grew older. The Liebling family's life was a model of serene, pre–World War I prosperity. Certainly little Abbott's childhood did not expose him to much of those other "worlds" that he would one day enumerate in a list of the microcosms that made up *his* New York: the worlds of "the weight-lifters, yodelers, tugboat captains and sideshow barkers, of the book-dutchers, sparring partners, song pluggers, sporting girls and religious painters, of the dealers in rhesus monkeys and the bishops of churches that they establish themselves under the religious corporations law."

As a boy, Abbott saw none of these colorful worlds, but he knew that his own bourgeois home did not represent the only way of life in New York City. He knew this because his father had told him about his own youth downtown, when "the carters left their wagons in the streets of nights and small boys would roll the wains away and burn them on election day, and of how he . . . boxed with the other furriers' apprentices using beaver muffs for mitts."

Anna Liebling, a pretty, pleasant soul, added gentility to the newly rich family. Her son was loyal and affectionate to her all her life, but it was his father who chiefly molded Abbott and left him with an image of old-fashioned manhood he would partly emulate and partly despise as long as he lived.

The father he loved "spoke New Yorkese perfectly" with its "neo-Corkonian" *dises* and *dats*. He had lived "the gay life of London and Paris and Leipzig in the late nineties when he was a bachelor buyer, although, he always protested, he had finished with that sort of thing when he got married. And early he introduced me to those worlds into which one may escape temporarily for the payment of a fee, the race course and the ball park."

That father was a sport and tough bird, who, as president of a furriers' association, hired the notorious gangster Monk Eastman to break up a mass meeting of striking workers. Abbott took perverse delight in talking about the Eastman caper, shocking liberal classmates at Dartmouth with it. He also liked the urban con man lurking behind his father's dignified exterior, the fast-footed fellow who used the good offices of an anti-vice crusader, the Reverend Charles Parkhurst, to help him promote a real estate venture on West Twenty-sixth Street. "Pop" Liebling wanted to put up three eleven-story loft buildings on a prostitute-ridden block between Sixth and Seventh avenues, where he predicted the fur industry would move as it migrated uptown. First "Pop" had to get the girls to move out of the neighborhood. He "made a substantial gift to Dr. Parkhurst's society, enclosing with his check a letter that called attention to the sinful conditions on West Twenty-sixth Street. Dr. Parkhurst raised hell with the police, who made the girls move on to another block, and then Father put up his buildings."

That happened around 1910. Joseph Liebling settled respectably into new offices in one of his own buildings. He lunched regularly at the posh Café Martin on nearby Madison Square. He was a success, and he could afford the luxury of expensive lunches for himself and occasionally for his precocious son, who doted on the yellow French vanilla at Martin's, ice cream with broken bits of real vanilla bean mixed in.

Joseph Liebling had risen a long way indeed by 1910. Three years earlier, in the fall of 1907, he had moved Anna and Abbott, the fräulein and a maid, to the spanking new Lassano Court at 307 West 79th Street. These elegant quarters on the seventh floor ran to nine rooms and two baths. There was an everyday sitting room behind green plush portieres, a formal parlor in lighter green for company and a dining room with a burnt-oak table over which hung a Tiffany dome, also green, with "a dependent skirt of beads."

Once the Lieblings had settled into this verdant, proper apartment, they consolidated their middle-class solidity still further with a second child. Norma Liebling came into the world at roughly the same time that her father was hatching his loft scheme on Twenty-sixth Street. Her arrival at this heady moment gave "Pop" the occasion for his only known literary invention. "Father," recalled Joe Liebling near the end of his life, "composing a corporate name for one of his buildings . . . had taken the first two letters, Ab, of my name and hitched on all those of my sister's, Norma. The result, the Abnorma Real Estate Corporation, suggested that we were both psychopaths."

While "Pop" Liebling sought his fortune downtown each morning, Abbott sought his around the corner and two blocks up the street, at P.S. 9. "My route," he later wrote, "lay up the Seventy-ninth Street hill as far as West End Avenue—the slope to the river is sharp here, and the wind in March howled through the draw between the solid rows of apartment houses. . . . The wind stung my face and made my eyes water, and sometimes made me clutch at area railings to keep my balance."

Having weathered this heroic passage, he would come to a small yellow-brick building "faced with white stone in the faintly Germanic style popular in New York during the eighteen-nineties." The upper floors housed a girls' high school. Downstairs, younger children studied in elementary classrooms segregated by sex. The teachers, at least all Liebling's teachers in the three years he went to the school, were female and Irish-American: the Misses Flynn, Costigan, Collins and McCabe. The vice-principal who ran the elementary school was a Miss Duffy. "What they taught me," he wrote, "was to read and write and do simple sums in my head—'mental arithmetic,' this was called. Once the reading came easy, the Misses lost control of my mind."

One of these Irish schoolmarms did foster Abbott Liebling's self-guided intellectual development, inadvertently, no doubt, when she discovered he couldn't read the letters on the blackboard. He was near-sighted. "As a pre-literate," he had "liked to fight, but now," he reminisced, "before I started to fight another boy in Riverside Park I would put my glasses on a bench. Then I would forget which bench, and not be able to see them. Losing the glasses caused such *histoires* at home that I fell into sedentary ways. As I turned intellectual, though, I retrogressed socially, and by my third year I stood barely in the middle of my class in fighting."

Norma Liebling Stonehill still remembers the *"histoires"* over lost glasses. "I used to climb around the rocks in the park with one of those awful fräuleins, looking for them. We were always protecting him." But their solicitude seems to have operated primarily after the fact, when the damage was done. Fräulein Marthe, for example, let the boy wander off in the park one day. "A goose grabbed him by the neck and shook him," Norma Stonehill recalls. "Mother was furious."

With his fistic career curtailed, Abbott began to read widely and energetically. By the age of eight, his sister says, he could recite the names of all Napoleon's marshals. And he browsed among the adventure books—novels by Henty and the works of the African explorer Paul Du Chaillu (whose name he then pronounced "Doo-shaloo")—on the shelves of the nearby St. Agnes branch of the New York Public Library, at Eighty-first Street and Amsterdam Avenue.

Generally precocious, Abbott was a model student at P.S. 9. He received virtually all *A*'s and his permanent record from P.S. 9 also shows that Abbott was a punctual student, late only once in all his time at the school. When the family moved to Far Rockaway, Queens, in the summer of 1913, Abbott entered the second semester of fourth grade, one term ahead of his age-group peers, because he had been double promoted going into third grade the previous year.

He was, then, a bright young lad, like many bright young lads, but Abbott's intellectual formation in those days of his early youth included two important influences peculiar to him. They were influences that opened him to wide areas of life, areas that even schoolboy prodigies do not normally come to know until they are older. And they were influences that pressed upon him ever after and pointed him in crucial directions. He went to Paris and he discovered newspapers.

Fortunately, the adult Joe Liebling wrote in some detail about both these watersheds in young Abbott's boyhood. Through the filter of the mature writer's nostalgia we see greedy Abbott in pre–World War I Paris, witnessing the "heroic age" of the giant appetites of French epicures and falling in love for life with France. We also see the future press critic "meeting the press," at a time when New Yorkers could choose luxuriously among seven evening newspapers to read on the way home from work. Both the French meals and the New York press, as Liebling portrayed them, were paradigms of abundance. He showed himself catching one quick taste of a way of life whose richness and variety he did not know then would vanish and haunt him forever after.

His first memories were of a European tour in the summer of 1907. Fräulein Marthe dragged him "at unforgettable speed" through "a mile of streets" in Wiesbaden to see "a tall man in a white uniform." That was the Kaiser. In Nuremberg, later in the trip, they glimpsed the Iron Maiden, "a hinged hollow figure with spikes," into which, the guide told three-year-old Abbott, prisoners were put "and then squashed and blinded simultaneously."

The Lieblings went all over Europe on those grand tours, but it was Paris that stood out as the "chocolate filling" between layers of sponge. Abbott was not happy during the four weeks the family spent in the summer of 1911 at a spa in Marienbad while Mother took off weight. This was "Europe proper, or *odiosa*, a place where the inhabitants spoke German, as did my oppressors, the Fräuleins." On the way home, they stopped in Paris. "The language," he wrote, "sounded better, although I couldn't understand what people said in it. We lived at the Hotel Regina, where the Place des Pyramides debouches into the Rue de Rivoli, and when we went out on foot we stayed under the colonnade because of the heat. We seldom got beyond the Place de la Concorde, because my sister, who in later years became as nimble as a roebuck, could not then walk worth a damn."

Joseph and Anna Liebling would abandon Abbott and Norma to the fräulein and go off in a horse-drawn carriage or a motorized taxi to dine "*en ville*," while Abbott, Norma and nurse ate in the room, ate "some uninspiring dish like cold cuts or an omelet." After much nagging, they obtained permission for an expedition to "Rumpelmayer's *confiserie* under the colonnade, near the Hotel Continental, for what we had seen advertised on a window card as an American ice cream soda."

They went, but even this treat was a disappointment. The soda did not match those obtainable on the West Side of New York. Already the gastronome, Liebling concluded that Rumpelmayer's had no genuine soda pump and used Perrier instead. "Boys," he recalled, "liked their sodas very gassy then, with a sharp, metallic bite that reminded me of the smell of a bicycle-repair shop." At any rate, he finished the concoction, and then watched tension build as Fräulein discovered she didn't have enough French money to pay the bill. Eventually the nurse and the management "reached a *Konkordat*." Fräulein would go back to the hotel to change money, taking Norma, "who was already howling," and leaving Abbott as "collateral." When she returned, the boy blackmailed her into an éclair.

What else did the young Liebling remember of the city he would later love so well? A statue of a cuirassier on horseback, the *"vespasiennes* where no Fräulein could pursue me," two toys—"a chef *legumier* who hacked away at a carrot with a big knife," a fire engine that pumped real water through its hose—and Napoleon's tomb, "where the gold light, the marble, and the massed battle flags made an image of Napoleonic glory that has always helped me understand the side of Stendhal that is least rational."

The Lieblings returned to New York on the *Kaiserin Augusta Victoria*. And shortly thereafter, in mid September, the future press critic and boxing annalist launched himself, modestly, by reading a story in the *Evening Mail* about a fighter known as Carl Morris, the Sapulpa (Oklahoma) Giant. This was, at least, the first thing Liebling, as an adult, remembered reading as a child. Typically, he remembered the story in impressive detail twenty-five years later. He also remembered that the *Evening Mail* carried Rube Goldberg's cartoons and that he had read the paper surreptitiously in bed, while his parents thought he was asleep. He had read other things, of course, but this article about the Sapulpa Giant was the first bout with literature he remembered, because it was crucial. It led on to a lifetime of similar, addictive scanning of newspapers, but the experience was more than a debut. It combined many elements that would attract Liebling to newspapers, sports and kindred reading projects all his life.

Abbott read newspapers with the abandon that most young sensualists reserve for food or the other conventional pleasures of the flesh. He recalled: "Their smell and texture had the same sensual immediacy for me as the taste of the cookies I ate while reading them. . . . For all that I loved them. I would spread them on the floor and lie down on my belly on them, or take them to bed with me, or into the bathroom."

This private debauch turned completely clandestine when the boy's appetite for comics and pop reporting led him to that paragon of Hearstian papers, the New York *Journal*. He had to "sneak out" and buy it, and then read it "surreptitiously." "My mother," he explained, "who had grown up in San Francisco, said it was a yellow sheet and would corrupt me." Despite this counsel, or perhaps in part because of it, Abbott came to prefer the *Journal* to all the other New York papers of the day, especially the *Times*, which he found dull and associated with his father, who "would monopolize" it "at breakfast and then carry it off to read on the subway on his way to the fur district."

"It is impossible for me to estimate," Liebling wrote in the auto-biographical sketch at the beginning of *The Wayward Pressman* in 1947, "how many of my early impressions of the world, correct and the opposite, came to me through newspapers. Homicide, adultery, no-hit pitching, and Balkanism were concepts that, left to my own devices, I would have encountered much later in life. Reading about Verdun, I formed francophile attitudes that were to become automatic by 1939. Seeing newspaper pictures of Irene Castle, I formed convictions about feminine good looks that were not to be shaken by subsequent changes in fashion. (My father, whose tastes had been fixed in the early Lillian Russell era, could never understand my views.)"

Reading these memories closely, we can hardly avoid noticing that they tell us much more about the young Liebling than the simple fact that he read many newspapers as a boy with extraordinary gusto. He appears to have a personality built explicitly around appetites; he conceived (or at least the mature Liebling conceived him as conceiving) the world synesthetically as a stew of information to be consumed. In an almost literal way, he devoured life through newspapers. And when he wasn't eating the news (or life; in context they coalesce), he took it to bed.

This panoramic appetite would stay with him to the end. It

prompted him to embrace all manner of subjects as a writer, gave him a special lust for the humble and unwashed, and helped him to see connections between the most diverse corners of life. It produced his later, ostentatiously metaphorical style, that orgy of unexpected images pulled into the same king-size sentence from Tunisian philosophy, the pugilistic academy of Eighth Avenue and the trenches at Fécamp.

One element behind it all, as he obliquely let us know, was a disagreement with his parents about values and standards. It was an amiable dispute, so far as we can tell. His overt relations with his mother and father always remained cordial and affectionate. Norma Liebling Stonehill dismisses altogether the possibility that her brother might have rebelled against the family. Yet we see him, from the very first, rejecting without second thoughts his mother's decorous, middle-class outlook. He went ahead to read the *Journal* behind her back.

Toward his father Liebling's feelings were more complex. The disagreement about women is a sign of his ambivalence. The matter of feminine style and Lillian Russell comes up again, more fully developed, in *Between Meals*. There Liebling speaks of the actress's ample figure, compares her variously to a "butterscotch sundae," "a tulip of beer with a high white collar" and San Simeon. She was plump, cinched her waist with corsets and wore big, feathered hats. She "embodied a style" and Liebling's mother imitated it. This was, of course, the style Liebling's father had opted for and admired. The son did not so much dislike it—he granted his father the right to the taste of his generation—as lament the fact that he himself had been born too late even to consider such an inclination. In 1911, "Irene Castle lurked just around the corner of history, light of foot, long-legged and sparse, and by the early twenties, when I began to look purposefully at females, I would not find a Russellinear woman anywhere."

Joe Liebling did, in fact, marry three thin women, all non-Jewish, none of them proper women and housewives after his mother's image. The disagreement about feminine style went deeper, then, than a generational change of mind about poundage. Still, the son admired the father, because he detected in him an unaffected coarseness which the furrier may be said to have buried when he married up to the higher, genteel social level of Anna Slone. Norma Stonehill recalls: "Abbott seemed to feel my mother and I were kind of sham. Father was real, down-to-earth."

Anna Slone Liebling had indeed grown up in politer circumstances than her husband. Her father was evidently prosperous and self-made. As Joe Liebling put it: "Her father had made *his* money—from scratch— . . . and had passed her to Father, like a beanbag, before he lost it."

Anna Liebling brought not only a touch of class to her marriage, but also an aura of superior education. Her husband was a grade-school dropout. She had "been a high-school valedictorian and had then attended extension courses at Berkeley," her son wrote. "She had had timid ambitions—which she had never got up the courage to exploit—to be a writer or an actress, and she attended the lectures, chiefly cultural, of the Women's League for Political Education every Wednesday afternoon, returning with full notebooks and enthusiastic reports on speakers like Rabindranath Tagore and Alfred Noyes and Nicholas Vachel Lindsay. 'Go down to Kew in lilactime,' she would spout when she came home from a Noyes lecture, even before she took her hat off, and 'in lilac-time, in lilac-time,' as she took out the hatpins. She would give me the whole poem, if I didn't dodge off."

There they were, then, a happy family on the eve of the First World War, blessed with a comfortable income and the grand style of life that comfortable incomes bought in those days. Their boy was reading whatever came his way, which seems to have pleased both parents, the mother with her suppressed desire for a creative career and the father with his residual Jewish veneration for scholarship and his dropout's awe of his own boy's sprint through school.

For his part, Abbott had already begun, amid such gentle, bourgeois promptings, to develop the subversive tastes and habits that would shape his adult life: his hate for the fräuleins, those emblems of the bourgeois household, his love of common, gutsy trash, the *Journal* and Henty, his disdain for his father's chosen life "among middle-class enterprisers with horizons slimmer than a gnat's waist," and his passion for the scheming, ranting, bickering, "real" street life his father had left downtown. These traits deepened as he grew up in the new family home outside Manhattan, in a seagirt new suburban town on the south shore of Long Island: Far Rockaway.

two

Oysters and Dolphins

"The years from 1911 to 1924 were plain sponge," Liebling wrote, looking back on his adolescence and early manhood. When the Lieblings moved to Far Rockaway in 1913, it was almost a rural village. The south shore of Long Island and the romantically endless expanse of the Atlantic were only a short walk from the Lieblings' "tall, gaunt house, painted dark green and darkened by oaks that stood too close." Inside, the family reposed in stuffy comfort, tended by the usual fräuleins as well as a German butler named Louis.

The house stood just inside the city limits of New York, where the borough of Queens borders Nassau County to the east. Before Abbott had finished high school, the Lieblings moved over that magic line to the even more prosperous Five Towns area, with its perfume of WASP aristocracy. But for Abbott, who never transferred out of the New York City public school system, it was the social context of Far Rockaway that mattered. And that boiled down to a mix of "comfortable" Jews and working-class Irish, whose children met in school.

From his parents, Abbott knew he was Jewish. There was never any doubt about the label and no question which of the two major ethnic groups at school he belonged in. At home, too, most of the friends of his parents whom he met were Jewish by background. But the Liebling household was not at all religious. There was no attempt to observe traditional dietary laws or the sabbath. In fact, the family did not practice any form of Jewish religion. Joseph Liebling had left behind the orthodoxy of the Lower East Side, had married an assimilated woman and had no interest in rabbis and synagogues. Norma Liebling Stonehill remembers that as a girl she had to wheedle permission from her father to attend a Jewish service with friends.

Apostasy was one of the many reactions to American life taken by large numbers of upwardly mobile Jews then as it is now. Without ever leaving a Jewish milieu, they fell away from Jewish religion. This was the comfortable choice for them, but it also put them in an intrinsically ambiguous position vis-à-vis both religious Jews and non-Jews. Growing up in such a home, Abbott seems to have tried to resolve this ambiguity. As a child will, he experimented with simple solutions to the paradoxical attitude of his parents. During his adolescence, he recoiled from the Jewish community around him and he idealized the gentiles whom he met. Later in life, he explored the traditional Jewish world his father abandoned, with curiosity and affection. He was never religious himself, but he was fascinated by piety in others. In Far Rockaway, Abbott fell in love with the local Irish.

Liebling—pudgy, precocious and outwardly a model young Jewish intellectual—emerged from P.S. 39 and Far Rockaway High School marked for life by his contact with his Irish classmates. Abbott came from a home where a boy could learn about sex by peeking into a set of Maupassant. They, the Irish kids, were unencumbered with such cultural baggage. They excelled in sports. He, according to a former chum, William Yankauer, was uncoordinated and couldn't compete athletically with his classmates. Nevertheless, he "tried very hard to play games," Yankauer recalls, but he was two years younger than his classmates, because of double promotions, and he couldn't keep up. Probably he would not have kept up even without the age differential, but as it happened he certainly cut a ridiculous figure with glasses askew and socks perpetually falling down from his knickers around his bare legs.

His social life was not brilliant either. He did not go to the beach with Yankauer's crowd, didn't skate, had no girlfriends for years and did not go to parties. He got excellent grades, however (with a few exceptions, mostly in math), and devoted even his free time to intellectual pursuits.

His youthful reading program was ambitious and advanced, ranging from Ambrose Bierce to the European classics. "He would hold it over me that he had read so many things," says his sister Norma. "I can remember dragging myself through Thackeray to keep up. I adored him, but he gave me a complex about writing for years."

Abbott himself wrote so much and so often at home that Norma Stonehill "can even remember my mother pulling him from under the bed; he was always writing in the darkest corner under there."

For the most part, however, Abbott's intellectual bent was encouraged. His father may have been stern and dour, and an arch-example of the successful self-made businessman, but he proudly encouraged his son's early efforts at writing and never pressed the boy to follow him into the fur business or any other business. "I guess," Mrs. Stonehill says, "it was the old Jewish respect for learning."

Abbott looked the part of the young, unphysical scholar. His feet were flat and made it painful for him to walk. It also appears that he was pigeon-toed. The humor page of a school publication carried this interchange:

> Liebling's feet must be awfully tired.
> Why?
> Because they're always turning in.

Then there were his hands, small, delicate and laughably out of scale with the rest of his oxlike frame. Liebling never allowed these *fines attaches* to embarrass him. He would always claim, when anyone noticed them, that they were a mark of natural aristocracy.

Even his mother ribbed Abbott about his tiny hands. His sister remembers that at one point "he had made plans to go to Europe on a cattle boat. His job was to feed the animals. My parents were sufficiently Jewish to have worried about his doing an excessive amount of manual labor. Mother assured him he'd be too seasick to feed the animals. Finally, she said: 'It's impossible for anyone with hands like yours to feed animals.' "

Joseph Liebling also made fun of his son's appearance. He frequently joked that it was a lucky thing that "Abbott looks like me and Norma like her mother. What if Norma had been a big clumsy thing like Abbott."

If that was the tone his family took, it is not difficult to imagine the way children at school reacted to Abbott. Somehow he avoided ostracism. And, perhaps in order to keep from being labeled a sissy, he turned into an obstreperous child, who flouted rules and mocked the manners and standards his proper family tried to enforce.

"He was moody and unpredictable," recalls Norma Stonehill. "You never knew if he would butt a guest in the stomach or say hello. He grew to be very critical of our family and their friends. We were too bourgeois for him."

As part of his rebellion, Abbott cultivated some mild vices. During the summer of 1914, the Lieblings vacationed at Schaefer's Hotel in Lake Hopatcong, New Jersey. It was, he wrote, "a German-American kind of place, as much roadhouse as hotel, built on the side of a hill with a dark cool bar on the lowest level. There was a fruit machine in this crypt, and I would play it every day, until I had lost the last nickel I could wheedle or extort from my mother. Then I would drink sarsaparilla and eat Swiss cheese sandwiches on rye while I read the Waverley Novels."

Gambling, drinking, begging, gluttony—he had formed the bad habits of a roué before he was ten. His intellectual interests also began to shade off into dubious corners. Through his addiction to popular newspapers he discovered a raffish world of "theater people and horse trainers" who seemed to him "as casually real as the fur merchants, lawyers, general agents for insurance companies, and cotton converters who formed the most numerous element in my parents' milieu."

He turned his voracious mind to popular music and, says William Yankauer, learned the field so well he "could tell you when a pop tune had been plagiarized." He also memorized the records and pedigrees of thoroughbred horses.

In school, Liebling was a notorious mischief-maker. Yankauer remembers him as "a rebel. He was always getting salmons, which were pink cards you took with you when you were sent to the principal's office. Teachers wrote comments about your behavior on them. Abbott was something of a jailhouse lawyer in the principal's office."

Abbott had the classic problem of the bright boy in American culture, feeling left out and unimportant because he was no good at sports. Liebling compensated by palling around with the class jock, the hero of the basketball team, Francis Xavier (Frank) Lenihan. In Yankauer's view, Abbott had a "crush" on Frank. He also wrote poetry to Irish girls a bit his senior and continued elegizing local Hibernian maidenhood at least through college. This poem is drawn from his Dartmouth notebook (1920–23):

> To Margaret
> Oh, lovely form I've never pressed,
> Oh, lips I'll never kiss!
> What fools are they who say "What you
> Have never had, you'll never miss."

The notebook, though written after he had finished high school, is substantially devoted to friends from Far Rockaway and to the place itself. To be sure, it reflects the mind of a somewhat older boy, but there was surprising continuity in Liebling's life and in his preoccupations right into the middle 1920s. In any case, the poetry notebook, a sewn school exercise book filled with a diverse and embarrassing collection of romantic outpourings and pastiches of French verse forms, is the most personal and unguarded piece of writing we have from Liebling's adolescence. The views of Far Rockaway expressed in it, though written from a distance and somewhat later, reflected the views he had formed on the spot, in high school.

The notebook reveals a Liebling who was intent on being a writer, and who was in love with love, especially with Jewish-Irish romance. In one poem near the end of the collection, after sketching out the similarities of "headlong" impulsive Irish and Jews (as compared with sensible, pleasure-denying "Teutons"), he comes to the point in the envoi, which he subsequently crossed out, but not heavily enough to prevent a reconstruction of the (partly emended) first draft:

> Princess, you are Hibernian and I a
> Jew; and so you'll understand just why a
> Love conceived and brought to light by me
> Must brilliant and illogical be.

Margaret [Paisley], also called "Peg," receives many other tributes in various other styles—one of them is in phonetically transcribed Irish brogue. These pro-Irish effusions are matched by exasperated diatribes against Jewish Far Rockaway. Witness the first two stanzas of "Conventionality at Far Rockaway":

> I'd like to sit beside the sea,
> And sing;
> In song to let harsh memory
> Take wing.
>
> But all the Jews, agape would form
> A ring.
> And mock at so mishugina
> A thing.

Similar anti-Semitic, anti-bourgeois verse, in which the poet once again seems to come out in favor of the sea, crops up a few pages later, in "Rara Avis":

> Where the roar of the great waves
> breaking and laving
> The shores, meets the roar of the
> Jewboy's shrill raving
> And the sound waves, rising 'round
> Meet in a great wild dance of sound

> In a wild, untrained kozatsky dance;
> There I found
> In the midst of that "knobby" rout
> One solitary man without
> White flannel pants.

In another poem, titled "Spring Song at Far Rockaway," Liebling mocked the "gross people," the "lewd, overdressed band" of soulless, moneyed Jews in his town. Some of this animus may also have had a literary background. The young poetaster of 1922 probably felt compelled to reject his own bourgeois origins merely in order to certify his poet's soul. It is undoubtedly not without significance that the notebook opens with a heavily morbid salute "To Baudelaire," the patron saint of rebellious young poets who hope to scandalize their parents.

On the other hand, Liebling's fixation on the polarity of Jew and Irishman did spring from real motives in his life. The Dartmouth poetry may give an overly charged impression of his normal mood, especially of his mood when he was only fourteen or fifteen, in high school. Still, it is clear that his friendship with Frank Lenihan was a symptom of his rebellion against conventional Jewish Far Rockaway and of his yearning for the normal joys of muscular Christianity.

This said, it must be added that Liebling's high school days were full of normal, untroubled moments. Lenihan was only one of the boy's friends. Frederick (Fritz) Berlinger claims Abbott Liebling as "my closest friend at that time," and remembers spending six days a week with him. Often, Berlinger recalls, he would walk over to the Liebling house—they were neighbors—and listen, spellbound, while Abbott would tell him stories of the First World War. Abbott would treat Berlinger to nickel sundaes at Mott's Drug Store and never expect to be paid back. And on one occasion, the two boys took the el in to Greenwich Village. Even then, Abbott "liked out-of-the-way places." On the way back, Fritz got deathly ill from his first clam. Abbott is likely to have bolted a dozen himself and egged on his friend.

Medically suspicious shellfish were to be a lifelong passion. Friends remember with real horror the perverse relish with which

Liebling would devour dirty-looking clams from street vendors. Such gastronomic slumming—typical of his attitude toward food and of his general passion for the lower depths of life—was no accident. It goes back directly to the most dramatic event of Abbott's childhood.

In the spring of 1915, while pursuing his studies in eighth grade and working himself into a small furor over the battle of Verdun, Abbott fell seriously ill with typhoid fever. One day he suddenly "began to feel queer and got sent home from school." He had eaten some bad oysters out of polluted waters in Jamaica Bay. So had his father. The old man "shook off" the disease. Abbott slipped into delirium and stayed in bed for weeks, attended round the clock by two nurses, Miss Galt and Miss McCarthy.

The war continued to fill his mind. He later wrote that he dreamed he had served "on several fronts" and "had a particularly arduous indefinite period as a Serbian army horse, being ferried across a river as one in a bunch of bananas. On arriving at the other side of the river I was presented at a formal review of cuirassiers, where General Nivelle, the heroic commander of Verdun's heroic defenders, decorated me with the Medaille Militaire, which he attached to my right horse-ear by a safety pin. I put the medal under my pillow."

Pleasant dreams, but they were the sunny side of a very serious siege of typhoid. When the crisis came, the family called in a Dr. Manny Liberman "as a last resort," recalls Norma Stonehill. "Abbott swore so that my mother apologized. Dr. Liberman said, 'You're fortunate that he can swear at all.'"

The boy did eventually rally, but he was out sick from April 24 until October 5, 1916. Yet the experience did not set him back in school. He entered Far Rockaway High School the next February, at twelve, thinner but apparently undaunted.

Cocky and fractious, he continued to collect his salmons and eventually turned his energies and budding talents as a writer toward subversive journalism. In the early months of 1919, with a group of friends, he wrote and published a satirical four-page paper called *The Weekly Groan.* Liebling was fourteen and a junior; the other *Groan* staffers were sixteen. Unfortunately, no copy of their waggish paper seems to have survived, but in William Yankauer's memory, it contained wisecracks about some of the Far Rockaway High School faculty, so the principal threatened to suspend the staff if another issue came out. Apparently, there was only one issue, printed on the presses of the local newspaper. But according to a magnificently pompous editorial in the May 1919 issue of the official school magazine, the *Dolphin*, the *Groan* was not only "a great success," but "it was read with much pleasure by all." On the other hand, continued the *Dolphin*'s archetypical high-school editorialist, "No paper made up entirely of flippant remarks will for long be a success," but "a paper such as the 'Groan,' toned down, with a regular editorial staff . . . will add a great deal to the school spirit by having all school activities always before the eyes of the students, in a diverting and interesting way."

This did not happen. The editors of that same issue of the *Dolphin* did, however, print a special section called "The Groan." It contains a spoof news article announcing a Bolshevik landing at nearby Belle Harbor, some dog Latin (Boyibus Printi Weakli Groanorum/Alli liki, wanti somorium. . . .") and an allegorical wrap-up of World War I in the form of a football game.

William Yankauer says that all the humor in the *Groan* was written by Liebling. This indictment cannot be proved. We can, however, point with certainty to the boy's official, signed efforts for the *Dolphin*. His first published piece had, in fact, already appeared in the November 1918 issue. It was a short story called "The Field of Glory," and it was about an American soldier wounded on a battlefield in Belgium. Surrounded by corpses and wounded men of various nationalities, Ned, the American, observes the atrocities near him: a German's "yellow pompadour . . . reddened with blood," a blond with no lower body whose "sightless blue orbs stared upward" in vain. The story ends happily, with news of peace, and if it was thoroughly conventional, it also showed that Liebling at fourteen had absorbed the clichés of war reporting. Also, the dialogue, which includes snatches of dialect from Irish, Gascon French, American black and British cockney soldiers, shows that Liebling's talent for mimicry developed early.

Two other short stories by Liebling appeared in subsequent *Dol-*

phins. In the same May 1919 number that accommodated "The Groan," Abbott published "Poor Barrett." The narrator, wandering "in a dingy side street on the East Side," comes upon a ragged man gazing at a medal in a pawnshop window. It is fighting Bob Barrett, once a celebrated boxer, now a penniless disabled war hero, who has been reduced to taking three dollars from "old Ginsberg, the pawnbroker," for his Distinguished Service Cross.

Cleanly written, "Poor Barrett" is the first of hundreds of Liebling pieces to take the form of interviews with fighters, soldiers, simple folk of heroic mold but humble circumstances.

"Pals," the final major Liebling contribution to the *Dolphin*, appeared in February 1920. It is a yarn about two rival players on a high school basketball team. The hero is named Regan.

Liebling meanwhile did so brilliantly in school that his history teacher, Miss A. M. Troll, thought he should take the New York State Regents' exam early, in the spring of 1920, when he was only fifteen. On June 20, he sat exams in two subjects only and received a 91 in English and an 86 in American history.

So ends Abbott Liebling's high school career. He did not graduate with the class of 1920 and was not pictured with them in the commencement issue of the *Dolphin*. Since he had completed only three years of high school, he would not have had enough credits to enter college in the normal way, even without a diploma. It appears, however, that this was unnecessary.

Liebling must have appealed to Dartmouth because of his obvious intellect and his precocious literary talents and background. As he neared sixteen, Abbott had already read widely in English and French, he was an impassioned student of history (especially military history), was widely traveled, sophisticated for his age and had learned to write clearly. In a day when college entrance was not the competitive drama it is today, he was an excellent candidate even a year ahead of time. For his part, Liebling, like so many restless boys before him, must have been relieved and excited to leave home and the "comfortable" community that oppressed him so.

three

Renegade "Indian"

7 West South St.,
Hanover, N.H.,
Sept. 22, 1920

Dear Folks at Home:

I am now occupying my room, having moved in last Saturday.
It is very nice and comfortable and Mrs. Bergeron is very nice and
obliging.

She sends my wash out with hers and helps me in many other
little ways. She has three of the cutest little girls imaginable. Some
time you ought to send them some little present of some sort as she
seems to appreciate gifts to them more than to herself. She is a
typical little New England woman but very good-hearted.

I am having a great time up here, as I already know about 30
fellows, all very good skates. Roberts, (of Mt. Vernon) and his
roommate Hagenbuckle, as well as Tremaine, a fellow from Chicago, Barker, a Massachusetts fellow, and of course Marks are some
of the best.

Saturday I moved in the morning, went to practice in the afternoon, and the movies at night.

Sunday I rose late, spent most of the day lounging around, writing letters and playing checkers (everything up here is closed) and in the evening walked to Lebanon and back with Roberts (14 miles).

We had a great time and got home at 1:30 A.M. Roberts had no blankets so we slept together and of course again rose late, just in time for lunch, in fact, and spent the afternoon making various small purchases (stationery, medicines, soap, etc.) and watching practice.

I sent a box of cigars (25) to Prof. Soldien.

In the evening Commons opened and I eat there for the first time in company with Marks and Uris, a friend of his from the city. We went to the movies in the evening and then I came home and read a book of Jack London's I had drawn from the library, which is very good.

Tuesday morning I registered and matriculated. Had lunch at Commons, went to practice, joined Y.M.C.A., and met Fritz Wolff, who had just arrived.

With Fritz all evening, talked a lot, went to bed late, but rose early as Commons closes for breakfast at 7:45 A.M., went to library and read essay on Merimee by Wright, met Hagenbuckle and Barker, went to lunch, came home, met my room-mate, who has just arrived, he seems a fine chap, sat down to write a letter to you—

And that brings me right up to date.

I received the jersey comforter, underwear, and tie, but not my trunk as yet. However I expect it soon and in the meanwhile lack nothing I need.

Send me a heavy, fleece-lined, mackinaw as it is biting cold up here even now and I have to wear my sweater under my coat.

Paid my bills for board, tuition, and room rent, but bank account otherwise pretty healthy.

Your loving son,
Abbott

P.S. Love to Norma, Grandma.

This energetic, kind, studious, friendly freshman is almost too good to be true. Years later he would sneer at himself and his, mostly older, 623 classmates as "indifferent." "The college was liberal," Liebling wrote, "there was an exemplary freedom of thought and speech, but we never bothered to think or say anything more than 'Hi' or 'Howdy.'"

His frequent letters home that fall and winter do paint a picture of luxurious contentment with the pseudo freedoms of pseudo adulthood in Hanover. He worked hard, too, and strove to match some boys'-book ideal of undergraduate life.

Completely installed by September 25, he exultingly described himself: "I am sitting at my own (newly purchased) desk, in my own room, decorated with my own pennants and stuff, with an impressive row of my own books (22 of them) facing me, and it sure gives me a terribly important and independent feeling."

As of September 25, 1920, Liebling felt fine and realized that he was passing over a sacramental threshold into a sanctified domain of late boyhood: College. All those repeated "fellow"'s in his earlier letter are in the stout-hearted Stover at Yale tradition. He had left the parochial shores of Far Rockaway for an older, more honored and freer community, whose fellowship he had joined, ritually, "With exercises in chapel, very impressive, the president making a long speech (no words less than 6 syllables), the dean making a less pretentious but more comprehensible one, the whole college singing 'Onward Christian Soldiers' (Grandma should hear us). . . ."

Next, he took part in the Football Rush. "It was the greatest night of my life," he wrote his parents. "As you can imagine, the shock of 1200 fellows coming together at top speed and then the terrible pushing and fighting for the ball makes football seem like child's play by comparison." Liebling threw himself into the melee with a vengeance. He was a "front lineman" and "badly bruised during the fray," too "used up," in fact, to take part in the snake dance afterward, although it was "wonderful."

Liebling also threw himself into academic life, taking courses in Latin, English, French, history, evolution (a kind of science survey that started with physics and chemistry) and phys. ed. His first-quarter grades were excellent. He received A's consistently on written assignments. His English professor advised him to submit one of his stories to a magazine. He went out for the staff of the *Jack O'Lantern*, the Dartmouth humor magazine, and saw several of his things published. A former staff member of the *Jack O'* (as it was called), Harland Manchester, remembers the day Liebling came to the magazine's office to put himself into the staff competition. "He was a shy little boy in a green beanie, mournful and brooding."

Even so, the letters all that fall and into the winter maintain their original exuberant tone: "With so many different things to do, I hardly find enough time for sleep." (January 12, 1921) He worked in the gym and had his heart examined in order to allay family fears that he wasn't healthy enough for sports. "My heart is *quite normal*," he wrote his mother. "So no more talk about 'let the *starke goyim* do it, you're not strong.'" In addition to gymnastics, his exercise program at Dartmouth included frequent horseback riding and boxing. He had been seriously interested in boxing from the age of thirteen, when a black-sheep bachelor uncle from California had taught him to punch and had told him about the great fighters of the 1890s and early 1900s. Dartmouth gave him a chance to follow in this appealingly unconventional relative's footsteps in a small but satisfying way.

His only complaint at Dartmouth was with the menu, which relied heavily on beans. The Lieblings supplemented this diet with frequent shipments of candy, anchovies, olives, cake and the like. And in moments of extremity, the future gastronomic writer would slip away to Boyd's, "the swell restaurant of Hanover, the waiters don't wear sweaters," for mock turtle soup, honeydew melon, porterhouse steak with onions and pie à la mode.

In all this flurry of activity, the prodigious sixteen-year-old had found a focus, in writing. He considered his teacher's encouragement to publish his stories premature, but by January 18, 1921, flushed with success over a string of *A* compositions (and perhaps from the discovery that he could "eat more than 2½ ounces of anchovies at a time"), he wrote his parents: "I feel more and more sure that by the end of my course I'll be ready to step out with the best of them. I'm improving steadily and I don't think I'm near my crest yet. However, *tout cela reste avec Dieu.* For all I know, I may have no more than a little talent anyway, so I'm not worrying over my career. I may wind up in the raw fur business after all."

He was writing steadily and passionately in his plain brown composition notebook. But it is only with the goal of learning about

Liebling's mind—and not with aesthetic hopes up—that one should poke among the remnants of his juvenilia. Liebling, nevertheless, thought enough of four of his mawkish lyrics to type them out on special theme paper with blue-ruled margins. It is doubtful, though, that he submitted "The Monkey God" as classwork in a writing course: "The poet fain would be a seer,/The courtesan a lady;/The self made man would be a peer,/Each Levy an O'Grady."

One short story, also typed, reworks material Liebling had used for the *Dolphin.* "Of All Bad Words" begins: "Tom Stapleton and Frank O'Brien were about as gifted and extraordinary a pair as ever came to Dartmouth." Like the two friends in "Pals," both boys are athletes. The Irish character, O'Brien, becomes a champion boxer; Stapleton teaches chemistry at Dartmouth. O'Brien then goes into a decline and dies penniless, an even more pathetic figure than the antihero of earlier "Poor Barrett." Meanwhile, the narrator of this moral tale, who has gone on to be the city editor of a newspaper, returns to Dartmouth to interview his old friend Stapleton when Stapleton announces a sensational discovery. Stapleton's study is filled with mementos of O'Brien.

In the short play "A Career," an intellectual is paired once again with a "big, healthy, husky Irishman." The slim, intense youth reads some of his poetry to John McBride and some other soldiers in a southern farmhouse in 1864. Afterward, he says he "can't afford to die until I know whether I'm a real poet—or just one of God's jokes on men." He then goes out to get a drink at the pump and is shot dead by an enemy bullet.

To these already familiar Liebling motifs—male friendship, violence in battle, the literary vocation, the Irish athlete—we can now add a few others, motifs that will crop up in his mature work and that were already in his mind in college. Fragments of an essay "On Taste" contains a windy argument against censorship and petty puritanism. He comes out for the ribaldry of Charles II and of Urquhart's translation of Rabelais.

His future interest in lowlife crops up in two handwritten themes submitted to an instructor called Baldwin. One is about a local farmboy whom the narrator, Joe, meets at the fair in White River Junction, Vermont.

Baldwin gave the paper an A. He did the same for a grandiloquent defense of New York City called "My Home Town," which
presages the similar efforts collected in *Back Where I Came From.*
"There is more honesty in any good New York burglar," Liebling
wrote on November 22, 1920, in the sixteenth theme he handed in
to Baldwin, "than in a thousand Hanover merchants, there is more
morality (and more beautiful immorality) in Chinatown than in
Lebanon. There are better fighting men on Tenth Avenue than . . ."

Liebling has turned his back on Far Rockaway. His home town is
Manhattan, or rather that side of Manhattan that always appealed
to him, the Manhattan of crooks and pugs and mysterious ethnicity,
the Manhattan of "beautiful immorality." The phrase rings splen-
diferously false. At his age, Abbott Liebling could not have had
much first hand experience with the seamy side of New York City.
He was a suburban kid who nipped into Manhattan by subway only
on special excursions. But he was also a suburban kid addicted to an
overrich diet of New York newspapers. And it is as much from
newspaper features as from his own teen-age firsthand knowledge
that he "defends" New York.

This habit of striking poses learned from reading came easily to
Liebling. His student themes are crippled by "literary" gestures and
rhetoric, tics acquired in a hundred-odd books and columns. It
would take him many years to slough off all these learned mannerisms and find his own limber yet convoluted style. But from the
start he was obsessed with matters of style, and was very sensitive to
other people's tones and cadences. He was a wonderful mimic all
his life. And he could manage wonderfully funny parodies of pompous diction, as in this letter from Dartmouth to his sister Norma,
dated January 13, 1921:

Dear Nonce:

I got your very edumacated letter yesterday and I was so astonished at your really astounding vocabulary that I was scarcely able
to realize that you were indeed and nevertheless my own naturally
inconsiderable and youthfully obstreperous juvenile relation com-
monly called sister. Your request for further suggestions as to your
progress in literature is therefore obviously impossible to fulfill,

since, prima facie, ipsa facta, your knowledge is so immeasurably
superior to mine that it would be ridiculous in the extreme for me
to venture any recommendations. However, the modern Russian
playwrights and the older German philosophers might satisfy your
intellectual requirements.

Aesthetically and educationally yours,
Your closely related male offspring
of the same parental progenitors,

Abbott Joseph Liebling

That may be the only time he voluntarily signed his full name.
He hated his first name. Like Isadore for Isaac and Marshall for
Moshe, Abbott was a hopeful but transparently pretentious Ameri-
canization of a Hebrew name. This is exactly the kind of genteel
Jewish greenhorn sham that made Liebling so uncomfortable in Far
Rockaway. And so, at Dartmouth, he gradually dropped Abbott and
became Joe. Officially, he adopted A. J. Liebling as his signature.
Fifteen years later, he met a non-Jew who had gone through the
same process. E. B. White had been christened Elwyn, but abhor-
ring the name, had shifted to Andy at Cornell. The two men always
felt that their unwanted first names (and subsequent transforma-
tions into double-initial men with folksy nicknames) were a kind of
bond between them.

It took a while, however, for Abbott to turn into Joe, and Leo
Stone, the best friend Liebling made at Dartmouth, still habitually
refers to him as "Abbott." The Dartmouth yearbook for the class of
1924 gives Liebling's nickname as "Lieb," but this was apparently a
mistake.

He was certainly still Abbott on registration day in the fall of
1920, when Leo Stone first met him. Stone was a small, chubby sixteen. Liebling, a taller boy, only fifteen, came over and struck up a
conversation. They remained lifelong friends and confidants. Stone
went on to eminence in psychiatry. Today he recalls his first impression of Liebling as "obviously very brilliant, but very awkward
physically, with flat feet that made it hard for him to walk; he
couldn't throw a football. We used to box, and even though I was

much smaller, I used to beat him. He kept on boxing for years, dog-gedly, and got to be quite good at it."

In that first semester of freshman year, Liebling and Stone saw each other frequently, even though they did not live near each oth-er. Stone lived in an old, wooden dormitory, later demolished, called Sanborn Hall. Liebling lived off campus in Mrs. Bergeron's rooming house, with a boy he knew from Far Rockaway. The room-mate turned out to be up to no good. He was a wealthy scapegrace who collected bootleg gin in his lodgings and sold it to other stu-dents. He was caught and expelled, and almost pulled Liebling down with him. Stone remembers that a professor sounded him out quietly, wanting to know if Liebling had had anything to do with the bootlegging.

Liquor was a very dangerous substance to play around with in the Dartmouth of those days. The year before, one student had shot an-other in a dispute over possession of some alcohol. Liebling, fortu-nately, was innocent and survived the purge of his roommate. He had, moreover, already shown a preference for the crowd at San-born Hall. "There was a whole group of tough Boston athletes, sec-ond-generation Irish," recalls Leo Stone. "They came to admire him, when they saw what guts he had. He used to get hell knocked out of him in gym. Joe Liebling became known as a regular guy."

This preference for Irish athletes was of course merely a continu-ation of a habit developed at home. It may even have partly worked to ward off homesickness. Stone recalls, and the poetry notebook confirms, that Liebling carried a torch all through college for his high school sweetheart, Margaret Paisley. To fawn on Irish athletes at Dartmouth—and fawn he did—was to call up happy memories of previous associations with Frank Lenihan and the rest of the "neo-Corkonian" Far Rockaway varsity. The Dartmouth squad was simply bigger and tougher, but they made Liebling feel at home. They may also have served as protective coloration and turned him into a goy by association.

The Jewish question did, in general, arise more pointedly for Jew-ish undergraduates at Dartmouth then than it does today. The Jew-ish influx into the college had just begun. There were no Jewish fraternities. A friend of Leo Stone's was told that he, as a Jew, had no future in the Dartmouth English department. And, as almost everywhere in the country at the time, Jews could count on meeting with frequent if mild instances of covert anti-Semitism and even an occasional overt incident.

There was, then, a definite social advantage to escaping the Jewish label. But Liebling's enthusiasm for Catholic toughs grew out of a different motive. He didn't crave social status; he wanted to cut himself off from the emasculating Jewish tradition that corrupted battling Abrahams into sissified pseudo-American Abbotts.

Liebling's way out, characteristically, led him to the brink of criminality, to the very dingiest Irish "slums" in Hanover. The obvious route to social respectability at Dartmouth did not attract him. He did not pal with Protestants, and as it happened, he came a cropper completely because he would not go to the Protestant college chapel.

"I could not believe," he wrote years later, "that the college could be serious about maintaining such an absurd vestige of its missionary days."

But Dartmouth took its chapel very seriously. Compulsory attendance was not abolished until a few years after Liebling's time. And as Abbott/Joe learned, the Puritan legacy, like a dead scorpion, still could sting.

They bounced him.

It was the depth of the New Hampshire winter. The second semester had just begun. And on February 26, 1921, a thoroughly penitent Abbott wrote home to explain:

> Dear Father:
>
> By the time this reaches you you will have probably received the Dean's and Mr. Baldwin's letters. Of course I can't expect you to look on this affair as anything but a disgrace, for it arose from pure carelessness on my part, and it means a great shock both to Mother and you. But I hope you won't feel too bad about it, for I intend to make good this winter in some line of newspaper work and make you proud of me. Of course I don't expect you to believe this after the way I've made a fool of myself up here, but you'll see.

I guess the whole business seems rather mixed up to you, so I'll have to explain it. We are supposed to attend chapel 65 times each semester. If we cut more than 18, we are separated from the college. Having, with my usual harebrained carelessness taken 23, I didn't even keep track of them, and so came home to celebrate passing everything. I did pass as you know, and pass quite well, but I had too many cuts and that puts me out until next September. The Dean has been quite decent about it and says he is mighty sorry, but a rule is a rule, and so I'm out. My profs have all advised me to tackle the newspaper game this winter and spring, just for the experience and I'm going to.

It's been a pretty tough blow, especially because it was absolutely unexpected, but I hope you won't take it too hard. After all I've done nothing dishonorable, I've made good in my work and I'll get credit for that when I return. You must be pretty angry and tired of paying my way through life, but I'll make it up this year. Until I do, don't think too hard of your son,

> Abbott

He must have hated writing that letter, and hated even more than that his ignominious return to Far Rockaway, shorn of his freshman beanie and his independence. For half a year he was feckless Abbott. He did not even get that job in the newspaper game. Who would hire a sixteen-year-old kid, inexperienced and certain to return to college in the fall?

That summer he took courses—at Columbia, most probably, but no one remembers for sure—and they earned him credit for his lost spring at Dartmouth. And so he returned to Hanover a full-fledged sophomore. Liebling continued his friendships with campus toughs and jocks. In later life, he invested this year and the following fall with a Stoveresque luster.

Those three semesters, beginning in the fall of 1921 and ending in the winter of 1923, were the heart of his college experience. He was well known on campus, respected as a writer and rarely seen in class. He was eighteen, had finally reached the age when most boys enter college, but he was already a junior and apparently headed for a precocious and successful graduation in 1924. He seems to have had an almost literary sense of this stage in his life. For instance, in a letter to his parents written the late fall of his sophomore year, he sounds like a novelist sorting out characters for a *Bildungsroman:*

> This is about the most sickly-sweet-sad period of calf-melancholy of my whole life. Nearly all the fellows I go with are also suffering from the same phenomenon, which is a sort of adolescent spring fever, or self-crush. You know how foolish boys of seventeen or eighteen are when they have a "crush" on a girl. Well, we're all "crushed" on ourselves, and we're all suffused with a sweet, solemn self-pity, because we are at the stage when we don't know where we're going but we *do* care. Leo doesn't know whether he wants to be an author, or a doctor, or a forester; a roué or a platonic lover. Ed is heartbroken because he says he "talks in platitudes" and cannot express his soul. Mick Uris is completely at sea. Other fellows are the same. We all realize how quickly the end of our schooling is approaching and none of us know what we're going to do. Now I know why the college sophomore is such a laughing stock. If I ever wrote a story now it would be "sophomoric" all right.
>
> Personally, the idea of writing still remains very strong with me. I am not writing much at present, but that is quite usual at this particular period in my life. I am absorbing impressions and, imperceptibly growing older and broader. . . .

All that fall and into the spring of 1922, he had been sending home bulletins whose constant theme was the boredom of life at Dartmouth. He was also quite candid—one might even say boastful—about his indolence. "Just been having a lazy spell," he wrote to his parents on May 18, 1922. His grades for the fall of 1921 had been worse than mediocre, but he stayed afloat, went off probation in the spring term and passed on successfully into his junior year in the fall of 1922.

No letters survive from that term. By then he was an established literary figure on campus, and he seems to have accelerated the pace of his indolence to the point where he devoted himself virtually full time to dissipation. In this area, his senior partner was a rogue named Fistere.

Now deceased, Robert Fistere was, in the view of one rather

strait-laced classmate, who has asked to remain anonymous, "a second-rate basketball player, a very tough New Yorker who had been
in the Navy and talked out of the side of his mouth, an assman and
a drinker." His "villainy" fascinated Liebling and repelled others.
Leo Stone, for one, couldn't understand Fistere's malign attraction.
"I used to say to him," Stone recalls, "Fistere's all right, but what's
so special? He would say, 'Leo, you know you're a moralist. You
don't like him because you think he's evil.'"

Liebling liked Fistere *because* he was "evil." This was a pattern
that would repeat itself in Liebling's life. He always formed friendships with deadbeats. Liebling loved crooks who had verve. And
Fistere seems to have had plenty of verve. Unfortunately, the details
of Liebling's escapades with Fistere are lost.

The association with Fistere and those other athlete-roughnecks
does seem to have turned Liebling into a bully with his roommate
Sol Levine. Levine was small but fierce, and he made a point of not
sucking up to gentile jocks. Liebling would ride him. "Look at
him," he would say in a disgruntled moment. "Do you think he
could ever pass for a typical Dartmouth man?" Levine, who took a
dim view of Liebling's "worship" of Fistere and the other rough-
necks, remembers that even after the two of them had left Dartmouth, when they met in New York, Liebling continued the old
routine. He said to Levine: "Jesus, I told everyone how big Dartmouth men were. You're a shrimp."

None of this seems to have fazed Sol Levine. He and Liebling
would argue fiercely, but that was why he had agreed to room with
him. "I thought it would be interesting," he recalls.

As it turned out, Levine found Liebling's interest in Fistere and
the rest of the muscular Christian crowd undignified and probably
homosexual: he thought so even though he saw that Liebling used
his special reader's privileges at the Dartmouth library to borrow
"advanced" books such as Havelock Ellis's *Psychology of Sex* and
circulated them among the jocks; even though Liebling had "arranged to meet a whore in Boston," arranged this by mail and later
bragged about his adventure, probably the same one he mentioned
somewhat differently in an avuncular letter to his sister Norma
written on her eighteenth birthday, March 5, 1927. The letter, sent

from Paris when Liebling himself was twenty-two, begins with some topical remarks and then turns to advice and reminiscence about those bright college months when he had been eighteen in Sanborn Hall:

> Above all avoid affictation of ilegance and don't take college activities seriously. I didn't when I was eighteen. Which gives me a thought. Maybe you'd like to know just what I was doing and thinking when I was your age. I was living in Sanborn Hall with Sol Levine as a roommate and I used to spend most of my time lying on the busted-down couch in Cupe and Red's room and making sarcastic remarks about every author save Ambrose Bierce and Christopher Marlow [sic]. We used to shoot a great deal of craps and Red would wrestle with Dan Staton. When Leo would come in we'd all pile on and tickle him. Fistere was rooming in the Sigma Chi house and planning several species of adultery and extortion. I had the enviable reputation of being his "brains" because I used to do his themes for him. At that rate the cow is the brain of the milkmaid. Quentin Pan had just arrived from China, and Ed Shnayerson was trying to become a Confucian philosopher likewise. Ray Kelly, the great liar and halfback, used to come up to sponge cigarettes and everybody got drunk once a week. I was bored to death with all my courses, including Italian (because the prof was about as Latin as codfish cakes) but used to read a lot. I didn't think that war was ever right, or God existed, or that anybody was half as intelligent as myself (except maybe Fistere) and *I wasn't even in love* because I was temporarily too sophisticated (I had spent a weekend with a girl in Boston). What seems queer to me now, I took very little exercise until the last month of that semester, when I started to box. I had the greatest contempt for people with superficial education, but I didn't yet realize that it takes half a century to acquire a real one. But, somme toute, I enjoyed myself immensely in my mental rags, because they seemed to me robes of imperial purple, and that's the main thing, isn't it darling? So go thou and continue doing likewise, now that you're eighteen, and don't let me ever tell you that I was any different, because, come to think of it, I wasn't.
>
> As ever and ever (except that we change continually),
>
> Abbott

P.S. I think much more highly of you now than when I began this letter. A little introspection raises our opinion of others—even our sister!

Anyone who has been to college in modern America will recognize the mischief and self-conscious self-indulgence—and the overweening intellectual arrogance mixed with childish playfulness—of Liebling's Sanborn Hall. We recognize it because we have been there, and because we have read about it. University life is a genre, and the author of the letter to Norma on the occasion of her eighteenth birthday was very much an "author" writing in a well-known manner.

But in the real life of dissipation and lazing virile Bohemia at Sanborn Hall in 1922, Liebling's pleasant routine came to a sudden halt.

He'd taken too many chapel cuts again. And this time around, that meant out for good.

Luckily, his family were abroad. He had some time to find work before they got home. Somehow, Abbott got a job as a reporter almost immediately.

On February 7, 1922, Liebling left Hanover, but he did not return home. He stayed in New Hampshire and went to work for the elderly female publisher of the Granite Monthly of Concord, at a salary of fifty dollars a month. The family in Europe had no idea anything was wrong, although Norma Stonehill remembers her mother's noticing that Abbott's letters had been posted from Lebanon, not Hanover, New Hampshire. Then a letter came from Grandma Slone in Lawrence, Long Island. She wrote that they had better come home right away, because Abbott was mixed up with some woman in New Hampshire.

The job, it turned out, was nothing if not respectable. He wrote a puff feature on New Hampshire's labor commissioner for the May 1923 issue, entitled "A Strong Man and a Big Job." This was the first professional article by A. J. Liebling, however, and it began with a bit of personal fanfare suitable to such an occasion. He was self-deprecatory, but he did announce himself: "Interviewing the Commissioner of Labor, when first suggested to the young journalist, seemed a terrifying task. . . ." But the plucky youth persevered and "long before the interview was over it had become a rare pleasure, for John S. B. Davie, practical creator and head of the Bureau of Labor, is not only a hardworking, fearless and successful executive, he is above all a great personality."

An article of some three thousand words followed that flattering overture. The text shows a firm grasp of the history, especially the legal history, of organized labor in the state of New Hampshire. The most sympathetic reader in the world could not say more.

Liebling himself, in the only account he ever gave of the episode, concealed the existence of this article. By December 8, 1956, when he wrote about the aftermath of his second expulsion from Dartmouth in a *New Yorker* article called "A Stranger in New York," he chose to emphasize the raffish side of what must have been a painful time. He starts off jauntily with a description of the coat he bought (no doubt as a gesture of defiance) immediately after his expulsion:

> The one I selected at Campion's, in Hanover, was an extra-pale-fawn gabardine trench coat with a belt. I was a premature Private Eye. I needed a new cap, so I bought one with large black-and-white checks. I was eighteen years old and pretty big, but I didn't look like a prizefighter, as I would have liked to, because I wore thick glasses. A professor whom I had had no opportunity to antagonize, since I took no courses with him, had got me a job on a small magazine called the *Granite Monthly*, in Concord, New Hampshire. The magazine was owned by Mrs. Robert Bass, the wife of a former Governor. She was wealthy.
>
> The thaw had not yet come, and it was cold in northern New England, but I wore my new outfit down to Concord. I would have made a hit with the publisher of a scratch sheet, but Mrs. Bass was unimpressed. My employment didn't last long, because I couldn't get interested in Oxford sheep, a subject the *Granite Monthly* had chosen for me. I offered to do a paper on Jose Maria de Heredia instead, but we could come to no agreement and soon parted. After the de Heredia impasse, I went back to Hanover and found several letters from my father and mother, who were off on a Mediterranean cruise aboard the *Rotterdam* and were not aware of my unattached status, since I had concealed the carks of care when last in New York, at the

short holiday after midyears. I won forty dollars in a crap game in South Fayerweather Hall, although winning was an unusual experience for me, and accepted promissory notes for my furniture and textbooks, which I sold at eviction sale prices to other inhabitants of Sanborn, where I roomed. I then bought a ticket for New York and departed, secure in the belief that my parents would not be home for eight weeks and that in the interim I could draw on any number of people for funds while I made a success as a short-story writer.

He planned to live like a "stranger in New York" in a neighborhood where he wouldn't see anyone he knew, a block such as Thirty-fifth Street between Fifth and Sixth avenues. Sometime in March, he did check into a hotel on Seventh Avenue in the upper Thirties, "because nobody I knew ever went there and I had heard it was fast." The bellboys surprised him when they offered him neither liquor nor women, but having set himself up in sufficiently déclassé style, he phoned his uncle, Charles Liebling, "to inform him I had left college in order to become a writer of short stories."

Uncle Charles, "a kind, vague man, always slightly in awe of my father," took Abbott to a serious lunch at Mouquin's. He gave the young man fifty dollars, after sounding him out on his plans, with evident suspicion. Abbott took the money and embarked on the first day of a new and lifelong role as, he liked to think, "the last Manhattan boulevardier."

He made his debut that evening, at Mouquin's, which was quiet at dinner, since the business trade had gone home and the Tenderloin district, which had formerly surrounded the solid old French restaurant in the West Twenties, had long since given way to the garment and fur industries. He wasn't quite sure what to do, but he had a fair idea from things he'd read: "I wanted to be like James Gibbons Huneker and H. L. Mencken." He ordered a "whopping dinner" with *canard aux olives* as the main course. He also worked his way through a pint of Sauternes and a full bottle of sparkling Burgundy, without a pucker, and then, after demitasse and Cognac, he "began to look harder at the women."

One in particular caught his eye. She was alone, and he began to think that she was smiling at him. But he wasn't positive; so he sent Roberto to ask if she would mind if he bought her a drink. "I shall always remember him with gratitude," Liebling wrote, "for not having made fun of me." The waiter returned, "saying that Madame would be most happy if I would join her."

> "I have been noticing your nice table manners all evening," she said when I sat down opposite her. "Your mother really must have taken a lot of trouble with you." I couldn't think of a good answer, and asked her if she would like some wine. She said no, it didn't agree with her, but she would just have a little bourbon-and-water. "I've been waiting here all evening for a very nice man who owns a paper mill," she said. "It seems there's some kind of a paper millers' convention in town. The first time he called up he was an hour late, but he said he'd be down right away; he and some other millers were just having a drink at a place on Fifty-second Street. The second time he said he was sorry but he was too stiff to move. What business are you in?"
>
> I said I wasn't in any, and she said she was glad, because she wouldn't have to listen to me talk about it. "It's all men ever talk about to us," she said, "and we have to pretend to be interested. About how they will fix the sales manager's wagon if they land something or other, because that will show the boss who is really the old he-coon, and if they quit the company, he may as well kiss off the medium-price market. Or sometimes gold scores." I told her I thought she was the only pretty woman in the place; I couldn't understand how any man would want to be with the others.

This patch of dialogue may have been an invention, a synthesis of similar conversations he had had in the interim with all manner of sporting women, courtesans, manicurists and other female waifs and professional veterans of the sex wars, but it may just as well be a radiant example of Liebling's often attested capacity for remembering conversation with the accuracy of a court reporter—minus notebook or Dictaphone. In any case, there is no reason to doubt that he did make that callow and grandiloquent gesture to a fading lady of the night, did buy her a drink, did pay her bill, doubling his 15 percent tip at her suggestion and thereby wiping out most of the working capital just donated by Uncle Charles. And it seems completely plausible that he did offer to lavish a last dollop of that precious fund on a cab to take his first Aspasia home.

She said she could walk, and then took him for a nightcap, on her, at Cavanagh's, across from her brownstone on Twenty-third Street between Seventh and Eighth, only a few short blocks from those other tart-infested houses his own father had demolished so shrewdly before the First World War. Liebling makes no mention of this curious geographic juxtaposition of important events in his life, but it is easy to imagine that he took secret pleasure from the coincidence.

The entire evening was, after all, staged in one of his father's favorite lunch spots. But he, the new-fledged boulevardier, was there, flush and spiffingly attired, to try his wings at an hour when his father was normally tucked away at home with the other solid burghers. That night his father was even farther away, and so his son could boldly tramp those same streets that were normally the old man's territory. And he could symbolically rescue a representative of the group his father had injured.

And so he was prowling through the old Tenderloin, his mind filled with lurid, nostalgic fantasies of an earlier New York, and like any high-class pimp, he went with his girl (who had just finished telling him how she preferred him to boring old businessmen, of his father's ilk) to a relaxed place where professionals hung out, for a drink at *her* expense.

It was lucky the woman had that generous impulse, for her "fancy man" had somewhere between $4.75 and $5.25 left in his pocket. Remembering his Maupassant, he knew he should then present her with a "lordly gift," but he couldn't even afford to hire her for the rest of the night. He improvised:

> "I'm sorry," I said, "but I think I'll have to leave you. You see, I'm in training for a track meet, and I have to get up at six o'clock in the morning and run ten miles."
> "It's perfectly all right, darling," Miss Griffin said. "You paid for my dinner, and you didn't tell me any stories about how you have the linen buyer at Strawbridge's in Philadelphia right in your pocket. Just don't get out of breath running."

The next day, this freshly minted lowlife phoned his uncle for more money. Charles Liebling had by then cabled his older brother in Beirut and apprised him of the bad news about his son. Joseph Liebling had instantly cabled back that Abbott should go and live with Charles and his wife in Bensonhurst, Brooklyn. His allowance was to be "waffles-and-coffee-size."

Suddenly, Joe had shrunk back into Abbott. He could spend the next few months as an apprentice writer, but his furious father was determined that his boy should have "some kind of career." Eventually a compromise was reached. Young Liebling entered the Pulitzer School of Journalism at Columbia (now the Columbia Graduate School of Journalism) and managed to stay the whole two-year course.

"In deciding to go to the Pulitzer School," he wrote, "I was influenced equally by my reluctance to go straight to work and by a feeling that to attend another undergraduate school after Dartmouth would be anticlimactic. The name of Joseph Pulitzer of the *World* may have had some slight influence upon me too." His "secret ambition" was to write fiction that would combine Bierce's "macabre qualities" with the "naturalism of the École de Médan."* Until he was ready to try that grand synthesis, he would "conquer journalism." He had told a Barnard girl in the summer of 1922 that it would not be within his powers to write anything great before he turned twenty-five.

He did clearly mean to write fiction, to write it seriously and to challenge the great novelists and short story writers of the past with his own work. The bragging may have covered up doubts. The basic plan was real. His Dartmouth notebooks prove that he was struggling to improve his skills and to force his soul through the sieve of poetic form, in order to learn the verbal discipline that poetry demands. His student essays and other pieces, even those from the *Dolphin*, show him as a dedicated apprentice to Prose. By the time he flopped himself down on Morningside Heights, he seems to have opted completely for prose—we have no explanation for the drying up of his verse, but it stopped flowing after Dartmouth—and he continued to write fiction.

Three manuscripts survive from the Columbia years. Two are typed with his name ("A. J. Liebling") and his address (606 West

* Médan was Émile Zola's country house, where he gathered about him a school of literary followers, including Guy de Maupassant.

116th Street) during journalism school. Perhaps these were the papers that got him exempted from the writing course at the school. "My queerest disillusion," he said, "came in a course in just straight writing. I was excused from it, on the ground that I could already write 'well enough.' I have often thought back on that 'well enough' with wonderment; well enough for what? The aim of a serious professional school should have been to teach everybody to write as well as Tom Paine or William Cobbett."

At any rate, there are two short stories written by Liebling at 606 West 116th Street. "The Princess of Capria's Hand" is a sub-Rabelaisian *conte* set in a medieval hall, replete with cold capons, drawbridges and kitchen wenches for occasional tickling. The hero has made a bet that he can win the hand of the imperious princess of the tale within the year. He strides back into the hall the next night, announcing himself with a stained-glass-shattering blast on a horn just before midnight. He has failed, but he wants to tell the story of his escapade. At this point the manuscript comes to an end.

The second, or rather the other, story is more interesting in its strange way. "A Painful Choice" is a castrational melodrama in which Tarik the Corsair is taken prisoner by a Phrygian captain and dragged to the palace of his brother Ali. The narrative is packed with vignettes of cruelty and sadism. Ali's court is a museum of Oriental sensuality, with divans bedizened with "a dozen Circassian girls and boys of surpassing beauty" lying in "amorous attitudes"; its sultan never stops stroking "the velvety skins and tender organs of his favorites." Tarik has to choose whether his punishment for rebelling against his brother's authority will be loss of his eyes or his genitals. This dilemma gives rise to much erotic daydreaming. The end of the story is also lost, but it does show a certain gift for pastiche and a taste for Moslem exoticism that Liebling would refine and sophisticate but never abandon.

Whether or not these stories were what sprang Liebling from the writing course, he did somehow demonstrate his writing competence and that gave him space in his schedule to take Old French from Raymond Weeks. And to keep his hand in with modern French, he seems to have translated several pages of elegant erotica by Restif de La Bretonne.

Otherwise the school was a washout for Liebling. In *The Way-*

ward Pressman, he complains about the exercises in "newswriting" and that the model he and his classmates were meant to copy was Adolph Ochs's "colorless, odorless and especially tasteless *Times* of 1923, a political hermaphrodite capable of intercourse with conservatives of both parties at the same time." The Pulitzer School, he concluded, had "all the intellectual status of a training school for future employees of the A & P."

Most of his classmates did not excite him either. He divided them into five categories: would-be creative writers looking for a paying trade that involved writing; fellows who expected to inherit or buy country papers and "were under the illusion they might learn something useful"; veteran reporters who had noticed that J-school graduates got thirty-five instead of thirty dollars a week for the same work; women with time to kill who "thought journalism sounded fascinating"; and Pan.

Hracia (Pan) Paniguian was a chubby, emotional, gregarious Armenian. He and Joe Liebling met on the first day of classes at Columbia (as Liebling had met Leo Stone on the first day at Dartmouth), became friends instantly and stayed friends for the rest of their lives. They spent luxurious hour after hour together during their journalism school days hanging out at Armenian restaurants. Pan was an exile from Armenia, and that must have appealed to Liebling's sense of the romantic. The friendship was interrupted after they graduated, when Pan couldn't get his visa extended and left for Europe. But the two men kept meeting at pivotal times in their lives for the next forty years.

Pan is dead, and little else remains from those two years that would throw light on Liebling's state of mind. His Columbia file shows that he caught a "grippe infection" in mid May of 1924 and had to postpone two final exams until the fall. That summer he toured England, France and Ireland with his family. His passport picture shows a solid young man in a three-piece suit of conservative cut and fabric. His expression is sullen. His ears protrude and his lips turn up on the left and down on the right side, forming an unpleasant compromise between sneer and scowl. The personal description on the passport states that he stood five feet nine and a half inches high, that his hair was brown, his nose flat and his forehead

high. He was already starting to bald. This may have been the trip
to Europe that, Norma Stonehill recalls, involved an expedition to
Alsace, to Hohwald near Strasbourg. They went to the convent of
Ste. Odile and drank the wine of the place, Lacrimae Sanctae Odi-
liae, the tears of Ste. Odile.

"I had chased after him the whole way," Mrs. Stonehill says. "He
was so big and loped along. We sat at a table in the orchard and
drank the wine. I asked him: 'Are these really the tears of Ste.
Odile?' He said: 'Sure, kid.'"

He did finally return to journalism school from this idyll, late and
without zeal. That summer was the last one he ever spent as the
ward of his parents.

Liebling's chapter on Columbia in *The Wayward Pressman* is
entitled "How to Learn Nothing." Still, his exposure to Romance
philology did really make an intellectual difference to him. Raymond Weeks was a fine scholar and a writer too. He put a certain
rigor into Joe's Gothic, fairy tale ideas about medieval France. And
that course must have been part of the impetus behind his studies
two years later, in Paris and in Normandy. The subject also gave
him a learned frame for his passion for Villon and Rabelais. But as a
whole, Columbia struck him as a pointless exercise. He said: "The
newspaper world is full of alumni of schools of journalism, but they
seldom admit it until their interrogator thrusts hot needles under
their fingernails."

The only journalistic training he got through the school that he
did value came to him at the other end of Manhattan Island from
Columbia. He got course credit in "reporting" by actually doing a
bit of it, at police headquarters downtown at Centre Market Place.

A Professor C. P. Cooper, known as "Coop," sent him downtown
to the newspaper shacks and promised to pass him in reporting if he
spent two days a week working on police stories out of Centre Market Place, which was "cold as a glacial crevasse in winter" and "hot
as a fat man's breech in summer."

Cooper told him to look up Max Fischel of the *Evening World*.
Fischel, "a plump, gray man with a round face and a psittacine
nose, was sixty" and "liked to call himself 'the dean of the corpse' of
police reporters; he had been legman for Jacob Riis in the nineties,

when that Danish-born *Sun* reporter had made slum clearance a national issue." Fischel became Liebling's mentor in the practical arts of reporting, both by precept and by example. And that chapter in *The Wayward Pressman* called "Max and the Corpse," in which Joe describes his down-to-earth apprenticeship, is a classic description of the nuts and bolts of old-time crime coverage.

Student reporter Liebling knew then, and understood even better when he wrote the chapter about his experiences with Fischel, that he had also stumbled onto the vestiges of a great tradition of investigative urban journalism and muckraking, which connected with his own family heritage.

Jacob Riis wrote about New York's Lower East Side, whose population was, in large part, Jewish. Riis, in his influential book *How the Other Half Lives,* described the very same neighborhood in which Joseph Liebling spent his youth and early manhood. Max Fischel was, therefore, a link with a moment in journalism that touched directly on Liebling's family and the impoverished conditions from which his father had risen.

But Joe Liebling, while omitting the Jewish side of his father's Lower East Side past, glorified it in general terms in "Max and the Corpse":

> I liked even the sociable smells of the East Side. It was something of a return to the manor for me. My father had spent his boyhood there, although by the time he married he had got five miles uptown and even further away economically. Yet he had often told me stories of this vivid world in which all his adventures, according to him, had been personal triumphs. My mother professed to find these stories boresome, and I don't think I had ever been sure, before I got down to Headquarters, that he hadn't made most of them up.

Clearly, Liebling did consider his stint with Fischel a return to his roots, but he refused to give us more than a vague economic sense of what those origins had been.

Max Fischel was a perfect guide to the neighborhood and to the craft of reporting. "Max," Liebling wrote, "knew the East Side so well that despite his advancing years and short legs he could beat almost anyone to the scene of a story when he really wanted to. He knew the roof pattern of every block by heart, for one thing, and by

travelling across roofs he could often arrive at an upper-floor tenement before less resourceful reporters had reached the street door."

More even than Fischel, Liebling's favorite among the police reporters was one Red Gallagher: "He was only five years older than I
but he knew everything. He wore a derby hat on the side of his
head and a chesterfield overcoat with a velvet collar; a colored man
had slashed one side of his face in a clip-joint brawl, he had a crush
on a woman who had been divorced five times, with bigger headlines over each reprise."

Joe sat in the newspaper shacks, watching Gallagher dash about
or Fischel sucker another reporter in two-handed pinochle. He must
have listened spellbound when Bob Patterson of the *Sun*, in Victorian white mustache and derby, or some other old hand, told of
"murders by perverts, then of rats eating babies, and how old Dan
Peabody used to beat more information out of stool pigeons than the
new cops would ever learn how to get in police college."

Young Liebling kept himself busy, playing reporter and handing
in "little stories" in class at Columbia. One was about a detective
who tripped up a confidence man by giving him a five-dollar bill on
which he had previously decorated, with a discreet inky stud, the
shirt front Abraham Lincoln wears in his portrait on the bill. Another story was about an unwed mother in an Episcopal home for
women on Mulberry Street.

Liebling's instructor, "the old raspberry-sherbet-faced biographer
of cardinals," pronounced both these efforts unfit for inclusion in
the *Times*. But that did not cut into Liebling's enthusiasm for reporting. He was learning how to handle himself, exploring new
worlds: "I liked to pound up tenement stairs and burst in on families
disarranged by sudden misfortune. It gave me a chance to make
contact with people I would never otherwise have met, and I
learned almost immediately what every reporter knows, that most
people are eager to talk about their troubles and are rather flattered
by the arrival of the *World* or the *Journal*."

Once he covered an actual death:

> There was a police slip about a wrecker's workman who had fallen
> from a building, a long walk east of headquarters—Pitt or Cannon
> Street, I think. Langdon Post, a Harvard man who had decided to en-

ter newspaper work at thirty, had been sent to Max at the *Evening World* shack to break in. We started out together on the story of the fallen workman. Both of us were in good condition, and I think we broke all records for walking through an obstacle course of children and pushcarts. We did not consider it sporting to run. By the time we reached the knot of curious people on the sidewalk in front of a half-demolished wall we had almost forgotten the nature of the thing we were racing to. Each of us had been concentrating on walking so fast the other fellow would have to run a couple of steps to keep up.

The crowd opened up before our evident urgency and the police cards we wore in our hats, and there the man lay on his back. He was gray with cement dust and there was no blood on his face. There was no blood in sight. Under his short white nails there was mortar; falling, he had tried to hold onto the top of the wall by his fingers. He must have lost his balance as he heaved to loosen a stone. The bloody old building had revenged itself. Many an immigrant must have died in it, and even going down, it was taking another European to the grave.

A cop standing by had the man's name already; the boss of the wrecking gang had furnished it. None of us knew how to pronounce the name, but Post and I copied it out of the cop's notebook. It was Polish, or Ukrainian, or Lithuanian, I forget.

The cop said: "Nobody but a Polack would take a job like that."

Liebling wound up his sojourn on the Lower East Side by translating an Italian book on Italo-American life for an *Evening World* series on the "different colonies of foreign-born Americans in New York." He was paid fifteen dollars, the first money he ever earned from a newspaper. And that was that. He had found significant experience on the Lower East Side, among Italians and poor "Polacks" and even in an Episcopalian home for unwed mothers, but there is no mention of Jews.

School ended anticlimactically: "As a maraschino cherry on the sundae of academic absurdity, the degree was entitled Bachelor of Literature, although what literature had to do with rewriting the *Times* paragraphs I never found out. I went swimming on commencement day."

four

The Road Back to New York

He swam a lot in the first six weeks of the summer of 1925. From time to time, he looked for work as a police reporter, but there were no such jobs. And the water was pleasant at Rockaway Beach.

Finally, in August or thereabouts, Professor Cooper, the Columbia teacher who had sent him to Max Fischel, found a way to launch Joe Liebling in the big time, so to speak. One Laurence J. Spiker, of the sports department of *The New York Times,* had asked Cooper to send him an ex-student with "the makings of a copyreader."

"By this," Liebling later quipped, "I presume, he meant a broad bottom and a captious disposition. Coop recommended me, and I went unromantically to work sitting down."

He hoped that he would eventually convince an editor that he had enough experience to "use my legs." This never happened. Instead, he spent his time at the *Times* among "frustrated reporters who know exactly how a story should be covered because they have never covered one" and "superannuated reporters who are just resting their feet" and "the congenital, aboriginal, intramurals." This

third group of copyreaders, he observed, were all "fated to be editors except the ones that get killed off by the lunches they eat at
their desks until even the most drastic purgatives lose all effect upon
them. The survivors of gastric disorders rise to minor executive jobs
and then major ones, and the reign of these non-writers makes our
newspapers read like the food in the *New York Times* cafeteria
tastes."

He went to work, then, without excitement. They paid him eight
dollars a day, six days a week. That wasn't much even in 1925, but
he lived with his parents, who had moved into town, in an apartment hotel near Central Park, and after five months on the job he
got a raise to fifty dollars a week. The salary was "adequate," but
the "clean, painless job" was "without any intrinsic interest." He
checked the statistics in sports stories, cleared the copy and gave a
"cursory look at the sports writer's text," which he rarely changed
much, because sportswriters guarded their verbiage so jealously.
Then he wrote a headline for the story, his "nearest approach to creative effort."

He worked nights, and he was bored, even though "there was, for
a man of twenty-one, . . . a fascinating sense of being a dashing
chap just because one was in the newspaper game." For relaxation,
after 1:30 A.M., the "gayer element" on the desk drank needled beer
in the speakeasies around Times Square. Liebling's most frequent
companion, Irish, of course, was John Muldowney, the next most
senior copyreader. Their most memorable experience, other than a
series of garrulous drinking sessions, was picking up a drunk lying in
the January snow on West Forty-fifth Street and returning him to
his hotel, the America, which they guessed was what he meant
when, after being asked where he lived, he murmured, "United
States."

The sports editor, Major Thomson, was an Anglophile and a florid
Canadian, who "acknowledged a profound dislike for sports of all
kinds." Thomson, at that time, was conducting a ludicrous competition with the *Herald Tribune* to print more scores from schoolboy
athletic contests. Thomson was also a stickler for printing the names
of every player, whenever possible, including referees, on the theory that the more names a paper printed, the more readers it would

attract. This misguided zeal for full high school basketball line scores led to the now famous Ignoto episode. "One night," Liebling's account begins,

> some boy with pimples in his voice called up from Brooklyn to tell the *Times* about a particularly unfascinating contest between two Catholic-school fives. I took the call and noted down all the drear details until I got to who was the referee. "Who was he?" I asked. "I don't know," the kid said, "and anyway I ain't got any more nickels." So he hung up. We couldn't use a basketball score in the *Times* without the name of the referee. So I wrote in "Ignoto," which means "unknown" in Italian. Nobody caught on, and after a while I had Ignoto refereeing a lot of basketball games all around town. Then I began bragging about it, and after a short while my feeble jest came to the ears of Thomson.
>
> "God knows what you will do next, young man," he told me after the first edition had gone to press on a bitter night in March. "You are irresponsible. Not a *Times* type. Go."

This is a somewhat embroidered account. For the record, that illustrious figment Mr. Ignoto appeared only two times in high school basketball line scores in *The New York Times* during the 1925–26 season. And a careful inspection of the same subliterature shows that many other line scores that winter were printed without benefit of referee. Over the years, it seems, Liebling improved the story.

He told it so well, in fact, that it was accepted as truth by almost everyone who knew him. Even the writer of his *Times* obituary reprinted Liebling's version of the Ignoto story. This would have been a delicious moment for Liebling if he could have been around to savor it, because he was one of the very few people who knew that the Ignoto story he had confessed to in *The Wayward Pressman* was not only an exaggeration but also a hoax.

Major Thomson did fire Liebling in March 1926. But the Ignoto business had nothing directly to do with it. What really happened, according to Joe Nichols, who was a young *Times* sports reporter at the time, is that Liebling played a little joke on the *Times* boxing writer, James P. Dawson, and the joke backfired. Dawson had attended the first meeting of the Boxing Writers Association of America at the Hotel Commodore, where he had been elected first vice president of the new group. Afterward Dawson called in with a short news item about the meeting. Liebling was on the desk and took down the story. He noticed that Dawson, evidently pleased with himself, had given his full name, James Patrick Dawson, in the announcement of his own election. Dawson's normal signature (and his *Times* byline) was simply James P. Dawson.

Liebling thought this act of self-inflation was absurd and he decided to make fun of it. He sent Dawson's copy down slightly altered. His name appeared as James Parnell Dawson in the morning paper.

Thomson noticed the made-up middle name. He was not amused by the spurious assimilation of his star ring reporter into the radical flock that venerated the nineteenth-century Irish nationalist Charles Stewart Parnell. The *Times* had no place for a copyreader who, for fun, would knowingly change the name of a reporter. And that was really why Liebling was fired.

Why did he camouflage the truth with Ignoto? It can only be that Ignoto made a better story. It was funnier and easier to tell. Inventing Ignoto was also a more outrageous jape than changing Dawson's middle name from Patrick to Parnell. Liebling ought to have been fired for Ignoto, he must have thought, if he was going to be fired at all for mischievous tampering with copy. Eventually, through slyness and the power of his own narration, he persuaded the world that that was the way it had really happened. In March of 1926, however, his main problem was not planting a creative version of his dismissal in the public mind. Liebling needed a job.

Getting fired from his job at the nation's most prestigious paper convinced Liebling of his own worthlessness, briefly. He recovered his spirits with great speed at the bar of a reporters' speakeasy called the Artist & Writers Club, near the *Herald Tribune*. After accepting, with pleasurable astonishment, the congratulations of the older reporters in the saloon, Joe sat down at a desk and wrote two letters on the free stationery provided by the club's founder-owner, Jack Bleeck.

The first letter was a long one, to a woman called Nat. Older than Joe and officially a manicurist, Nat was a part-time courtesan kept, in order to brighten his visits to New York, by "a department-store owner in a Southwestern state." Joe, desperately shy with women, in those days frequented manicurists because they were professionally obliged to talk to him and hold his hand. With Nat he had evidently found the courage to push the relationship further than a mere manicure. And before the end of his stint at the *Times,* he had even "cherished a project of rescuing her from what" he had "considered her equivocal status." Now jobless in early March 1926, he wrote to warn her that he was a "ne'er-do-well" and wouldn't be able to make "a living for her." Actually, he would continue to see Nat in later years, after he had rescued and married another woman. But for the time being, he thought he had to sever the tie.

The second latter went to Vic Bernstein, a former classmate at Columbia working at the Providence *News.* Joe assumed that the Ignoto debacle had spoiled his chances of finding work in New York but hoped that word of his "irresponsibility had not yet reached New England." It had not. Bernstein spoke to another Columbia alumnus, Claude Jagger, at the Providence *Evening Bulletin.* Within three days a firm offer arrived in the mail from Rhode Island: forty dollars a week to cover general assignments. Liebling took it. His parents, whom he had not told he had been fired, were shocked that he was leaving the *Times* so abruptly. "It's a dirty trick," said his father. "They'll never hire you back."

He took the train up to Providence in mid March, in time to go to work on March 18. That very same day, Edward Radding, a real estate speculator, hanged himself in his cell in the Providence County Jail. Liebling jumped right into the story, which ran on page one the next day. He tracked down the Radding family and got them to talk about the deceased. "This was the kind of assignment that," Liebling subsequently wrote,

> if I had not had my experience at Police Headquarters, would have caused me to throw up my job then and go home. But I remembered how welcome ghouls usually were in such circumstances and set out with equanimity.... They were all glad to see me, because they wanted to say that the dead man had been double-crossed, framed, and crucified, and they hoped the same thing would happen to the whited sepulchre of a banker who had put him on the spot.

Liebling's career had finally begun, anonymously, but it had begun. Buoyed by this initial success, he rented an apartment with Vic Bernstein on State House Hill, a tiny place with a folding bed and a tub in the closet. Bernstein slept on the couch. The two young men spent their nights off at the Empire Theatre watching burlesque and at an Italian speakeasy downing homemade wine and dollar dinners. "Providence," Liebling found, "was a lovely place to work in. There was nothing you could do about anything, but then nothing was so bad that you felt a burning urge to do anything about it."

In short, he prospered. After two weeks at the *Bulletin*, he substituted for another reporter at a hearing in a Prohibition case. A German bootlegger named Sigmund Rand had been chopping down a tree in his front yard when the revenuers nabbed him. There was a still in his cellar, which he claimed he hadn't known existed. Liebling wrote that he may have chopped down a tree, "but he was no George Washington." This light touch convinced management that its newly acquired reporter was "primarily a writer" and he was transferred to the *Journal*, the *Bulletin's* sister paper, a morning daily where, he later wrote, "there was more space for the leisurely deployment of my talent."

He then "oozed prose over every aspect of Rhode Island life," from shipwrecked mariners to a society charity drive. None of these articles had bylines, but it is possible to identify four of them from references he let drop in the autobiographical sketch in *The Wayward Pressman*. Every one is, in its way, a parody of conventional reportage.

"WEEDEN, LUNATIC,/FLEES ASYLUM FOR/FOURTEENTH TIME" reads the column-one, page-one headline from the *Journal* of April 19, 1926. Frank Weeden was an officially dangerous psychotic who, Liebling noted astutely to himself, had become over the years a fixture of Providence journalism. "I decided to take a new line," he wrote in *The Wayward Pressman;* "it was obviously a funny story." Liebling lovingly rehearsed the Weeden legend. "Romance and the sinister mingled strangely in his life story," he wrote, and then proceeded to undermine Weeden's reputation for violence by showing that he timed his escapes to coincide with warm weather and that he had never done anyone harm during his outings. Finally, in the time-honored reportorial tradition of relying on expert quotations, Joe phoned the superintendent of the State Hospital for Mental Diseases and got him to say: "I guess he simply has the wanderlust."

Ten days later, Liebling invented a page-one news item. The New York State Athletic Commission had just declared that it would not condone a heavyweight championship bout between Jack Dempsey and Harry Wills, the Brown Panther. Joe contacted the newly created Rhode Island Boxing Commission and got the commissioners to agree that they would not oppose the match or any other interracial fight. The joke was that there was no practical possibility that provincial Rhode Island, where no fight had ever drawn more than $15,000 in gate receipts, could attract Dempsey.

Liebling continued this mischievous approach a few weeks later in a long page-one story on the annual horse show at the Jacobs Hill Hunt in nearby Seekonk, opening puckishly with a tribute to the animals:

> King horse regained his throne yesterday at the Jacobs Hill Hunt in Seekonk. Five hundred automobiles were parked around the clubhouse during the show, but they came only to do the old monarch homage.

The standard sports lead would have mentioned the names of winning riders. Liebling, typically, chose an unorthodox angle, one that glorified Jacobs Hill's normally unsung equine "working class." His lead also allowed Liebling to express the authentic affection he felt all his life for horses and his nostalgia for the pre-automobile age.° By the third paragraph of the story, he did get around to naming the stable that had produced most of the day's winners. But even that concession to conventional news judgment became a pretext for blatant idiosyncrasy. "The victory of Chantry," he wrote, ". . . followed the finest contest of the day, in which Chantry, his stablemate, Tradesman, and Miss Alice Stuart's Blue Fern all performed perfectly." The first two horses came from the stable of C.

°At his death, Liebling was under contract to write a book about New York City in the era of the horse. See page 315.

V. B. Cushman, which captured most of the show's events. Normally, a reporter would have focused on Cushman and his triumphant mounts. Liebling shifted his attention to the hapless Miss Stuart:

> Although her horses were beaten by narrow margins in all their classes, Miss Stuart's riding made her the popular heroine of the show, and the applause when she rode out for her later classes were like those heard when Babe Ruth walks to bat.

Altogether, eight paragraphs, more than half of all the space Liebling was given to work with on page one, are devoted to Miss Stuart's graceful failures. Was Liebling using the columns of the Providence *Journal* to declaire his interest in a society equestrienne? More probably, in raising such a question, he meant to amuse readers (and himself) by paying exaggerated attention to a woman in a sports article. The comparison to Babe Ruth is noteworthy. Liebling went on to say that "Miss Ann Kenyon, about as big as a mustard seed and looking twice as sharp, was the heroine of the junior events." Although his remarks never exceed propriety, they suggest that an erotic interest lurks in the mind of the reporter. Whatever Liebling's true feelings may have been about the Misses Stuart and Kenyon, his story about their performances at the horse show was like a wink in their direction, a wink committed in public and one that was particularly noticeable because it occurred in a setting where women were not normally noticed at all.

As he had in his other pieces that spring, Liebling here made mild subversive fun of journalistic convention. Tacitly, he wrote against the grain; he performed in an original manner which implicitly called into question the faceless, formulaic mannerisms of daily journalism, while at the same time he made the acute reader wonder for an instant who the person was behind the undoubtedly personal tone of his writing.

Liebling was no rebel. But he had begun to ask himself serious questions about his profession almost as soon as he had entered it. After spewing out five thousand words on a big fire in Fall River (he was the rewrite man for a group effort) in one hectic night without, as he proudly remembered, once stooping to write the word "holocaust" as a synonym for fire, he wondered how long he could last in the newspaper business:

> This is the kind of thing that newspapers in all times and cities are largely made up of, and I've nothing against it, but I can't see that it means very much. Within a couple of months I was sure I could do it as well as anybody anywhere, and better than most. This was a pleasant thought in one way, but in others less so. How would it feel, I wondered, to be doing the same thing at forty or fifty? And how could a man of forty or fifty, with dignity and responsibilities, make a living at it, when there would always be kids of twenty-one able and willing to do the same job for peanuts? The run of the news is repetitious: the lunatic's escape, the embezzler's suicide, the conflagration, the rescue are prototypes of continually recurrent stories. In times when great things are happening, young men have to cover earthshaking events. In ordinary grubby times, the city editor can find no more important assignment for the most sapient reporter in the shop than the opening of a new wing at the municipal art museum.

If this reminiscence written twenty years after the fact accurately recollects Joe Liebling's thoughts in Providence in the spring of 1926, then at twenty-one he had already formed basic opinions that later guided his criticism of the press. Newspapers were founded on repetition; reporters were the slaves of low pay and of their assignments. On the other hand, he was "having a fine time," treating life like a "spectator sport," keeping fit by jogging, swimming and boxing at the YMCA, taking long walks at night with new friends. He was hooked. "The taint was on me," he wrote, echoing the words of Max Fischel. He would never leave journalism, and he would always feel equally delighted and trapped. But it was only to last a few months, this Rhode Island debut. Joe's father made him an extraordinary offer.

"You always used to talk about going to Europe to study," he said one day when Joe was visiting his parents in New York, "and I have always thought that a man should. If you don't go now, you never will. You will get a good job and then you won't want to give it up, or you will get mixed up with a girl."

"As a matter of fact," Joe replied, hoping to confirm his father's resolve, "I was thinking of asking a woman to marry me. She's fifteen years older than I am, and she isn't Jewish, and she hasn't any money, and she has been divorced four times and she has a child by each of the four husbands, but I am sure Mother and you will like her."

The dialogue sounds made up. Indeed, in another version of the same episode, Liebling quotes himself as saying, "the girl is ten years older than I am, and Mother might think she is kind of fast, because she is being kept by a cotton broker from Memphis, Tennessee, who only comes North once in a while. But you are a man of the world, and you understand that a woman can't always help herself."

Perhaps it is safe to conclude that Liebling did con his father in one way or another with the specter of a disreputable girlfriend. And both versions of the story do reflect the truth of his erotic inclinations toward tainted non-Jewish women in need of rescue. On the other hand, his father may have needed no encouragement; the dubious fiancée may never have been conjured up. At any rate, Joe Liebling soon found himself the bearer of a letter of credit on the Irving Trust for two thousand dollars and a reservation on the *Caronia* for the late summer, when the rates fell. Meanwhile he continued to work in Providence, and his family sailed for Europe at full fare and in first class so that his sister could spend her school vacation with them abroad. The plan was that Abbott would enjoy a few days with them in Europe and then begin his studies after they left.

With prophetic improvidence, Liebling began drawing on his letter of credit during the summer. He went through eight hundred dollars of it before the *Caronia* sailed and several hundred more were gone after he spent a week in Paris at a hotel off the Champs Élysées. He wired ahead to his parents, who were by then at Lake Como, announcing that he was on his way to join them. Once in Italy, he negotiated a two-hundred-dollar-a-month retainer for the coming year. He confessed to his father that he had almost run through the original lump sum and that without more money he would have to return home and marry the cotton broker's girl. The ruse probably did not fool Joseph Liebling, but he recognized it as a face-saving device and went along with it because "he had a very good idea of the value of leisure, not having had any until it was too late to become accustomed to it, and a very good idea of the pleasure afforded by knowledge that has no commercial use, having never had time to acquire more than a few odd bits."

So it was agreed upon. His family left for America, and Joe Liebling began his *Lehrjahr*. It marked him deeply, lay at the heart of half his books, for France and the Villonesque life of the literary vagabond that he led on the Left Bank during the next year permanently shaped Liebling's imagination and style. Never again would he have the leisure to pursue knowledge and experience without the justification and prod of a deadline. He was not in debt. He had no dependent women's costs to defray. On his modest stipend he managed to explore medieval French literature, introduce himself to French food from the ground up and carry on his first recorded love affair. It was a year without restraints, a time of pleasure and self-indulgence, a golden parenthesis. He began it with a trip to Normandy that later assumed mythic proportions in his memory.

Writing in the middle fifties about this Shandean "sentimental journey," he explained:

> I had two months to spare before the opening of the Sorbonne in 1926, and I wanted to travel in some part of France that wasn't Paris. Lower Normandy was easy to get to, it had a historical cachet, and I had heard that it was agreeable, but not spectacular. Because it was not spectacular, it was not tourist country, and I was terribly afraid of being mistaken for a tourist. At that remote period of my life, I liked to walk fifteen or twenty miles a day, but I wanted a good bed to sleep in at night, and I was a great glutton. I had read Guy de Maupassant in English when I was still in short pants—I was in them again in 1926, but I called them plus fours—and this gave me a feeling of confidence about plunging into Normandy.

He plunged in with gusto. For a typical light lunch, Liebling polished off "a dozen *huîtres de Courseulles*, an *araignée de mer* (spider crab) with a half pint of mayonnaise on the side, a dish of *tripes à la mode de Caen*, a partridge Olivier Basselin, poached in cream and cider and singed in old Calvados, a *gigot de pré-salé*, a couple

of biftecks, and a good Pont l'Evêque." Between meals, he feasted
on the Bayeux tapestry. He stopped at Avranches in "the hotel on
top of the hill that has a view over Mont-Saint-Michel and a garden
with fig trees." From there, he passed to the village of Genêts and
hired a carriage to take him over the sand to Mont-Saint-Michel at
low tide. "There was," he conceded, "already an automobile cause-
way to the Mont, but it seemed more authentic to cross the sands in
the calèche with its wide-rimmed sand wheels."

He revisited these sites during the Normandy invasion and again
in the mid fifties. They had a magic resonance for him, haunts of
his youth's only golden moment, but no Norman town held quite
the place he reserved for tiny, drab little Vire. To this stopover popular with traveling salesmen he came in search of a literary phantom, Olivier Basselin, the putative author of some medieval drinking lyrics. Liebling quickly discovered that the work of Basselin had
actually been composed by a seventeenth-century hoax artist, a Vi-
rois named Le Houx. Basselin had, however, lived, drunk and perhaps written poetry, now lost, in the fifteenth century, but Liebling,
having unmasked Le Houx's deception, took pleasure in it as well as
in the partridge dish that bore his name. It tasted, he said, "like a
partridge that had been fed all its life from a bottle of Calvados fifty years old." Fortified by such fare at the Hotel du Cheval Blanc,
next to Vire's sixteenth-century clock tower, he would tramp as far
as Mortain, seventeen miles away, down a brook trout and then cab
home to Vire. On these rambles he would have passed the sinuous
rills known as the vales or Vaux de Vire. This local scenery is usually
said to be the source of the word "vaudeville," because of satirical
songs written long ago in Vire, songs probably attributed to Olivier
Basselin. No doubt this is what sent Liebling, a lifelong aficionado
of modern vaudeville, to Vire in the first place. He also felt a literary attraction for Vire's principal product, the *andouille,* a smoked
sausage filled with tripe. Rabelais mentions the gutsy, big and phal-
lic prize of Norman charcuterie often, and Rabelais was a Liebling
hero.

Classes at the University of Paris did finally begin in November.
Liebling returned to the capital, 150 miles to the south but a world
away from Vire, in late October. On the way back, he stopped near

Vendôme to visit his journalism school friend Paniguian, who had found a job at an Armenian orphanage. He wrote home, from temporary lodgings at the Hotel des Théâtres de Champs Élysées, 6 Avenue Montaigne, on the Right Bank, on October 24, to acknowledge receipt of the first monthly check, and later that week he wrote again:

Dear Folks:

This is the last letter you will get from this address as classes start next week and I have found (after much trial and trib) a room near the Sorbonne, where I hope to remain for the winter. The new address is Hotel Saint-Pierre, 4 Rue de l'Ecole de Medicine, Paris (VI). Like most of the small hotels in the quarter, it is really a students' lodging house during the university year, all the rooms except those "au premier" being rented by the month to students and instructors. Naturally there are many medical students at this particular hotel, for it faces the Faculte de Medicine, but the Sorbonne is within three blocks. I am paying 450 francs a month for my room, which is a good size, comfortable and has running water. I do have to climb four flights of stairs to get at it, but then you can't have everything. There are 22,000 students at the five faculties and rooms are at a premium. I tried nine places before this one and saw two rooms, neither of them any good. The price of 500 francs, for a room I didn't like, indicates that I am not being gypped.

Matriculation took two days because they have only two men to inform, interrogate and matriculate 5,000 students at the faculty of letters. As they charge only 100 francs a year, however, one can't complain. For the 100 francs you are allowed to take all the courses you can carry. Dartmouth has raised its tuition fee to $400 a semester. Just now I have in mind four courses at the faculty of letters, two at the Ecole des Chartes, and one (lectures only) at the College de France, but one of the courses at the Ecole covers pretty much the same ground as another at the Sorbonne, so I shall drop one or the other after giving both a trial. This is the general policy advised by M. Champenois before I left New York. The Quartier Latin seems as fascinating to me now as the Boulevards did two years ago. Hope the charm doesn't wear off as soon. . . .

It will take me a month, I suppose, to get adjusted to my new surroundings, probably longer than that to "find out what it's all about" at the university. I got my biggest shock when I produced my Columbia diploma and was not thrown out on my head.

I think of you surprisingly often (when you consider what a hard-boiled son I am). There are some nice new hotels on the Boulevard St.-Germain. This morning I picked a couple for you to choose between next spring so you can be near me. As ever—
Abbott

During this same period, while he waited for classes to start, he applied for a job at the Paris *Herald*, but turned up nothing. By November 5, however, he had plunged into university life.

Liebling fell into a routine of study, found a gymnasium and habituated himself to the Left Bank. Thus settled, he also pursued his gastronomic education under the ideal conditions (as he later pontificated) of a limited budget. Short funds forced him to pick and choose among a variety of cheap new foods and to weigh with great seriousness the merits of each. "The consistently rich man," he wrote, "is . . . unlikely to make the acquaintance of meat dishes of robust taste—the hot *andouille* and *andouillette*, which are close-packed sausages of smoked tripe, and the *boudin*, or blood pudding, and all its relatives that figure in the pages of Rabelais and on the menus of market restaurants." In *Between Meals*, he expatiates on his strategy for maximizing his remittance from home. Despite every precaution and the most astute weighing of one dish or wine against another on the menus of his favorite bistros, he always ended up broke at the end of each month and would drop in at the main office of the Crédit Lyonnais, on the Right Bank, arriving on foot, to see if the next check had come in. This hand-to-mouth policy became a habit with Liebling. For the rest of his life, he was constantly short of money. He was certainly never guilty of the bourgeois virtue of deferred gratification. He wrote at a Defoe-like pace, spurred by insatiable appetites of all sorts that required expensive support. He was never "comfortable," prided himself ruefully on living at the edge of his resources, but always lived well by his own standards of elegance and gourmandise.

It was in Paris in 1926 and 1927 that he refined those standards.

He cadged a bit of the best of everything available, on the cheap or for free. When Arthur F. Jacobs, an old chum from Far Rockaway High School, came over to Paris on his honeymoon with his wife, Ruth, in December 1926, Liebling met them every day for lunch at the Dôme in Montparnasse. The three of them went on endless walks around the city. "One day" Arthur Jacobs recalls, "he refused his *fine* at lunch. We asked what the matter was. He said: 'You know these French, how carefully graded everything is. An orange with a bruise is one price, one in paper is another. Women are just as carefully graded. My father told me to watch out with women. Last night I was in Montparnasse, and I didn't have enough money to get a decent woman.' "

Jacobs made him go to a doctor at the American Hospital. When he came back, he announced: "The doctor told me to take it out. I took it out. He told me to turn it over. I turned it over. Then he said: 'The prophylactic you used was too tight.' "

It was a kind of lesson. In the course of his hundreds of hours of girl-watching at certain Latin Quarter cafés, he became attached to a bevy of young women who were not exactly professionals nor precisely virtuous either:

> The girls were like country artisans; they took money for their services, but only when they felt like working. On occasion they would accept payment in kind—a dinner or a pair of stockings . . .
>
> Our girls were not intellectuals. None was a geisha primed with poems, nor were there hetaerae who could have disputed on equal terms with Plato, or even with Max Lerner.

One night, while trying to live his "idealized notion, formed at home, of how a Frenchman lived," he met a girl named Angèle at Gypsy's Bar on the Rue Cujas. Angèle's torso was "solid Renoir." "Her neck," Liebling wrote, in one of the few pieces of his ever rejected by *The New Yorker*, "was also a bit short and thick—a good point in a prizefighter but not in a swan. She had a clear skin and a sweet breath, and she was well jointed—the kind of girl you could rough up without fear of damage. Angèle had a snub nose, broad at the base, like a seckel pear tilted on its axis."

Best of all, she thought that Joe was *"passable."* His "brain reeled under the munificence of her compliment." If she had said he was handsome, he "wouldn't have believed her." As it was, her plain but credible tribute saved him "a debt the size of a small Latin American republic's in analysts' fees" over the ensuing decades.

Angèle encouraged Joe's disdain for Montparnasse and the resident American colony that camped out in the *terrasses* of its cafés. The Lost Generation reminded Liebling of "monkeys on a raft," dabblers in Parisian life who were "not in the water at all." Instead of looking up Joyce (whose *Ulysses* he had admiringly read), he drank in obscurity with Angèle or with M. Perès, his landlord at the Saint-Pierre. In part, this total immersion in the plain, permanent life of the Quarter was a defense mechanism. He "hated" the expatriates at Le Sélect because "they had all decided they were writers, or painters, or sculptors, and I didn't know what I was."

The crisis of identity was upon him in a particularly virulent form. Was he a writer or an urban lowlife who made a living working for newspapers? Was he an artist or a hack? He wasn't sure; the perplexity would not lift. And so he despised others who sidestepped vocational malaise and blithely declared they were writers or painters. While he tried to make up his mind, Liebling retreated into the lazy life of the Sorbonnard, emerging rarely from the role he had chosen. No further letters home survive, which suggests that he wrote none or only the most routine communications. He did, however, stay in touch with a French family he had first known on Long Island.

The Salens had lived in Lawrence for several years and had just returned to France upon the completion of Herman Salen's stint with the American office of Duplan, a Lyonnais silk concern. Mme. Salen had filled her time on Long Island by giving French lessons to local ladies. Anna Liebling, always eager for intellectual self-improvement, became one of her students and then her friend.

As a family, the Salens offered Joe Liebling a surrogate home in Paris that roughly matched his own family's. They were also in the garment business, and they treated Joe with familial affection. During his first few weeks in Paris, he visited them twice in the space of three days, "coming around as often as O'Grady's wife." And he couldn't reciprocate because grandmother Salen protested the one time he took her granddaughter Suzette out on a date.

Suzette Salen Namin recalls that Joe "came a lot to the house" the whole time he was a student and, in her opinion, was heavily influenced by her father. The two men went on long walks together.

With Suzette, then seventeen, he alternated between periods of memorable silence and playfulness. "He would make fun of the French, while loving them. He could be *très moqueur.*" Liebling also used Suzette to perfect his knowledge of French. She was bilingual (and even today speaks French with an American accent) and would make a game with Joe out of "looking for the right equivalent for French and English words." In general, Joe seems to have amused the Salen family, but never more than on the occasion of a large dinner they gave for some American businessmen, when Liebling put an entire Camembert on his plate, and made everyone giggle around the table in the Salens' vast apartment on the fashionable Avenue de La Motte-Picquet.

It was also through Herman Salen that Liebling joined a lackadaisical rowing organization, La Société Nautique de la Marne. His career as a French oarsman, as chronicled in *Between Meals*, seems to have been mainly a dry run. The crew spent most of its time at water's edge, apéritifs in hand, waiting for rain to stop. Joe did exercise, at the American Baptist Center's gym on the Rue Denfert-Rochereau. In the tradition of his Uncle Mike, a rough-and-ready character who had taught him to box as a boy and recommended "accidentally" butting opponents in the mouth, Liebling collided head to head, but intentionally, with a young Mormon missionary:

> The blood ran as from two faucets; there was no pain, but the mess was ridiculous. Amateur first aid was hopeless. It would have posed a problem to a professional cut man like Whitey Bimstein. So we set out just as we were, in sweat shirts and gym pants, and ran to the hospital on the Avenue de l'Observatoire, not far away. We left a bloody trail as we jogged.

The doctor pulled the lips of the cut together with clamps, using an "instrument like a stapler." The laceration was too close to the eye for stitches. The scar that this procedure left looked like a dent and increased the oddity of Liebling's appearance. He accepted the mark with mock pride:

> The skin in time grew over [the clamps—which were never removed], and the hair-thin white line, gravelly to the touch, is the nearest thing that I have to a duelling scar by which to remember my university days. It is also the nearest thing I have to a mining claim; grains of metal have continued through the years to work their way to the surface, and I sometimes suspect that they breed or multiply by parturition.

Liebling had found the Center gym through a tiny ad in the Paris *Herald*. He was later pleased, in his self-deprecating way, that he had not sparred at the more glamorous American Artists' Club on the Boulevard Raspail, "where literary figures like Hemingway and Morley Callaghan and Bob Coates beat each others' brains out constantly," and then wrote up the combats in their memoirs. "Raspail," Liebling said, "was far off my beat, and I don't suppose they would have boxed with anybody who hadn't published."

Liebling's isolation from the expatriate crowd "dispensed" him, as he put it, from defending his "whims." These passions for unofficial, popular cultural events led him to operetta theaters and to the Grand Guignol "without being reminded that it was *démodé*" or "corny." As always, he experienced such traditional fare from a well-informed, historical perspective. He fancied himself in the original first-night audiences of 1877 when he saw a retreaded performance of *Les Cloches de Corneville*.

Even boxing put Liebling in mind of the past, of similar moments of style in the ring and of unpreening artistic records of those moments. Watching Georges Carpentier fight an exhibition at the Salle Wagram, he thought, first of all, of Dunoyer de Segonzac's line drawings, which had caught Carpentier's fluent fighting style with "a grace unequaled by any other draftsman of the ring." Segonzac was the best practitioner of a genre with a history. "A hundred years after Thomas Rowlandson's 'Cribb and Molyneux,' Segonzac made his fighters move like fighters. There was nobody in between. The lugs in 'A Stag at Sharkey's' are just pushing. Bellows painted fights the way Jack London wrote about them."

Such art-historical judgments may have matured in Liebling's mind during the thirty years after he saw Carpentier and before he wrote down his "memories" in *Between Meals*. Still, the seeds had been planted; a way of looking at the world had taken shape in Liebling's mind. In Paris, he gravitated naturally toward traditionally humble crafts and invested them with the luster of art. This democratic view of life searched out a lineage for every pursuit, located aristocracy of endeavor in previously unheralded professions, honored craft and spurned established high art except when, as in the novels of Dickens, it too embraced all levels of society in a popular, accessible and not consciously "artistic" style. This attitude would eventually lead Liebling away from fiction, the most established and officially exalted mode of prose writing, into other, plainer genres (or, one may speculate, Liebling's lack of talent for fiction may have soured him on the novel and crystallized his zeal for the kind of journeyman work at which he excelled). In the spring of 1927, however, Joe still wanted to be the Tolstoy of the New World. But even then his subject was taken from the unromantic, low-flown world he had settled into. "In a sixth-floor room in Paris," he wrote in 1947, "I began to write my version of the great American novel (148 typewritten pages, unfinished). . . ." It was about a newspaperman who "wanted to cover Police Headquarters but had to make his living writing feature stories."

Typically, Liebling set up a conflict between two genres of writing within journalism, between the plain craft of police work and the fancier, artistic feature story. His sympathy, of course, went to the police beat, or so he implied. The manuscript, at any rate, is lost. And after a summer and part of a fall in France, which included a visit from his family, whom he took to Maillabuau for classic, ungussied cuisine, and visits to Angers and to Paniguian's orphanage in the Vendômois, he headed south to catch a liner home.

He chose Marseilles for the sailing because it came after Burgundy. He had just enough money left to eat very well and to ply his now well-grounded palate with the great wines of the Côte d'Or. He could afford to splurge, because his future was more or less secure; he had arranged to resume his old job at a higher salary, sixty dollars a week.

His ship deposited him in Providence harbor, where, with the help of a reporter from the *Journal*, he smuggled several bottles of wine and brandy through customs and past the Prohibition agents.

This time around, he lived in a "rowdy nest" on the ground floor of 304 Benefit Street, at the edge of the Brown University campus and across from the imposing First Congregational Church. The apartment was furnished, had "three great rooms with peeling wallpaper and vast fireplaces." He and one of a series of reporter roommates "used to stoke the fireplaces with cut lumber [they] stole from the site where the new Superior Courthouse was building."

Older and more discriminating than he had been during his earlier stint in Providence, Joe began to have even stronger misgivings about the quality of work he was assigned:

> When I resumed my work I began thinking up feature assignments for myself, as well as taking them from the desk. Straight news might have taken precedence over such stuff if there had been straight news to cover. But newspapers in those somnolent days (while the train rushed toward the open switch of October 1929) had turned increasingly toward the exploitation of the inconsequential, since advertisers insisted upon a certain minimum of editorial to advertising matter and people had to read something while they ate breakfast.

Liebling found a way out of such fluff with a classic piece of investigative reporting. He exposed an unqualified Indian pathologist at the Rhode Island State Hospital for Mental Diseases at Howard. In order to prove his case, Liebling went to New York and tracked down the quack's earlier places of employment, where he had worked as a mere lab technician. The man had no medical training, and in the wake of the scandal that his unmasking raised, he was fired. The article appeared April 13, 1928, without a byline, and it can only be identified as Liebling's because he mentioned it in *The Wayward Pressman*.

Two entire years passed before the name A. J. Liebling appeared on a Providence *Journal* story. In all that time, Liebling apparently wrote nothing he deemed worth mentioning in his Providence memoir; and so it is impossible to follow his career in concrete terms until April 13, 1930, when he emerged from reportorial anonymity

on page eight of the *Journal*. The very personal feature is head-lined: "REPORTER DISCOVERS MYSTICS/ENTERTAINING BUT INACCU-RATE. ONLY THING ALL AGREE ON IS THAT HE HAS 'IT.'—STAR/READ-ER DASHES PREDICTION OF OTHERS THAT HE WOULD OBTAIN RICHES."
The article itself, a diary of several visits to seers—fortunetellers and an astrologer—is first-personal with a vengeance. Every one of the sentences in the opening paragraph begins with "I":

> I shall be rich in June (creditors please note). I shall be rich at 35. I shall inherit money. I shall gain money by speculation. I shall be-come rich by inventing a small shiny object in two parts. I shall never be rich at all.

He goes on to relate, as if in a short story, the actual dialogue of his encounters. He also reveals several facts about his personal life, in-cluding that he was single and had produced no children. Reading closely, one can even follow Liebling on his reportage. He lets read-ers know what time of day he went to see the clairvoyants and what day of the week. Suddenly, he, Liebling, was news.

The star turn didn't last. He got no by-line on a funny feature that ran on June 28. Anticipating the arrival in Providence of one Zaro Agha, who claimed he was 156 years old, Liebling produced a small feature full of preposterous quotations from the venerable Turk. " 'Wallah,' " he quoted, apparently from a press agent's inter-view (or possibly from a press release), " 'unless the pictures which move and talk have lied, the women of America are as sweet-mouthed gazelles. The first I see [I] shall certainly wed. But I hope it is the one called Crawford Joan.' "

The Zaro Agha story was big news. Despite the Depression, Alva Johnston came to cover it for the New York *Herald Tribune* and Harold Denny was assigned to Agha's Providence landfall by *The New York Times*. Liebling went up against these stars as the omni-bus reporter for the North American Newspaper Alliance, the New York *Evening Post* and, of course, the *Journal*. Unawed, he got closer than anyone else to the non-English-speaking Agha; he found a French-speaking Turkish doctor among the passengers and used him as an interpreter. On July 19, 1930, Liebling's byline reappeared, under the headline "156-YEAR-OLD TURK ARRIVES/SEEKING WIFE, TEETH, CASH." The piece began: "Spry as a lad of 90-odd, Zaro Agha, who has a nice new certificate giving his birth date as 1774, arrived in Providence from Turkey yesterday."

During that same summer, the Liebling byline also ran on four other articles in the *Journal*. Three were reported from Block Island and the fourth from the Rhode Island shore. He seems to have been on vacation. Possibly Sevellon Brown, the "over-editor" of both the *Bulletin* and the *Journal,* had decided to court Liebling with this sudden shower of bylines and with the chance to cover lobster and crab fishermen at the beach. Joe was "fed up" with his job; "the seasonal repetitiousness of assignments" had begun to weigh on him about a year after his return from France. So by the late summer of 1930, he must have been showing signs of restlessness that Brown could not fail to notice.

The final break occurred in September, when his roommate, a recent graduate of Brown named Lou, was fired just after he had been given a raise and on the pretext that management was reducing the size of the staff. When Lou was replaced by the son of an officer of a large local utility, Liebling exploded. "I got mad as hell," he wrote, "and went down to Sevellon Brown's office and asked for my pay."

Suddenly, he was a free agent again. He had no job, no debts to speak of, no children and no wife. He did, however, have a girlfriend.

Ann McGinn (formally Anna Beatrice McGinn), ravishing redhead, Providence-born Irish waif, was working in a movie-theater box office when Joe Liebling came along and took her away from everything she knew. Her education, by all accounts, had been brief and thin—no college, certainly. She was at odds with her family. Her father had died when she was three. She had grown up afterward in an orphanage until an uncle took her in as a young teenager. Her mother worked as a store detective. And very early in her poor, grim and unanchored coming of age, Ann began to have what one close friend calls "scary experiences" with men.

She was an odd match for Liebling, but she was the great passion of his life. Even after her mental instability forced them to divorce,

Ann and Joe remained in love. Only their almost simultaneous deaths really ended their affair. But in 1930 all that darkness lay far ahead, unseen or at least unheeded. Joe went off to New York. And not long after, Ann joined him. Liebling's boyhood and his provincial apprenticeship were over. It was time for life in earnest.

five

Hire Liebling

Joe Liebling returned to New York in September 1930, with plenty of bravado and no immediate prospects. Over the years he had applied for jobs on New York papers without any success. Once he had written to Stanley Walker at the *Herald Tribune:* "I have been informed that you are looking for a good reporter. I am one." Walker replied: "You have been misinformed."

During periodic visits to New York from Providence, Liebling had called several times on Walker, with no better result. He had also frequently accosted James W. Barrett, the city editor of the *World,* at a bar called Racky's, across from the paper on Frankfort Street. Barrett had had nothing for him either. The *World* was on its last legs, but Liebling didn't know that. He thought of it with reverence. "It had," he wrote, "more talented writers than all the other New York papers put together—F.P.A., Lippmann, William Bolitho, Deems Taylor and then Chotzinoff doing music, Laurence Stallings and then Harry Hansen on books, Frank Sullivan, James M. Cain, Milt Gross (on Sundays), and cartoonists like Rollin Kirby and Denys Wortman."

More than anything else, Liebling wanted a job on the *World*, the writer's paper. But he had tired of the direct pitch. As a fresh alternative, he hired a sandwich man, a full-bearded retired Norwegian seaman named Larsen. For three afternoons, Larsen walked up and down in front of the Pulitzer Building on Park Row, where the *World*'s offices were. The sign (which Liebling ordered from a Hungarian sign painter near Grand Central Station) was bright orange and, in bold blue letters, it demanded: "Hire Joe Liebling."

The idea was to catch Barrett's attention on his way in and out. It failed. Barrett never even saw the sign. He used the back door, on William Street. Liebling found this out when he dropped in to see Barrett on the fourth day. The editor was amused, but he had no job for Liebling or anyone else.

Eventually Liebling sold the "story of the misadventure" to the Sunday *World* "Metropolitan" section, and then in January 1931, he sold it again, to *Editor & Publisher*, the newspaper trade magazine. Meanwhile he had taken stock of his situation and moved in, sheepishly, with his parents in their apartment at the Hotel Olcott, on West Seventy-second Street. He filled his time walking all over the city, mostly downtown. Tompkins Square, a Lower East Side park, suited his mood best. His wanderings also led him to a few feature stories, which he wrote and then took to the *World* Sunday department.

Happening upon "a tall young man with an undershot jaw, buckteeth, and yellow hair and mustache" near the door of the Sunday room, he asked him who to see about story ideas. The future playwright Paul Sifton answered, "Me."

The two men had chatted for a while, when Liebling suggested a piece on the Cape Verdean islanders who worked in New England. Sifton said he would like to see it. And the next day Liebling astonished him by bringing in two thousand words on Cape Verdeans. The piece never ran—it had no New York angle—but Sifton, the Sunday feature editor, arranged for Liebling to get regular freelance assignments. Soon he had a seventy-five-dollar-a-week drawing account and plenty of work from the Sunday "Metropolitan" section and the *World* Sunday magazine.

It was a storybook outcome. Liebling had taken the direct approach and been rewarded for his hard work and willing nature. It made him feel sheepish; he would have preferred to get the job by hook or crook. "That's the way it goes sometimes," he commented. "You plan a flashy gag, and all it gets you is nothing. Then you go through the routine motions, give it that old college try, and you maybe get a break. It's the same thing whether you're investigating a hospital or looking for a job. Afterward, however, you like to give yourself credit for being devious."

At any rate, he had arrived at the summit of American newspapering, but he was only just in time to witness the end of his beloved *World*. While the paper steadily failed, during the last months of 1930 and the early days of 1931, Joe Liebling scurried around town, churning out features at the frenzied rate that every free lance has always been obliged to maintain. He jotted down actors' chatter in a saloon and anatomized the tricks of the ticket scalper's trade. He brought a breezy tone to sports, watching fifth-rate fighters in a gym and interviewing a matador from Brooklyn named Frumkin.

Liebling listened carefully to little people, small-time nightclub promoters and bicycle racers. He interviewed Ogden Nash, then just at the start of his career. He even ruminated at length on some painted portraits of five clipper captains on exhibit in mid-Manhattan.

Reading through these pieces almost half a century after they were published, one still feels Liebling's exaltation and amusement over the life of the city. A little awed, however, at the thought of writing for the writer's newspaper, he worked hard, sometimes too hard, at writing well. Straining for an epigram, he wrote:

> The period that always comes off with a clean bill of health from the lovers of simon-pure or Simple Simon sport is the middle ages. Somehow everybody believes that Lancelot was an amateur, and that Tristram used to battle Palomides for the benefit of the Round Table Athletic Fund.

Paul Sifton seems to have given Liebling his head. He let him experiment with those bathetic conceits, those preposterous mixtures of high and low subjects and styles that he would eventually refine into a brilliant personal manner. But in February 1931, Liebling's mouth was still full of verbiage. "Ton for ton," he wrote, "grimace for grimace, polysyllabic name for barbaric appellation, two dynasties of wrestlers are striving for public favor in New York City. . . ." Refusing to drop the trope, he continued it in the second paragraph of a Metro-section page-one feature on rival wrestling teams:

> Dynasties is the word, because each troupe includes one champion, several ex-champions and several heirs-apparent, besides a horde of hairy-chested court jesters. Each champion has a belt, and the promoter is chancellor of the exchequer.

Though they let that aria go into print, the *World* Sunday editors did, evidently, apply themselves to the task of tightening Liebling's prose. "They battled over the way things were written," he later recalled, "in a manner I never saw approached until I came to the *New Yorker*. Sifton and Mike Herman Michelson, Sunday editor, both did a lot to get the superfluous scroll-work out of my writing and make me 'pack things tight.' "

Later (in the full, controlled effervescence of his mature style), Liebling described his colleagues as "Pompeian lapidaries, putting a careful polish on their last bits of carnelian while the lava bubbled like a rarebit on the threshold."

The inevitable eruption came at the end of February. Liebling recognized that his short stay at the *World* gave him only limited license to expatiate on that legendary paper and its fall, that his memory might seem "as limited as an account by the ship's cat of the sinking of the Titanic." Yet the debacle marked him deeply, gave enduring nourishment to his animus against newspaper publishers and the other avaricious forces that killed newspapers and bred one-paper towns. He saw his mentor Max Fischel and nearly three thousand other journalists thrown out of work, many of them permanently. It was the Depression, and Liebling easily concluded that a greedy management without concern for either the welfare of its workers or the public importance of the *World* had milked his paper dry and then junked it. Still, he mainly felt regret that a good time in his career had ended:

> The pattern of a newspaperman's life is like the plot of "Black Beauty." Sometimes he finds a kind master who gives him a dry stall and

an occasional bran mash in the form of a Christmas bonus, sometimes
he falls into the hands of a mean owner who drives him in spite of
spavins and expects him to live on potato peelings. The *Sunday
World* was a dry-stall interlude in my wanderings (without bran
mash), but I was soon to be put between the shafts of the ragman's
cart.

The ragman was Roy Howard, who had bought the *World* and
merged it with his *Evening Telegram* to the *World-Telegram*.
Liebling subsequently labeled this hybrid a "hermaphrodite-rigged
craft." His scorn for Howard grew with the years. But it had already begun in pre-merger days, when Howard's *Telegram* had
seemed to him, variously, "a punch-drunk enterprise" and "a ludicrous rag, written for the most part in an idiom I once described as
Oklahoma Byzantine, to the specifications of an owner who had
placed on the bulletin board a notice saying: 'Remember, New York
is Baghdad on the Subway!' "

Despite these misgivings, and after yet another unsuccessful job
interview with Stanley Walker at the *Herald Tribune*, Liebling
slunk down to the *World-Telegram*'s "crazy old building at Dey
and Washington Streets, south of Washington Market" and signed
on as a reporter for seventy-five dollars a week.

He went to work in March 1931, and proceeded to crank out hundreds of features about every conceivable aspect of New York life,
emphasizing the eccentric and unofficial side of things, as always.
By his own count, during the next four years he wrote "between
seven hundred and fifty and one thousand" pieces, "nearly all under my own byline." This seems to be a highly exaggerated claim.
Even allowing for a liberal number of un-bylined second and third
stories on many days, it is hard to see how Liebling could have written more than five hundred articles. That total, of course, would still
constitute a respectable body of work. Unfortunately, there is no
way to trace Liebling's unsigned *World-Telegram* pieces. He kept
no scrapbooks; the *World-Telegram*'s morgue is locked away in a
unlit and remote building in Missouri awaiting cataloguing funds so
that the University of Missouri's journalism school can put it to use.
And a close scanning of all issues of the *World-Telegram* published
during Liebling's tenure turned up fewer than 350 signed features.

Liebling conceded that "some of them were good," and he collected a few in 1938 for an early anthology of his work called *Back Where I Came From*. On the other hand, he came to look back on the *World-Telegram* years as a waste of time. He insisted that his "sojourn" on the paper taught him "nothing about writing."

This is a complicated and disputable claim. Anyone reading through all the dozens of identifiable Liebling *World-Telegram* pieces cannot fail to admire his indefatigable verve, his humor, and his broad and sensitive reportorial scope. But Liebling, in deprecating his *World-Telegram* phase, had in mind both a literary standard that transcended the criteria of feature reportage and a conception of literary craft that implied a long apprenticeship. He was twenty-six when he started at the *World-Telegram* and thirty when he left. He had enough experience at writing by then to know that he could, or at least ought to be able to, do more with his talents then slap together an amusing short glimpse of life in readable prose. The *World-Telegram*, he told his fellow reporter Joe Mitchell at the time, did not give him space to stretch himself. He thought he should go to *The New Yorker* to find new challenges and opportunities for creative growth. At the *World-Telegram*, Liebling coasted on his previous experience, plied the feature writer's trade with uncommon skill and a commitment to plain folk and lower-class rascality. But he resented the constrictions of his situation, and his work, subtly rebellious, showed it.

Humor is always subversive, especially in conventional newspapers, with their basic commitment to straight-faced fact. Almost all of Joe Liebling's signed *World-Telegram* features were funny. But that was only the beginning of his tacit campaign against the supremacy of Objective Truth. Other feature writers on the *World-Telegram* had a light touch. Liebling went further. He chose and then manipulated subjects so that his articles often emerged as parodies of normal journalism. He was, it is true, perfectly capable of bird-dogging a news story in the classic, value-neutral manner. His coverage of the Lindbergh kidnaping case shows that. But over and over, he picked assignments and then executed them so that the finished work made a joke of the sacrosanct notions of news and truth on which newspapers insist.

Liebling, after his Ignoto tangle at *The New York Times*, knew firsthand what happened to reporters who made things up and slipped them into the paper. Perhaps because of this, he was fatally drawn to stories that sounded implausible, features that invited disbelief or raised the issue of falsehood. Impostors and con men crop up again and again in Liebling's *World-Telegram* features. He found dozens of ways to get other men's lies and fictions into print. The voice of the pitchman—the mountebank's spiel—is the typical voice of dozens of articles. His subjects all had their lines; they kidded and ranted. Nothing, under the Liebling byline, was quite what it seemed. For instance, he interviewed a Marx brother who had left the Marx Brothers to run a company in the garment district but who still sold dresses with a vaudevillian's patter:

> The Marx Brothers had two openings this week. One, as is modestly advertised on the marquee of the Rialto Theatre, visible for less than ten miles in any one direction, was that of "Horse Feathers," featuring Harpo, Groucho, Chico and Zeppo.
>
> The other, at 1375 Broadway, was that of Gummo Marx, Inc., dresses.
>
> "I attribute their success entirely to me," said the eldest Marx brother, as he observed the gyrations of a mannequin in front of a resident buyer. "I quit the act. That is No. 923, a burgundy crepe with full bell sleeves. $10.50 wholesale. You couldn't buy it for fifteen in a larger house.
>
> "Were the Marx Brothers always funny? I don't know—we never gave me a laugh. That is a black afternoon dress with erminette cape. Sure it's a nice dress, but there's nothing in it for you," following the direction of the buyer's glance. "Harpo was in this morning to chase the model, but she wouldn't run.
>
> "What is erminette? Listen. I'm trying to look busy and you come in to talk zoology. . . ."

This is a relatively straightforward case. The *World-Telegram* copy desk would not have doubted that Gummo really did have a dress company or that he talked like a stand-up comic. It did not, probably, occur to those resident guardians of journalistic style and standards, however, that the "resident buyer" in the Gummo feature was a humorous way of putting the reporter anonymously into his own story. "Resident buyer" was a journalistic joke, a play on the usual formula for avoiding the first person: "this reporter."

On another level, the entire article was a sly concoction, a tongue-in-cheek collaboration between Marx, who came up with some bright lines in order to publicize his dresses, and Liebling, who staged his visit to Marx's showroom in order to produce a funny piece with a subversive spin on it. The joke, in other words, was about journalism and its assumptions. Liebling had slyly attacked three basic tenets of his trade. News, he implied, was not an objective phenomenon reported on by passive observers; it was simply what reporters and editors decided was news. Interviews were not random affairs, didn't just occur, but were arranged and staged by reporters and interviewees, both of whom almost always had something to gain by their association; quotes, then, were a form of dialogue, lines in an artificial conversation from which every other speech (the reporter's questions) had been suppressed. Finally, reportorial anonymity was a convention and nothing more; reporters were not cameras but people who participated in news events—sometimes even caused them for their own purposes—and later wrote about them in highly artificial accounts called news stories. To put it plainly, Liebling implied that journalism was a confidence game like all the other arts. News was a contrivance; reporters were mountebanks. The facts in newspapers were a kind of fiction.

It was only a step from the Gummo piece to more blatant forms of reportorial invention, notably the invention of people. Asa Wood and Elmer Chipling, totally fictional creations, appear in several Liebling articles, saying what he wants "men in the street" to say.

They made their most outrageous appearance in a facetious article on poker on December 14, 1931. The piece was a parody of the bridge columns that had come into vogue in newspapers at about that time. Liebling printed bridge-column-style diagrams of each player's hand, complete with symbols for the suits. Among the other players were Sidney L. Cumbersome and Hans Wasserspritzer. Near the end of the article, Liebling introduced a real person into the imaginary proceedings. He reported that C. C. Nicolet, a *World-Telegram* staffer who actually did write about bridge, interviewed Chipling. Chipling allegedly told Nicolet: "Whatever small success I have had I owe to my mother."

Real toads in such imaginary gardens let Liebling play havoc with conventional journalistic strictures. The *World-Telegram* must have knowingly indulged him in this unorthodox funning. His editors must have known at least part of the time that he was making things up. Even if they did not see through the comic names, even if C. C. Nicolet was in collusion with Liebling and asserted that he had really interviewed a man called Elmer Chipling at a poker game, still there was the completely unbelievable Liebling series on pinochle, which nobody could have taken as truth.

The basic context of the articles was plausible, if barely so. Downtown ethnic neighborhoods really did have unofficial leaders known as locality mayors—the Mayor of Mulberry Street or the Mayor of Hester Street. Joseph Mitchell recalls that he and other feature writers cultivated locality mayors as sources of human interest stories. The mayors were ideal for Liebling's special purposes, because they combined lower-class exoticism and urban cunning. They were, moreover, figures whose real lives bordered on the improbable. Nevertheless, the typical locality mayor feature was still within the bounds of probability. During January of 1932, however, no one who read Liebling's seven stories on the mayors' pinochle match closely could possibly have believed in the factuality of this flight into surreal hokum. The series began more or less credibly. The headline on page six, January 14, read: "PINOCHLE PALADINS WILL MELD INTO TOWN SATURDAY,/ AND LORD MAYORS PLEDGE AN EVEN BREAK—LESS 10 P.C." The story began in the customary vein of locality mayor items:

> Louis Abrams and Elmer Dupree, the pinochle paladins of Toledo, Ohio, will sweep down on the Metropolis like eagles, via the air lanes, Saturday or Sunday. Such was the purpose of a telegram received by the Knickerbocker Pinochle Club of Locality Mayors last night.
>
> "And they will swoop right back again, like stocks what went up in 1928!" thundered Mayor Abe Haimowitz, of Forsythe St., as he took the last trick and ten points from the infuriated Lord Mayor Stitch McCarthy in scrimmage practice in Mayor John Leppig's near beer house on Avenue A.

Day after day, the hype mounted. Liebling reported on the mayors' training camp, eliciting much bravado from the pinochle players and the news that Oswald Jacoby, the bridge expert, had snobbishly declined to serve as their referee. So far the series merely went further than previous Liebling efforts in stretching credulity, mainly because it stretched over several days, but it did not absolutely defy belief. Then came a brief squib on Saturday, January 16, that spilled over into pure fantasy:

Set to Greet, Mayor-at-Large Eyes Sky from Rooftop for Flying Pinochlers Meanwhile Local Defenders Train for Match by Inhaling Cigar Smoke.

BY A. J. LIEBLING   World-Telegram Staff Writer

A stout gentleman of aldermanic appearance rolled out of a horse blanket on the roof of a midtown skyscraper today. He wore a frock coat, striped trousers, spats and a stovepipe hat, and when he had rubbed his eyes three times he applied them to a telescope as big as a water main.

It was Wireless Looie Zeltner, Mayor at large of the Locality Mayors, Inc., and he scanned the western sky for the United Airlines plane bearing Elmer Dupree, from Toledo, Ohio, to play for the world pinochle championship.

HUNDRED ACES GROUNDED

Weather conditions held the plane, which has been christened the Hundred Aces, at Toledo last night, and the Weather Bureau could not say whether there would be proper flying weather today, but Looie is on the alert.

When he spots the Hundred Aces—with his telescope, which he rented from a guy on Columbus Circle, Looie can see like a swarm of eagles—he will wave his large embroidered red silk handkerchief to Mayor Angelo Rizzo, of Mulberry St., waiting in the street below at the wheel of his fastest hearse. Mayor Rizzo will dash off like a pinochle Paul Revere, gathering Mayors here and Mayors there, and finally heading for Newark Airport, where the Hundred Aces is scheduled to land.

At the airport the Mayors will rush out on the field to greet the

Twin Eagles of pinochle, and Mayor Ruby, Pittsburgh, chairman of
the reception committee, will make a speech. So will Wireless Looie,
and so will Lord Mayor Stitch McCarthy. They will all make their
speeches at the same time, because as Stitch explains, "It saves time
and nobody listens to dem spiels anyway."

During the intervening uncertainty, while Looie and Mayor Rizzo
keep their vigil, the athletes are not letting themselves go stale.

Under the expert direction of Head Coach Mayor John Leppig, of
Ave. A., they are sleeping in telephone booths filled with cigar smoke
to harden themselves to the atmosphere of championship pinochle
play.

FOOD BY THE TON

By day they practice counting wrong fast. Mayor Abe Haimowitz
of Forsythe St., who is maintaining the training table, volunteered
the following list of comestibles consumed by the squad, which con-
sists of Stitch, Mayor Izzy Einstein, of Ridge St.; Mayor Isadore
Pinkowitz, of E. Broadway; Mayor Haimowitz and thirteen kibitzers:

"Twelve sides of beef, out of which will be carved 500 juicy
steaks; 400 chickens, 600 pounds of lamb chops, ten boiled hams and
fifty pounds of bacon—"

"Hey: wait a minute!" interrupted the reporter who was taking
this down. "Are the mayors eating bacon?"

"No, no," said Mayor Haimowitz in some confusion. "To tell you
the truth, I had here an old program of the Six-day Bike Race, so I
was reading the part which says 'What the Riders Eat.' This is on exactly the same principle."

This high-flying pseudo sport story may have been a collaboration between Liebling and the locality mayors. But it was obviously
90 percent fiction. There may have been a pinochle team drawn
from the mayors; there may even have been a match planned with
two visitors from Toledo, but there the factuality ends. Liebling had
written a short story with his favorite Lower East Side characters in
it.

The pinochle series, which ended in an ignominious loss for the
home team, was not really typical of Liebling's work at the *World-
Telegram*. He never again ventured so far into zaniness and make-
believe. But over the four years he worked for Scripps-Howard, he

gravitated toward a relatively small number of subjects or categories
of pieces.

Far and away the largest quantity of Liebling articles were about
show business, about popular entertainment in all its aspects from
vaudeville to the circus. He wrote series on comedians, on the old
vaudeville team of Weber and Fields, and a scholarly six-part investigation of old-time performers, rep actors, Wild West rough riders,
minstrels and Uncle Tommers. This interest in old-fashioned acting
and shamming shaded off into a fascination with all kinds of serious
fakery, swindles, patter and rant. He wrote about a jongleur and a
man who claimed to have cornered the market on cockroaches. He
interviewed fast-talking athletes like Casey Stengel and Philadelphia Jack O'Brien. He wrote a half-dozen pieces on harebrained in-
ventions such as the "two-piece four-piece suit." He covered the
New York Aquarium's fish as if they were Broadway novelty acts
and treated avant-garde intellectuals with the same wry humor he
applied to theatrical mountebanks. Thomas Mann, in a boastful
mood about his authorial abilities, sounded, in Liebling's hands,
much like the other celebrities with an image to sell, the Tallulah
Bankheads and Paderewskis whom the saturnine, roundish reporter
from the *World-Telegram* caught coming down the gangplank of a
transatlantic liner.

He interviewed the French novelist Louis-Ferdinand Céline during his American tour in 1934. Liebling had undoubtedly read *Voyage to the End of the Night* by then (he eventually came to the
view that it and Céline's second novel, *Death on the Installment
Plan*, were "two of the best books written between the wars"), and
it must have been with trepidation that he went to his appointment
with the wild man of French prose. For some reason, Liebling does
not seem to have written up the interview, but a decade later, in a
survey of collaborationist French writing, he tried to come to terms
with his memories of the visit and his reactions to Céline's later,
Fascist ravings:

> It is easy for a Céline reader to imagine the furibund and fear-strick-
> en Céline; few other authors have so well described paroxysms of
> rage and terror. For myself, I shall always remember him as a big-
> shouldered man, unexpectedly rugged and tweedy for a Frenchman,

sitting in the dining room of the Hotel Vanderbilt in New York in 1934, eating strawberry ice cream after rare roast beef and at intervals pausing between enormous mouthfuls and great, gasping swallows to shout obscene regret for the Middle Ages, when the Church assured the common people that they would go to hell after death and be miserable in the meantime. "Then, at least, there were no false hopes," he said. He will die, I think, like a character in a Céline novel, perhaps like the professor of medicine in "Death on the Installment Plan," who preached stoic dignity and then, stricken by angina, died in humiliating contortions at the feet of his students.

Liebling listened to Céline with the same strategic passivity he applied to all the people he interviewed. He goaded his subjects into conversation by remaining completely silent himself. He enticed strippers and sidewalk poets and evangelists for Esperanto to do their spiel for him. He drew out the confidence man in nearly everyone. His memory, by legend, was so keen that he could recapitulate quotations word for word at his desk.° In any case, his zeal for direct quotation was a central part of his own performance as novelist manqué on the hunt for characters. Quoting helped him define characters without putting himself, as reporter (or narrator), on the line. In this way he could color the story through the subject's own tone and biases and dialectal inflections. Quotation was a way of shading the journalistic requirement for value-free neutrality without submerging entirely his own autonomy and judgment. At the same time, by repeating without comment the preposterous and comic lingo of Asa Wood or the mother of Sing Sing prison's football hero, Liebling adopted a stance of Olympian detachment.

There was, of course, no deity inside the reporter's suit, only an extremely devious and rebellious young man of almost thirty. The rebellion spilled over into Joe's work, made him play games with the rules of newspapering and bend the form to fit the fictional impulses he was unable or unwilling to work off directly in a novel.

If his program had been less serious and less complete, it could be dismissed as slumming. But Liebling's symbolic and actual trip back

° Some actual Liebling notes do survive, barely legible scrawls, with only the scantiest fragments of information. Eyewitnesses confirm that he could remember long passages of conversation with amazing accuracy, and it seems quite likely that he depended very little on conventional note taking.

to his family's old neighborhood and his aversion to polite or official people and places were not part of a superficial pose. Ann was the proof of that. Wasted and beautiful Irish Catholic out of nowhere, she was every Jewish parent's nightmare in the flesh—and worse. Ann McGinn was a schizophrenic.

It isn't clear when her trouble started. Her condition definitely grew worse with time. But Liebling knew the truth before he married her on July 28, 1934, when he was twenty-nine and she was twenty-four. They had been living together in New York for several years. She followed him down from Providence. And for a while, she coped quite well. His parents accepted her reluctantly—it was not the religious but the "class" difference that bothered them, says Norma Stonehill with some embarrassment—but accepted her nonetheless.

In the early years, while Joe was still at the *World-Telegram*, Ann was reasonably tranquil in a world not very different from the poverty-line simplicity she had known in Providence. Joe's career at first continued the shape it had had when she met him. Some of their old friends from the *Bulletin* and the *Journal* had even moved to New York at the same time and helped give her a feeling of continuity with her own past.

Vic Smith, Leo Fontaine and Frank Money were all on their uppers, grown-up waifs. Joseph Mitchell remembers: "Joe and Ann would help them out. They fed them and lent them money for their rented rooms. Ann would wash clothes for them. She had an instinctive concern for the waif."

Ann had long periods of lucidity, even gaiety. From her days as a cashier at a Providence movie theater that featured vaudeville acts between films, she had picked up a Fifi d'Orsay routine. Mitchell recalls that "she danced a lot when she was drunk." She and Joe would squabble amiably, "like an old Providence couple," over salt-cured Scotch ham, a Providence specialty which had to be soaked properly before it lost enough salt to be eaten. Liebling would say, "There's too much salt in the Scotch ham." Ann would snap back in mock anger: "What do you mean? I was born in Providence."

She was very proud of her cooking. Indeed, Ann Liebling was generally proud in defense of what was hers. In February 1934, she showed her mettle at a publication party at the Claridge Hotel for *They All Sang*, a Tin Pan Alley memoir by Edward B. Marks, the music publisher. Joe Liebling was the real author. The title page reads "They All Sang, From Tony Pastor to Rudy Vallee, As Told to Abbott J. Liebling by Edward B. Marks." But at the party, the celebration focused on the old song plugger, not his youthful ghost. Ann seethed until she boiled over. She got up and asked in a loud voice: "Would you mind telling me who wrote this book?"

Joe was embarrassed. The book was a job of work, with only an occasional phrase or literary allusion to show that he had shaped it. His journalism of the same period was far more personal, more "his" than *They All Sang*. Liebling must have known this, but, Mitchell recalls, he was still very glad that Ann cared enough about him to make a public scene. His commitment to her was strong and unwavering, even though he knew by then, only a few months before their marriage, that Ann had serious mental problems. "Very early in my *World-Telegram* life," he wrote, "I acquired a human responsibility, which through circumstances beyond the control of either of us became at times exceedingly heavy. This took the care-free, juvenile jollity out of journalism for me definitively."

The "human responsibility" was obviously Ann, who, while remaining his wife, had also become his charge. This dual relationship lay at the center of their problems together. "Ann," says Mitchell, "had trouble sorting out whether Joe was her father or her lover." That confusion had been present from the start, and it may well have fed Liebling's love for Ann. He had rescued an uneducated orphan and taken her in. If she excited him as a woman, she also satisfied other needs, for she would always be dependent on him as her savior, always be his intellectual inferior. Ann did not prosper in this wife-daughter role. Periodically—and with greater frequency as Liebling's career brought him and Ann in contact with more sophisticated people—she fled into psychosis. These episodes reinforced Liebling's sense of obligation and allowed him to rescue her again and again. It is fruitless to speculate about the meaning of rescue in Liebling's life. Rescue fantasies are notoriously complex, and in acting them out with Ann and two other wives, he did not repeat a simple pattern, nor did he discuss his actions in any depth with friends.

His Dartmouth pal Leo Stone, who by 1934 had already embarked on his career as a psychoanalyst, tried to raise the issue of Ann's illness just before the marriage. Did Joe really know what he was getting into? Liebling cut him off, gently but firmly.

The only direct evidence of Liebling's attitude toward Ann's illness comes, strangely, from a passage in *The Wayward Pressman* that is basically an informal Marxist analysis of the class system in newspapers. His domestic burdens, he said, taught him "that society is divided, not into newspaper people and non-newspaper people, but into people with money and people without it." His consciousness raised by the high cost of Ann's treatment, he went on:

> I did not belong to a joyous, improvident professional group including me and Roy Howard, but to a section of society including me and any floorwalker at Macy's. Mr. Howard, even though he asked to be called Roy, belonged in a section that included him and the gent who owned Macy's. This clarified my thinking about publishers, their common interests and motivations.

Liebling had joined the proletariat more or less by choice when he entered journalism, but he had gone further. He had married a working-class woman whose therapy bills impoverished him and removed forever any illusions he may have held that a reporter's low income would permit him to lead the carefree, Bohemian life of his youthful dreams. He was a wage slave. The debts would not go away. Under the circumstances, it became easier and more natural for him to write with understanding and without condescension about poor people scraping together a life with their wits. Their desperate scrambles and spiels were like his own daily con game at the typewriter.

That was how it must have seemed to Liebling in mid Depression. With more personal justification than most bourgeois intellectuals, Liebling shifted his views to the left. He became a charter member of the Newspaper Guild. And he built up a hatred of newspaper publishers that would endure until he died.

At the same time, nevertheless, that his work and his marriage were nourishing his identification with the working poor, Liebling continued his passionate, idiosyncratic reading of English and French literature. In Villon and Dickens he found models. But Liebling had no one to share these enthusiasms with, until one morning late in his first year at the *World-Telegram*, when he happened to walk out of the office at the same time as a new reporter who had previously worked at the *Herald Tribune*. Liebling and Joseph Mitchell stopped off for a cup of coffee at a luncheonette near the paper, at the northeast corner of Barclay and Washington streets. It was, for New York journalism, a meeting of young giants. For Liebling and Mitchell, it was the beginning of a deep, enduring friendship, the most important either man would ever have. They talked about books. Mitchell remembers:

> At that time, both of us were interested in George Borrow, the nineteenth-century British picaresque writer, the author of *The Bible in Spain* and *Lavengro*. He was an agent for the British and Foreign Bible Society, a desperate man, an anti-Catholic and extremely interested in pugilism. He was a forerunner of Joe's and my interest in what they called lowlife at *The New Yorker*. Joe was surprised I knew Borrow. We found a mutual bond in other authors concerned with lowlife—Villon, Rabelais, Sterne, Dostoevsky. And we became fast friends. We used to gorge on oysters in the Washington Market.

Mitchell and Liebling talked and drank and ranted at each other for the next thirty years. Mitchell remembers Liebling as a very argumentative man. He loved to debate with Mitchell and other cronies in saloons and speakeasies. One of his favorite hobby horses was Christopher Marlowe. Liebling believed passionately that Marlowe was a better writer than Shakespeare. Marlowe had been unjustly neglected. Shakespeare was the darling of schoolmarms and other polite people Liebling couldn't stand. Marlowe had just the right touch of evil and extravagance.

Liebling's other great fascination in these barstool bull sessions was religion. He had an obsessive and scholarly interest in religion, in the arcana of Christian heresy and factionalism. It blended into— or perhaps it partly lay behind—his interest in the Middle Ages and the early history of Islam. He was never a believer in religion himself, of course, but other people's dogmas were a serious business for Leibling. He would even pay for masses when practicing Catholic friends died. Mitchell, who had been brought up as a Protestant, would sometimes preach mock country sermons when he was in his cups, and that bothered Liebling.

Mitchell's and Liebling's professional interests coincided so completely that they found themselves writing about some of the same people. For instance, there was Samuel J. Burger, the promoter who ran cockroach races and rented monkeys to people so they could talk to them instead of to psychiatrists. They both wrote about the locality mayors. Mitchell now thinks that his personal involvement with his subjects was greater than Liebling's, whose concern for poor people grew more out of his sense of economic injustice. Mitchell says Liebling "had real animosity toward Wall Street. He had read Engels on the working class of Manchester and had been influenced by him as a reporter."

He also must have taken encouragement from Mitchell. Although the two men were different in many respects—Mitchell is a subdued, courtly North Carolinian from a rural, Protestant, landowning family, a notoriously slow writer, happily married, thin—they had both gravitated to the "low life" beat and would stick with it, in their separate ways, through decades of close association.

Mitchell was not only a colleague, but he also appealed to Liebling because of his exotic (to Liebling) southern origins and because, despite his outwardly mild manner, he had earned a reputation in New York journalism as a rebel. At the *Herald Tribune,* in a fit of rage, he had once thrown an inkwell at the newspaper owner's office wall. Mitchell had acted out the rage against management that Liebling would be able to express only as a member of the Newspaper Guild and, years afterward, in his "Wayward Press" columns. At the *World-Telegram,* he confined himself to covertly subversive features and an occasional piece that directly broadcast radical views.

At the end of 1934, when his stint at the *World-Telegram* was almost over, Liebling abandoned his usually light-hearted tone for a group of straightforward political articles. On November 12, he launched a four-part series titled "Passing of the East Side," which was a detailed survey of "the housing problem in the slums" on the occasion of the centennial of Manhattan's first housing reform. Part one began with a grim, factual and coldly ironic paragraph:

> The first trace of snow this year speeded up the annual east side migration, now in progress, from the "cold-water" flats, where pipes freeze early and rents for three months run as low as $10 a month, to the luxury tenements, where tenants may enjoy hot running water in their stove-heated rooms, but must pay from $15 to $20.

Part Two, the next day, led off with a concise, Marxist history of the Lower East Side:

> The tenements of the east side furnished the capital for the development of a great part of America. Here rose to wealth the Astor, Goelet, Wendel, Fish, Gerry and other clans. The money which was poured into Western railroads, oceanic steamship lines, sawmills in Oregon came out of the sweaty half dollars and cartwheels turned over to rent collectors by cockney butchers and German ragpickers and Jewish capmakers and Italian laborers.

Economic determinism and the exploitation of labor by capital had been on his mind all that year. In a more jocular vein the previous winter, he had given humorous vent to his own discontents as an exploited worker in journalism. The *World-Telegram* seems to have missed the underlying bitterness of Liebling's front-page piece for Groundhog Day:

> STRIKING EDITORS LET GROUNDHOG DO OWN SHADOWING
> IN DESPERATE EFFORT TO MAKE A HARD WINTER EASIER

> *Mr. A. J. Liebling, selected as Groundhog Day Editor for 1934, achieved the following:*
> A momentous decision was reached after an all-night conference of the Amalgamated Union of Saps Who Have Had to Write Groundhog Stories in the past and the Amalgamated Union of Saps Who Have Had to Read Groundhog Stories. Both organizations voted a strike.
> Secaucus Jack Dudelsackpfeiffer, president of the Jersey Pork Sau

sage Association (groundhog), opened the session with the announcement that the troop of Boy Scouts who never seem to grow up would
visit the Bronx Zoo today and chivvy a woodchuck, as is their annual
custom. He said they would bury it in the snow and then wait for it
to emerge, while editors all over New York held the presses for the
gag about the shadow.

"Two courses of action are open to us," said Dudelsackpfeiffer.
"To exterminate the groundhogs or to exterminate the Boy Scouts.
Both are protected by law. Let us, therefore, exterminate the story."

It was resolved.

Telegrams of congratulation recieved today include:

"This is the greatest advance in the newspaper business since I got
out of it."—Joseph Lilly, secretary to the comptroller (Groundhog
editor, '33).

"This is the greatest advance in the newspaper business since I entered it."—Lou Wedemar (Groundhog editor, '32).

*P.S. The story goes that if this groundhog comes out of his hole
on Candlemas Day (today) and sees his own shadow, he goes back
for six weeks, and it means a hard winter. Nobody needs a groundhog to tell him that this is a hard winter. That is why we have omit-
ted the story.*

It took Liebling several months to follow his predecessor in the
Groundhog editorship out of the newspaper business. Liebling was a
man with responsibilities and not many options in a shrunken, Depression job market. Another Candlemas passed. By then, the other
Groundhog editor, Lou Wedemar, had also quit the *World-Telegram.* Wedemar had scooped the world in 1934 by obtaining facsi-
miles of the signatures on the ransom notes Bruno Hauptmann had
used after kidnaping the Lindbergh child. Wedemar was rewarded
by the *World-Telegram* with "a due bill on a chain clothing store
entitling him to a thirty-dollar suit of clothes." The sùit gave him
the confidence to go out and find a new job with a much higher salary. Wedemar's example gave Liebling the courage to quit.

Or maybe [he wrote] it was all the pugnacious music I heard at the
St. Patrick's Day parade, which I attended in company with my
wife, who is redheaded. Anyway, on March 22 I told Lee Wood that
I had been with the *World-Telegram* for exactly four years and that

if he didn't give me my first raise I would quit. "No raise," he said.

So I went up to Mr. Hearst's King Features and got a job that lasted just eight weeks, at eighty-five dollars a week. This was exactly enough time for me to negotiate a steady job on the *New Yorker.* I had done both reporting and rewrite for the Talk of the Town department in the front part of the *New Yorker* while I was still at the *World-Telegram.*

I am glad I worked for Hearst once, because that completes the gamut. The editor of the *Evening Journal* magazine, to which I was assigned, used to hand me a couple of clippings about a sex murderer in Altoona who had inherited an ancestral estate while awaiting the electric chair. Then he would say in a cavernous voice: "*Dream* about it for a while, Liebling. Just *dream* about it."

Liebling seems to have done just that during those eight weeks. Only one feature by him appeared in the *Evening Journal Home Magazine* in that period.

It was midsummer 1935. Liebling was thirty. His newspaper days were gone forever. Now his real career would begin.

six

There at *The New Yorker*

All moveables of wonder, from all parts,
Are here—Albinos, painted Indians, Dwarfs,
The Horse of knowledge, and the learned Pig,
The Stone-eater, the man that swallows fire,
The Bust that speaks and moves its goggling eyes,
The Wax-work, Clock-work, all the marvellous craft
Of modern Merlins, Wild Beasts, Puppet-shows,
All out-o'-the way, far-fetched, perverted things,
All freaks of nature, all Promethean thoughts
Of man, his dullness, madness and their feats
All jumbled up together, to compose
A Parliament of Monsters, Tents and Booths
Meanwhile, as if the whole were one vast mill,
Are vomiting, receiving on all sides,
Men, women, three-years Children, Babes in arms.

  Oh, blank confusion! true epitome
Of what the mighty city is herself . . .

—WORDSWORTH, "Bartholomew Fair" (VII, 685–723)

Joe Liebling came to *The New Yorker* when the magazine was already at the end of its first decade and changing unobtrusively from its original superficiality as the house organ of the Algonquin Round Table to a more diverse and even, inadvertently, serious publication. The change had something to do with the Depression, but it chiefly coincided with the arrival of new writers such as Liebling and Mitchell and many others who brought a view of the world and their profession to the magazine that was much wider than the outlook of snappier first-generation staffers: Dorothy Parker, Alexander Woollcott, that crowd. There seems to have been no conscious change of editorial policy. Harold Ross, the mercurial and philistine founding editor, did not change his ways (although he did hire such people as Katharine Angell, E. B. White and William Shawn, all of whom, variously, helped push Ross away from the smart set and onto higher ground), but he did attract the writers who improved his magazine. As one of his outstanding recruits, James Thurber, put it:

> I might as well admit, right here, that I have done a lot of brooding about the mystery that some literary scholars have wrought out of, to quote one of them, the central paradox of Harold Ross's nature; that is, his magic gift of surrounding himself with some of the best talent in America, despite his own literary and artistic limitations. Without detracting from his greatness as an editor, it must be pointed out that the very nature of his magazine, formless and haphazard though it was to begin with, did most of the attracting. Writers and artists of the kind Ross was looking for decided that here was a market for their wares, and to say that the head of such an enterprise, personally unknown to most of those who came to work for him, was the attracting force is to say that the candle, and not the flame, attracts the moths. I think the moths deserve most of the credit for discovering the flame.

Like nearly every one of Ross's writers, Liebling admired him greatly but stintingly. Ross, he wrote in a memorial sketch in 1959, "was as great as anybody I ever knew, in his way." The two men never became friends. Indeed, one gets the sense that they tolerated each other, acknowledging their respective talents but basically conceding that they were stuck with each other. Ross, said Liebling, "never let his notion of what he wanted get in the way of what was to be had. In the late thirties, when all his new writers came from newspaper staffs where they had sweated through the Depression, he said to me, 'Liebling, I wish I could find some Conservative young writers who could write, but there aren't any.'"

Liebling was undoubtedly one of the liberal younger writers Ross had had to settle for. He continued to write about the same lowlifes and poor folk he had covered at the *World-Telegram*. Perhaps it was not fundamentally politics, but age, that separated Liebling and the other younger writers from Ross. Liebling wrote:

> I think that all the reporters of my *New Yorker* generation—Mitchell and Jack Alexander and Dick Boyer and Meyer Berger and I—had the same classical ambivalent son-to-father feeling about him. We were eager to please him and cherished his praise, but we publicly and profanely discounted his criticism. Especially we resented his familiarity with the old-timers—the Companions of the Prophet—and his indulgence for them. Our admiration for their work was not unqualified or universal. (I still think *The New Yorker*'s reporting before we got on it was pretty shoddy.)

Liebling's own strong background in reporting for newspapers was at first a handicap on *The New Yorker*. "Personally," he admitted, "I had a tough first year on *The New Yorker*, from the summer of 1935 to the summer of 1936, because I brought to it a successful newspaper short-feature method that was not transferable to a magazine, especially in long pieces. It would have been like running a mile in a series of hundred-yard dashes."

William Shawn, now Ross's successor as editor in chief, was then the editor who handled all of Liebling's copy before it went through Ross, and he disagrees about Liebling's difficulties that first year. Shawn says:

His problem was one of tone or style, not length. At that time the "Talk" stories all had a fairly accepted tone. They sounded pretty much like Thurber or White. Liebling, who was very individual, had his own style. There was also the problem of the way the assignments came. He didn't get one every day. He was left on his own. He had trouble finding his way that first year. But Liebling, more than almost any writer I've known here at the magazine, improved his writing. He had trouble putting sentences and paragraphs together, but he learned in a remarkable fashion. I don't know how. He absorbed something—he wasn't taught. Something developed in him. He became fluent and extremely stylish, a master in journalistic terms.

Liebling's awkward early "Talk of the Town" pieces support this judgment. But, as Shawn says, he learned fast. There is a hiatus of thirteen months (May 4, 1935–June 13, 1936) between Liebling's last piece as a newspaperman and his first signed article in *The New Yorker*. He did not, however, write his debut *New Yorker* piece, only reported it. He was, in effect, the legman for St. Clair McKelway, who did the actual writing of what turned out, in the event, to be a distinguished debunking profile of the black evangelist Father Divine.

Liebling did not regard the double byline on the profile (with his name second, out of alphabetical order) as demeaning. At least, he took the opposite view in print. He said, in the Ross memoir, that he had "rescued" himself with his reporting. Before McKelway stepped in, Liebling had written a first draft of the profile, but he went out of control on this first long piece and seemed to have embarked on "a million-word book on comparative religion." Evidently, Liebling scrutinized what McKelway did with his material and learned what to do himself the next time round. At any rate, it is clear that Liebling's reporting was crucial to the success of the piece, and he proudly held it up in later years as an example of the investigative thoroughness that newspaper publishers were too cheap and narrow to support:

Divine had been aided rather than defined by newspaper stories accenting the mystery of his origin and wealth, and repeating, without analysis, his claims of a vast international following. I traced him back to the earliest beginning of his ambition to be God, described the main source of his income, with proofs, and worked out pretty accurately the relatively small number of followers he had, but had absolutely.

At the very center of the profile, and its most telling evidence of Divine's fraudulent exploitation of his followers, is a vignette about the experiences of a black couple named Thomas and Verinda Brown, who gave Divine their savings, moved in with him and later, disillusioned, sued him to get their money back. The Browns (their names, or at least their surname, may have been altered) gave human weight to the crushing indictment of hard facts Liebling had assembled. Liebling was able to persuade the Browns to talk because of his connection with Katharine Angell (later Mrs. E. B. White), who presided over fiction for *The New Yorker*. Her vivid and typically meticulous recollection of the circumstances, written in a letter shortly before her death in 1977, also draws a succinct portrait of Joe Liebling in the thirties:

He was neither short nor tall but he was very broad and heavy. His balding head, spectacles and his look of sheer benignness and good humor made him attractive to everyone. He suffered badly from gout even in his early days and his walk was that of a person whose feet hurt. (Yet I learned later that he could walk fast and for long distances over the pavements of any city—New York, London, Paris—rolling slightly as he walked. Perhaps this was after the new medicine for gout was discovered. But I think he walked whether in pain or not.)

Anyway, one day in the early '30s he appeared in the doorway of my office smiling, this time, as if he was very much amused. It was a smile of triumph and almost of mischief because he knew he was going to surprise me. He asked me if I had time to talk to him and I said of course. He came in, shutting the door behind him, and then sat down and said, to my utter astonishment, that all roads on Father Divine led to me. "What on earth do you mean?" I asked. Then he told me that the Ordway Teads (who lived in Forest Hills and were friends of my first husband and me prior to our divorce in 1929) had a Negro housekeeper who was the key to the Divine story and who would talk to him (Liebling) only if I said it was OK. . . . Verinda and I had a long conference and I reassured her and from then on Joe ferreted out the real story.

At the time of publication, it was the details of the Browns' connection with Father Divine that were the high point of the Liebling-McKelway exposé. Today, however, one also notices the dignity, the affectionate care, of the portrait of the Browns themselves:

> Verinda is a very tall, very healthy-looking middle-aged woman, the color of a fine mink coat. Her features are large and frank—a great nose, an enormous jaw, a mouth that opens and shuts decisively. Her natural expression is an expansive grin. Thomas is shorter, darker, less vivacious, a sort of understatement of Verinda. His eyes are drowsy and slow-moving. He is deliberate, methodical, and thoughtful by nature. Verinda comes from Barbados, Thomas from the Bahamas. Both have been in this country thirty years or more and they have been married ten. Both are excessively neat; Thomas is even something of a dude, and at one time owned sixteen suits of clothes, all of them in fair condition. Verinda is a fine cook and a capable children's nurse; as a butler and house man, Thomas is efficient and has a soothing manner. They are decent, honest people. They estimate that during the time they were Angels in Sayville they gave Father Divine, freely and of their own accord, something over $5,000 . . . .

Such lavish and loving attention must rarely have been paid to a pair of black domestics in *The New Yorker* or any other American publication aimed at a general white audience up to that time. The specific items of fact that build the portrait—Verinda's physiognomy, Thomas's sixteen suits, "in fair condition"—are early gems of Liebling reportage: a novelist's perceptions in the service of a journalist's task.

Ross liked what he saw. He took Liebling off his salary of sixty-five dollars a week and started him on a ninety-dollar drawing account. For the rest of his life, Liebling was in debt to *The New Yorker*. But in the summer of 1936, the accumulating liability made him feel flush. It also spurred him into writing more profiles, long portraits of his favorite Broadway sharpsters and antic con men. From the fall of 1936 until the fall of 1939, Liebling put *his* New York on paper. He took the same "parliament of monsters" he had delineated in miniature at the *World-Telegram* and enlarged the canvas. Many of these pieces were collected in *Back Where I Come From* and *The Telephone Booth Indian*. As a group, they are an album of lovable undesirables, many of them Jewish, all sly, the real denizens of the city's modern Bartholomew Fair.

Fairs, in fact, crop up several times in Liebling's prewar *New Yorker* features. In the fall of 1936, he wrote a profile of George A. Hamid, a Syrian ex-acrobat who furnished "acts of skill and daring" to county fairs all over the Midwest and East. From his office in New York, Hamid arranged for the bedazzlement of rural folk. Liebling was obviously amused by the Levantine agent's behind-the-scenes role as purveyor of flimflam to the boondocks. He quoted from Hamid's florid catalogue with mock sympathy for the man's workaday problems:

> He has to make sure, for example, that the Relmutt Troupe, described in his catalogue as "a quintet of nimble-footed artists performing spectacular and breath-taking feats of daring on a slender steel wire in mid-air," gets to Kennywood Park, near Pittsburgh, on the right day, and that the Albino Sensation, "thrilling, nerve-racking, death-defying feats originating at the dizzy height of seventy-five feet while four aerial artists defy nature's law of gravity," arrives safe and sound at the New York State Fair in Syracuse. In any week, through the summer and early fall, the fair committee at Toronto may decide that the farmers up there won't be happy without Pallenberg's Wonder Bears, "huge bears that walk and act like men, trained to a perfection that only Pallenberg's genius can achieve," while our own Suffolk County potato growers are clamoring for Weir's Elephants, "a prodigious performance by the pachyderms of the show world," and the managers of Enna Jettick Park, named for the shoe factory at Auburn, New York, demand that Alf Loyal's

Dogs, "still the greatest act of its kind in the world," be sent up there right away.

He savored the pitchman's rant, the completely unabashed language, so different from the lubricated and tonsured *New Yorker* style he was having to ape. But in the rich sentence above, he had found a way to satisfy Ross, with a prose that flowed impeccably but still, thanks to quotation marks, could incorporate the wildness and cheapness of Hamid's manner, without infringing on the magazine's sense of its own style.

Carnival production was only a small part of the multifarious, antic bustle radiating from the dingy offices around Times Square. Entrepreneurs, whom Liebling called telephone booth Indians,° and their more successful, non-nomadic brethren, were building a factitious cosmos of popular theater, nightclubs, race tracks, wrestling matches in their scheming imaginations. At the margins of polite society was a secret culture. Its members frequented Izzy Yereshevsky's all-night tobacco store. Their hero was Hymie Katz, a con man whose principal dodge was starting new night clubs.

" 'Hymie is a tummeler,' " Liebling wrote, quoting the boys at the I. & Y. tobacco store. " 'Hymie is a man what knows to get a dollar.' "

Hymie sometimes operated an audacious horse-race tipping service over the phone with unsuspecting doctors and ministers fifty to a hundred miles from New York. But his chief work was nightclubs. Liebling recorded his M.O. in loving detail. It was a marvel of leverage and fast patter. "Hymie," he observed, "has been around Broadway since 1924. He is a good talker." Armed with a lease on a nightclub (as yet unsigned), which cost him fifty dollars in legal fees—his only risk capital—he goes to a hatcheck concessionaire:

> This is the really critical phase of the enterprise. He must convince the concessionaire that the place has a chance to do business ("Look at the figures in the lease, you can see what we're expecting"). He

---

° The telephone booth Indians were impecunious promoters, first described by Liebling in an article called "The Jollity Building." They hung around Broadway office buildings and used the lobby telephone booths as offices.

must fill the concessionaire with enthusiasm for the entertainers, who have not yet been engaged. For it is up to the concessionaire to provide the cash that will make the enterprise go—three thousand dollars in advance, in return for the hat-check and cigarette concession for six months. Hymie is a great salesman. He does impersonations of his hypothetical acts. He tells about the Broadway columnists who eat out of his hand and will give yards of free publicity. While Hymie talks, the concessionaire distills drops of probability from his gallons of conversation. In his mind he turns Hymie's thousands of anticipated revenue into fifties and hundreds. If the club runs three months, the concessionaire knows, he will get his money back. If by some fluke it runs six months, he will double his money. If nobody financed night clubs, there would be no concession business. So the concessionaire lets Hymie have the three thousand.

This is more than a job description. It is also a character sketch, and read together with other, similar sketches, it forms part of a loosely structured account of a coherent world, a factual picaresque in which the picaro, the reporter, is rarely visible but always present, both as a narrative sensibility and, sometimes, in his own guise ("he reminds me whenever I see him"). Liebling's reporting stints in the Broadway demimonde were a series of personal adventures. It is clear that he immersed himself in the life of the I. & Y., that he knew Hymie Katz. It is a matter of abundant record that he was a habitué of Stillman's gymnasium on Eighth Avenue, where boxers trained. His own life and inclinations led Liebling to his stories, and so, in a direct sense, his *New Yorker* lowlife sketches accumulated into a selective autobiography. Some of his subjects became lifelong cronies. The feel of these pieces is personal, because Liebling had made the world of New York lowlife a part of his own universe. Without, in the strict sense, becoming a Broadway character himself, he had found a way to spend time among those promoters and scalawags. It was an alternate world he could enter at will, a society that was the mirror image of settled, bourgeois life. Here were dozens of pointed alternatives to conventional upper-middle-class careers and life styles.

Instead of the proverbial Jewish doctor, Liebling found Whitey Bimstein practicing the healing arts at ringside. He was the "best-known prizefight second in New York" and in place of a doctor's black bag, he carried "a bundle," "a small affair, flat on one side," containing, among other useful objects, a roll of adhesive tape, gauze, petroleum jelly, "a tube of liquid cement known as carpenter's wax" and various styptics. Whitey Birnstein was not only a man of consummate skills; he was also handy with the language. "I like the country," he told Liebling. "It's a great spot." He started his career training a boxer called Frankie Jerome. "Being associated with a man like that, you get known," Bimstein said. "He was a regular hoodlum."

Like many of Liebling's heroes, Bimstein had some of Liebling's own qualities. He was Jewish in a non-Jewish trade, a trade requiring great skill but, like journalism, one without class. Bimstein was also a failed boxer with "a passion for frankfurters and charlotte russes which he would indulge even a few minutes before a fight, and all his roadwork was done at a walk, selling boxing tickets to neighbors." Furthermore, he had returned to the Manhattan demimonde (professionally; he, like Liebling, lived in a conventional residential neighborhood) although his parents had fled it. "Shortly after Whitey's graduation from public school," Liebling wrote, "his father, a small cloak-and-suit manufacturer, moved the family uptown to Brook Avenue and 138th Street, in the Bronx. The idea was to remove Morris, as Whitey's parents insisted on calling him, from the raffish associations of the East Side. Morris took to hanging out in the basement of St. Jerome's Catholic Church on Alexander Avenue, where Father Ryan, the pastor, gave boxing lessons."

One cannot fail to see similarities between a Morris who hated his name and an Abbott who hated his, between a boy in Far Rockaway with a furrier father who had rescued the family from the East Side, to his son's dismay, and a boy in the then orderly Bronx whose father, also in the garment business, had fled the old neighborhood against his son's will. Abbott and Morris had both tried, with comic results, to play sports with the Irish in their neighborhoods and then found ways of making a living at the peripheries of professional sport.

Liebling's interests were, obviously, wider than Bimstein's. He hovered on the sidelines of all proletarian sports and all kinds of popular entertainment, from cockfights to journalism.

Inevitably, any reporter is a spectator at the event he covers, but Liebling chose to look at life from the wings. He was still interested in the ostensible performance at issue—the boxing match or the Broadway revue—but he nearly always spent the bulk of his energies, especially during this prewar period, on producers and other nonperformers whose work made the performances happen.

Other writers covered the fights. So did Liebling, after the war, but in the late thirties he covered the gyms or Bimstein at ringside stopping cuts. Typically, he made a professional sparring partner into the hero of the Louis-Schmeling fight. "Louis," he wrote, "trained for Schmeling with the best colored heavyweights his handlers could hire. They included a man named George Nicholson, who is considered the best sparring partner in the business." Louis, subsequent innuendo makes clear, was not half the technician that the languorous Nicholson was. Only the lack of a killer instinct kept Nicholson out of main events. But he had made the crucial difference in Louis's victory.

Philadelphia Jack O'Brien was also on the sidelines, too old to fight, but not too old to teach or talk. As with Bimstein, Liebling could fasten delightedly on O'Brien's backstage life and on his surprising gift for speech. But where Bimstein had made poetry of low diction, O'Brien was a master of "high-toned language." He once told "a friend," probably Liebling: "I have always loved to hear the verbiage that flows from an Englishman, whether he be an Oxfordian or otherwise. It is a beautiful thing." This is bathos, and it appealed mightily to Liebling, with his instinctive dedication to the obliteration of barriers between high and low genres or classes or styles.

Liebling heroes came from all social levels. He paid, for instance, much admiring attention to the Shuberts. They had a very successful business—dominating legitimate theater in New York by dominating theatrical real estate—but they still had the manner and speech of telephone booth Indians. Clifford C. Fischer fitted the bill even better. He produced trashy, "spectacular pseudo-Gallic revues" and made a fortune at it without ever becoming famous like the Shuberts. Fischer was also a master of rant, in French, German and English, all at once. Liebling attended his rehearsals not for the show on stage but for Fischer's performance.

The Fischer profile, in fact, opens with the statement that "a rehearsal by Clifford C. Fischer . . . is one of the finest shows imaginable." The brief scene, based on an actual rehearsal, that follows immediately on the lead paragraph of the article is itself a hilarious, frenzied little playlet that illustrates the ironic way in which Liebling meant "finest":

> "Get out of here on the next boat and go back to Paris!" Fischer will yell at a show girl, a vision of ecstatic beauty, who has failed to switch her hips. "The next boat—out!" Then, with a sweep of his hand toward any three or four acrobats or stagehands present, he will shout, "And take them jackasses with you! Im-MED-jutly!" His voice sinks, and as he slumps into his chair, he gurgles, "Quick. Before somebody kills you, already." Odette Puig, a calm, blonde Frenchwoman who is his secretary, provides him with a glass of water. Then an electrician misses a cue, and Fischer is up again.
>
> "Rudy," he screams, "Rud-y, did you forgot again? I want here ma-GEN-ta! Not PINK! Ma-GEN-ta! Oh, my God!"
>
> At this point two stagehands, providing the motive power for a property horse and carriage, bring the vehicle onstage too soon. Fischer goes clumping up on the stage with head thrust forward, shoulders hunched, and hands flapping away from his sides, looking like an angry penguin. "For five months I choke myself," he howls, "turning around, breaking my neck, jumping up and down and thinking—and two swines—like you—the effect—ruined! It's too much. *Vous m'emmerdez, tous. Mais tous!*" Mlle. Puig brings him another glass of water.

Betting also fascinated Liebling. During the summer of 1937, he looked into two of the turf's outstanding insiders. Augustine J. Grenet flourished at New York tracks in the days before the parimutuel system mechanized odds-making. Grenet invented "the profession of making prices" and worked at it for fifty years. He was the experts' expert, the man who told the bookies what the odds were. "The average bookmaker," he told Liebling, "has as much idea of horses as a hog has of heaven."

Perhaps Grenet would have made an exception for Liebling's fa-

vorite bookie, the redoubtable Tim Mara, who was the subject of
another Liebling profile a few weeks later. Both men were "fine"
examples of free-wheeling commercial enterprise, operating in relative obscurity. But they were the real show at New York race tracks.
The horses were only an excuse, a come-on for Grenet's and Mara's
acts.

Almost every Liebling subject in this period fits the same pattern
of behind-the-scenes operators milking popular entertainment in a
coolly logical manner that Liebling unmasks in a friendly spirit.
Usually the subjects are prone to rant; they are almost always comical, or seen from a comic perspective. Occasionally, however, his
tone darkened to deal with the pathos of obsolescent forms of entertainment and of restaurants that had passed their heyday. In Jack
Pfefer, the wrestling promoter, he found a classic case of a con artist
whom history had shunted aside. Pfefer had promoted the last wrestling match in Madison Square Garden in the spring of 1938. By the
time Liebling wrote about him in the summer of 1939, professional
wrestling had gone into "spectacular" decline. But Pfefer continued
to hold neighborhood shows in places like Ridgewood, Queens, and
felt that these smaller events were, "from an artistic point of view,"
superior to the extravaganzas of his and wrestling's prime.

"From an artistic point of view"—the words are Liebling's and
they are meant seriously, although they include a bit of mockery at
Pfefer's mountebank pretension. Liebling, in all these early pieces,
was studying, with great seriousness, the art of popular entertainment. He was systematically exploring the business of organized hokum. And it was a sign of his scholarly interest in the arcana of
amusement, as a kind of history of fakery, that he pursued fading
practitioners to learn their secrets before they were gone. It was this
historical impulse that led him to Bluch Landolf and the subject of
clowns.

The ancient art of clowning had gone into decline because of the
three-ring circus. "It is as hard to be an outstanding clown in an
American circus," he wrote, "as it is to be a distinguished artisan in
an automobile factory. The vastness of the arena, the remoteness of
the audience, work no hardship on the aerialist or the man shot out
of a cannon, but the clown's grimaces go almost unperceived; his

words, if he bothered to speak any, could not be heard."

Still, Landolf and the others continued to perform, although for less money and less fame. What else, after all, does an artist have to do but practice his art? This principle applies even to restaurateurs, like Maria Bulotti, who ran a speakeasy in the West Forties which Liebling had frequented during Prohibition. After repeal, Liebling lost track of the place, and when he later noticed that Maria had not hung a sign in front of her place like the other legitimized speakeasy owners, he assumed she had closed down. Still, he wondered what had happened to her, and one day in 1937 he rang the bell and discovered that nothing at all had changed. Behind the drawn shades, Maria was still running a speak:

> It seemed to me that time in its flight turned backward to 1928. "Come in the kitch', Mista Lieba," she said. "Maybe you like a drink. Bruno!" She yelled down the hall. "Itsa Mista Lieba!" I followed her. The door to the front room was ajar, and I could see the familiar tables laid with their white cloths.

Maria still made wine at home and took care of her faithful clientele in the old way. Bruno the chef made "rather good" cannelloni. The secret, informal speakeasy atmosphere continued to suit customers, and the economics of unlicensed business suited Maria. Like Pfefer and Landolf, she was keeping at it and doing well enough. They were all redeemed by their loyalty to an old and skillful way of doing things. The moral is clear. The Liebling hero—Liebling's version of the good man—is someone who practices his art for its own sake, however humble the art, however small the reward. In French, this ideal professionalism is described as *sérieux*, without overtones of solemnity. Clifford C. Fischer at his most hysterical and profane was *sérieux*. Any good clown is *sérieux*. Worldly success or prestige has nothing to do with it, at bottom.

Liebling never used this terminology. But he meant the same thing, with an ironic nudge, when he said "fine." Invariably, the "finer" things in life for him were superficially mediocre or low-class, but with fundamental qualities of seriousness that recommended them to the discerning person who could see beyond middle-class standards of "fineness." It was this sort of inverse snobbery that impelled Liebling to eat dubious clams and to frequent down-and-out ethnic restaurants specializing in lamb's head.

The acme of his search for authenticity-in-squalor and for humbled but persistent seriousness of craft is a piece written in 1937 about a shore restaurant in the Rockaways. The original title was "The Old Man," but it was collected in *Back Where I Came From* as "What Do You Expect for $2.00?" The opening is an eerie, Dickensian evocation of seediness:

> There never were many people in the finest restaurant I ever discovered within the city limits (it was at one of New York's bathing beaches) and most of those there were seemed unwanted. Sometimes a party of four sunburned adults and maybe three children would sit around a table uneasily for half an hour, the men in shirt-sleeves, the women in cotton dresses, and no waiter would come near them. Three or four waiters, old, acrid fellows, would be standing in the farthest corner of the vast room, talking and laughing bitterly, and looking over at the people at the table. The waiters wore black alpaca coats and round tin badges with numbers on them. Once we saw a man at a table grow angry and bang on the water carafe with a knife. There was only yellow tepid water in the carafe. A waiter shuffled to his table from the far corner. He seemed to take an interminable time getting there, and the slup, slup of his broken old shoes on the floor sounded loud in that almost silent place. The man said something to him, and then the waiter said in a loud, contemptuous voice, "We don't serve sandwiches or soft drinks here." The party went out, the men looking ashamed, the women scolding their males for subjecting them to such embarrassment.

Liebling and his party were better treated:

> The restaurant was so obviously decadent and unprosperous that we had not ventured into it the first few times that we went to the beach to swim. It was only after investigating the possibilities of the Greek lunchrooms, the Japanese waffle shops, and the saloons that we had dared that ghostly pavilion, deciding that we had nothing to lose. The food in the old restaurant had astonished us. The steamed clams were small, clean and accompanied by a stiff sauce of butter with tarragon vinegar and curry powder blended into it. The chicken

fricassee was not smothered in a white flour paste, but yellow and succulent. The three-and-a-half dollar steak, for two, was perfect. As long as we ordered substantially, took cocktails before dinner, and drank plenty of beer with the meal, the waiters tolerated us.

There, in capsule, is the essential Liebling reportage. To engage his full sympathies, a subject must appear déclassé, even dangerous. In this case, he "dared that ghostly pavilion." The adventure ends well, because he finds that in this unlikely place, the chef is a serious artist who provides an ample, sensual experience without frills. That he should have found this "finest" of New York restaurants in his old neighborhood adds an oedipal fillip, and the mere fact of discovering a restaurant in an outer borough, beyond the New Yorker's Manhattan-bound purview, also gave the place reverse cachet. Typically, too, the staff behind the scenes had its own, raffish style, as Liebling learned in conversation with a tipsy, cantankerous waiter. When Liebling asked him for the green salad which the menu said would come with his shore dinner, the old man snapped: "What do you expect for two dollars? A *gold* watch?"

On another occasion, the same waiter confided dyspeptically:

> The cook is forty-nine million years old. Some day he'll fall into the clam chowder. At the end of every season the old man says to him, "I never want to see you no more. You're dead as a doornail." And at the beginning of the next season he sends a taxicab for him. He used to cook at Burns's. The old man is in his second childhood. That's him setting up on the high stool by the bar. He ain't got no cash register, only an old wooden cash box. He sets there from ten o'clock in the morning until closing time, to see that no waiter gets away with a glass of beer.

This eccentric portrait of the artist as old codger is a pure distillation of Liebling's sensibility. His range grew wider, and he wrote better with time and practice, but his fundamental outlook did not significantly change. Low life, rant, dedication to an art of low social prestige in a déclassé setting, and the presence of a demonic creative person, usually someone unknown to the public (here, the old man, in the background, obstinately running his restaurant his way)—these are the themes that attracted Liebling. It is, further-more, no stretch to see that they amounted to a projection of his idea of himself as an anonymous, committed artist in a low-prestige profession. As a reporter, he operated behind the scenes and con-trived popular entertainments. Like a theatrical producer, he found others to caper for him and speak his speeches. And like Jack Pfefer or the old man at the shore restaurant, he was obstinately plying his trade in historically reduced circumstances.

Perhaps it may seem wrong-headed to say that a job at *The New Yorker*, in what were bright days for the magazine and a renais-sance of opportunity for those of its reporters drawn from newspa-pers, was somehow a diminished situation. But Liebling habitually looked back to a golden age of literary adventures that had begun in the eighteenth century and ended, by and large, with the rise of the novel in the middle of the nineteenth century. From this perspec-tive, with such models as Defoe and Cobbett and Borrow before his eyes, the world of New York journalism, even with the haven for se-rious prose provided by *The New Yorker*, must have struck Liebling as decadent, constricting and second-rate. All the same, Liebling en-tertained grandiose dreams of reviving the golden age of his favor-ite writers. He would explore the city's stews and dives like Defoe. He would make friends with society's outcasts like Borrow. There were non-English models too: Rabelais and Villon for rugged sensu-ality; Stendahl for war and romance. But Liebling's program fo-cused most sharply on British writers who had written in great quantity, as journalists, pamphleteers or popular essayists. Liebling's program was unproclaimed. He did not declare his ambition, which was to follow in the footsteps of great writers of the past while os-tensibly just doing his reporter's job at *The New Yorker*. He did, however, discuss his aims and ideals with friends, over many years, at lunch and, principally, in New York bars. He clearly had a vision of the kind of writer he wanted to be, and that vision was intimately bound up with his idiosyncratic reading of English literature.

Standard literary history does not make a pantheon out of Cob-bett, Borrow, Pierce Egan, Defoe and Hazlitt. What drew Liebling to these writers? Joseph Mitchell, who discussed them with him over the years, points to an affinity of approach and subject matter. Defoe, for instance, Mitchell says, was important because of *A Journal of the Plague Year*, which purports to be a firsthand account but was actually a reconstruction of the plague of 1665, written half a century later. It was important, Mitchell says, "to those of us who were trying to do the same thing," stretching the conventions of realistic prose, within journalism.

Defoe was an ideal model, too, because he, like Liebling, had operated outside polite literary society. J. H. Plumb has written:

> Defoe did not achieve acceptance among the writers of his day. Addison called him "a false, shuffling, prevaricating rascal"; Swift sneered at him. Pope scorned him; the majority ignored him. His work was alien to the polished elegance that they admired. His literary gifts were as great as theirs, if not greater; certainly they were more original, but he wrote for a different public. He did not write for a coterie, for the fashionable, polished upper middleclass or for the aristocracy. He wrote, like Bunyan before him, for shopkeepers, artisans, clerks, yeomen, for ordinary men and women, and he wrote as one of them.

So, too, in their disparate ways, Borrow and Cobbett and the other Liebling favorites wrote for the general public. They were great writers but not generally recognized as such. They wrote enormous amounts, without pretension. Liebling easily felt a bond with them, for they were early examples of himself, with the advantage that they wrote in a period when popular prose covered a wider territory than it did in Liebling's day. He could point to all these important writers, who would have been classified in this century as journalists, who would today have found work as reporters, as Liebling had. But in their time, they were not so narrowly pigeonholed. Cobbett and Egan were, in effect, their own publishers. They wrote what they pleased, and they didn't particularly worry about crossing lines between fiction and nonfiction.

Liebling looked back nostalgically to Egan and Borrow because they were great writers in his vein who had not written novels. And Liebling was a writer determined to be great who *could* not write a novel. He had tried.

From boyhood, Liebling had written short fiction of no special merit. His first stabs at writing were almost all either short stories or poetry. Early on, probably at Dartmouth, he gave up poetry altogether. But he continued to write stories well into middle age. Some of these thinly disguised autobiographical sketches ran in *The New Yorker*, and they are passable pieces of work, but no more than that. Still, they do show that Liebling never did quite abandon the fictional impulse. It glimmered in some dark corner of him like a pilot light.

He wrote fiction in earnest in the fall of 1936, at the same time that he was having so much trouble getting used to *The New Yorker*. Perhaps because he felt insecure at the magazine—he had begun to sign features, but only just begun—he turned to his alma mater the *World-Telegram*, and arranged to contribute a regular page of humorous fiction to the paper's "Week-End Magazine Section."

The protagonist of most of the stories is Crash Bernstein, "the educated cabby." On the Saturday before New Year's Day, for instance, Telly readers came upon a timely Liebling story that began:

> Crash Bernstein, the talented taxi driver, was wearing such a wide grin when he entered the Klytemnestra Koffee Potte that Brakeless Brennan, his colleague, dropped a cruller in astonishment.
>
> "You must of got something good for Christmas," Brakeless politely observed. "Did your wife leave you?"
>
> "Naw," said Mr. Bernstein. "It is just that I am glad it is over. A guy got into my cab with a Christmas tree about thirty feet high Thursday night. Made me open up the sliding roof so he could get it through. Then when we had gone about a block I heard a yell and there he was climbing the tree, yelling he was Tarzan and knew no fear. When I got to the address he give he wouldn't come down. Said he was afraid. I had to stop at a firehouse and the boys shook the tree until he fell into a life net. His wallet and all the change in his pants must of fell out on the way down. So I was skunked for the fare.
>
> "Then I tried to borrow a axe from a fireman to chop the tree down, because it was the only way I could think of to get it out of my cab. The fireman says no, I would have to get permission from the Forestry Bureau of the Department of Parks, which is closed over the holidays. I could not get rid of this Christmas tree until this morning."

This is not memorable stuff. The adventures of Crash Bernstein do not merit further quotation. Bernstein was an unsuccessful fictional device. Through his cab passed all the urban lowlife characters whom Liebling had been covering as a journalist for years. As straight fiction, they lost their plausibility. Liebling strained for a humorous, proletarian tone and fell flat. The Bernstein stories were, nevertheless, a serious experiment. He wrote more than a dozen of them, and then, in the same spirit, sat down and wrote ten chapters of a novel entitled *The Girl with the Cauliflower Ear, A Romance.*

The typescript survives in ninety pages, which were apparently submitted to publishers by an agent named W. K. Wing, whose name and address, 205 East 42d Street, are typed under Liebling's name on the title page. *The Girl* is chaotically plotted as a New York picaresque, and is set in some of Liebling's favorite haunts, nightclubs and agents' offices, gyms and the aquarium. The heroine, Eula, is a lady boxer who falls in love with an ichthyologist after diving in a suicidal moment into one of the big tanks at the aquarium.

Under unaccustomed pressure to "make things up," Liebling tried too hard and produced an awkward story. The stiffness of the language of *The Girl* is a sign of Liebling's own unease with fiction, especially fiction on a large scale. Here he describes Eula's first time in the boxing ring:

> Although she was angry at Sam, Eula found this new mode of combat unsatisfactory to her emotions. As she advanced, the girl struck her in the face with her left hand. This caused Eula to shut her eyes and confused her, yet she had not the least notion of the mechanics of the retaliatory left jab, and the large gloves precluded hair-pulling. Once when the anticipation of being struck in the face grew unbearable she turned her back, but the other girl, much smaller than she, deliberately whacked her on the rump. At this there arose a chorus of baritone laughter which filled her with such humiliation that she fell to her knees and pretended to be exhausted.

Having produced an unsalable manuscript, Liebling must have drawn the obvious conclusion. He should forget about writing novels and stick to the novelistic journalism whose tricks he had already mastered. This decision (one assumes he made it; there is no evidence beyond the undoubted fact that he never attempted another novel) pushed him definitively into the camp of Egan and Borrow, reinforced his original impulse to carry on their antique tradition of personal journalism.

Nineteen thirty-seven is the year his *New Yorker* work picked up speed. It was then that the remarkable improvement in Liebling, which so astonished Shawn, began to show in his lowlife pieces. Liebling had at last found his calling. It was, ironically, what he had been doing all along.

If Liebling's disappointment about his failure at fiction did not seep into his work, this is all the more surprising, since it was also in 1937 that Ann Liebling's condition worsened and she had to be hospitalized for long periods. Liebling took her illness very hard. Ann went in and out of madness; the woman he loved was always still there, ready to emerge from the psychotic's body. On many idyllic occasions, the Lieblings and Joe and Therese Mitchell would go to Rockaway Beach together. They were the foursome that ventured into the "old man's" broken-down shore restaurant. Therese Mitchell took photographs of them on the sand, a strange but happy-looking couple, Ann ravishing, Joe all pudge, she weirdly vacant, he with an amused glint in his eye. They spent many hours on the sand at this faded resort. Joe Mitchell and Ann, who weren't good swimmers, watched while Liebling and Therese Mitchell went in the water. All of them eavesdropped voraciously on their neighbors. Joe Liebling would mimic them later. Mitchell recalls: "He would imitate some old woman sitting on a canvas beach chair, presiding over a circle of other old women. He would even get the gasps between words and the pitch of her voice, the mixture of sorrow and pleasure she felt because of her daughter's troubles."

At Rockaway and the even scruffier Manhattan Beach, the two Joes would overhear "whole novels." "You had the feeling you were in the midst of life," Mitchell says. "Joe could remember the spiels from the freak shows they had there. There was a well known hermaphrodite, Albert-Alberta. He would come out and say, 'I am half man, half wo-man,' and then go into a long spiel, showing one hairy leg and one delicate one, and so forth. When Joe was drunk or bored, he would start it: 'My name is Albert-Alberta. I was born in Marseilles, France. I am half man, half wo-man. On this side . . .' "

Ann Liebling also never forgot the magic of those city beaches. On February 15, 1959, she wrote her ex-husband an extended thank-you note for roses he had sent her at Christmas. By then they had been divorced for a decade and were only in contact, by mail, about once a year. Ann's twelve-page letter, written in an elegant hand in green ink, switches in the second paragraph from his gift to the bookends she had bought him in a department store and then to her memories of the beach in the late thirties.

> I'm so glad you liked the bookends. You know when I held them up to the light in Tilden's to get a good look, I thought I spotted a little sea horse & to me & I may be wrong but I remembered a sea horse as a symbol of love. Then of all things I thought of Rockaway & I hadn't for years, the days you, Joe Mitchell, Therese and myself went swimming. We were always pretty broke, but not too unhappy. After the swim, maybe we would have a hamburger, frankfurt, soda or beer, then for a nice walk, then dinner later on. We would forget to worry those days. Let tomorrow take care of itself, at least that's how I felt & then, relaxed & feeling wonderful we would head for the train and back to New York.

When Ann was lucid, she did her best to make a go of life in the walk-up apartment she shared with Liebling at 159 East 33rd Street. She even braised a pheasant with sauerkraut for a dinner whose guests included Philadelphia Jack O'Brien. But all the while, and especially when she had had something to drink, her life was punctuated with psychotic episodes.

On the surface, she was competing with her "famous" husband (as she proudly referred to him in the 1959 letter), by asserting herself irrationally. Liebling confided to Emily Hahn, another *New Yorker* writer, that Ann repeatedly got involved with Irish policemen. Once, Hahn recalls, he came home to the apartment and found her with one of them. "What are you doing here?" Liebling asked the policeman.

"I don't mean no harm," he replied, "but a piece of tail is a piece of tail."

In public, Ann frequently got up abruptly and fled, ran out of bars and restaurants into the street. Even sometimes while she and Joe were walking together down the street, she would tear off and disappear for a day or two at a time. These episodes, which were usually diagnosed as fugue states, involved visual and auditory hallucinations. She would return from them haggard and claiming that she had been with relatives in Brooklyn. It turned out, Mitchell says, that she kept money on her and would stay at the Hotel Carteret on West Twenty-third Street. Sometimes she would end up at Bellevue, heavily sedated. Liebling would go and get her. Because Ann would then return to normal, he could "never accept a verdict of incurability" from doctors, Mitchell says. Instead, he immersed himself in the literature of schizophrenia, Ann's usual diagnosis, searching for a way to help Ann back to permanent stability.

Ann did not improve. She was periodically institutionalized at great expense. At some point in the late thirties, she spent time at Chestnut Lodge in Maryland, which was the most advanced private mental hospital of its day, and a place that pioneered in psychotherapy for schizophrenics. The head therapist was Frieda Fromm Reichman, the model for the doctor in Hannah Green's novel *I Never Promised You a Rose Garden.* Dr. Ralph Crowley was Ann Liebling's administrative physician at Chestnut Lodge and oversaw her movements in and out of the hospital, on passes and leaves. He recalls:

> She was damned sick. It wasn't easy to know whether she was simply a schizophrenic—out of touch with reality—or whether she also suffered from a mood disorder and was schizo-affective. She was probably the second. She swung from depression to manic uncontrollable behavior. She would run away from the hospital and then come back. She was very impulsive, but she also felt terribly inferior to Liebling intellectually. I met him there when he would come to visit. He was extremely patient, kind to her. I think the patience was hard on her.

More than that, Ann seems to have wanted to extricate herself from her marriage, to get away from Liebling, for what she saw as his own good. In a letter she wrote in the fall of 1958 to thank him for sending her a copy of his book *Normandy Revisited*, she said: "I used to feel that you really didn't want me & in a way didn't need me, some years ago & I was always trying to find a way to step aside & become just anonymity or something. . . . I knew a woman like my own sickness and sadness would have been only a hindrance . . . ."

Leaving Ann was also very painful for Liebling. He remained loyal and, in an important sense, in love with her always. He sent her money, even after their divorce, in 1949, but they had to part. Even while they were still married, he began to see other women during Ann's absences in institutions. In particular, he spent time with the journalist Maria (or Marie Louise) Van Slyke and with the psychotherapist Janet Rioch.

By the fall of 1939, Joe Liebling had no authentic ties holding him in New York. His father had died two years earlier, which helped to free him further from his rootedness in the city. And with the publication of his collected urban lowlife pieces in *Back Where I Came From* in 1938, he had saluted New York lavishly enough to leave it gracefully for a while.

History helped things along. By October 1939, there was a war on in Europe. Ross sent Liebling to France to cover it.

Liebling's explanation of how he landed the job is typically flip. He was eager to pass off this plum assignment as the result of a trick he had played rather than a reward for meritorious service. He alleged: "I attracted the assignment by telling McKelway how well I could talk French. McKelway could not judge. Besides, I was a reasonable age for the job: 35."

seven

Liebling
at War

He left town in a snarling rush to make a flight to Lisbon on a Pan American Clipper. His friend Fred Schwed drove him out to the yacht club basin at Port Washington, where the transatlantic seaplanes took off in those days. It was early in the morning; they got lost, but he did arrive in time, swearing like a sailor, until he saw his mother in the ticket office. "Sucking back four bloody oaths that I could already feel pressing against the back of my teeth," he wrote later, "I switched to a properly filial expression, embraced the dear woman, and got aboard the Clipper feeling like Donald Duck."

The flight was almost deserted. Few people were heading east to Europe that October. But at least Liebling and his eight motley fellow passengers flew in comparative luxury. The Clippers had pullman berths and even staterooms. Landing in Portugal on October 10, he took the train into Spain and north to the French border at Irún, where, waiting a couple of hours for Spanish passport inspection, he had his first brush with fascism. "From the manner of these strutting sparrows of men," he observed, "you might have got the

127

idea that they had defeated France, the United States and Great
Britain, which they had in a way, of course, but by default, and that
we were captives."

Formalities completed, Liebling carried his fifty-five pounds of
airline luggage across the bridge into France, caught the Sud-
Express, with its blacked-out windows, and got to Paris on October
12 in time to check in at the Hotel Louvois, which was to be his
headquarters until the fall of Paris, as well as on future visits to his
second-favorite city. The Louvois looks out on a small square across
from the Bibliothèque Nationale. From his second-floor balcony
Liebling had a view of a fountain with "heroic allegorical figures
representing the rivers of France." In particular, he cherished the
sight of "the Garonne's navel, which was nearly big enough to hold
a baseball." The Square Louvois also offered him trees, flowers in
season, and a functioning *pissoir* all year round. The immediate
quartier included a high density of good restaurants and an even
higher density of prostitutes. It was, he said, the "national lupanar."

Liebling had moved up in the world since his student days. The
Louvois was a second-class, comfortable pile favored by traveling
salesmen. By staying there, he had traded up from the Quartier Latin to the Second Arrondissement, which was on the Right Bank and
had also been the home of the chief hero of Liebling's adulthood,
Stendhal. That great *bon viveur* had written *Le Rouge et Le Noir*
around the corner from the Hotel Louvois.

Liebling, in short, established himself to perfection. Within a
week, he had his credentials in order (*carte d'identité* number
7.607.298) and he was ready to cover the war. But there was no war.
Refugees from the initial alarm were already seeping back into Paris. It was the period soon to be known as the phony war (or the *drôle
de guerre* or the *sitzkrieg*), when all Europe waited for the German
armies to continue the march they had begun in Poland in September. For Liebling, it was a time of professional frustration and personal loneliness. He was prepared to eat fire with Stendhalian detachment, but the best he could manage, after weeks of begging the
authorities, was a stage-managed tour of a tranquil section of the
Maginot Line at Christmas.

He had replaced the glamorous and refined Janet Flanner, who, as Genêt, had been covering European high life for *The New Yorker* and had gone on extended home leave. Liebling had hoped for a more down-to-earth approach than hers:

> I knew very little about Lady Mendl, Elsa Maxwell, Mainbocher and Worth the dressmakers, Mr. and Mrs. Charles Badeaux, or a number of other leading characters in Genêt's Paris dispatches. But since it seemed probable that they would lam anyway, Ross was willing to overlook this deficiency and even agreed in a halfhearted way with McKelway's idea that I write about the reactions to the war of ordinary French people. "But for God's sake keep away from lowlife," Ross said.

As it turned out, Liebling had to scramble to write about anything interesting at all. From his arrival until the beginning of the German offensive in early May, he did manage to turn up material and to produce acceptable copy regularly. He revisited Vire, and found life unchanged. He went out to Angers, because the Polish government in exile had settled there. Mostly, however, his budget and the restrictions on foreign correspondents' travel to the front kept him in Paris cobbling together the latest political gossip and chronicling the rebirth of popular theater, which had closed down after the war scare and was slowly reviving as the prospect of hostilities began to seem more and more remote. In a typical "Letter from Paris," cabled to New York on October 29, Liebling hopscotched from Nostradamus (whose astrological prophecies had emerged as a surprise best seller in Paris) to political street singers to the rise in anti-German sentiment among "the French" to a Gallic Tokyo Rose broadcasting pro-German propaganda. It was thin stuff, redeemed by Lieblingesque touches here and there. In that same letter, for instance, he related amusing items of popular gossip, especially an anecdote told, he said, by Parisian women:

> They circulate with grave optimism the story that a gipsy woman got into an autobus and sat down next to a Parisienne who moved her handbag out of the gipsy's reach. The gipsy said, "Why do you do that when you have only eighteen francs in your bag?" The woman had exactly that sum. Then the gipsy told each of the other passen-

gers how much he or she had, down to the last sou. "Since you know so much," one passenger asked, "tell us when Hitler will die." "On December second," said the gipsy, and got out at the next stop. A story like this gains currency here not because Frenchwomen are silly but because they refuse to believe that their sons and husbands will be killed—those sons and husbands who until now have been so unexpectedly preserved.

It is hard for one to believe in the imperialism of a country where the army and the people are physically identical, where the bourgeoisie, which, by Marxist theory, is supposed to fatten on the profits of war, is the same bourgeoisie which has to shut up shop and move into the advanced zone.

By the way, cooties have reappeared at the front and have been rechristened. The French call them "breadcrumbs on springs."

The only substantial piece Liebling was able to write during the entire phony-war period was a two-part profile of General Gamelin, the chief of staff of the French Army. It took him months of politicking to obtain a brief interview with Gamelin. Meanwhile he read French military history and brooded. Waverley Root, the future author of *The Food of France* and then a stringer for the Paris edition of the Chicago *Tribune*, recalls walking in on Liebling at work one night when the two men had a date to eat dinner: "He had piles of paper spread everywhere. He looked up from that chaos and said, 'You know, this is the 259th article I've written for *The New Yorker*. They've printed every one of them. But I'm still afraid they won't print this one."

Liebling's letters home were filled with worries, which turned out to be well founded, about the Gamelin profile. He wrote Joe Mitchell on February 13, 1940:

> . . . the anecdotal material is just no good. It will certainly be a test
> of my theory that a profile ought to tell what makes a man skillful
> whatever he is; this one won't tell anything but. All it is is an
> interview and a lot of military history, which has begun to
> fascinate me but probably won't anybody else . . . the French have
> decided that the Gamelins' domestic life is sacrosanct.

Over and over, in letters to Mitchell and to his mother, Liebling debates whether to leave France and go home, or wait and mark time on the chance that a shooting war really will break out. He was anxious about his work, but he was also lonely and anxious about Ann, who was in Chestnut Lodge. Root found his new friend "capable of going into long periods of silence, for several days at a time. He'd say yes and no, but he didn't make any real conversation. His wife weighed on him heavily."

This is the earliest documented instance of Liebling's habit of brooding silently when he was depressed. In the winter of '39–'40, the cause was almost certainly Ann, who was a constant subject of his letters. Both the Mitchells and his mother were watching out for her. On March 12, he discussed her at length in a letter to his mother:

> I had very encouraging letters about Ann from Leo, Joe Mitchell and her doctor at the Lodge. If she continues to improve, Leo says, she will be able to leave the Lodge. Of course, there is some risk involved, but he thinks it justified, because if she is kept there too long she'll lose all confidence in herself. They say that Ann wants to go back to Providence for a while. My only fear is that she will not find a proper welcome there, and that she is not in good enough physical condition to live alone. I have written to her already suggesting that she come up and visit with you first. I told her that you would get in touch with her and invite her, as cordially as possible to come to Woodmere for a week or so. . . . It's all a very delicate diplomatic problem. Ann really loves me, but she may do better (she *has* done better, it seems) when I'm not there for her to cling to. Also she is a very affectionate, domestic sort of child who craves love (I mean the kind of love mothers and sisters give most girls) so much that sometimes she appears to run away from it. You can't force yourself on her, but you might convince her that you really want her around—that would make her very happy. Me too. If she insists on going off by herself, you'll just have to let her go, but try to make her feel that she'll always be welcome. If she has a few months of independent existence she may be able to find herself again, and to decide for herself whether 1. Life in New York with me is too much for her—which she thinks sometimes—or 2. Life without me is impossible—which she thinks at other times. I would feel very guilty about having left her to the mercies of my friends and relatives—except that, as I wrote before, my absence from the country may have been the very

stimulus she needed. I am sure that she wouldn't have got well so soon if I had been in New York, so that she could call me every time she had a cross word from a doctor. Joe writes me that she keeps all my letters in the handbag I sent her from Paris, and puts the bag under her pillow at night. Sort of like a father and an only child who is at boarding school. You realize, of course, that I love Ann in a quite different way from anything else in the world. You don't realize, though, how good she is at heart. She must find herself, and perhaps she will do it this spring.

Such high hopes came to nothing. Within a few days there was news that Ann was worse again. The pattern continued, and would continue in these wrenching ups and downs, always. Gradually, in years to come, they both adjusted to it, by paying less attention to the problem and to each other. In France, he found temporary surrogates for her, as he wrote Mitchell:

Once or twice a week, I make a round of whorehouses with my friends in the champagne business. There are houses of all types, from the quasi-palatial to the quiet-provincial trade, the cloak-and-suit men's kind of place and the damn-near-Apache. Some of the girls are darlings, but they don't take the place of real women. I mean you can get screwed regularly and still feel lonely. . . . I'm beginning to get impatient about the Gamelin interview—maybe the damned war will end before I write the profile. I saw a madame bet twenty bottles of champagne that it would be over by Christmas. The sooner the better, I sez, so I can write a nice piece about the celebration and come home.

He filled his free time quite convivially even so. In a way, the winter of '39–'40 provided Liebling with his happiest moments in Paris. He had the money and the leisure to eat where he liked, whenever he wanted. That winter was also the twilight of traditional haute cuisine, and Liebling squeezed out the juices and sucked the bones of the gargantuan meals he elegized later in *Between Meals*.

Some of those dinners he ate with Waverley Root, who says, "He was a very good eating companion. He knew a lot of small restaurants that were not well known and that had a faithful clientele that all weighed over 100 kilos."

Liebling himself weighed almost exactly 100 kilos (220 pounds) at this time, which for him, by comparison with later years, was almost fighting trim. Even so, he did not look well. Root says, "He always looked unhealthy." Liebling himself was worried about the effects of his overindulgence in food and wine. He sensed even then the danger his appetite brought with it. But he invariably yielded to it. Over the years, this compulsion to eat became a plainly suicidal drive. During the *drôle de guerre*, when he was still young, it was merely an aberration, amusing enough, that didn't help his looks.

"*Il ne respirait pas de la santé*," says Yvonne Michel, who met Liebling when she was working in the Section Amérique du Nord of the Information Ministry in Paris just before the war. Not exactly exuding health, as she puts it, Liebling would hang around her office for hours, while she worked. "He knew more than I did. I finally asked him, 'Why are you sitting here?' He said, "*Je m'imprègne*. I'm impregnating myself."

For Liebling, the *Sitzkrieg* was indeed a total immersion course. He imbibed France through his pores.

Liebling's political insights, both in print and in letters, were, nevertheless, superficial and inaccurate, if they are judged by hindsight. But in his very vacillation from optimism to pessimism about German intentions, or in his constant theorizing about the war to come, he is still a good witness to the mood of Paris in that time. He was a mouthpiece for ordinary French opinion in all its uninformed helplessness.

He was, in fact, trying to cover France and the French "war" in the same way that he had covered New York. Today, this sounds like an obvious approach. But in 1939, foreign correspondents usually did not treat their assignments so informally. They were pseudo diplomats, emissaries from their papers who covered the high and mighty developments—parliamentary debates and grand shifts in foreign policy or military planning. In 1939-40, Liebling was inventing the lower-key, more sociological reportage that papers like *The New York Times* have subsequently adopted as the standard business of their foreign staffs.

Liebling felt his way, and sometimes he stumbled, because he could not quite get away from the assumption, held by everyone else, that foreign reporting was a very serious job. He gained confidence in his own impressions, from ground level, as time went on. He was also limited by *The New Yorker*'s timidity in the area of sex and by Ross's aversion to lowlife. Consequently he had to wait until 1944 to publish certain gamier experiences, in his first war book, *The Road Back to Paris*. For example, he was then able to write:

> One Sunday I was walking in Montmartre with my old friend, Henri, whose American silk firm had folded its Paris office during the depression and who had lost all his money, and on the Place Blanche we saw a great crowd of soldiers and strollers around a song plugger who was selling a new ballad. The plugger, a youth about fifteen, wore four hats one on top of another and howled into a megaphone with indelicate gaiety:
>
> > *"Hitler n'en a pas*
> > *Du tout, du tout!*
> > *Hitler n'en a pas*
> > *Pas même un tout p'tit bout!"* °
>
> ° Hitler hasn't got one
> Not at all, not at all!
> Hitler hasn't got one
> Not even a tiny little tip.

The lyrics were about things like ammunition and beefsteaks and gaiety. The plugger's gestures weren't included in the lyrics.

There was an evening when I heard two pimps arguing about the war in the bar of a brother. Each was in fact the protector of one of the two *sous-maitresses* of the house, and each was waiting until his particular protégé accumulated enough capital and good will to start in business for herself. So they were men with an assured future. It must have been in early October, when the French still held a minuscular strip of German territory in the Saar. "Them, they're not here!" one pimp shouted. "Us, we're there! So we must be winning." A moment later, to emphasize some point or other, he started showing off his World War I wounds and yelled, "I bet I am the only pimp in France with three citations." The proprietor of the house in which they were arguing was a naturalized Italian who, his wife always said, was a perfect gentleman because he never drank anything but champagne. "Not even in the morning!" Madame Lucie would say, looking adoringly at the fat procurer—"Not water, not coffee, not beer, not even *mousseux* have I ever seen him drink!" I sometimes used to watch a drop of sweat gleaming on his fat ear and wonder if it tasted of Irroy '28, his favorite. Madame Lucie never told me.

Even in 1944, Liebling still felt it necessary to apologize for this kind of reportage. He followed that anecdote and another pimp story from North Africa with this disclaimer:

"I don't want to give the impression that I covered Paris for the *New Yorker* entirely from cafés and brothels. I took the responsibilities of my new career so seriously that I joined the American Press Association of Paris and went at least once a week to the Hotel Continental, where the French had set up their equivalent of the British Ministry of Information, although they did not give it the status of a full ministry until the following spring.

If he pretended to feel or even really did feel a conflict between the classic role of the foreign correspondent and his personal, Tolstoyan inclination to look for the truth among little people far from the ostensible seats of power, both impulses worked together (in combination with his long-held anti-German bias) to make Liebling hate Hitler and to convince him that the American government should oppose the Nazis with shipments of war matériel, if not with troops. This was a very controversial issue at home, but Liebling, echoing official and unofficial French opinion, was eloquent in letters to his mother about the need for direct American opposition to Hitler in Europe.

Now, this stance might, to a degree, be explained as the typical foreign correspondent's picking up of local sentiment as his own. But Liebling's view of Hitler was complicated, because he was a Jew. More than that, he was a Jew with divided feelings about Jews. J. Anthony Lukas quotes Jean Stafford Liebling as saying: "Even Hitler didn't make him an intensely self-conscious Jew."

Hitler did, nevertheless, make him an intensely anti-Nazi person. His letters to his mother in 1939 and 1940 are filled with his revulsion for Hitler's policies, including his anti-Jewish policies and atrocities. But Liebling continued to bear ill will toward certain

kinds of establishment Jews, even to such Jews under Nazi control in
Germany and Austria. He wrote his mother on April 20, 1940:

> Mother darling,
>
> I had a letter from you in which you asked about coffee here.
> We have had plenty of it ever since about January 10. There was a
> temporary shortage around Christmas time. It made me wonder if
> you had been hearing any propaganda from your no-good Ger-
> man-Jewish friends. One still eats better in Paris than in New York.
> Since coming here I have often wondered about the refugees in
> America. In my book they are just Germans, although if they stay
> in the U.S. and die there their children and grandchildren may
> eventually be human beings. The French are quite sure to win this
> war. You can bet your cards on that and make more than 2 per
> cent. Nobody born in Germany, Jew or Christian, is worth the
> powder to blow him to hell, and I wish you would spread the good
> news. . . . I am staying here at least until things settle down. Paris is
> very beautiful now—the terrasses are full, the trees on the
> Champs-Elysees are in leaf. Stefan Zweig is staying at the Louvois
> and I wouldn't spit on him. I am so thoroughly fed up with *all*
> kinds of Germans that as the French say *je peux pas les sentir.*
>
> > I love you,
> >
> > Abbott

This wild indignation borders on hysteria, the hysteria of someone thrown into confusion by the nearness of war. Liebling sounds
like Céline raving and flailing against anyone who isn't French. His
considered views before and after the time he wrote this letter were
surely different. After all, his own father had been born in a Ger-
man-speaking country. He had written sympathetically about many
Lower East Side Jewish immigrants from Germany. Once, in an extremely compassionate article called "Frau Weinmann and the
Third Reich," he had shown sensitivity to the loyalties that a Ger-
man-Jewish immigrant in New York had continued to feel toward
German culture even after Hitler threatened members of his family
still inside the Fatherland.

Part of Liebling's anger was the result of reports he had heard that Jewish refugees from Germany were acting as German agents in the countries that had offered them asylum. This sounds exactly like the kind of cynical, xenophobic rumor one always hears in France. Liebling was particularly susceptible to believing it because of his childhood animus against Germans and German Jews which was nurtured under the thumb of the fräuleins. In the April 20 letter to his mother, he was not, in any case, referring to all German Jews, only to those with enough money to have escaped. The letter shows Liebling letting himself go in private, after six frazzling months of waiting to be attacked.

When the German bombers finally came in early May, Liebling reported the first air raid from his hotel window. His "Letter from Paris" cabled May 12 was the piece he had been waiting to write, calm and factual, but also a miniature short story set in the Square Louvois when Paris was under attack. Always prone to see real life as a seamless sham, he easily fell into a theatrical comparison and then extended the metaphor, turned it back into reality with a dramatic shouting woman and a closing slapstick vaudeville turn performed by a milkman:

> The new phase of the second World War was announced to Parisians at daybreak Friday. People had gone to bed Thursday night in their habitual state of uncertainty; the governmental crisis in London was still the chief subject of preoccupation. With the dawn came the air-raid sirens, startling a city that had heard no *alerte* during the daytime since the first week of the war. At once, each of the innumerable residential squares in Paris took on the aspect of an Elizabethan theater, with tiers of spectators framed in the opened windows of every building. Instead of looking down at a stage, however, they all looked up. All wore nightshirts, which, since the prosperity of tenants in a walkup is in inverse ratio to their altitude, appeared considerably dingier on the sixth and seventh floors than on the second and third.
>
> The anti-aircraft guns, which nobody heeds now unless an *alerte* has sounded, were intoning such an impressive overture that startled birds flew out of the trees in at least one of the squares and circled nervously in squadrons over the roofs. As they did so, a large, formless woman in a gray nightshirt, making her entrée at a top-floor

window, waved her right arm toward them and shouted, *"Con-fiance!"* putting all her neighbors in hilarious good humor.

The guns kept up their racket, and a number of tracer shells were fired to light up the early-morning sky. The noise of airplane motors was distinctly audible, but there was no way of telling whether they belonged to bombers or to French pursuit planes looking for Ger-mans. At last, one airplane appeared, flying so high that it looked like a charm-bracelet toy, and as it passed overhead, there seemed to be a deliberate lull in the firing. (The disadvantages of knocking down a bomber directly over Paris was obvious.) People stared uneasily at the plane, as they would at a stinging insect near the ceiling, but it went away harmlessly enough, and then the guns opened up again.

The morning air was chilly, so most of the spectators soon closed their windows and went back to bed. In the Square Louvois, the neighborhood milkman, with his wagon drawn by two enormous old gray stallions, came along a few minutes after the plane, and the crash of his cans on the cobbles brought a few nervous folk back to their windows under the impression that bombing had begun.

With that double take, Liebling announced himself as a new kind of war correspondent, new for the twentieth century, at least. Sten-dhal would have recognized an imitation of his own ironic, close-up, anti-grandiose war writing.

For the next month, Liebling's work did not again rise to such heights. He did his job, reporting on the mood of France and the fears and trembling of the people he saw. In his private life, there was less and less to do. Restaurants closed early, because of the blackout and because the city was emptying out. Liebling visited the Salens often and tried to cheer them up. They were both fearful that their son Jean would die at the front.

For his part, Liebling was frightened too, frightened, says Root, as a Jew who might be captured by Nazis, frightened to walk through dark streets home from the Salens', because he might be mistaken for a German parachutist. In the letters he kept writing to his mother, he called these weeks in Paris the toughest of his life.

Still, he remained optimistic. The French were brave. They were his team. They wouldn't lose. The Minister of Information, Jean Prouvost, who also was publisher of *Paris-Soir*, said as much to a convocation of American correspondents he assembled in his office on June 9. "From a military standpoint," he said, "it is improving steadily. Disregard reports of the Government quitting Paris. We will have many more chats in this room."

Minutes later, Prouvost left Paris for Tours with the rest of the government. Liebling went to bed thinking all was well. In the morning, he went to the Spanish consulate and the prefecture of police to get his papers in order for his return by Clipper, via Lisbon, to New York, for home leave. His plan was to return as an official war correspondent for a newspaper, accredited to the American forces which would, he thought, inevitably be sent to save Europe for the second time.

Stopping at the Crillon bar on the Place de la Concorde, he ran into a Canadian general he knew, who told him the news. Paris had been abandoned. Liebling thought he'd better leave town.

Waverley Root had had the same idea all morning. He and Liebling, who didn't drive, and John Elliott of the *Herald Tribune,* who had an ankle in a cast because it had been broken during an automobile accident in a blackout, had all agreed to leave Paris together in case of emergency. Root had a Citroën 11.

By 1 P.M. he had found Liebling and Elliott. Roads were clogged for the first twenty-five miles out of Paris. It took them until 9 P.M. to cover the seventy miles to Orléans, where there were no beds, not even any benches free. Root and Liebling, two big trenchermen, and Elliott, with his cast, all slept in the Citroën. "Every time I dozed," says Root, "my elbow would hit the horn. At 4 A.M. there was an air raid siren. Joe said, 'Good. I hope they blast this place. I'd like to see it.' I said, 'You'll have to get out, then. This car's going to Tours.'"

Official France had already shoehorned itself into little Tours. For four days, confusion paralyzed life there. Liebling made the rounds, saw his favorite American aristocrat, Anthony J. Drexel Biddle, Jr., the boxing Philadelphia millionaire and ambassador to Poland. Liebling had met him first in Angers, where Biddle had fled with the Polish government. Now Biddle was also envoy extraordinary to the government of France, fleeing again and keeping Washington posted about the collapse. "His dispatches," said Liebling, "must have read like a play-by-play account of a man falling down-stairs."

After three days in Tours, the government and the Root party and everybody else who still had a functioning vehicle pulled up stakes and drove to Bordeaux.

Midway there, at a town called Barbezieux, Liebling conned a garageman into letting the three of them sleep in his house. He claimed that Elliott had been shot at the front. The patriotic mechanic pulled out three mattresses and let them sleep on the floor of his dining room.

They got to Bordeaux and hung about briefly until France finally fell, on June 16. "There was a climate of death in Bordeaux," Liebling wrote, "heavy and unhealthy like the smell of tuberoses." For once in his life, he found overeating decadent: "Men of wealth, heavy-jowled, waxy-faced, wearing an odd expression of relief from fear, waited for a couple of hours for tables and then spent all afternoon over their meals, ordering sequences of famous claret vintages as if they were on a *tour gastronomique* instead of being parties to a catastrophe."

These gorging refugees had betrayed France. Everyone had betrayed France, including the United States. Liebling and Biddle and every other American in France were all ashamed. Liebling wrote Suzette Salen Namin a letter, proclaiming: "I will return. We can't let your country die."

He took the train through to Lisbon. *The New Yorker* had made him a reservation on a Clipper and so, on June 25, Joe Liebling landed at La Guardia, full of forboding—and confidence—about the great battle to come.

No one else he met seemed to care. For New Yorkers who hadn't just been there, Europe and its war seemed almost fictional. Isolationism and apathy were rife everywhere he turned.

"Getting off the plane and meeting people who had stayed in America was a strange experience," Liebling wrote, "because they hardly seemed to know that anything was wrong. When you started to tell them they said soothingly that probably you had had a lot of painful experiences, and if you just took a few grains of Nembutal so you would get one good night's sleep, and then go out to the horse races twice, you would be your old sweet self again."

Other returned correspondents understood. Dick Boyer, back from Berlin, where he had been working for *PM*, told Liebling at lunch: "I don't feel like a man from Mars but like a man from earth who has landed on another planet. Don't the damn fools know what is happening on earth?"

They knew at the War Department in Washington, where Liebling went to do a profile on General George C. Marshall, Army Chief of Staff. Marshall, with his old clothes and old-shoe manner, was a Liebling favorite. But there was no news value in the Army in the fall of 1940, and the piece turned out dull.

Liebling had fallen into another phony war situation, even worse than the last. At least in France, everyone had expected a fight. America, Liebling knew, was just as certain to end up at war with Hitler, but no one else seemed to realize it. Harold Ross protested: "You forget about the three thousand miles of ocean and the time Hitler will need to digest all the countries he has already taken."

Faced with such unreasoning apathy, Liebling didn't know what to do. His work record for the year following his return from France shows this concretely. He wrote only eight articles, a career low. The bulk of what he did manage to write was designed to round out a collection of lowlife pieces which appeared in 1942 as *The Telephone Booth Indian*. The best of these articles was a three-part series called "The Jollity Building." The last of Liebling's pre-war Broadway lowlife pieces, it should be read straight through for the full effect of its accumulating absurdities and the sense it gives of an enclosed antiworld of swarming tricksters. Chief among them was Maxwell C. Bimberg a.k.a. Count de Pennies (a character based, in fact, on the promoter Samuel J. Burger):

> What was perhaps the zenith of the Count's prosperity was reached during the brief life of the Lithaqua Mineral Water Company. Lithaqua was formed to exploit a spring on the land of a Lithuanian tobacco farmer in Connecticut. The water of the spring had a ghastly taste, and this induced the farmer to think it had therapeutic qualities. A druggist who was related to a murderess the Count had formerly managed organized a company to market the water. He gave

the Count ten per cent of the common stock to act as director of publicity. The Count "sent out the wire," as the fellows in the Jollity Building sometimes say when they mean that a promoter has had a third party act as go-between, to Johnny Attorney and Boatrace Harry. "Why be thick all your life?" he had his intermediary ask Johnny. "The Count has something big this time. If you will call it square for the few hundred he owes you, he will sell you ten per cent of the mineral-water company for exactly one grand." The Count had the same offer made to Boatrace Harry, and he sold his ten per cent of the stock to each of them for one thousand dollars. He sold his share in the enterprise to five other men, too, and was just beginning to think he had better go to Florida again when a chemist for a consumers' research group discovered that seepage from the vats of a nearby dye works accounted for the bilious flavor of the farmer's water. This got the Count out of a difficult situation. Even Johnny and Boatrace could understand that ten per cent of a worthless business was not worth quarreling about.

In order to make a full-length book of his uncollected *New Yorker* lowlife pieces, Liebling added one article that was not about a telephone booth Indian. His profile of Roy Howard, the newspaper publishing magnate, was sweet revenge. Howard had bought the *World* and folded it into his *Telegram*. Liebling had toiled for him at a low salary for several years. Now he could interview him and demolish the vain little tyrant with a lethally careful job of reporting. He buried Howard in an avalanche of facts and quotations. He even found an old private memo that Howard's mentor and employer, E. W. Scripps, had written in 1917: "Right from the start, Howard's self-respect and self-confidence was so great as to make it impossible for it to increase. . . . Gall was written all over his face. It was in every tone and every word he voiced."

Liebling allowed himself an occasional facetious swipe too. The *Telegram*, he said, "was losing a million dollars a year. It was steadily losing readers, too, many of them people who had developed hallucinations from reading its prose and were dragged from subway trains slapping at adjectives they said they saw crawling over them."

Finally, he was able to use the profile to attack, indirectly, the isolationist faction that had opposed lend-lease and the Roosevelt third term. Howard had backed Willkie and tried to get him to fight lend-lease. Attacking Howard, then, was like striking a blow at Hitler, at one remove.

This vainglorious attempt to set the United States on its proper, belligerent course did not obviate the need for Pearl Harbor. But it did help Liebling's reputation. He was getting known. *McCall's* commissioned him to write two thousand words on propaganda in the United States. He traveled to Chicago for the piece, to interview the leaders of America First ("I am not sure yet whether all these people desired an Axis victory consciously," he wrote later, "but the irrational stubbornness with which they denied its possibility made you think of certain women who continually and compulsively talk about the impossibility of rape"), and to Washington to meet the official propagandists. The article itself is of no lasting interest, but the headline is a sign of Liebling's new celebrity: "PROPAGANDA— One of America's crack reporters discloses what we are being told, who is telling us and how they are doing it."

When he was in New York, that year and during his other wartime stint at home the next year, he rented a room in Fred and Harriet Schwed's house at 8 East 10th Street. Fred was a childhood friend and adult drinking buddy of Liebling. Harriet Schwed, now widowed, remembers that Liebling suffered from terrible sieges of gout, that the principal decorative item in his quarters was an etching of Eddie Arcaro, whom he had interviewed, and that he was an untroublesome tenant except for the times when Ann, on her own in Providence by then, would visit him.

On those days, he would go to the station and wait for train after train until she arrived. She drank heavily and sometimes became violent, threw things. One Christmas Eve, she became hysterical at a party and went back to the Schweds' house without Joe. She told him later that she had scared Fred Schwed when she came in.

Ann tended to overdramatize herself and her effect on other people. The maid from an upstairs duplex apartment had dropped some dead roses on the stair. Ann said that she had done it to mock her.

More happily, this year at home gave Liebling a chance to renew his friendship with the Mitchells, with Philip Hamburger, a younger *New Yorker* writer, and with Hamburger's wife-to-be, Edith Iglauer, as well as with Emily Hahn, Richard Boyer and other *New Yorker* writers. Despite their companionship and the relative relaxation of this low-key year, Liebling must have been grinding his teeth, hoping Roosevelt would take the country to war. He had tired of making the case for American intervention to liberal friends.

Finally, unable to wait for his government to join him, Liebling went back to war on his own in July 1941. He flew to the United Kingdom to cover the London blitz.

This time he flew by bomber. It was faster, twice as fast. Also it flew direct and bypassed overcrowded Lisbon. His flight, from Montreal, was on an American-built Liberator run by the RAF. Liebling was doubly a VIP, with an invitation from the British and official permission to travel from the State Department. In a big brown flying suit with a hood, he made the crossing cramped together with other passengers on shelf-like beds. They didn't sight one enemy plane on the way. But this was a great adventure for the time, involving high speed and altitude in an exciting new aircraft that was in danger of attack at any moment.

He landed in Scotland, spent the night in battered Glasgow and traveled by rail down to London the next day in a train filled with soldiers in uniform. At the suggestion of one of them, he took a room in Fleming's Hotel, Half Moon Street, Piccadilly. The address sounded swank—it is—but the unpretentious hotel, which Liebling made his headquarters during wartime visits to England, appealed to him primarily because it was so close to Shepherd's Market, tucked away in a nearby mews. It reminded him of the neighborhood's raffish, Eganesque past.

There was plenty of time to look around. The blitz had faded to practically nothing. "I rather doubt that I'll send any sensational stories from here," he wrote his mother on August 10, 1941, "but I'm learning a lot." He was definitely a neophyte in Britain and never really felt as fond of the country as he did of France. Fortunately, his old Journalism School buddy Paniguian was in town. He had lost his business and his Rumanian-Jewish mistress on the Continent and, having recovered from a nervous breakdown, was scraping together a life in London. The two men saw each other once a week, and Liebling was able to help him celebrate his engagement to an English girl later in the year.

Liebling's other major contact in London then was *The New Yorker's* resident correspondent, Mollie Panter-Downes. She met him for lunch at Fleming's just after his arrival. "He won my heart," she recalls, "by producing a present from the office—dozens of nylons. They were like gold during the war. When he arrived we got the impression he was anti-British. He was so pro-French and we were holding out on them. He was unpopular with people. He was not at home with a certain type of Englishman. But he was a great figure with the staff at his hotel."

Liebling had plenty of time to scour London for his kind of Englishman and for offbeat places in which to dine out, and he came up with a short list of pubs that served plebeian things like haddock and egg. He would splurge at the supernal Wilton's, an upper-class British shrine off St. James's which still serves the best British food in England, at phenomenal prices in deliberately unglamorous surroundings. To work off the extra poundage, Liebling would jog in Hyde Park. He also found time for two girlfriends, one of whom was a Wren, a lady sailor. The other came from Hull and was known behind her back as the Yorkshire canary.

It was she who got him to travel up to Hull and write a *New Yorker* piece about the bombing damage there. She had lambasted Mollie Panter-Downes for not paying tribute to the particularly heaving pounding Hull had taken—the heaviest of any place in England—so Liebling went there and tried to redress the balance.

He wrote several other pieces during the fall, most of them touching on proletarian aspects of the war effort. He visited a munitions factory, interviewed an RAF ace. The best of these was a feature on the "V for Victory" campaign that had sprung up with tremendous international success at the BBC. Foreign-language programs had spread the "V" symbol across Europe. It had become a rallying point for resistance sympathizers everywhere.

Ross and Shawn kept sending him congratulatory telegrams for each of these efforts. And they pressured him to do a profile of

Churchill. Still, in almost every letter home to his mother, he complained that he was bored in London. The Churchill piece was a trap—too complicated and impossible to write objectively without sounding like an isolationist. Other subjects were minor and not worth staying on for. Ann had not written him since August. He was lonely and made continual plans to come home, plans which pressure from *The New Yorker* made him postpone several times through the fall. While he marked time, and cursed the United States for staying neutral, he put together two outstanding articles. In each of them, he found ways to translate the New York lowlife approach to wartime subjects in Europe. Or rather he found two telephone booth Indians living abroad.

"The Colonel of the Ship" is a great war yarn, an escape saga told to Liebling in London by a Free French air force colonel who had conned his way out of a Vichy prison camp by pretending to be mad. On another occasion, he had commandeered a five-hundred-ton armed trawler and turned it over to the British in Gibraltar. The colonel was a natural grifter worthy of the Jollity Building.

So, in his way, was Anthony J. Drexel Biddle, Jr., who had followed the Poles to London and been additionally assigned as ambassador to exiled Belgium, Norway and the Netherlands, while also assuming ministerial duties toward Czechoslovakia, Yugoslavia, Greece and Luxembourg. Although Biddle was inescapably a blueblood, with hand-tailored suits and his hair parted down the middle, he had grown up with Philadelphia Jack O'Brien as a constant dinner guest at the family manse on the Main Line. O'Brien was a Liebling favorite, and some of his gift for gab had been picked up by young Biddle, who talked, Liebling observed, "with a blarneying facility." The ambassador was, in effect, a reporter for the State Department, a reporter of such talent that some U.S. newspaper correspondents in London liked to call him "the best leg man they ever saw." At any rate, he could run, which was a lucky thing in a man with so many embassies and legations to visit:

> The eight governments Biddle services are all in London, but an eight-credential diplomat has to hustle to keep up with his schedule of widely scattered visits. This explains why Londoners passing the

apartment house at 40 Berkeley Square, where Biddle's multiple embassy is situated, are sometimes mystified by the appearance of a tall man in a black overcoat, a Homburg hat, striped trousers, and long, square-toed pumps who looks hurriedly right and left for cruising taxis, then darts to the corner of Mount Street, turns, and sprints toward the cab rank in Grosvenor Square. Biddle has long legs and runs like a man in first-class physical condition, which he is, usually doing the distance between the squares in less than a minute and sometimes exciting the interest of a constable as he runs, for his looks evoke memories of Raffles, the amateur cracksman. At Grosvenor Square, he leaps into the cab at the head of the rank. It gets under way just as the baffled constable is deciding that perhaps he should do something about the suspicious character.

One leap ahead of the law, Biddle was as much a hustler, and in the same line of amiable thuggery, as that other aristocrat the Count de Pennies. Biddle would have liked the Count. He and Liebling had similar enthusiasms. There was an element of the slummer's mentality, perhaps, in their attachment to classes below their own— a faint element, though, because the enthusiasm was carried off without condescension. Indeed, they were both suffused with admiration for the natural qualities and skills they found in their scruffier friends. Standing in a posh London hotel bar, Biddle told Liebling, with a certain swagger that is not difficult to imagine, "You know, old sport, the best thing you can do if you get into an argument with a fellow at a bar is to grab his lapels and drop your forehead against the bridge of his nose. You'll break it every time. Bob Fitzsimmons taught me that one."

If Biddle was swank, as well as tough, he was also a relative nonentity in the world of London diplomacy. No one else in the Foreign Service had wanted his job. Typically, however, Liebling had picked Biddle for a profile and not the United States ambassador to England or, despite continuing pointed requests from Ross and Shawn, Winston Churchill. He did finally convince them that the Churchill profile was a bad idea, and arranged to start home again for New York.

On December 1, Liebling boarded a westbound Norwegian tanker. He fell into easy rapport with the crew, and eventually transcribed the closed, intimate world of the voyage into a three-part *New Yorker* piece. The series did not run until late March 1942, which may explain why its most crucial event is treated with such sang-froid. By March, the Japanese attack on Pearl Harbor was old news. On December 7, 1941, the day of the attack, Liebling, who since October 1939 had been waiting with religious fervor for war to break out, was on board the *Regnbue* in the middle of a gale:

> I turned in early and put my watch and fountain pen in the desk drawer, where they rattled like dice in a nervous crapshooter's hand. There is a difference of thirteen and a half hours between the time in Hawaii and Great Britain, and I was asleep before Grung, the radio-man, picked up the first bulletin about the attack on Pearl Harbor. I heard the news when I went up on the bridge the next morning. Bull, the third officer, pumped my hand and said, "We both allies now!" It felt more natural to be a belligerent on a belligerent ship than that anomalous creature, a neutral among belligerent friends.

Another reason for Liebling's restrained reaction in the article may have been some unprintable feelings about being on a slow boat to New York at the very moment when Congress had at last declared war, and when the least interesting destination in the world for a reporter was the United States. Before Pearl Harbor, Liebling had begun "to feel more curious about the front in the United States," where "there was still a great decision to be taken. . . ." He had gone home by sea, moreover, because, hungry for action, he "wanted to experience what the British press liked to call the Battle of the Atlantic."

As things turned out, the great decision had been forced upon America before the *Regnbue* even reached the open ocean. The trip took forty-two days, and all was quiet on the Atlantic front.

Liebling's chief accomplishment on board was growing a beard. He looked like a Barbary pirate when he debarked at New Orleans on January 11, 1942. He had expected the country to be in a galvanic state, but found that "Pearl Harbor had left slight trace on the public mind."

He moldered in New York all spring, writing nothing, while his London pieces ran in *The New Yorker*, one by one. There is no direct evidence of how he spent his time in those months, only that he stayed with the Schweds, dined out with the usual friends and saw Ann occasionally, in the same painful way as before.

At the start of the summer, he took another Norwegian ship, a fast one, back to England. Landing at Liverpool on July 13, he reestablished himself for the next four months in London at Fleming's, whose restaurant had been transformed by a new manager into a noisy popular pub with a British swing band and crowds of American colonels. The U.S. Army was already pouring in personnel. Liebling devoted himself to this historic and vast troop movement. He wrote about the logistics of it; he looked in on newly arrived precision bomber crews; he spent some time with a black regiment billeted in a picturesque country town. The blacks had some trouble with white American soldiers in the immediate neighborhood, but they were amazed at the color blindness of the British locals. The piece (called "The Rolling Umpty-Seventh") made a nice, implicit point about American racism, but it lacked the edge, the spirit of skulduggery of Liebling's best work. He was not inspired by "inspirational" material, but needed sly and sensual subjects to prime the flow of his best prose. Once again he was waiting, distracting himself with visits to Paniguian and his new wife, Mary, getting together with old friends and reporters who had just arrived in town. Liebling was now an official correspondent attached to the Army, with a uniform he didn't wear in London.

Liebling's letters grow increasingly restless at this period. He wanted action and considered volunteering for official Army intelligence work. He ordered a helmet and gas mask (his third set since 1939) and collected other field equipment for the future. His tone waxed optimistic and patriotic. "We" were going to win the war. But when would we start?

By the end of October, Liebling knew he had been picked to go with the Army on an invasion. For two weeks he was subject to twelve-hour notice at his hotel, waiting for the call that would summon him on an expedition to an undisclosed destination. The mystery faded on November 8, when the first North African landings were announced in London. The next day, limping from a gout attack, he sailed for Algeria with a bevy of other reporters on a troop ship. They landed at Mers-el-Kebir, November 21. From that port it was a short trip to Oran, where Liebling was "assimilated" to the First Infantry Division for the next four weeks. He was able to go on one uneventful reconnaissance mission into Morocco, but he mainly used his time "getting the feel of North Africa and gaining a gradual and unforced familiarity with the First Infantry Division. . . . "

The First was full of New Yorkers with Bronx and Brooklyn accents, whose sounds reassured Liebling. Oran itself infuriated him because he quickly learned that the Allied occupation force had left most of the old, fascist-leaning leadership in place and was looking the other way when these Vichy leftovers continued to harass the local anti-fascists, most of them Jews, who had just risked their lives to assist the Allied capture of their city. The old fascist censors were also still in place and prevented correspondents from filing "negative" political information to the outside. As a result, Liebling's "Letter from Oran," radioed out on December 7, reads almost like a travelogue. So does his "Letter from Algiers," radioed on January 2. Liebling's real experiences in the beginning of his North African tour had to wait a year before they could be printed, until he published *The Road Back to Paris.*

He found collaborationists everywhere, found them shored up by American authority, which they continued to mock and publicly oppose. These official reactionaries represented the landowning class, Liebling said, a group "reactionary to an extent only possible in a country where a few white men live by the exploitation of a large native population." They also offended Liebling's francophilia; here was the last unoccupied remnant of France, and it reminded him, in its racism, of Mississippi. And Harlem: "There was in truth a violent anti-Semitism in the city of Oran, but it was the same kind as the anti-Semitism of Harlem', the result of deliberately inciting one exploited race against another." For perhaps the only time in his life, Liebling found himself solidly lined up with Jewish people in a political scrap. This did not imply any fundamental change of heart. The North African Jewish anti-fascists were, as he said, an exploited underclass, and they were early heroes in the fight to free France from German domination. They were on his side.

He found more of them in Algiers, when he flew there in a C-47 transport plane on Christmas day. First, however, he found a room in the deluxe Hotel Aletti, or rather he found an empty bed in a room there which he shared with Dave Brown of Reuters. Then, strolling about the city, he turned up no evidence of Allied propaganda, no caricatures of Hitler, only pro-German apologetics in bookstore windows. There had been a few patriotic street demonstrations after the Allied landing, but these had been discouraged by local officials as "examples of Jewish bad taste."

In a crowded restaurant, he was seated next to a Syrian-Jewish jeweler who said he "didn't know what to make of the Allies' 'desertion' of their pre-landing 'friends.' . . . " The jeweler arranged a meeting that afternoon with other anti-fascist Jews in the apartment of Dr. Henri Aboulker, a seventy-eight-year-old Jewish physician. Aboulker was the leader of the resistance group that had seized power in Algiers and held it until the Allies arrived a day later. A half hour after Liebling left the apartment, the government police pushed their way in and arrested fifteen people for plotting to assassinate General Giraud, the Free French commanding officer in Algiers. News of these arrests galvanized the thirty reporters in town. They insisted on a meeting with Giraud, who coldly dressed them down for meddling. An American diplomat then entertained them and tried to gloss over the affair, while defending the need for press censorship. This was the same diplomat who had used the Aboulker apartment as a clandestine headquarters during the months leading up to the Allied landing. His sudden switch to the side of the Algerian ruling class disgusted Liebling. Some of his anger got through the censor and made its way, as buried irony, into the *New Yorker* "Letter" published January 16, 1943. He wrote: "Probably no one will ever be able to explain why up-to-date films presenting the best aspects of American life were not rushed in almost with the first assault wave. Perhaps the omission was the result of a reluctance to indulge in propaganda which might put our cause in too favorable a light. . . ." Even this mild and involuted critique of American policy upset Harold Ross, just as Liebling's leftism would continue to frighten him over the years. Shawn, it appears, took Liebling's side. Today, Shawn credits Liebling with raising *The New Yorker*'s political consciousness, with helping to push the magazine out of its original apolitical joviality. Shawn recalls: "In those days, the magazine was more innocent than it is today. We didn't get into politics as much. At that time, to say anything against the government was very daring here. In North Africa, Liebling knew who was on the right, and who was on the left; he spotted the tendency of our government to side with the far right abroad. Ross sometimes thought Liebling was taking too liberal a stand. I would argue for Liebling. I began to get a little more sophisticated about politics."

In early 1943, this process of politicization had barely begun at *The New Yorker*. But the magazine's readiness to send a feature writer like Liebling to cover a shooting war was in itself a sign of Ross's brilliance and of his extraordinary instinct for the right way to use the staff of a magazine of entertainment to cover a war with seriousness and distinction. As Shawn observes, "There hadn't been a real tradition of magazine war reporting. Liebling adapted the Reporter-at-Large form in a most original way to war correspondence." In effect, Liebling treated war as if it had been Times Square with bullets. This was exactly the assignment that Ross (whose experiences as Paris editor of *Stars & Stripes* in World War I had taught him valuable if unofficial lessons about war—he had got his job while technically a deserter) had intended. Liebling was to let the newspaper boys handle the top brass and the press conferences. Liebling was to cover ordinary people and ordinary events. Liebling simply interpreted this mandate more broadly than Ross may have wished. He plunged into the mundane Stendhalian confusion of combat and wrote home about it with a novelist's eye. To do that in North Africa, he had to leave the political mess in Algiers and go to the front, which, by early January, was in southern and central Tunisia.

He hitched a ride with a courier plane, whose pilot navigated with the help of a Michelin guide and confessed, as they took off from an interim stop at a place called Telergma, "Up to here it's all right, but I've never been to your field, and it's said to be difficult to find, in between some mountains."

That first night Liebling stumbled into a tent he had picked for himself, thinking it was empty, and discovered two enlisted men already there. One of them apologized, "I hope you don't mind, but the tent we were sleeping in got all tore to pieces with shrapnel last night, so we just moved our stuff in here." The other said, "You can thank God you wasn't here last night."

For several months after that, Liebling lived in various locations at the shifting front line in the Tunisian desert. In January, he covered the air war, principally from a Godforsaken base near Thélepte. In February, Liebling returned to the Aletti to write and to get away from the discomforts of the front. In March, April and early May, he followed the ground campaign with the First Division. And at the end of May, he returned to New York by ship. This rough chronology can be extracted from Liebling's published war pieces, but they are almost wholly devoid of specific dates. The material in the pieces overlaps and seems to have been arranged almost purposely to keep the reader from knowing how the events Liebling narrates fitted together with the day-to-day history of the North African campaign. On the other hand, the basic feeling of all Liebling's Tunisian reportage is that of a diary. He worked hard to convey the atmosphere of normal life in combat, with its uneven, unsettling mix of banality and random violence.

At Thélepte, a Private Smith started to tell Liebling about some plumbing he had once installed for Liebling's friend Sam Spewack, the writer, in New Hope, Pennsylvania: "'His wife, Bella, couldn't make up her mind where she wanted one of the bathroom fixtures,' Smith said, 'so I said—'

"I never heard any more about Bella Spewack's plumbing," Liebling continues, in the leisurely, unflappable voice that he adopted for all his combat work,

> because Major Robert Christman, the commanding officer of the squadron, came up to me and said, "Well, it's a nice quiet morning." He had his back to the east. I didn't get a chance to answer him, because I started to run like hell to get to the west side of the mound. A number of soldiers who had been scattered about eating their breakfasts off the tops of empty gasoline cans had already started running and dropping their mess things. They always faced eastward while they ate in the morning so that they could see the Messerschmitts come over the mountains in the sunrise. This morning there were nine Messerschmitts. By the time I hit the ground on the lee side of

the mound, slender airplanes were twisting above us in a sky criss-crossed by tracer bullets—a whole planetarium of angry worlds and meteors.

Liebling had teamed up with Boots Norgaard, an AP correspondent. Their life together (or at least their life as recorded in Liebling's articles) held to this rhythmic alternation between routine life in the desert and spurts of potentially fatal excitement. In between German strafing attacks one Wednesday, Norgaard and Liebling went down to the Arab village to haggle for eggs. They returned at dusk and were hungry. Liebling decided to cook the eggs:

> I took the lid off the hole in the top of the stove, put the mess tin over the hole, and broke all the eggs into the oil. I think there were eleven of them. They floated around half submerged, and although I stirred them with a fork, they didn't scramble. We decided that I had used too much oil, so we added some cheese to act as a cement. Before the cheese had had time to take effect, we heard a loud explosion outside—plainly a bomb—and felt the shack rock. Norgaard grabbed his tin hat and ran out the door to look, and I was going to follow him when I reflected that if I left this horrible brew on the stove hole a spark might ignite the oil and thus set fire to the shack. I carefully put the mess on a bench and replaced the lid on the stove. I put on my helmet and followed Norgaard out into a kind of foxhole outside our door. More bombs exploded, and then all we could hear was the racket of the Bofors cannon and .50-caliber machine guns defending the field. I went back inside, removed the stove lid, and put the eggs on again. Just as some warmth began to return to the chilled mess, another stick of bombs went off. In the course of the next minute or so, I repeated my entire routine. Before I finished cooking dinner, I had to repeat it three times more. Finally the eggs and the cheese stuck together after a fashion and I drained the oil off. Then, since no bombs had dropped for a couple of minutes, I poured half the concoction into Norgaard's canteen cup, I put what was left in my mess tin, and we ate.

By insisting on this matter-of-fact style, Liebling called special attention to the unpredictable wildness of life in the New Mexican–Hollywood Western landscape around Thélepte. Civilization was a universe away; its rules were suspended. A certain type of man flourished at the margins of civilized society and knew how to improvise and live without laws. War, Liebling determined, favored the telephone booth Indians. They knew how to gamble and plunge by instinct. The basic difference between the Jollity Building and Thélepte's airfield was in the stakes. Failure in a civilian hustle was survivable and comic. Failure at Thélepte was lethal and tragic. But the successful operator in both situations looked at the world with the same angle of vision.

Liebling found many of *his* people in combat in North Africa. He wrote profiles of two of them. There was a bloodthirsty guerrilla pilot, Major Philip Cochran, already famous as a model for the aviator Flip Corkin in the Milton Caniff comic strip *Terry and the Pirates*. Cochran, an Irish maverick who never changed his clothes, could predict when German raids would come, as if, he told Liebling, he were "sensing when to hop on or off a guy who is shooting craps." Cochran had disobeyed orders to ground his squadron at a rear area airfield and had flown to Thélepte and started fighting on his own initiative. He had been left alone because he was so good at the job he had grabbed for himself. Liebling observed: "The situation called for officers who were good at guessing, bluffing and guerrilla tactics, and Cochran found himself in the spot he had dreamed of all his military life."

So did Major General Terry Allen, who commanded the First Division with "shrewdness and dash . . . not acquired from textbooks." Allen had flunked out of West Point, had boxed professionally, and he was a consummate actor who, to get his way, could "throw himself into or out of a momentarily genuine mood as quickly as a soldier can shift the gears of a jeep."*

Such amiable thugs became Liebling's war heroes. The Cochrans and Allens, he felt, were winning the war, with shrewdly channeled savagery and daring. Liebling admired them fiercely, rode with

---

* In another metaphor comparing human sensibility to motor vehicles, but in reverse order, Liebling described the movements of tanks in the desert in poignant terms drawn, doubtless, from memories of his younger self: "They advance hesitatingly, like diffident fat boys coming across the floor at a party to ask for the next dance, stopping at the slightest excuse, going back, and then coming on again, and always apparently seeking the longest way round."

them into battle, and in writing about their exploits, he tried to re-
draw the public's idea of heroism and manhood, tried to reshape it
after their image. These bandit-soldiers were his serious examples of
modern military behavior. Liebling put himself in the North African pieces for comic relief.

Shortly after Liebling returned to Algiers from Thélepte, in late
January, he wrote Leo Stone:

> I have at last joined the large legion of Hairbreadth Harries who
> have narrow escape stories to bore people with. . . . At dawn on the
> morning of our scheduled departure eight Messerschmitts came
> over the field as if to strafe and our planes on patrol engaged them
> in a pretty spectacular dogfight in which one of our pilots, a
> Frenchman of the Lafayette Escadrille, was killed. I was standing
> next to Major Phil Cochran, one of the shrewdest fighting men I
> ever saw, who was taking a piss while we watched the dogfight
> and I was brushing my teeth, and Cochran said, "There is one
> fucker way up high just stooging around and not joining in the
> fight at all and he is casing the joint for a strafe job later in the
> day." American transport planes drop in on the field at least once
> every day, but of course never on any scheduled time, and Nor-
> gaard and I intended to go back to the big city on one of them
> that day. The transports landed shortly before noon. There was a
> small dust storm raging so it was hard to see anything on the field.
> We put our baggage in a jeep and a Major named Christman
> drove us down to the transports to put us aboard. The two trans-
> port planes lay close together, which is against all orders, but the
> pilots get careless. The jeep was under the lee of one of the planes
> and we were just saying goodbye to Christman before getting out
> when Christman said "Jesus!" and vanished into the dust and can-
> non shells began to explode all around us. I leaped out of the jeep
> and lit running and somebody yelled "Down!" and I dived for the
> ground so hard I tore a lot of skin off my hands and knees and el-
> bows and lay there wishing my ass didn't stick so far up in the air
> while the Messerschmitts made their first pass. . . . All I could think
> of was "Joe Liebling has been a nice guy and it's been a pleasure
> knowing him," and I was awfully sorry that I would never know
> how Liebling's life was going to come out. I really did not think of
> anybody else. After the first pass I got up and ran off the runway

and got to a slit trench that a soldier had dug for himself and jumped in with him and then I felt safe. . . . There were parallel lines of small shell craters right along past us and past the transports, like the marks of a rake, but the teeth of the rake had missed us. . . . I was very much excited.

Liebling rewrote the incident and used it in a piece called "The Foamy Fields," minus some of the gamier Cochran language but still as strongly self-mocking. Liebling was, in his own terms, an antihero, in the comic tradition of Stendhal's Fabrizio del Dongo at Waterloo. He cast himself as a naïve. Liebling's helplessness was authentic, to be sure, but was also a pose struck self-consciously by a man who knew he was an actor in a traditional form of drama called war. As a war reporter, Liebling had an established role: to observe and portray the battle personas of others. For his part, Cochran played his macho role to the hilt, knew he was doing it, and kept exclaiming that life at Thélepte was just like a movie.

For Liebling, then, war stories were, at bottom, stories about how men in combat reacted to the idea of themselves in combat. As the man who wrote the stories, Liebling began to report on himself playing the role of war reporter. This preoccupation with himself as myth-maker was, in its involuted way, really a straightforward result of his meticulous concern for reporting the truth of events. If he had kept himself out of the stories, that would have been truly artificial. If he had merely recorded the air skirmishes and tank battles he saw, and had left out the grandiloquent personalities of the soldiers, that too would have been a false account, because it would have suppressed the most important cause of their bravery, which was their grandiloquence itself, their willing acceptance of the role of hero.

It was in such an introspective frame of mind that Liebling came, in early May, upon the corpse of an American private named, by legend, Mollie. Mollie, according to some GIs, was short for Molotov. But that wasn't his real name. Some friends of the dead man thought he might have been called Carl Warren, which also turned out to be wrong. Whoever he was, Mollie was reliably said to have talked six hundred Italian soldiers into surrendering. Well, he hadn't really done that. He and an Italian-speaking GI friend, who interpreted for him, had crawled up to an Italian position and persuaded 147 soldiers to give themselves up. Later, under continued artillery pounding, the rest of the total Italian force of 537 surrendered. Mollie's wildly valorous harangue had given them the idea.

But who was Mollie? Why did no one know his name? Where did he come from? What made him so brave? Such questions ate away at Liebling as he sailed home from Casablanca on the troop ship *Monterey*. Back in New York on May 31, Liebling began to root out the truth about Mollie. In the piece he eventually wrote, he painstakingly relates the details of his own legwork and how he gradually discovered Mollie's true name, Petuskia, how he tracked him down to a Greenwich Village bar, where he had worked as a busboy. At every stage of his search, Liebling turned up some sign of Mollie's drive to disguise himself, to hide his low origins and status and to glamorize himself. Eventually Liebling answered all his questions about Mollie, but by that point he saw that the literal truth (and, by implication, the sort of investigative reporting that could uncover it) was inadequate to explain Mollie, who was much more than his official dossier and more complex than the best legwork could ever show. It was the myth of Mollie that finally mattered, and that myth had turned into an obsession in Liebling's mind:

> When I walk through the West Side borderland between Times Square and the slums, where Mollie once lived, I often think of him and his big talk and his golf-suit grin . . . he bragged, but when challenged, he would not back off. The brag was like the line a deckhand throws over a bollard—it pulled performance after it. I lived with him so long that I once half-convinced myself he was not dead.

The piece ends with a series of fantasies Liebling had, in which he imagines that Mollie was miraculously alive:

> Suppose . . . that the corpse with the face shot away that I saw by La Piste was not Mollie at all, but that Mollie had put his uniform and dog-tags on a dead goumier and gone over the hill wearing a Moroccan *djellabah*, to wage a less restricted kind of war, accumulating swag as he went? And suppose he was living in Morocco now, with a

harem, a racing stable, and a couple of Saharan oil wells? . . . Or suppose he had switched uniforms with a dead German, and thereafter, as a secret agent, confounded all the Wehrmacht's plans? He liked to operate in disguise, as he proved when he fooled the French officers at Casablanca, and superior officers of foreign powers confided in him on sight.

These alternate Mollies popped into Liebling's mind when he had lived with the real man's story so long he had "half-convinced" himself Mollie was still alive. He started to write a play, using one of the fantasy Mollies, but never got anywhere with it. In his mind, however, he crossed the line from nonfiction to fiction. This is important, because it shows how near he had been coming, in his work and in his attitude toward it, to the procedures and sensibility of fiction. No evidence proves that Liebling consciously considered the theoretical implications of his North African writing. But the work itself shows him over and over again telling the news of the war through dramatic incidents focused with novelistic detail on his own adventures or on those of telephone booth Indians who were exaggerated versions of himself.

With "Mollie," Liebling went further. He broke beyond his usual covert experimentalism. Not only did he draw a full-dress character "out of an old-fashioned boy's book," but he cast the piece in the form of a personal memoir that chronicled his own dramatic confrontation with Mollie. He showed himself, the reporter-as-hero, in a grail-like quest for Mollie's truth. The search begins as reportage but ends in overt fantasy. The reporter has gone so far into his subject that he has merged with it. Still, through all this narcissistic narration, Liebling never allows the line to blur between his objective, reporter's perceptions and his subjective reactions.

Implicitly, then, "Mollie" depicts a reporter in the classic dilemma of all reporters, coming to terms, in a superficially impersonal manner, with experience that was, inevitably, personal. But in "Mollie," Liebling forces this issue. Having established himself as a traditional legman, he shows that the reportage would never have taken place without the personal obsession with Mollie which ultimately led to an outpouring of sheer fantasy. The same impulse, variously shaped, could, he implied, produce a news story or a play.

"Mollie" was, at bottom, journalism about journalism and its limits.

Liebling had been tacitly commenting on the nature of his craft while practicing it. These inchoate acts of journalistic analysis were really unlabeled bits of press criticism. With them, and with Mollie in particular, Liebling, unwittingly or not, had been pointing toward the explicit press criticism he would write during the postwar period.

But in the summer of 1943, his first "Wayward Press" piece was still almost two years in the future. He was a war correspondent taking a breather in New York, camping out at the Fifth Avenue Hotel in Greenwich Village for five months, during which he wrote up his North African adventures and poked into the Mollie case.

In mid fall, he crossed the Atlantic eastward for the fourth and last time during the war. A speedy Norwegian fruit ship dropped him in Liverpool on November 6. "My notion," he wrote, "was to get to England early in order to be sure of a good spot in the invasion. I did not want to get caught up in some ancillary theatre and then not be able to transfer out in time for the main event, and as the lone correspondent of *The New Yorker* I had to fight my own campaign against red tape and the stuffy lay bureaucrats of the large press organizations, who wanted to make the battle an exclusive feature for their employers, like *Gasoline Alley* or Arthur Krock."

This "sordid guerrilla," as he called it, did not busy Liebling until the last month before D-day. He had, in other words, almost half a year in London with virtually nothing to do. His major work there seems to have been foraging, finding a way around the food scarcities. This Liebling accomplished with customary panache. The man who had found eggs in the Tunisian desert found gulls' eggs in wartime London. He kept them for 11 A.M. snacks on a broad, book-littered mantel in his sitting room at Fleming's. Gulls' eggs were unrationed and plentiful for those who didn't mind the fishy taste. Liebling also had made a special connection with the purveyors in Shepherd's Market, who sold him black-market lobsters, oysters and kippers. He was a past master at circumnavigating official drink restrictions and found his way to several speakeasy-type restaurant-clubs. There was Toby's, a black-market restaurant in Piccadilly, which you entered through a totally dark passage before reaching a smoky room frequented by racing people, fight promoters and some reporters willing to pay for the steaks, Idaho potatoes and other rare delicacies. He also ate at the Gargoyle Club in Dean Street, which took up the top two floors of an old house, where a good chef did his best with limited materials for the benefit of the Free French. On New Year's, Liebling went to a party there and descended the staircase from the upper floor in a Napoleonic hussar's shako.

He seems to have kept up relations with both the Yorkshire canary and the Wren. But the Wren had got pregnant while he was gone. Even so, he went up to Nottingham to visit her in a snowstorm after she gave birth and wrote his mother her address so that she could send a gift. The baby was, evidently, illegitimate and not Liebling's, but this did not curb his affection for the Wren, especially now that she had authenticated herself as a woman in distress. Her Irish name, Kay O'Brien, had probably helped the romance too.

He was thick with Mollie Panter-Downes and the Paniguians, not to mention the Biddles and half the American press corps. Gardner Botsford, a young *New Yorker* staffer just mustered into the First Division, came up and visited Liebling on weekends from a training camp in Dorset. Likewise, Fred Schwed's brother Peter (who later became Liebling's editor at Simon & Schuster) dropped in for a visit when he was on leave from his artillery unit in Devon. Schwed brought a bedroll and slept on Liebling's floor at Fleming's. "It was my first experience with bombing," he recalls. "Joe was hardened to it. We pulled down the shades and kept going with the poker game."

In the midst of this social whirl, Liebling wrote his mother: "I am still waiting around, having a comfortable time, and have almost forgotten what work feels like, since there is very little to write about."

He did file a longish account of a parliamentary by-election ("not as exciting as battle pieces"), but his most exciting experience did not get written about at all (until the fall of 1945, when he built a short story around it called "Run, Run, Run, Run"). In early March, Liebling went along for the ride on a bombing mission over France, "and got shot at quite a lot; a perfectly empirical procedure, like . . .

electric shocks for melancholy, but it worked, and made me feel much better when I came back," he told Mitchell in a letter dated April 2, 1944. "It confirmed my opinion that the blood-and-guts correspondents are a lot of shit and just make that stuff up; there's nothing much to it unless you get hit and maybe nothing much to it if you do get hit either." He had, in any case, promised himself he wouldn't write about the mission. He seems to have gone on it out of some private feeling of obligation to "some dead people," presumably lost friends from the North African air war.

At the same time, Liebling collected a large sampling of the French clandestine press. Friends on the British Political Welfare Board and with the Free French supplied him with hundreds of issues of these resistance papers, from which he attempted to reconstruct what life was like in occupied France. This "time-killing expedient" came out in *The New Yorker* in April as "Notes from the Kidnap House." It was a worthy effort, Liebling's first serious stab at press criticism, and further evidence of his breadth as a correspondent. His collected dispatches from France and North Africa had just been published in the United States as *The Road Back to Paris*. The book sold an unspectacular five thousand copies, probably because it was obsolete as battle news, but it helped to establish Liebling among his colleagues and with the serious reading public as the leading intelligence and stylist covering the European theater of the war. The reviews were almost uniformly favorable, but he made light of them in the April 2 letter to Mitchell: " . . . they took the slant 'what a relief to find a correspondent who can treat the war in the New Yorker manner' . . . Two reviewers independently hit on the idea of calling me the intellectual's Ernie Pyle, and another a sophisticated Ernie Pyle. Thank God no one suggested I was a poor man's Ernie Hemingway."

About then, in the late spring, it was clear that the great Allied invasion of France was not far off. Liebling began his "guerrilla" against the Army Group press officers in London who were refusing to let him join the First Division when it crossed the Channel, even though he had been invited by the divisional commander. He worked off his frustration, cursing, as he jogged each morning from Hyde Park Corner to Kensington Palace and back.

The Navy came to the rescue. Two old friends, Barry Bingham of the Louisville *Courier-Journal* and the literary critic John Mason Brown, were in charge of naval press relations for D-day. They got Liebling a front seat for the festivities.

LCIL 88 (Landing Craft, Infantry, Large) was a smallish, 155-foot, 300-ton, flat-bottomed craft designed to drop soldiers on the beaches of Normandy. It could float in only five feet of water. Compared to the destroyers and even the LSTs in the D-day flotilla, it was a dumpy little boat. It "made me feel proletarian," Liebling wrote. He loved his "working-class vessel." And better yet, the LCIL's skipper was Lieutenant H. K. (Bunny) Rigg of the U.S. Coast Guard Reserve.

Rigg, a jovial big man of thirty-three, was not just any skipper. He had written a yachting column for *The New Yorker* before the war. Liebling had known him only slightly, but it was a marvelous coincidence all the same, an omen.

True to form, Liebling spent his five days on board LCIL 88 before D-day insinuating himself into the friendship of the crew. As a result, "Cross-Channel Trip" builds to the climax of the actual landing with characteristic Lieblingesque attention to mundane and undramatic detail: snatches of proletarian dialogue and reams of information on the workings of the ship, its special rear anchor and winch and so forth. Once again, this technique worked through mosaic accumulation. By the time the ship begins unloading soldiers at H-hour plus 65 minutes, 7:35 A.M., under significant German fire, on Easy Red Beach, Omaha, near Port-en-Bessin, the reader feels as if he were there with Liebling on the upper deck, huddled next to a pharmacist's mate named Kallam. Continuing to observe with maniacally deliberate intensity, Liebling actually slowed down the pace of his narration as the drama of the action raced ahead:

> Just about then, it seems in retrospect, I felt the ship ground. I looked down at the main deck, and the beach-battalion men were already moving ahead, so I knew that the ramps must be down. I could hear Long shouting, "Move along now! Move along!" as if he were unloading an excursion boat at Coney Island. But the men needed no urging; they were moving without a sign of flinching. You didn't have to look far for tracers now, and Kallam and I flattened our

backs against the pilot house and pulled in our stomachs, as if to give
a possible bullet an extra couple of inches clearance. Something tickled the back of my neck. I slapped at it and discovered that I had
most of the ship's rigging draped around my neck and shoulders, like
a character in an old slapstick movie about a spaghetti factory. The
rigging had been cut away by bullets. As Kallam and I looked toward
the stern, we could see a tableau that was like a recruiting poster.
There was a twenty-millimetre rapid-firing gun on the upper deck.
Since it couldn't bear forward because of the pilot house and since
there was nothing to shoot at on either side, it was pointed straight up
at the sky in readiness for a possible dive-bombing attack. It had a
crew of three men, and they were kneeling about it, one on each side
and one behind the gun barrel, all looking up at the sky in an extremely earnest manner, and getting all the protection they could out
of the gunshield. As a background to the men's heads, an American
flag at the ship's stern streamed across the field of vision. It was a
new flag, which Rigg had ordered hoisted for the first time for the
invasion, and its colors were brilliant in the sun. To make the poster
motif perfect, one of the three men was a Negro, William Jackson,
from New Orleans, a wardroom steward, who, like everybody else on
the LCIL, had multiple duties.

The last passenger was off the ship now, and I could hear the stern
anchor cable rattling on the drum as it came up. An LCIL drops a
stern anchor just before it grounds, and pays out fifty to a hundred
fathoms of chain cable as it slowly slides the last couple of ship's
lengths toward shore. To get under way again, it takes up the cable,
pulling itself afloat. I had not known until that minute how eager I
was to hear the sound of the cable that follows the order, "Take in on
stern anchor." Almost as the cable began to come in, something hit
the ship with a solid clunk of metal against metal—not as hard as a
collision or a bomb blast; just "clink." Long yelled down, "Pharmacist's mate go forward. Somebody's hurt." Kallam scrambled down
the ladder to the main deck with his kit. Then Long yelled to a man
at the stern anchor winch, "Give it hell!" An LCIL has to pull itself
out and get the anchor up before it can use its motors, because otherwise the propeller might foul in the cable. The little engine which
supplies power for the winch is built by a farm-machinery company
in Waukesha, Wisconsin, and every drop of gasoline that went into
the one on our ship was filtered through chamois skin first. That engine is the ship's insurance policy. A sailor now came running up the

stairway from the cabin. He grabbed me and shouted, "Two casualties in bow!" I passed this information on to the bridge for whatever good it might do; both pharmacist's mates were forward already and there was really nothing else to be done. Our craft had now swung clear, the anchor was up, and the engines went into play. She turned about and shot forward like a destroyer.

Four minutes had passed. The deck was covered with blood and condensed milk. And away they sped to safety after taking part in the most heroic episode of modern warfare. In a series of almost Shandean divagations, Liebling had stretched out his story, stopping here for a freeze frame of the ship and its flag, there for a look at himself, foolish under his cloak of rigging, even stopping to explain how the fuel for the winch motor was filtered. All this magnificently unhurried and antiheroic information flowed from Liebling's determination to tell only what he saw during the landing and to set down his state of mind. It is this doggedly real account that gives the passage its tremendous excitement. By avoiding martial rhetoric altogether, and by refusing to clog the scene with cosmic observations about the overall movement of an offensive he couldn't possibly witness from one small boat, Liebling compressed the drama of D-day into a few feet of deck. He made time stand still, while an almost unbearable suspense built up. Would the LCIL get away in time?

It did, limping back to get more groups and ferry them from bigger to smaller ships on D-day plus one and D-day plus two. On D-day plus three, Liebling thumbed a ride ashore on a rocket-firing speedboat, which transferred him to a still smaller craft, which dropped him on the beach. He made a brief tour of the installations, then rejoined Rigg's LCIL and sailed with it back to Britain, where the ship was to be repaired. Arriving late on D-day plus five, Liebling returned to London to get his dispatch written and sent. If he had stayed with the invasion, he would have risked a greater delay and extremely difficult, not to mention distracting, work conditions, as well as the interference of Army censors in the field. In London, he had only the first of the V-1 rockets to face.

While Liebling wrote about D-day, the doodlebugs buzzed overhead. Too gouty to feel much like going out and watching them from the street, he kept on working through the automated blitz, determined to tell only what he had seen, even after he found out that the assault on Easy Red had been bloodier than he'd thought when he was there. He had witnessed enough blood and guts as it was, and twenty years later, when he was putting together *Mollie and Other War Pieces*, he made fun of the "Cinemepic called *The Longest Day*," its "swashbuckling magnificence" and its jaunty theme song. "Everybody, of course, had his own D-Day," Liebling wrote, but some versions were simply false. "Anybody who thinks there was a theme song should have his head examined," he said.

Two weeks in London gave him time to finish his tuneless report and push it through the censors. One morning as he was getting ready to rejoin the troops in France, toward the end of June, the Paniguians came for breakfast. Mary Paniguian recalls:

> We got a direct hit at 8 A.M. by a doodlebug at our flat in Buckingham Gate. We had come out of the shelter in our pajamas to have tea before a moving van came to move us to a new place. Pan saw the V-1 coming, belching fire. There was a terrible explosion, and then we were up to our knees in rubble. The flat was on the top floor; so firemen had to take us out on a ladder. In the bedroom I saw the nasty dirty remains of the bomb. We arrived at Fleming's in our pajamas. Liebling was the same size as Pan and fitted him out completely. Someone gave me a tweed skirt. We joined Joe for lunch as planned. The van didn't have to remove anything.

On June 24, Liebling returned to France on an LST (Landing Ship, Tanks) and began two months of hopscotching from place to place in Normandy and Brittany. His dispatches are full of the anarchic flavor of the advance through the hedgerows of the *bocage normand*, littered with corpses of cows. He spent little time at briefings and wrote almost exclusively about the effect of combat and liberation on the French peasants he met and lived with. He was frequently in mortal danger, but he filed, as usual, only scenes from daily life. His own movements are now impossible to trace with chronological exactitude, but the vignettes that have come down to us show Liebling in rapid motion from one part to another of the northern France he revered as holy ground, circulating among the

GIs he loved and admired. In a sense, he treated the Normandy invasion like a great open-air party spread over wonderful terrain, which he was paid to tour in a chauffeured jeep, dropping in on familiar places and old friends.

Shortly after his arrival in France, Liebling pulled up to the howitzer emplacement of the 955th Artillery at Omaha Beach. "Is this Lieutenant Schwed's outfit?" he asked. "Yes," someone said. "Where is he?" "Down there in that slit trench."

As Peter Schwed recalls the incident: "He was our first press visitor. Our commanding officer, a southern West Pointer, a son-in-law of General Marshall, Colonel James Winn, had noticed him in his press jeep and had immediately begun combing his hair. Joe strode right by Winn, came up to me and pulled out a bottle of Calvados. He spent a half hour and left. It cost me a promotion. Winn didn't like it."

Not far off, at Caumont, at a First Division observation post, Gardner Botsford had a similar visit from Correspondent Liebling, bottle in hand. Botsford remembers him vividly "dressed in low brown quartermaster's shoes, canvas leggings right up to the knee, wool olive drab pants with that enormous stomach on top of his belt, and on his head he wore a wool helmet liner."

He visited Rennes after it was liberated, dropped in on Cardinal Archbishop Roques, a prelate and *résistant*, and then ("not directly, for I have a sense of fitness") dropped in at a brothel called La Feria, which he had liked in 1926. He drove up in his chauffeured jeep with a press officer, Lieutenant Roy Wilder, Jr.

Liebling's relations with the rest of the press corps were amicable in the extreme during this time of happy confusion. At one press camp in a cow pasture near Caumont, he shared a tent with Ernie Pyle and three other correspondents. Pyle cooked breakfast from the food the others would scrounge. One of Liebling's other companions, Don Whitehead, recalls coming into the tent on a warm day in June and finding Liebling on his cot, wearing nothing but his shorts, with a French classic propped on his hairy chest, "and on his rounded belly was an open box of ripe Camembert, which he dipped into occasionally with a finger."

Liebling reached the height of his career as a forager when Cherbourg fell to the Americans. He, Pyle, Whitehead and Clark Lee of INS happened to be near the entrance of Fort du Roule, where the Germans had stored ammunition, food and liquor. Whitehead says: "The Germans surrendered and after they had marched out—we marched in. In one huge storage room just off the main tunnel, we found case after case of brandy, Cointreau, Benedictine, champagne, etc., etc. Joe advised us on our choice of liqueurs. . . . So we loaded ourselves down with bottles and stored them in the jeep just before the MPs placed guards at the entrance of the fort. That supply of booze liberated at Cherbourg lasted us almost all the way to Paris."

In the course of his zigzag travels, Liebling watched generals exhorting troops. He watched reporters compete with each other for marginal newsbeats. He attended a historic press conference held by his hero General Omar Bradley after the breakthrough at Saint-Lô. He even attended a first communion party in Barneville, at the invitation of the local electrician, whom he had met in a shabby café the same morning.

Normal life was reasserting itself behind the lines, just behind the lines. Liebling and two other correspondents stopped for lunch in Barneville on July 9, a lunch consisting of sole bonne femme and tournedos Choron, and then began driving the twelve miles to La-Haye-du-Puits, where VIII Corps was cleaning out a pocket of German resistance. They walked the last five miles, passed numerous German corpses and eventually found themselves under fire. Liebling took it with sang-froid, or so he said:

> . . . street fighting, in my limited experience is not particularly dangerous unless you want to fight personally. Observation for marksmen is limited, and there is defilade everywhere. You sprint from shelter to shelter. Even while I was running, I felt that it was a game that did not in any way affect survival. . . . Sprinting, nevertheless, through the burning town, we reached a company post in a wrecked café. . . . We stayed around awhile, rather at a loss for conversation, and then left, feeling that we had atoned for our good lunch.

In August, Liebling passed through his beloved Vire, but spent only a few minutes there, because it had been so badly shelled he could not bear to stay longer. He made other stops at old student haunts, now battle sites: Avranches and Mortain. Other correspondents had settled in at Mont-Saint-Michel. Hemingway had made the Hôtel de la Mère Poulard his headquarters, and Liebling visited the place a couple of times, running into Charles Wertenbaker, a Time-Life correspondent, and the photographer Robert Capa.

As the weeks of the mopping up after D-day drew on, it became more and more definite that the Germans were crumbling and that any day might bring the final march on Paris. Every reporter who gathered at General Bradley's special press conference on the night of Monday, August 21, in Laval in western France felt the same excitement. A great moment was at hand, and more than that: a great story. But for Joe Liebling the recapture of Paris meant more still, for he had taken the war personally, as an affront to his Paris. The Axis, the Pacific theater, even the subjugation of Germany—these were secondary matters. "In my mind," he had written, "the war would pretty well end with the road back to Paris. The rest would be epilogue."

Bradley told the reporters it would take a little while still. So Liebling and his "fellow-sybarite" Lieutenant Wilder drove off to a little hotel at Ernée, where they spent the next day in pursuit of pleasure. Liebling did not, however, manage to seduce an attractive woman from Cherbourg.

On Wednesday, Liebling and Wilder returned to the press camp at Bagnoles-de-l'Orne in central Normandy and found it deserted. While they had been cavorting at Ernée, the race for Paris had unexpectedly begun. "I was consequently," thought Liebling, "in a fair way to being scooped on the story I had been looking forward to for four years, two months and thirteen days."

He broke into tears. Briefly.

Then he ran inside and rolled up his kit inside his sleeping bag and raced out to hitch a ride to Paris. The word was that the road was clear all the way to Paris. But Wilder had been grounded, for arriving back late from Laval. So Liebling had to hunt about for a willing chauffeur among the rapidly diminishing remainder of the press relations detachment at Bagnoles. A former reporter from Philadelphia named Jack Roach welcomed him into his prewar

Chevrolet touring car, recently liberated from the Germans, and the two set out.

All the way to Chartres, about one hundred miles, they sped unimpeded, and even acquired a stock of K rations, tossed with quarterback proficiency from a moving truck by a GI whom Liebling compared to "an Old Black Jove hurling well-meant thunderbolts." But in Chartres, they ran into a military traffic jam. While waiting, they picked up a *Stars and Stripes* reporter, Allan Morrison, who was hitchhiking. And then Liebling talked the First Division lieutenant colonel directing traffic, whom he had known in North Africa, into letting them through.

On the other side of Chartres, the road was empty. A wild and chilling thought came over Liebling. Perhaps they had leapfrogged over the Allied front lines and were driving straight into the German defenses:

> . . . our 1937-or-so Chevrolet was no armored division. As an assimilated captain (the grade bestowed on all war correspondents), I was the senior member of the expedition. Lieutenant Roach, the ranking active soldier, had received most of his battle training in the Philadelphia Bureau of the United Press, and his combat effectiveness was not enhanced by an oversized helmet that was likely to fall over his eyes if he moved suddenly. Pfc. Morrison's attitude was that of an objective observer, exactly as it is taught in schools of journalism. He was our whole enlisted strength.

They drove on "in a mood of modified rapture," past the road north to Rambouillet, where most of the press had gone and where Hemingway was playing general with a platoon of resistance soldiers. They drove on until twilight and stopped for the night at an exurban hotel filled with resistance *effectifs*.

In the morning, they began the last twenty miles of the trip to Paris, weaving through a column of French half-tracks. Clearing that, they were once again by themselves, until they pulled up on two jeeps, one of them bearing a general's star. A shell fell two hundred yards to the right of them. The general's jeep stopped. He got out. It was General Leclerc, the man who was officially leading the liberation of Paris. Leclerc got back in his jeep, turned around and started driving toward the Chevrolet. He had seen an antitank gun and had decided to try another route. The Chevrolet followed him.

The Liebling squadron continued zigzagging about for the next few hours, each time running into enemy fire and turning back. They saw Leclerc several times. Finally, they stopped for the night at Montlhéry, still fifteen miles from Paris, but within binocular range from the town tower.

It took all day the next day, August 25, to negotiate the vehicle-clogged roads into Paris, and when they got there, there were still a few resisting Germans. They drove through the city as well as they could and then they parked at the Gare Montparnasse, the temporary headquarters of the French Forces. Inside the railroad station, the Liebling platoon congratulated themselves further on their valor and their instincts as war reporters. They had stumbled on the surrender of Paris. The German military governor, von Choltitz, surrendered to Leclerc and de Gaulle, while they, Paul Gallico and Harold Denny of *The New York Times* witnessed the historic moment. Gallico worked for a monthly, which meant that Denny was the only reporter present from a daily newspaper. Roach, who was a public relations officer, took Denny's dispatch to the press center at the Hotel Scribe. The center, however, somehow never transmitted the story and Denny lost the scoop of a lifetime.

Liebling did not learn about the foul-up for several days. And so he was still in a triumphant state when a detachment of French Forces press people led him to a billet reserved for foreign press at the Hotel Néron in the Fourteenth Arrondissement. Their "dashing cortege" was "a cross between an Arab fantasia and the reception accorded Adah Isaacs Menken by the silver miners of the Big Bonanza." French soldiers, weighed down with weapons, hung from the sides of his jeep. Volkswagens fore and aft escorted the jeep.

At the Néron, Liebling took a cold bath—there was no hot water, but it was still a luxury after weeks in the field—and put on fresh socks, his only change of clothes. Then he did what he liked best to do. He went for a walk in Paris, looking for a place to eat. This was not a simple quest: shots could be heard regularly in the distance; a blackout was in effect. But after some wandering, he came upon that Montparnasse landmark the Closerie des Lilas, where he had gone often before the war.

The place was deserted except for four staff members, who welcomed him with open arms and invited him to join them for dinner: potato soup, Bordeaux wine, salad and an omelet "as big as an eiderdown." The owner had been saving two bottles for the arrival of the first American after liberation—one Pernod and a fifth of Black & White. Liebling chose the Scotch because he knew he could drink more of it. "It was," he wrote, "the only trophy or award I won during the war, and I wouldn't have traded it for the D.S.O."

The next morning, the city was calm. Liebling dropped his bags at the Scribe and walked to the Square Louvois. He went into the lobby of the Hotel Louvois:

> Mlle. Yvonne was sitting behind the desk, going over her accounts. *"Bonjour,* Monsieur Liebling," she said, barely looking up. It was as if I had just stepped out for a walk around the fountain.

The rest *was* just epilogue.

On the day after liberation, Bunny Rigg arrived in Paris and looked up Liebling at the Scribe press center, where they had arranged a rendezvous when Liebling had left the LCIL in England in June. Rigg had wangled a two-day leave and hitched a ride over on a military DC-3. Liebling got permission for Rigg to eat at the Néron mess and then helped him solve the problem of money. The Allied forces had been foraging and making do with their own scrip until liberation, but in Paris that wouldn't do. Liebling, however, like Hymie Katz, the tummeler of the I. & Y. Cigar Store, was "a man what knew to get a dollar." As Rigg recalls the incident:

> "Do you know Charlie Wertenbaker?" he asked.
> "I do," I said. "His father brought me into the world in Wilmington."
> Charlie had liberated the Paris bureau of Time-Life. He opened the safe and found $100,000. The Nazis had never discovered it. Wertenbaker reported the windfall to New York by cable. The reply came back: "Dispose of as you will—insurance company already paid off."
> Wertenbaker gave me $1000. Just then Ernest Hemingway came bursting in. He'd heard about the money. Wertenbaker denied he had any; so Hemingway went out all red-faced and blustery. Wer-

tenbaker said: "I wouldn't give that son-of-a-bitch the sweat off my balls." Hemingway had been trying to scoop everybody and get credit for liberating the city singlehandedly.

Liebling took Rigg all over Paris with him, looking up old friends and dropping in on favorite restaurants. He even fixed him up with a ballet dancer.

By September, normalcy had already set in sufficiently so that Liebling could return home. He wrote three more "Letters from Paris," notable mainly for their focus on the transition of the French press from collaborationist to resistance control. He visited a village in the Côte d'Or region of Burgundy and wrote about a massacre of civilians which the Germans had perpetrated there on August 21, just before the area was liberated. Liebling wrote this final, brilliant piece of narration in November and left for New York, sad because his replacement as *New Yorker* correspondent with the troops, David Lardner, son of Ring Lardner, had been killed in his jeep at Aachen by a mine, and troubled on many other levels. For one thing, he was sorry "his" war was over. In the foreword to *Mollie*, he wrote:

> I know that it is socially acceptable to write about war as an unmitigated horror, but subjectively at least, it was not true, and you can feel its pull on men's memories at the maudlin reunions of war divisions. They mourn for their dead, but also for war.

Shortly before leaving France, for a week in England (prior to embarking on a liner at Cardiff that sailed on December 9 and got him to New York just before Christmas), Liebling wrote Joe Mitchell a letter that sums up his thoughts and feelings as he moved into the civilian world again and on to a new phase of his life:

October 23

Dear Joe,

I started to write a long letter to you Saturday night shortly after I heard of Dave's death, but it didn't go very well—I felt like cry-

ing rather than writing. I had been meaning for some time to write
you about a lot of things, and on that particular night I couldn't
write about anything but Dave and my first reaction—that if I
hadn't asked to come home he wouldn't have gone up to Army
and wouldn't be dead. The same thing would never have happened
to me: it was only because of his inexperience that he was killed. I
think sometimes there is a "sin" attached to taking the easy way
out; this concept is so antithetical to all my past predilections that I
want to get home before I get any more hooks like it in my brain.
. . . If you stay in a war long enough you become a believer in ju-
jus; I want to forget all about it and burrow into a nice manure
pile of writing which will keep me busy in New York for years to
come. I have a feeling that I will never learn anything more from
the experience of war, and that as far as I am concerned as a
would-be writer the time I spent in the war from now on is wasted, like my last two years on the Providence Journal, or my last
three on the World-Telegram. My writing is getting progressively
sloppier and needs to be worked over before I can even get back to
the pitch of "Frau Weinmann" days—and I want to go a hell of a
lot better than that. My feelings during the past five years need to
be thought over now. Is this true or am I just fed up with Europe?
I want to go home by way of England. There are two girls there
who love me and whom I could easily love. I will leave them and
go back to the old idiot uncertainty at home. I haven't heard from
Ann in months and according to Shawn nobody in the office has
either. I will go crawling around to Janet for sympathy, wearing
my expression of "a big fat baby looking for a tit to suck on"—Janet's best-inspired line. I will not even talk to Marie-Louise, but I
will find a couple of new dames to fuck up my days and nights
worse than ever. I don't think there's anything left for me to do
with my life except write, and since that has been my idea from
the beginning, it is just about time I shut up and get started. I will
start a chapter of my life to be entitled "Or Get Off the Pot." But
I will at least start it in great comfort. I will get me subscription
seats for the opera and some good concert society, alternate weeks.
I will get tickets for all the shows I haven't seen, and go to them
one after another. I will join George Brown's gymnasium, which
Hemingway says is good, and maybe I will even continue my exercises with Colonel Koritzky. I will also join a freehand drawing
class, and have dinner at the Lafayette every night except when I

eat at Shine's or the Red Devil, and in the summer I will go to some good beach in Rhode Island or North Carolina for weeks, except when I am sitting on the porch of the Hanover Inn, reading Stendhal items from the College Library. And I will write like hell and not make any small talk and hate whoever I feel like hating and go to the races and think of Broun, and just not be bothered about anything. . . . I was forty years old last Wednesday, and that's time to be getting some sense. Today is another anniversary—one year since the last time I sailed from New York, from Erie Basin. We've done about everything I expected we would. I have D-Day now for all my life, and the day we got to Paris. Nobody can ever take them away from me, but nobody can give me another D-Day either. What the hell am I waiting around here for?

Love to Therese and Nora

Joe

eight

Wayward Pressman

Back in New York, at the Fifth Avenue Hotel, with no more battles to fight and no steady assignment at *The New Yorker,* caught in an impossible marriage to a woman he loved and couldn't have a life with, Liebling at forty in 1945 did not easily find a way to focus the ambition he had felt just before leaving France. He had decided not to return to his prewar routine of lowlife and entertainment reportage. In his personal life, there was no continuity, or very little, with the old days. Ann was in limbo, his father was dead, his mother had moved to Norwalk, where she lived with Norma and her broker husband.

Joe Liebling was cut off from his past and even his present. Like all foreign correspondents returning home after a long absence abroad, he was an immigrant in his own country. And like many immigrants, he carried the ideas and the style of his mother country around with him. Liebling continued to write about France and the war all through the first half of 1945, in a sort of mopping-up operation. At the same time, he decided to make use of his collection of clandestine French newspapers, to excerpt them for a textbook that would teach American students French and teach them an unforgettable lesson in which the Germans were villains and the French heroes. While Liebling was arranging this project with Harcourt, Brace, he also was reading American newspapers, but with a new perspective. He read "foreign news with constant, involuntary reference to what I had seen in Europe and to my knowledge of the men filing the dispatches." He also devoured everything else, from turf news to music reviews, just as he had always gourmandized among the daily papers since childhood. But the Liebling who had just finished surveying a free French press edited by Camus and written by the likes of Sartre and Mauriac read American newspapers with a higher standard in mind. He had previously found, in the French resistance press, a "mosaic of what life must be in France under the occupation." He had also found a level of literary accomplishment in *Combat* and *Le Franc-Tireur* that had not existed in English-language papers since the heyday of Cobbett and Egan in the nineteenth century. Full of hope for himself as a writer-in-journalism, Liebling read the American press and it made him angry:

> Some of my reactions resembled severe attacks of mental hives or prickly heat. Occasionally they verged on what psychiatrists call the disturbed and assaultative. So I suggested to Bill Shawn, the managing editor of the *New Yorker,* who relayed to Harold Ross, the head man, that we revive the Wayward Press department.

"The Wayward Press" already had a distinguished tradition as a forum for press criticism when Liebling took it on. Robert Benchley started it in 1927 and, from light-hearted beginnings, turned it, during the Depression, into a platform for what Liebling remembered as "some pretty hard socks at injustices and misrepresentations." Eventually, however, Benchley moved on to other work, and "The Wayward Press" (with the sole exception of a piece by Wolcott Gibbs on a murder case in 1944) did not run for eight years.

In May 1945, Liebling did his first column, on the flap that occurred when Ed Kennedy of the Associated Press broke a press embargo and reported the news of the German surrender at Reims.

Over the next two decades, indeed for the rest of his life, Liebling
continued to dissect the press with the furious and pained concentration of a lover. He railed against publishers who starved their reporters and who were turning the United States into a country of
one-paper towns. He lampooned clichés, ferreted out blunders and
illogicalities, and took some pretty hard socks himself at injustice, as
he defined injustice. The personal bias in his columns is clear—that
is, clearly liberal, pro-labor, and on the side of the underdog. Some
people today would call Liebling an advocacy journalist, a cant
term he would have hated. But the irony is that Liebling despised
editorialists and other experts who marketed their opinions at the
expense of hard fact and firsthand observation. He was "a chronic,
incurable, recidivist reporter," who wrote:

> There are three kinds of writers of news in our generation. In inverse
> order of wordly consideration, they are:
> 1. The reporter, who writes what he sees.
> 2. The interpretive reporter, who writes what he sees and what he
> construes to be its meaning.
> 3. The expert, who writes what he construes to be the meaning of
> what he hasn't seen.

Liebling belongs in category 2. His underlying liberal attitude did
not keep him from scrutinizing the world before him; it merely
gave him a standard for interpreting the facts he observed. Even as
a *critic* of the press, he based his analysis and his judgments on solid
reporting. Every morning, he went through a heap of newspapers,
ripping out stories that interested him and stuffing them in his
pockets. Then he would take this raw material from many sources—
usually competing versions of the same story as it had run in several
papers—and subject it to scrutiny. As a result, Liebling's press columns often read like a variorum edition of the news. By comparing
several treatments of the same subject, he could arrive at a highly
concrete and persuasive opinion. Sometimes this process led to a
synthetic super-version of the basic news event—a description, actual or implied, of the ideal story that Liebling would have liked to
read. Of course, this Aquinian sifting of competing texts amounted
to a complicated judgment about the best way to cover a particular

event—a judgment, in other words, about matters of journalistic craft. Liebling's political liberalism surely affected these judgments, but he was a critic fundamentally occupied with questions of technique. His opinions grew organically out of a mass of closely observed details—culled from newspaper clippings—just as his war reporting had accumulated to drama through a series of close-ups and technical expatiations on the daily life and craft of war: how to find eggs in the desert or where the winch on an LCIL was made. Similarly, he had taken pains to explain exactly how Hymie Katz financed his fly-by-night nightclubs on Broadway.

"The M.B.I." is a triumphant case of careful observation leading to an outraged and important conclusion. Typically, Liebling puts himself in the forefront of the "action." He is the main character in what amounts to a fable about a man who reads newspapers. "A couple of months ago," he begins casually, "I had occasion to subscribe to 20 out-of-town newspapers, and the copies have been piling up in my office ever since." From time to time, Liebling explains, he would read four or five of the papers, and find articles of pluperfect banality, about homicides or a man fed by a tube for twenty-six years. Then, in the New Orleans *Times-Picayune*, he read with a start that " 'Over some protests of "Gestapo" in both houses, the Mississippi Legislature today gave final passage to a far-reaching measure granting the Governor police power through investigators to suppress violence.' "

Mississippi had just voted itself a secret police force to be called the Mississippi Bureau of Investigation. The M.B.I. had been created to suppress violence in a strike against a bus company, and it was armed with several new oppressive criminal statutes expressly drafted for its use. One of these laws made it a capital offense to place a bomb in a bus.

"The story of the M.B.I.'s creation," said Liebling, "and of the establishment of a new crime subject to capital punishment seems to me to have merited space in any American publication pretending to be a newspaper." But it hadn't. The story had run in New Orleans and just about nowhere else. In New York, only the *Times* had had coverage, but only in a condensed and misleading squib. Something had gone wrong with the "fine-mesh news net." Either editors all over the country had mysteriously blackballed the story, or the press associations, the AP and UP, had somehow slipped up, Liebling concluded in consternation.

After his "Wayward Press" piece appeared, Liebling continued to dig. He discovered that both wire service systems had failed to route the M.B.I. story properly. The full version had not made it past their southern regional networks, except in a form so terse and choppy that editors had not understood its significance. Liebling's piece provoked belated interest in the M.B.I. around the country. By then, and partly because of this sudden national attention, the governor of Mississippi had announced he no longer needed the M.B.I. The AP meanwhile conducted an internal review of its southern routing system. This made Liebling happy, but the whole affair, which he discussed in a second column, still worried him because of its general implications for American newsgathering:

> What impresses and depresses me, though, is that by looking through a few old newspapers I was able to find a pretty big story that the main organs of news distribution had completely muffed. I can't help wondering how often stories of general importance appear in full solely in local papers and get out to the rest of the country only after they have been compressed into insignificance. I wonder how many important stories never get into the newspapers at all. The American press makes me think of a gigantic, supermodern fish cannery, a hundred floors high, capitalized at $11,000,000,000, and with tens of thousands of workers standing ready at the canning machines, but relying for its raw material on an inadequate number of handline fishermen in leaky rowboats.

There was no way of discovering how many sins of omission the nation's press was perpetrating, but Liebling found plenty of sins of commission to expose. He was especially alert to those waves of collective hysteria that sweep epidemically through city rooms. One paper covers a confusing story confusedly, takes an approach that distorts the facts, but at least it is an approach, however shallow or hyperbolic. Other editors, equally confused, copy and compete with the paper that broke the news, accepting its concept of the story but striving to do better along the same lines, because there is less risk and less trouble that way. Editors, like most human beings, feel safer in a pack than they do blazing a trail all alone. Liebling, with his stack of newspapers, would gleefully detect these slothful, unacknowledged conspiracies.

In "The Great Gouamba," he exposed the misguided frenzy with which the press responded to a meat "shortage" in October 1946. In fact, the scarcity of meat in stores was an artificial scarcity. Meat producers were holding meat off the market, hoping to bring about an end to official price ceilings. Most newspapers, taking the scarcity at face value, ran piece after piece, fanning the national meat hysteria. Liebling called this meat hunger "gouamba," an African term for "the inordinate longing and craving of exhausted nature for meat." He remembered the word from a book by the explorer Du Chaillu that he had read as a child. In his "Wayward Press" survey of the situation, he catalogued a hilarious profusion of scare headlines. In the *Times* alone, he found "QUEENS RESTAURATEUR, WORRIED OVER MEAT, DIVES OFF BROOKLYN BRIDGE AND SURVIVES"; "BURGLAR IN BUTCHER SHOP FINDS CUPBOARD BARE"; "MEAT HUNTERS BEAT PATH TO JERSEY HAMLET." The *Sun* shrieked: "SCARCITY SWELLS HOURLY!" Bludgeoned by such headlines, Congress voted out price controls. The press had been successfully manipulated by the meat industry. Meat at higher prices filled the stores straightaway. "The Great Gouamba" was a triumph of the comparative method, showing Liebling at the top of his form, assessing "The Press" as a single multiform phenomenon.

For roughly four years, until he left for Chicago in 1949, the great bulk of Liebling's work for *The New Yorker* was press criticism. The "Wayward Press" column gave him a simple source of copy. He wrote more than ever, under the usual pressure to pay Ann's bills as well as his own. But the column did much more than earn money. It was a power base within journalism that won Liebling the respect of his profession. Even today, when a great many of the columns have dated, nearly every one is still in print, in a fat anthology called *The Press*. No other area of Liebling's work has weathered so well.

Liebling himself fell eagerly upon the press assignment. He produced a constant flow of "Wayward Press" pieces right up until his final year, but the great period came at the beginning, when the job was fresh. He had few other assignments to distract him from the joy of giving the world urbane object lessons in how opinion could grow naturally out of a good reporter's notes. In "The Wayward Press," Liebling had found an ideal platform for his views and a showcase for his writing that even William Cobbett would have envied. He was his own man and he had discovered a new way to fulfill his ambition, to write well within the limitations of a strict and unpretentious form. More specifically, he must have received a special push and felt particular inspiration in his new endeavor, in those early days as a press critic, because of his total immersion in the French resistance press.

For five weeks during the summer of 1945, Liebling pored over the two suitcases full of documents he had brought back with him from France, making the selections for *La République du Silence*. Having arranged the contract for the book with Harcourt, Brace, Liebling had gone to Columbia University, looking for a collaborator who could do scholarly annotations. The Romance Language Department referred him to Eugene Jay Sheffer. The two men hit it off immediately and agreed to work together. Liebling arranged that they should share all royalties equally, which he was not required to do under his contract. And at Sheffer's insistence, they repaired in midsummer to East Hampton, to the Sea Spray Inn, at water's edge.

This was Liebling's first time in the Hamptons, at the extreme eastern end of Long Island's south shore. East Hampton was to play an important part in his later years, as a second home, a kind of ideal landscape near the part of the ocean he loved best, and, finally, as a burial place. In 1945, it turned out to be an invigorating place to work. Each morning, he scribbled away at a furious rate on yellow foolscap, writing continuity for the anthology, setting the dozens of letters, broadsides, poems, short stories, news articles, exhortations and editorials into a historical and, sometimes, a personal framework. Sheffer would "put in his two cents." After lunch, his head full of the glories of the resistance as set down by Aragon and Vercors, Sartre and Camus, Liebling would plunge into the water.

By the time the book came out in 1946, Liebling had only just begun to hit his stride as a press critic. He had written, of course, about the flap over Ed Kennedy's German surrender scoop. And he wrote a puckish piece on the seventeen-day newspaper strike that had just ended. He noted that there hadn't been much news of importance during the strike, and that therefore even an addict like himself had not missed much: "the effect was the same as it would be if restaurants stopped serving the chalky white cheesepaste they now put on your butter plate. In a word, unnoticeable." In a footnote to this passage, written somewhat later for an anthology, Liebling added: "Sometimes news disappears for years at a time. . . . News is like the tilefish, which appears in great schools off the Atlantic Coast some years and then vanishes no one knows whither, or for how long."

His tongue-in-cheek solution was to recommend a radical reform: getting out large newspapers only on big news days and "supplementing them on the intervening days with small bulletins containing such essential matter as race charts, market reports and weather information."

Next, in "Obits" in early 1946, he pointed out the inflation of General George S. Patton's reputation in his obituary notices, and he showed how, in the same week, the death of Theodore Dreiser had called forth minor, grudging notices tainted with ill-judged smears, aspersions on Dreiser's writing talent and unfounded allegations about his membership in the Communist Party. The piece showed that obituaries are really biased artifacts of the obituary-writing process, which is itself the result of the twin tyrannies of newspaper clip files and the frame of mind of the obituary writer. In effect, Liebling was attacking the anarchy of the process, and its staleness. Tired anecdotes and views were repeated yet again. No fresh effort was made to reassess a man's life or to decide on the correct editorial priorities between one death and another. There was nothing, he remarked, in the *Herald Tribune*'s mingy Dreiser obit "to indicate that Dreisers outrank four-star generals."

Liebling then occupied himself with the phenomenon of "papers within papers," advertisements that were really editorials. Here again, he found newspapers taking the side of established wealth and power. Just as they had puffed a general and maligned a leftist writer, so too, in their advertising acceptance policies, they favored big business and discriminated against labor and liberal views. In one column, he showed how the Hearst papers were refusing to reprint ex-mayor Fiorello La Guardia's liberal *PM* columns when a department store wanted to buy space for them as the text for its ads. In another, later column, Liebling proved, by meticulously counting every line of political opinion advertising, that business "opinion" advertisers had outbought labor advertisers six to one.

Already, then, in these early columns, Liebling was exercising his power as critic to expose the tendency of newspaper publishers to favor capital over labor and to distort the truth. He must have received some helpful moral support early in 1946, when he saw Jean-Paul Sartre. Albert Camus also visited New York that spring, to publicize *The Stranger*, and Liebling interviewed him for "The Talk of the Town." Camus had just retired as editor of *Combat*, at thirty-two. He exemplified Liebling's idea of the tough, liberal writer who could range from news to novels to plays. He took press criticism very seriously, and even proposed to Liebling that there be "a critical newspaper, to be published one hour after the first editions of the other papers, twice a day, morning and evening. It would evaluate the probable element of truth in the other papers' main stories, with due regard to editorial policies and the past performances of the correspondents. . . . After a few weeks the whole tone of the press would conform more closely to reality."

They met at Camus's hotel, on West Seventieth Street, the same kind of apartment hotel, in the same neighborhood, as the Olcott, where Liebling had once lived with his parents. And it is not difficult to imagine the warm and familiar atmosphere that sprang up between them, the young French writer dressed "like a character in 'Harold Teen,' " delighted to spend the afternoon nattering facetiously about newspapers with a bright and francophone American who admired him and was eager to hear him talk about his work. For his part, Liebling must have gone back to the office brimming over with self-esteem. Camus had shown respect for Liebling and for press criticism. He had, in effect, certified Liebling and made it possible for him to see himself as part of a confraternity of self-sufficient, unpoetic writers like Camus.

French people made Joe Liebling feel good. They reminded him of the freedom of wartime and his student days. He could speak French with them and overeat in their company at a nondescript West Side restaurant like the Du Midi. In the late forties, in New York, he made two important French friends. Pierre Guedenet, a cultural officer at the French embassy, asked Liebling to sponsor an evening of French journalists and writers at Columbia. Camus was among them; so it must have been in the spring of 1946. Guedenet and his American wife, Charlotte, were together with Liebling regularly from then on, usually over meals at the Du Midi, The Lobster, Bleeck's—places convenient to the *New Yorker* offices on West Forty-third Street, all of them unfrilled and not, with the exception of The Lobster, restaurants where epicures were wont to forgather.

Guedenet stayed on in the United States, as a professor of French. He and Charlotte were part of Liebling's inner circle of friends until the end. So was Jean Riboud, who came to New York in the fall of 1946 to seek his fortune on Wall Street. Riboud, a propertied resistance fighter, who had weathered two years in Buchenwald (by one account, he spent more time in the camp than any other survivor), was introduced to Liebling by Henri Cartier-Bresson, who was in New York for a show of his photographs at the Museum of Modern Art and must have thought Riboud could use a French-speaking American friend.

"Our relationship was a relationship of love," recalls Riboud, now the head of the international oil firm Schlumberger. "It grew and grew and grew, so naturally. I could never understand why. He couldn't stand Wall Street. I wasn't a newspaperman."

Riboud lived in New York until 1951, and during those five years he spent "endless" evenings with Liebling, drinking at Costello's on Third Avenue, consuming "so many lobsters," going to boxing matches, hockey games and the races. Riboud, after his long siege at Buchenwald, was more than ready to cut loose, to live for pleasure, and Liebling must have found him an ideal companion. They continued to see each other off and on after 1951, in New York and in Europe, but the height of their friendship was in the late forties, before Riboud's marriage. Liebling liked to call Riboud "Mr. Excuse." He used him as an excuse to beg off boring dinner parties. And Riboud was a living link with France and the resistance. Hard-boiled and by no stretch an intellectual, Riboud was a Gallic version of the masculine and unpretentious tough-guy hero Liebling had always liked. Riboud had another special attraction, perhaps, since he was a non-Jewish survivor of Buchenwald. He was proof that the concentration camps had gathered in all of Germany's foes, not just the Jews. Liebling, who had thought of the war, essentially, as a conflict between France and Germany, with American troops thrown in for good measure, must have liked the idea that an ethnic Frenchman, an Aryan and not a Jew, had been the champion survivor at one of the worst camps.

It was at about this time, too, that Liebling began his second major romance with a woman in dubious and difficult circumstances whom he would rescue with affection, money and the cleansing agent of his name. When Joe Liebling fell in love with Harriet Lucille Hille Barr Spectorsky in 1946, she was thirty-five and still beautiful, leggy enough to model for magazine ads and in dress houses. By then, Lucille Spectorsky had come a great distance, in every sense, from Clinton, Kentucky, the jerkwater bypass town near Paducah where she had been born into a family of small landholders. Her mother died when she was twelve, and that was the end of normal family life for Lucille. Her father, who had worked as a newspaper editor in Clinton, deposited her with his mother in St. Louis and moved on to a new life. Lucille never finished high school. She ran away from home at seventeen to escape ill-tempered Grandmother Hille. Money from a male cousin in Atlanta paid her way to Chicago. Shortly thereafter she moved again, to New York, possibly to join her father.

Dramatic and ambitious, this tall girl from nowhere was pursued by a British writer of fiction, Stephen Barr. They married when she was in her early twenties and divorced a year later. Quickly afterward she married another writer, or rather someone who would become a writer. A[ugust] C. Spectorsky worked as a fact checker for *The New Yorker* in the middle thirties. After the war, he wrote *The Exurbanites*, prospered and acquired great influence as the fiction editor of *Playboy*. When he met Lucille, Augie Spectorsky was mainly full of prospects. He spent time with a group of writers and artists who lived in Woodstock, New York, a pretty spot at the edge of the Catskills, about two hours drive from New York City. Lucille was part of the group, already a confirmed culture moll. Spectorsky married her, and in 1938 they had a daughter, Susan.

By 1946, that marriage had also collapsed. Liebling rushed into the vacuum and began courting Lucille with his usual worshipful fervor. It was a love match in the beginning. Lucille did not tire of Joe for several years and took a while to turn into the carping narcissist all his friends learned to dislike. Toward the end of the forties Joe and Lucille lived together, and he found himself enthusiastically playing the role of father to little Susan. Theirs was a deep and lasting relationship. Liebling doted on the sensitive little girl and also paid for her keep and education right through Radcliffe and graduate school, since her father never sent Lucille money for child support.

Liebling was still married to Ann, of course, and sent her money regularly. He referred to her as his wife, obliquely, in a comic letter to the editor that ran in *The New Yorker* in May of 1946 under the heading "Department of Amplification." Commenting on an ambiguous explanation of the rules of surname hyphenation in a previous *New Yorker* piece by Rebecca West, Liebling signed himself A. J. McGinn-Liebling. The jocular implication was that he had married a woman of property.

The reverse was painfully true, and it is likely that the financial pressure of maintaining wife, mistress and mistress's daughter forced him to moonlight, starting in November 1946, as the book critic of *Esquire*.

Liebling had written book reviews regularly for *The New Yorker* since his return from France, but he had concentrated almost entirely on war subjects. He applauded, for example, Ralph Ingersoll's *Top Secret*, an attack by the editor of *PM* on the reputations of Generals Eisenhower and Montgomery. He lampooned a respectful memoir of Ike produced by Harry Butcher, a "landlocked naval officer" who

> has written the first account of the important high-level campaign that led from Claridge's in London to the Dorchester, to the Hotel St.

George in Algiers, to a palace near Caserta, back to London, and across to the Hotel Raphael in Paris. The gold-laced armies of the eighteenth century bequeathed to historians the phrase "*La guerre en dentelles.*" Mr. Butcher's book suggests a new one—"*la guerre en hotel.*" The book is called "My Three Years with Eisenhower" (Simon & Schuster), but it must have been a struggle for Mr. Butcher not to call it "Me and Ike." Almost the only time the General is called by his last name is on the title page.

Liebling had also shown himself at ease with more scholarly works, with a study of the effect of war stress on soldiers' minds and bodies, as well as a biography of his hero Stendhal by Matthew Josephson. The editors of *Esquire* must have been attracted to this mixture of wit and seriousness.

During the same period, Liebling had been modestly showing his literary skills in a string of "Wayward Press" pieces, turning ironic on the occasion of the death of Joseph Medill Patterson, publisher of the *Daily News*. Training his satirical sights on a series of articles about a cross-country drive by the drama critic of the *Sun*, he also looked closely at the diction of those pieces, so closely that he sometimes sounded like a new critic doing a "close" reading of a modern poem. Quoting extensively, he demolished Morehouse of the *Sun* by exhibiting his mannered prose. He savored Morehouse's galumphing phrases, his creaky circumlocutions for such things as Washington ("Potomac city of the incommunicable beauty") and for his own car ("the doughty little coupe, WM 125"). Liebling, in effect, turned into a textual editor, adding his own terse, barbed critiques after several quoted passages. Morehouse wrote, "It's wet, as wet as only north Georgia can be during a cloudburst." Liebling asked parenthetically, "How wet was that? I wasn't sure."

In "Antepenultimatum," Liebling continued to focus on the abuse of language in newspapers. When the U.S. government demanded that the Yugoslavs free the survivors from two planes they had shot down, free them within forty-eight hours or be the target of a complaint to the United Nations, most newspapers called the "conspicuously civilized note" an ultimatum in hyperbolic headlines that made Liebling think "we had left the diving board and would hit the surface of the third World War any second." His article amounts to a scholarly investigation of the meaning of the word "ultimatum" as well as a reasoned attack on the insobriety of headline writers' lingo.

In "The Scribes of Destiny," he went after journalism's most egregious offenders against good literary taste, the sportswriters:

> Newspaper people speak of a police reporter, a City Hall man, and a Washington correspondent, but always of a sports *writer*. The sports writer is not expected merely to tell what happened. Upon small, coiled springs of fact, he builds up a great padded mattress of words. His readers flop themselves down on this Beautyrest and escape into a dream world where most of the characters are titanic heroes, devouring monsters, or gargantuan buffoons. . . .

Liebling quoted maliciously from the mixed metaphors of the sports pages. What pleasure he must have taken in finding in the sports section of the *Times* a sentence beginning: "Not since Ellsworth Vines . . . has a tennis gallery seen such electrifying maceration of a fuzz-covered ball. . . ."

These amused attentions to journalistic style suggested that if the standards of good prose could be abused by journalists, then they could also be sensibly observed. Reporters were, undeniably, writers. Only a degraded tradition and laxity kept them from being good ones. The potential was there.

Behind this general implication lay a veiled and boastful assertion. The man who saw the potential for literature-on-newsprint must know how to produce such stuff himself; was, in fact, if you had the wit to notice, already doing so, in the witty piece in front of you. Perhaps Liebling meant to convey that if or when he resumed reporting (which he gave up almost entirely until 1949), he would be able to spin gold instead of the usual straw.

At any rate, the editors of *Esquire* admired his "steady wit and learning" enough to hire him as "writer and critic," as they described him in the paragraph that introduced his first column as staff book reviewer in the issue dated November 1946. They perceived him as he wished to be perceived. He took the occasion to describe himself raffishly in a biographical headnote. "I have never ridden the rails," he wrote, "preferring parlor cars." He was, he said, "married, bald, overweight and gluttonous." His books were all out of print, but he was proudest of *The Road Back to Paris* because "it is out of print in England too." He concluded the squib lamely: "I live in New York City; can't stand country air because it isn't pasteurized."

The first *Esquire* review is remarkable only because it reminded readers of Liebling's enormous knowledge of the history of boxing (he wrote a short essay on two forgotten boxers in the course of reviewing two books on the ring) and presaged his return to ringside as *The New Yorker's* fight writer a few years later. Fifteen more columns followed, in a series that did not end until January 1948. Liebling's range was typically vast. From boxing he hopped to the theater, using the publication of a play by Irwin Shaw as a way of ridiculing Wolcott Gibbs, the *New Yorker* drama critic who had helped to kill it on Broadway. He moved from there to *All the King's Men* and then to the *American Racing Manual*. He spent one column sardonically picking apart the publishing industry and wove a personal memoir into his review of Lee G. Miller's *An Ernie Pyle Album*.

Perhaps because the *Esquire* of the forties was a men's magazine, the reviews are littered with macho and sports metaphors. But in an omnibus fiction review, titled "The Superfluous Obbligato," Liebling must have surprised *Esquire* readers in barber shops all over America when he came out against superfluous sex in novels. "A belief seems to have arisen," he observed, "that a novel without a bedroom scene is as incomplete as a sentence without a verb." Liebling went on to enumerate various metaphors for orgasm from recent literature: the moving earth, electric blue flashes, etc. Then he concluded that sex-prone modern authors thought, erroneously, that they had had a unique and superior sexual experience which they were compelled to describe. He cites an example of this solipsistic tendency that must be thinly disguised autobiography:

> Once, while I was at Dartmouth, I knew intimately a young freshman who returned from a visit to Montreal dizzy with the conviction that he had had an experience that was unparalleled in all of human history. On subsequent reflection, however, he decided that it was open to anybody else who had five dollars.

Liebling was certainly no prude, but he was, according to Jean Riboud, a man of *pudeur*, reticent about sex. Given the far more candid sexuality of today's novels, his reservations (based primarily on his reaction to *Mister Roberts*!) now seem quaint. And like all but one of his *Esquire* columns, "The Superfluous Obbligato" is not of lasting interest.

The exception is an inventive, brilliant flight of whimsy pegged loosely to the American publication of Jean-Paul Sartre's plays *No Exit* and *The Flies*. In "Mr. Existential Brooks" (April 1947), Liebling opens with a characteristically flip and sports-minded lead that appears to accomplish nothing beyond an overly bumptious tip of the cap to modern phenomenology:

> Kierkegaard, Husserl, Heidegger and Jaspers (pronounced Yaspers), whose combined names sound like a University of Wisconsin backfield, are four Teutonic-language philosophers from whose muddled musings a Frenchman named Jean-Paul Sartre has extracted a way of looking at life celebrated under the name of existentialism. The name in itself is attractive; everybody feels a participating interest in existence and a competence to argue about it. A public in Paris, which could have easily refrained from talking about something called Neo-Platonism or J. K. Willis' Universal System of Picking Horses, plunged into endless café-table squabbles about Monsieur Sartre's version of the backfield's ideas.

Breezy, yes, but this lead is also a carefully condensed and gauged introduction to a then unfamiliar and mostly untranslated author for an audience normally nurtured on Petty girls. And Liebling was up to something more complicated than the Esquirization of *Being and Nothingness*. He had evidently been well briefed on Sartrean existentialism and was able to write:

> Sartre's existentialism is less an original philosophy than an attitude for which he has borrowed a philosophical basis. Man is compelled to exist, which is disgusting and absurd, and to continue to exist after death, which is humiliating. He exists in the same involuntary way as a flat stone or a chestnut tree, and yet he must assume full responsibility for his absurd, disgusting, humiliating, involuntary existence. . . .

Liebling had also met Sartre and caught his measure as a man sly enough to pretend he knew no more English than the phrase "Scotch and sodah," a "stubby, applecheeked little man with a bad eye and a bundled up way of dressing, as if he were continually afraid of catching cold."

Liebling had also met Sartre's "friend and sparring partner," Camus. He brought up this "former amateur middleweight who has bad lungs and looks younger than he is, in a thin, caved-in way," in order to show how Camus had taken the same grim notions about life and come up with a competitive theory of the "absurdity" of existence.

Having completed this *tour d'horizon* of current French philosophy in four paragraphs, Liebling came to his real point, or rather he revealed the outrageous "thesis" that was the nominal justification for the whole column. Liebling announced, with what might be called calculated absurdity, that the "father, or at least the foster father of the whole existentialist movement, lives right here in the United States, in a place called Fontana, California," and that this half-black, half-Cherokee was a songwriter and an early practitioner of jazz piano born in 1886 in Amesburg, Ontario.

How could this be? Liebling, with a mischievous glint, holds back the answer and plunges into a plot summary of Sartre's novel *La Nausée*, then untranslated, in which the protagonist, Roquentin, reaches the depths of despair and sees no point to his life. Then, in the final scene, which is meant to stand for Sartre's own discovery of existentialism, Roquentin listens to a record of Sophie Tucker singing "Some of These Days," and speculates about the man who wrote the song. Liebling quoted the passage in his own translation:

> I think of a clean-shaven American with heavy black eyebrows, smothering in the heat of a twentieth-floor apartment in New York. . . . Above New York the sky is burning, the blue of the sky is on fire, enormous yellow flames lick at the roofs; the kids of Brooklyn, in swimming trunks, huddle in the spray of the fire hoses. . . . The black-browed American . . . is in shirt-sleeves, seated before his piano; there is a taste of smoke in his mouth and vaguely, the ghost of a tune in his head. *Some of These Days.* —It happened like that. Like

that or some other way, it doesn't matter much. It's like that that the song was born. It chose the weary body of that Jew with coal-black brows to be born in. —I think of that guy. —He did that. He had beefs of his own—bills to pay, probably, and there must have been a woman somewhere who didn't think as well of him as he would have wished—and then that heat wave. —He had luck. Probably he didn't know it. He just thought, "With luck that tune will get me fifty bucks." —I'd like to know more about that guy—it would interest me to know what kind of troubles he had; if he had a wife or if he lived alone. —Just to be able to think of him, now and then, listening to this record. —But maybe he's dead. Me, I'd be happy to be in his place. —Maybe one can justify one's existence? A little bit, perhaps?

Roquentin decides to go out and write a novel. Liebling casually dismisses this solution to the existential *crise* (and with it dismisses Sartre's philosophy, by implication). "Camus and I agree that it is only a temporary solution at the very best." Roquentin would never know if the finished novel was good enough to justify his continuing existence. But that is not (or Liebling claims it is not) Liebling's real point. In the next paragraph, he delivers the *coup de grace:*

I don't know if Sartre ever did find out anything about the man who wrote *Some of These Days*, words and music. If he did, the awakening must certainly have been rude. Brooks obviously isn't the kind of composer Roquentin visualized, and he couldn't have lived in a twentieth-floor apartment because Jim Crow landlords wouldn't have rented him one. He's a slender, small-featured colored man. I once saw him playing the piano in Murray Bennett's saloon on Eighth Avenue, but that was some time ago and I assume that now he is retired.

Liebling proceeds to relate the actual circumstances of the composition of the tune, which were quite unphilosophical and not very dramatic. Brooks had a tune in his head but no words to go with it. Then he heard a woman in an alley behind the Cincinnati vaudeville house where he was working shout at her lover, "Some of these days, you're going to miss me!"

"Brooks," Liebling observed, "like Villon, took his inspiration where he could find it."

The implications ramify. Brooks was a poet who made art out of what he actually saw and heard. Liebling, it went without saying, was in his camp. Sartre, on the other hand, shied away from life, went about "all bundled up" against the cold, and he didn't "report." He surmised, for he was an intellectual posing as an artist. He wrote a novel as a foil for an idea.

Liebling spelled out very little of this in "Mr. Existential Brooks." Instead, he performed as a reporter on many levels: giving the news about existentialism, dashing off little feature vignettes of Sartre and Camus, writing a capsule review of La Nausée, and digging out the facts of the Shelton Brooks story. The real point of the column was not its Yahoo claim—that Brooks was the father of existentialism. Nor was Liebling seriously asserting that his facetious bit of investigation into Tin Pan Alley history constituted a refutation of Sartre's philosophy. The true purpose of Liebling's article was Liebling's own performance, which was a counterpoise to Sartre's. Without actually saying so, Liebling was setting up his own work, his own journalistic investigation of Sartre and existentialism, as a challenge to Sartre's work. He meant to contrast, in the most exaggerated way, the armchair intellectual with the down-to-earth reporter. The result was satire, in the bluff, faux-naif manner of Mark Twain, but it was also an unlabeled manifesto, an unavowed advertisement for Liebling, the reporter-artist. Liebling, reticent about himself and his purposes, as conventional reporters are reticent, never came out directly and said so, but he was using "Mr. Existential Brooks" as an object lesson whose unstated point was that reporters, writers-in-the-world like himself and Villon, were the moral and aesthetic superiors of writer-intellectuals like Jean-Paul Sartre.

Liebling's reticence was also a defense. It allowed him to dangle himself in front of his readers, to create a cosmopolite persona, without showing his full face. He could tacitly claim worlds of complexity and mastery without boasting or literary pretension. This kind of authorial peekaboo also let Liebling conceal his conflicted feelings about his own writing.

In the beginning of his career, in Providence, and at the World-Telegram, Liebling had played much the same game but for a different reason. Then, he had found oblique ways of inserting himself into his articles because he wanted to rebel against the newspaper profession's narrow notion of authorship. By 1947, he was still teasing readers with veiled glimpses of himself, even though the external pressure for concealment had long since vanished. Neither *The New Yorker* nor *Esquire* encouraged anonymity. But Liebling persisted in his calculated, dissembling suppressions of self. Now you saw him, now you didn't, and the man you thought you knew was never the real thing anyhow. It suited him to camouflage his real identity with the various masks of boulevardier, sportsman and faceless reporter. He could wrap himself up in these roles and ignore the fact that he was obese, Jewish, tragically married, often depressed.

By 1947, Liebling had one more important blemish to hide. He had spent two and a half years in New York without producing a major work. He had, to be sure, in that time written voluminously and sharply, but he had not written *The Red and the Black* or *Romany Rye*. He was still putting together short pieces, and they were about other people's work. Although he was certainly proud of what he had accomplished after the war, Liebling must have felt that he had not lived up to the high hopes he had held for himself in the letter he had written to Joe Mitchell before leaving France in 1944.

Committed as he was to the reporter's career, Liebling still craved the recognition that only books could earn a writer. This ambition, later declared openly, must have been in him much earlier and must have made him defensive in the late forties about the work in journalism that he had done so well. While he refused to concede that his articles were inferior to writing in other genres, he knew that the straightforward case for journalism as art, baldly stated, would sound like an empty boast. And so, when he came to spar with Sartre, an author fertile in genres of the highest prestige, Liebling opted for the feint instead of the punch, kept his guard up and hoped the smart money would detect the quality of his moves.

Liebling's comic *guerrilla* against Sartre was an oblique and hedged bid for public recognition. It must have been at just the same time, in the early spring of 1947, and in a contrastingly expansive frame of mind, that Liebling wrote the long autobiographical essay that forms the first half of *The Wayward Pressman*, the collection of his press columns that appeared toward the end of the year. In more than a hundred pages, Liebling forsook his usual reticence and told the story of his life with newspapers from childhood until he went to *The New Yorker*. The essay was explicitly an attempt to lay out his credentials for writing about the press, but it went well beyond a mere professional *curriculum vitae*. It is enriched with newsroom anecdotes, with outcries against publishers and blinkered editors, with everything Liebling thought fit to print about his early days. Whether or not this ebullient, entertaining but highly idiosyncratic self-portrait really does establish Liebling as a *bona fide* authority on the press, it certainly works as a character study. In it, Liebling finally found an outlet for his previously cramped ego.

In twenty years of journalism, he had been an autobiographer manqué, filtering Rhode Island and Broadway and France through his own sensibility, but never wholeheartedly giving way to the impulse to write directly about himself. The assignment had always been about someone or something else. But in *The Wayward Pressman,* he broke free of formal journalistic restraints altogether. The prose is exhilarated, hyperventilated by this new freedom.

The essay was also the longest piece of writing Liebling had ever published. Not quite a book in itself, it turned what was otherwise a collection of columns into the public debut of a writer. It was the beginning of the career he had planned in the letter to Mitchell.

Nineteen forty-seven was also the year that *La République du Silence* came out. With two books under his belt in one season, Liebling could begin to think of himself as a literary figure of substance. In the "Wayward Press" pieces that followed, he spoke with increased confidence and he wrote more freely and pointedly about the evils of monopolistic newspaper publishers and of right-wing, witch-hunting anti-communists, of anti-labor reactionaries and of threats from all sides to freedom of the press and other First Amendment rights.

In August, a serenely self-assured Liebling began a "Wayward Press" column by referring smugly to a "principle" he had previously "denominated" Liebling's Law: "if a man is smart enough, he can kick himself in the seat of the pants, grab himself by the collar, and throw himself out on the sidewalk." The law had proved its validity once again, Liebling gloated, when "the press rooted home the Taft-Hartley Act" although it contained a provision that was, in effect, a gag rule against political comment in the press. Belatedly, the *Times* and *Herald Tribune,* which had both backed Taft-Hartley, began to squirm editorially and view the overlooked section with alarm. Why this sudden reassessment, after the bill had passed? Liebling, an out-and-out foe of Taft-Hartley, concluded that "the newspapers, in their preoccupation with something that promised to 'curb' labor," had waved the bill on to passage without reading the fine print.

A month later, returning once again to his preoccupation with headline diction, Liebling collected several examples of headlines with words "that primarily express physical violence":

BOSTON ARCHBISHOP HITS 'APOLOGISTS FOR TITO'

or:

PR FIGHT LINKED TO U.S. RED PURGE

But as he moved on, from headline to headline, Liebling seemed to forget the original premise of the piece. Continuing to quote rebarbative headlines, he included several that weren't metaphorically violent, but only absurd in the way they overused the omnibus verb "probe." These headlines were funny enough to cite for their vapidity alone, but the list of six has a special coherence of its own, an unavowed political coherence. It culminates with:

GREEN ASKS FIRING OF PROBE SLUGGER

William Green, the president of the American Federation of Labor, had demanded that a congressional committee investigating labor problems dismiss its counsel because he had roughed up an AFL lawyer during a hearing in Hollywood. Liebling's ostensible reason for including this headline was misuse of the violent word "slugger." In a remarkably long stretch of exegesis, Liebling wonders "how anybody could slug a probe." He goes on to quote contradictory accounts of the incident. The AP story under the "slugger" headline had one lawyer choking, but not "slugging," the other. In the UP story, three blows were struck.

This sort of inconsistency was fair game for a press critic, but on the other hand, it did not belong in a piece about the phenomenon of violent words applied to nonviolent situations. There had been real violence at the hearing. To be sure, "slugger" might have been less accurate than "choker" or, as Liebling suggests, "gozzler," but all this only adds up to a quibble, and still leaves the reader wondering why so much attention has been paid to such a small point, and one that, furthermore, bears only the slimmest relationship to the explicit subject of the article.

Is it excessively ingenious to suppose that Liebling had orchestrated a long section on "probe" headlines and then expatiated on technical problems in the coverage of a "probe" story so that he could devote space to a government lawyer manhandling a labor attorney? Wasn't Liebling really making a veiled reference to the rise of political reaction in America when he said, twice in the same piece, that the "temper" of the times was violent? Perhaps all this was the result of unconscious processes or of a sincere belief that the mood of the country had turned pugnacious. If so, why then was he unable "to leave the subject of headlines" without quoting this one:

ATOM ROLE HEIGHTENED BY STUDY OF RED AIMS

Admittedly, the language of the headline is absurd, and it does call attention to violent weaponry. But the real pattern into which it fits is a pattern of headlines that illustrate the rising pitch of right-wing paranoia that was leading to the McCarthy era. Perhaps Liebling hoped to satirize the trend covertly. Or perhaps Harold Ross had told him to keep politics out of the "Wayward Press" pieces, and this was a way for him to sneak politics back in. At any rate, with one exception, every column Liebling wrote about the American press from August 1947 until early 1949 discussed the rise of right-wing, reactionary feeling (or the Truman-Dewey-Wallace presidential election, which focused on the same issue).

On October 11, 1947, Liebling devoted a column to cold war restrictions on foreign correspondents' travel in the United States and Russia. The next week he returned to the matter of pro-capitalist press bias raised by his earlier "Great Gouamba" piece. Meat prices had risen, as he had predicted they would, and he called on the press to admit that it had been traduced by the meat industry and had slighted poor consumers. On November 1, Liebling began a column about anti-labor bias in the coverage of a strike of grooms and exercise riders at the Jamaica race track with a humorous if unrelated reminder of the cold war hysteria abroad in the land:

> The headline on the first page of my copy of the *Daily News* on October 21st was:
>
> ### PROBE REVEALS HOLLYWOOD REDS
>
> Next morning's front-page head in the same paper was:
>
> ### REDS GRIP B'WAY FILM QUIZ TOLD
>
> —apparently denoting an advance of three thousand miles in twenty-four hours.
>
> While waiting for the Crimson Wave to reach a point on Forty-fourth Street about midway between Sixth and Fifth Avenues, where it will presumably sweep over the New York Yacht Club and the Harvard Club before engulfing my office, I have decided to set down a few notes on the press treatment of the recent strike of grooms and exercise riders. . . .

On November 8, Liebling acerbically surveyed the largely approving and amused press reaction to the House Committee on Un-American Activities hearings that investigated communist subversion in Hollywood. Liebling showed, first, how the proceedings were getting wide coverage because they were directed at glamorous people, and because some of the witnesses fell into bizarre and quotably humorous patter. He also reproduced a series of scare headlines from the *Journal-American,* "one of those cascades of front-page streamer heads that are calculated to make a terrified reader buy several editions of the same paper on the same day—a sort of typographical 'Shut the door, they're coming through the window; shut the window, they're coming through the door,' the 'they' in this case being the Hollywood Reds."

As 1947 drew to a close, the reactionary fever continued to rage, and the press reflected it. Liebling, retaliating against the trend, debunked a widely reported welfare scandal which he called "Horse-feathers Swathed in Mink." The *Times* and other papers had been quick to jump on what looked at first glance like a flagrant abuse of public assistance. A women with a mink coat and, allegedly, sixty thousand dollars in her pocket was receiving welfare payments. Eventually it transpired that the coat was in tatters and the woman authentically destitute. Liebling saw the precipitous newspaper yowling as one more example of the press contributing to the growth of conservative public opinion. He laid the blame for this misjudgment, as usual, on the newspaper publishers, saying "there is no concept more generally cherished by publishers than that of the Undeserving Poor."

Not all of Liebling's press criticism during the period leading up to the McCarthy era and the Korean War was political. He took time out from the witch hunt to write in a lighter vein about press coverage of the wedding of Britain's Princess Elizabeth. He vacationed in the Caribbean and took two indulgent looks at the local press. In the winter of 1948, he traveled to France with Lucille and Susan Spectorsky, renewed his acquaintance with Albert Camus, who rode up to the Hotel Louvois on a motorcycle, and with other ex-resistance writers, including François Mauriac. These meetings ultimately led him to write an essay on the post-liberation history of the resistance press. Liebling's ten-day visit to Paris was also, in personal terms, a chance to escape the political turmoil in America and to reimmerse himself in his own past. Mary Paniguian came over from London. She and Liebling, Lucille and Susan, took long walks through the city. It was like the old days, but the trip made him wistful. Paris, he wrote a few years later in *Normandy Revisited*, "made me feel a bit like a man returning after a dozen years to a former love and finding that she is married, has four children, is worried about money, and devotes all her afternoons to the Parent-Teacher Association, the Ladies' Village Improvement Society, the Friends of Krishnamurti, and the American Red Cross."

There was not enough time to get up to Vire, which he had lovingly "revisited" the previous fall in a "Wayward Press" piece based on copies of the local paper, *La Voix du Bocage*, which he had been receiving in New York. But Liebling did go to Oslo, wrote a "Letter" from there to *The New Yorker*, and interviewed his old companions from the tanker that had carried him across the Atlantic during the war, in preparation for a three-part article that ran in *The New Yorker* a year afterward.

After this month among old friends and old haunts, Liebling returned to an America more politicized than ever by an exceptionally bitter presidential campaign and by rampant paranoia over communist subversion. Liebling, like many other left liberals, detested the witch hunters. As a press critic, he had naturally begun to poke fun at the excesses of anti-communist rhetoric and to excoriate the role newspapers played in fomenting public fear of the Red Menace. It was natural, too, for Liebling to connect inflammatory anti-left journalism with capitalist publishers, whom he lumped together with the whole gang of businessmen and other wealthy, conservative oppressors of the poor, proletarian plain folk that he loved and sentimentally identified with.

And so it was in every way inevitable that Joe Liebling would pay close attention to the press coverage of the HUAC hearings that began on August 3, 1948, shortly after his return from Europe. This was the crucial session that brought two star witnesses to the stand, two communist recusants eager to confess their pasts. They were Elizabeth Bentley and Whittaker Chambers. They both asserted that they had been involved in the subversion of the United States Department of State. Chambers, an editor at *Time*, named Alger Hiss, a former high State Department official, as a communist.

Liebling reacted with indignation. In a "Wayward Press" column in the August 28 *New Yorker*, he called the session a "long, dreary exhibition of prosecution-by-innuendo." What "staggered" him more, however, "was the great, crashing newspaper display accorded a set of hearings that, it was evident from the first day, were reminiscent of a group of retarded children playing deteckative." Liebling then quoted a spate of headlines that repeated the "character murder" of Bentley's and Chambers's accusations. He closed his column with a stream of righteous indignation attacking the news judgment of editors who had overplayed the hearings:

> If it should be argued that newspapers don't aim mudballs in their news columns—that they simply report upon the mudballs other people throw—I should be tempted to reply that this defense is a tri-

ple-distilled extract of Bulgarian fusel oil, turpentine, molasses, potato skins and grain hulls. The importance that a newspaper attributes
to a story depends upon the editor's judgment. An editor who
couldn't smell an odor of burning synthetic rubber about Miss Bentley's inside-policy data has an extremely insensitive nose for news.

It would be—it is—unnecessary to suppose that Liebling needed
any more than the facts of the situation—the tawdry hearing mer-
etriciously covered—to make him heap such abuse with such unaccustomed vehemence. In fact, Liebling had a personal interest, very
slight, but an interest nonetheless, in the HUAC proceedings. Liebling knew Alger Hiss.

As Hiss himself recalls it, they had met at lunch at the Harvard
Club of New York after Hiss had taken over the presidency of the
Carnegie Endowment. The lunch was arranged on the spur of the
moment by a mutual friend, and it occurred between Hiss's arrival
in New York in January 1947 and the HUAC hearings of August
1948. In other words, the two men met in a friendly way before
Liebling could have known that Hiss was under suspicion as a spy.
There is no reason, at any rate, to believe that Liebling was aware of
anything unusual about Hiss until Chambers testified before the
committee. There is also no reason to suppose that Liebling's friendship with Hiss up to that point was anything more than a chance acquaintance. But as the Hiss case exploded into a major political
scandal, Joe Liebling himself became more and more involved, became convinced that Hiss had been unjustly tried and, worse, that
he had been tried in a prejudicial atmosphere concocted by a hostile
press. At the same time, Liebling and Hiss became good friends,
and stayed friends until Liebling died. Furthermore, Liebling was,
Hiss says, "helpful during the investigation state of my case. He put
Rosenwald in touch with Malcolm Cowley and others who had
known Chambers."

"Rosenwald" was Harold Rosenwald, a former classmate of Hiss's
at the Harvard Law School and a junior member of the team of
lawyers whom Hiss had assembled to represent him. Liebling used
Rosenwald as a source throughout the Hiss case, and the two men
became good friends and drinking buddies. As Rosenwald recalls it:
"Liebling got in touch with me early in the Hiss case, around August of 1948. He didn't follow the trials on a day-to-day basis, like a

newspaper reporter. Instead, he called me for background and insights."

Liebling also gathered information elsewhere, from acquaintances of Chambers, from Mark Van Doren, the English professor, from Malcolm Cowley, the literary critic and editor, and from Richard Simon, the publisher. He passed on these findings to Rosenwald, along with the text of some poems that might have been written by Chambers and published pseudonymously. These bits of doggerel had been ferreted out by Liebling's research assistant at *The New Yorker*. Perhaps Liebling was exploring the possibility of writing a profile of Chambers. Perhaps the research was merely part of a general effort to gather documentation about HUAC informers and victims in anticipation of further hearings and a future need to write about them. At any rate, Liebling passed on some relatively benign information about Chambers to Rosenwald and offered to put Rosenwald in touch with two left-wing editors who had known Chambers. On October 7, 1948, Rosenwald dictated a memo outlining the substance of the information Liebling had given him.° On the basis of this one act of low-level and trivial collaboration between reporter and source, Allen Weinstein in his *Perjury: The*

°Here is the text of the most important section of Rosenwald's memo:

> Mark Van Doren was a teacher of Chambers at Columbia and was very friendly with Chambers during that time. Chambers was a very promising writer and his talent was the basis for the friendship with Mr. Van Doren. Mr. Liebling gave me Mr. Van Doren's file of letters which he had received from Chambers, certain newspaper clippings, chiefly involving the blasphemous play written by Chambers, and a copy of the play.
> The letters to Mr. Van Doren from Chambers indicate:
> 1. His joining the Communist Party in 1925 and his enthusiasm for the Communist Party at that time.
> 2. His interest in writing heroic couplets.
> 3. His acquaintance with Rorty (apparently James Rorty) who was on the Executive Board of the New Masses in 1926.
> 4. His written admission that he lied to the Dean of Columbia upon returning to the college to continue his undergraduate work.
> 5. His trip to Europe during a summer vacation.
> 6. A well developed literary melody in the writing of the letters themselves.
> Early in the year 1939, Chambers called Mr. Van Doren and told him that he wanted to see Mr. Van Doren.
> Chambers inquired whether Mr. Van Doren was alone and Mr. Van Doren replied that his wife and a lady friend of his wife's were at home with him. Chambers seemed unhappy about this and was rather reluctant to come to see Mr. Van Doren while other people were present. He finally decided to come and appeared at the Van Doren residence. He insisted upon being hurried by the two ladies although he knew Mrs. Van Doren quite well from his student days. He asked Mr. Van Doren whether he could get him some work doing translation. Mr. Van Doren stated that he did not think this kind of work very worth while for Chambers and asked him why he wanted to do it. Mr. Chambers replied that he wanted to "establish an identity."

Hiss-Chambers Case (Knopf, 1978) smears Liebling, calling him an "adviser and tipster for Hiss's lawyers."

Weinstein's extremely condensed and misleading account of Liebling's involvement with Hiss and the Hiss case (*Perjury*, pp. 166–67) concludes, in a tendentious footnote, that Liebling, as Hiss's friend, had "abandoned journalistic objectivity" and adopted "an advocate's position in the case." This apparently straightforward charge actually conflates two separate ethical issues and two quite different moments in Liebling's relationship with Hiss.

It is clear from many articles he wrote about redbaiting well before the beginning of the Hiss case that Liebling was, in a general way, an advocate of the left-liberal position (and, as it happens, the constitutional position) on the rights of communists and so-called communist sympathizers. He thought they had a right to their views and a corollary right to freedom from public harassment by publicity-hungry officials making hay out of "Subversion." Liebling used his press critic's platform in *The New Yorker* to bait the redbaiters. He attacked their hollow rhetoric and showed how their inflammatory language had infiltrated newspaper headlines and articles; how the Red Scare had taken over the judgment of editors; and how HUAC was manipulating the press. This is all surely advocacy, but it is not wrong, just as it is not wrong for Professor Weinstein, as a historian, to advocate, in seven hundred pages of "objective," scholarly prose, that Alger Hiss was guilty.

Professor Weinstein was not, however, a personal enemy of Hiss, whereas Liebling and Hiss so warmed to each other as the Hiss case drew on that Liebling and Lucille Spectorsky spent several weeks during the summer of 1949 with the Hisses at their summer home in Peacham, Vermont.° Now, since all the evidence suggests, as Weinstein says, that "Liebling became a good friend of the Hisses and the defense lawyers during the year that follows" (his original contacts with Harold Rosenwald in the summer of 1948), we must

---

°Hiss, in an interview in early 1977, could not remember whether Liebling had visited him in 1948, 1949 or 1950. Nineteen fifty is impossible, since Hiss had gone to jail by then. Nineteen forty-eight is unlikely, since the first HUAC hearings that mentioned Hiss were in August and the two men did not become real friends until after Hiss was under fire. At any rate, Hiss recalls a pastoral visit unmarred by discussion of the case and enlivened by periodic appearances of the village idiot, Old Ned, who ogled Lucille when she wore a bathing suit at nearby Harvey's Pond.

look to some later time, after this friendship had truly ripened, before the charge of friendly bias can be legitimately applied.

In the immediate aftermath of the August HUAC hearings—between, that is, the first Chambers accusation and the "discovery" of the "Pumpkin Papers" in early December of 1948—Liebling wrote directly about Hiss only once, in the August 28 article already discussed. The next week, he returned to mock philology, exploring the recent history of the phrase "red herring." President Truman had dismissed congressional concern with subversion as a "red herring." Republicans had then seized on this indiscretion and made the phrase notorious. Liebling had great fun with the absurd piscatorial furor and used it to satirize the redbaiters. The piece was opinionated, certainly, but it did not mention Hiss, nor did its temperature rise above the level of Liebling's pre-Hiss liberalism. Similarly, on October 23, 1948, Liebling uncovered a particularly complex smear tactic that HUAC members were using to leak their then-secret sessions into the papers. No mention of Hiss is in that piece either.

On November 13, 1948, Liebling wrote about the full transcript of the HUAC hearings. His basic point in the review was that this complete text contained crucial testimony that had not been reported in the press. The full transcript showed congressmen badgering witnesses, subjecting them to anti-Semitic innuendo and denying them their constitutional rights. Liebling's main example of unreported but important testimony was "the tangled story of the relationship of Alger Hiss and Whittaker Chambers." Whether Hiss, in his initial testimony, failed purposely to identify Chambers as a former acquaintance (who then, in 1933, had gone by the name George Crosley) is still a matter of controversy. Liebling summarizes the dialogue in the various HUAC sessions that bore on this point. The synopsis is indeed friendly to Hiss: it does not conclude that Hiss was lying, and it does try to impugn the motives of the committee members. Liebling wrote: "For a person reading the record merely as a play, the statements of the Committee people in their attempt to stall Hiss should stimulate a certain amount of curiosity as to their motivation."

The remark is, however, entirely appropriate and within the

bounds of fair comment for a press critic arguing, from facts he pre-
sents in his article, that press coverage of HUAC had been biased
(by the omission of important testimony) against witnesses such as
Hiss. It did not require any special relationship with Hiss for Liebling to write as he did. His opinions flowed from his own political
make-up and from his careful reading of 878 pages of transcript. In
any case, it is unlikely that Liebling's friendship with Hiss had pro-
gressed very far during the heated months of the fall of 1948, when
Hiss had concerns more pressing than the cultivation of a sympathetic magazine writer.

If Weinstein's slur has any merit, it rests on "Spotlight on the
Jury," an article that Liebling wrote many months later, on July 23,
1949, just after Hiss's first perjury trial had ended in a hung jury. By
then, Liebling and Hiss had definitely cemented their friendship.
But it is important to note, as Weinstein does not, that from the time
in November when he reviewed the HUAC transcript until the end
of the first trial—in short, during the entire period of the emer-
gence of the Hiss case as an actual case (as opposed to a juicy episode in the HUAC espionage hearings)—Liebling had refrained
from writing about Hiss. He did not, even in this valedictory comment on the Hiss case, take a position on the case itself, but confined
his remarks to the role the press played in the aftermath of the trial.

"Spotlight on the Jury" shows, through a detailed examination of
New York newspapers, how, collectively, the press exposed the
members of the hung jury and the judge to a hailstorm of publicity
and vilification. Liebling concluded, "This sort of thing obviously
and apparently lessens the chance of a fair trial next time. Perhaps
the secrecy of the jury room, like that of the voting booth, should be
protected by law."

A sensitive reader of "Spotlight on the Jury" might have conjec-
tured that Liebling thought Hiss was innocent, but that would have
been no more than a guess. The column itself nowhere, directly,
suggests that Liebling was anything other than an agnostic where
Hiss was concerned.

In private life, where reporters and scholars are universally conceded the right to partisan opinions, Liebling did eventually side

with the Hiss forces. But even this gradually evolved position did not mean that he thought Hiss was innocent of espionage. All anyone can say at this stage is that Liebling was convinced Hiss had been unfairly tried. Also he was Hiss's friend, and he despised the reactionaries on the other side of the fight, the Nixons and Strykers and Mundts.

After July 1949, Liebling never wrote about Hiss again (except in 1961, when he supplied some retrospective amplifications to the pieces collected in *The Press*). In the fall of 1949, he did also apparently do some additional investigation of Whittaker Chambers as part of the series on Time, Inc., that *Collier's* had commissioned him to write. This reporting coincided with the second Hiss perjury trial. Liebling handed in the first two parts of the series in November. The trial ran from November 17, 1949, to January 20, 1950. Meanwhile *Collier's* refused to accept the Time series, rejecting it as libelous. Liebling's row with *Collier's*—indeed, the fact of his relationship with the magazine—was not widely known. And so it was that some confusion arose as to Liebling's reasons for looking into Chambers's past and then not publishing anything about him. On December 31, 1949, Liebling wrote Harold Rosenwald:

> That time I called you I had received a telegram from Tom O'Neill [of the Baltimore *Sun*] saying: Government at Hiss trial suggested today you used subterfuge of preparing New Yorker profile of Whittaker Chambers to gather derogatory information regarding him when you were really acting as agent for defense lawyers, specifically [Edward D.] McLean and Rosenwald stop appreciate comment wired collect.

Liebling sent O'Neill this telegram:

THANKS FOR PROMPT INFORMATION STOP ANY SUCH SUGGESTION FALSE STOP EYE WROTE AT LEAST TWO PIECES REFERRING TO CHAMBERS BEFORE EYE EVEN MET ROSENWALD OR MCLEAN IN FACT MET BOTH OF THEM WHILE GATHERING DOPE ON CHAMBERS STOP INTRODUCTION OF ROSENWALD TO COWLEY WAS INCIDENTAL TO MY PRIMARY JOB COMMA ACQUIRING INFORMATION ABOUT ONE OF MOST CUR-

IOUS CHARACTERS OF OUR TIME STOP PERHAPS BETTER MAKE THAT
READ OF OUR TIME INC STOP HAVE NOT YET WRITTEN MY DEFINITIVE
CHAMBERS PIECE BECAUSE GUY KEEPS CHANGING HIS STORY SO OFTEN
EYE DONT KNOW WHAT TO DISBELIEVE MOST FIRMLY STOP REGARDS.

There is no longer any means of determining (nor is it of any real
interest to do so) how Liebling's curiosity about Chambers was first
aroused or at which points in time specific interviews were related
to specific article assignments. Perhaps Liebling did hope to write a
New Yorker profile of Chambers. At any rate, his telegram to
O'Neill quashed any press follow-up on the government lawyer's allegation. O'Neill must have concluded that it was quite believable
that a liberal press critic such as Liebling would have turned of his
own volition to the subject of Chambers, because Chambers was a
politically and morally corrupt journalist. O'Neill must have decided that Liebling was no "agent" for Hiss's lawyers. For some reason,
however, Professor Weinstein chose to revive this hoary prosecutor's
smear in a long footnote. Harold Rosenwald denies the allegation
out of hand.

Liebling did, nevertheless, come to side with the Hiss lawyers in a
private way. In his letter of December 31, 1949, he asked Rosenwald to "tell Claude [B. Cross, the chief Hiss lawyer in the second
trial] to be of good courage." But Liebling's firm conviction remained that "newspapers had made a fair second round impossible
in New York."

The defense lawyers had petitioned unsuccessfully on this ground
for a change of venue to Vermont for the second trial. And the deni-
al of the petition was part of the substance of the motion for a retrial that was eventually argued, to no avail, before the Supreme
Court. In early 1950, a request for funds to pay for this last-ditch
maneuver was sent to previous contributors to Alger Hiss's legal expenses. According to Hiss, Liebling, who helped "with some P.R.
work" at the time of the motion for a retrial, may have written the
text of a fund-raising letter. Richard Field, the attorney who super-
vised the appeal, is now dead, and no copy of the letter seems to
have survived. Even if Liebling did write it, he had long before that

taken himself off the Hiss "beat" and turned his journalistic energies to other topics.

Indeed, Joe Liebling's work written for *The New Yorker* during
the first half of 1949 did not differ noticeably from the work he did
before his "involvement" with the Hiss case. Shortly after Alger
Hiss was sentenced to a jail term, Liebling wrote "Toward a One-
Paper Town," an obituary for the New York *Star* which reiterated
his concern for the local and national drift toward an end to competition in the newspaper business. Liebling had hoped that the *Star*, a
mediocre successor to the liberal *PM*, would improve itself and suc-
ceed. "I think," he wrote, "the *Star* was making progress toward a
successful change-over, although the process resembled changing
clothes under water."

Later that spring, he made fun of Louella Parsons's "coverage" of
the Ali Khan–Rita Hayworth wedding in Europe. He also reviewed
the American edition of Sartre's *La Nausée* in a sober rehash of his
Esquire piece on the same book. In all those months of pumpkin papers and triumphant statements by Richard Nixon, Liebling turned
to the Red Scare hotbed only once, on April 9, 1949, in a "Wayward
Press" column called "100,000—Count 'Em—1,000." It was a classic exposé of inflated crowd statistics and sensationalizing headlines
that predicted mob violence on no basis whatever.

"Calmly handled," Liebling said, "the story would have had all
the thrill of an account of a Unesco meeting." Speakers from the Soviet bloc were scheduled to participate at a ho-hum affair at the
Waldorf-Astoria called the Cultural and Scientific Conference for
World Peace. The *Journal-American*, however, predicted that
100,000 anti-communist pickets would ring the hotel. Liebling,
"alarmed by the prospect of a mob tearing the delegates into fragments suitable for shashlik," took a stroll past the Waldorf at six-
thirty on the evening the conference convened. "There were about
a hundred and fifty pickets on the Park Avenue side of the hotel
and only a handful on Forty-ninth Street down near Lexington, and
nobody seemed particularly excited." The papers all gave out
sharply reduced counts for the picketers the next day, but went on
to report the ideological squabbles at the conference with what

seemed to Liebling an excessive zeal. He preferred the drab prose in the *Times:*

> The *Times* report of the panels confirmed my opinion that the best way to describe how dull a dull event is is to tell it straight; the trouble with writing ominously about this sort of thing is that you make it sound ominous, and the trouble with being amusing about it is that you make it sound amusing. The best way to kill Communism is to give it several pages in the *Times* every Sunday. This is also the best way to prevent war. Nobody can fight while he is asleep.

Liebling himself had, however, just invigorated the Sunday *Times* with some genial invective in the *Book Review*. In late February, he had reviewed a British war novel by Alexander Baron, sneering at its romantic, wartless portrait of an impossibly heroic battalion as "suet pudding." The following week, J. Donald Adams devoted his column in the *Book Review* to an attack on the Liebling review. He dismissed the notion that in real warfare not all men were heroes; he wondered "what troops" Liebling had seen as a war correspondent that had convinced him that ordinary soldiers could develop battle psychosis. Adams ended his diatribe with a schoolmasterly hiccup:

> This is an angry piece, I know. But it does not arise from a momentary irritation. It has its roots in a long-existent conviction that American realism is the realism of a spoiled child.

Liebling's surrebuttal appeared in the *Book Review* letters column the next week, on March 13. He defended himself on various specific points and then rose to a pitch of real eloquence:

> The one portion of Mr. Adams' piece that I am tempted to take seriously is his query about the kind of troops I associated with during the war, in which I sensed a reflection on their quality. I was with very good troops indeed, among them the First, Ninth, and Twenty-ninth Divisions, the Thirty-third fighter group, the Corps Franc d'Afrique and the Fourth Indian Division. I have seen tank battalion soldiers dragged yammering back toward their own lines along the sunken road that led through St. André l'Epine on the way into St.

Lô, and seen fine big stolid Midwestern infantrymen frozen to a wall in the fighting to take La Haye du Puits, unable to move, or be moved, forward or back, although the front had moved a thousand yards ahead of them. I have seen good pilots arrive at a point where nobody could make them get into a cockpit, and a man on a landing craft on D-Day make the most heroic rescue—and then blow completely several days later, when the pressure was off. This, as I don't expect Mr. Adams to understand, is because every man has a threshold of endurance, although no two thresholds are of identical height, and, when the flood of experience piles high enough, it comes over.

"This," Liebling concluded in a sardonic echo of Adams, "is not an angry piece, but one written in pained amazement, from the point of view of one who is invited to tea and then jabbed with hatpins by his host's aunt."

Liebling had been rejected again by *The New York Times*. But now he had been able to turn the rejection to his immediate advantage. His indignant reply to Adams was, in effect, a chance to publish again in the *Times*. And it was at precisely this moment that Liebling was preparing to break away from *The New Yorker* and strike out on his own as a free lance.

The spring of 1949 was, in general, a watershed in Joe Liebling's life. He signed a lucrative contract with *Collier's* to write articles about two press lords, Henry Luce of Time, Inc., and Colonel Robert Rutherford McCormick, editor and publisher of the Chicago *Tribune*. He was to finish the Luce series by September 1 and then move to Chicago to work on McCormick in the fall. Having severed his connection with *The New Yorker,* probably by the end of May, he began research on Luce in New York in June, while at the same time making plans to divorce Ann and marry Lucille Spectorsky during the summer in Nevada.

Cutting the *New Yorker* umbilical was a serious risk. But Liebling saw the move as his chance to capitalize on his reputation as a press critic, to operate on his own in the world, without Ross looking over his shoulder. As a free lance, he could run his own shop and begin to write book-length projects, or at least work on longer pieces than the "Wayward Press" format allowed. Mostly, however, it must have pleased him to throw over the traces, to rebel against the coziness of his *New Yorker* arrangement. And he expected to make more money, while reaching a larger audience through a mass-market magazine.

How much pressure Lucille may have exerted, how important she was in pushing Liebling into these momentous decisions, is impossible to say. But her ambitious nature must have supported Liebling's own craving for wider recognition, more money and more independence. Lucille and Liebling had been living together at 131 Riverside Drive, while Ann Liebling continued her inpatient/outpatient existence at the fringes of normal society, far from her legal husband. Lucille, meanwhile, with an adolescent daughter to think about, quite reasonably wanted her lover to marry her and to give up the pretense of being married to Ann. Liebling, always sensitive to the plight of women in distress, agreed to make an honest woman out of Lucille, whom, at any rate, he found physically irresistible, and whose daughter he had come to love as if she had been his own. There was, then, a superficial logic to all the changes Liebling made in the summer of 1949, but they all turned into failures. It was as if nothing Liebling did west of the Hudson turned out well. And while he suffered that fall in Chicago, he remembered what Harold Ross had told him when he had asked to be sent to the Midwest just after the war. "You wouldn't like it, Liebling," Ross said. "You wouldn't like it."

nine

By
Way of
Chicago

July 26, 1949

Mr. Joseph Liebling
Riverside Hotel
Reno, Nevada

Dear Joe:

I didn't know you'd gone until the end of last week, although I expected it. That damned Reno is unique and one of the crazy places of the world, and stories are lying in the street there, unquestionably. I was told, for instance, that the Harold's Club, which is nationally advertised by billboards—you see the damned billboards in New Jersey, etc., set up a nursery when it opened its second floor a few years back, where mothers could leave infants in competent hands, while they gambled. . . .

One item that has always stuck in my mind: Even the drug stores out there have slot machines—you go in to buy some suppositories and stop at the door on the way out to gamble a couple of quarters. Well, Lucius Beebe told me that he called a surgeon's office to have some wound taken care of, and found a slot machine in the surgeon's waiting room.

Another fellow that knows the ropes out there is a gent named Standersick, who I looked up while in Reno last summer. I worked with him on a newspaper in Sacramento thirty years ago, or maybe it's forty. He's been practicing law there for years; that is, he's been getting divorces for people. He told me that marriages run away ahead of divorces in Reno and that the weekend line-up of couples getting married is an amazing sight: The marrying is done by the judges (two in number, as I recall it) who do the divorcing. They get seven or eight thousand a year for being judges, but they have a monopoly on the marriage business and that brings in thirty or forty thousand a year.

I'm full of things like that, but I was only there two days and you are a better reporter than I am (like hell) and have more time.

Good luck and God bless you.

As ever,

H. W. Ross

Liebling must have cherished Ross's letter. It is one of the very few letters from a friend that he preserved. Ross, writing as if Liebling were on an extended *New Yorker* assignment instead of waiting out the residence requirement for a Nevada divorce, must have made Liebling feel that he had not cut himself off completely from his old life.

But for the most part, those weeks of "lingering" in "implausible little" Reno were a difficult time in a desert limbo. He tried to finish the Time series and saw he couldn't come close. The steady rhythm of work on shorter pieces was gone, and with it, for the first time in years, the reassuring momentum of constantly seeing his work in print. And at some level of importance no one can judge, he felt the guilt of divorcing the wife he still loved but couldn't live with.

When Joe Liebling told Ann he was divorcing her, she said in her addled, poignant way, "I thought I was so nice." And he felt even then, as he later confided to Emily Hahn, that he would never love anyone as much as Ann. He never did actually abandon her, since he continued to send her money for the rest of his life.

Ripe for a serious attack of separation anxiety, Liebling kept himself in balance by roaming about Reno and uncovering raffish riffraff who reminded him of similar cronies in New York. In "Slot Machines and Repose," a piece he wrote for *The New Yorker* the following spring, he summarized his wanderings through Reno's lower depths, where he found an appealing anti-America based on the legalization of all the vices the rest of the country repressed: drink, prostitution, gambling and sloth. Liebling, who had suffered through Prohibition and covered it as a reporter, took happily to the nocturnal, bibulous freedom of Reno:

> Once, walking down Lake Street in Reno at eight o'clock in the morning, I looked in at the door of an old hotel called the Mizpah and saw that the length of the bar, about fifty feet, was packed tightly with battered men and women, elbow to elbow and shoulder to shoulder. (I was awake at that hour because I had been up all night, and so, I presume, had they.) I went in and, since I could find no place at the bar, observed them from one end of the room. I ascertained that they had packed themselves together in that fashion in order not to fall down.

On his very first day in Reno, Liebling met an ex-telegrapher turned judge, who sat on the bench in the morning, in divorce court, and whiled away the afternoon at the Elks Club or the movies. The judge spoke in a sub-Shakespearean rant that any of Liebling's Broadway con men would have admired. He warned Liebling against a visit to Las Vegas, which, he averred, was, in comparison to prim and serious Reno, "all froth, no substance, dust and wind."

Reno was for Liebling what the Abbey of Thélème had been for Rabelais, a utopia of innocent sensuality and well-meant corruption devoted to the systematic suspension of puritanical rules. And wherever he turned he heard the kind of extravagant talk he loved:

> It was at the Toscano Cafe and Hotel, on Lake Street, that I heard an Italian rancher, in town for the day, say, "I want a filet mignon with very mushroom. Very, very mushroom." All the juices of beef were

in his voice, and the filet sounded better than anything I have ever tasted. It was at another Lake Street place that a tall girl a bit worn at the edges entered with a farmerish-looking man and, leaving him at the door end of the bar, came over to a group I was with, placed her hands on the shoulders of two of the women in it, strangers to her, and said, "I must love that man. He gave me two dollars and I put twenty cents in the juke box because I feel so good." Reno is a lyrical place.

Liebling and Lucille also killed time gambling and went to the horse races at Ely, Nevada, several times toward the end of August. Finally, on August 31, he divorced Ann, and two days later, on September 2, he and Lucille were married sixteen miles from Reno in Virginia City, Nevada. The ceremony took place in the beer garden of the old town brewery (by then converted to a private residence) under the auspices of a certain Justice Matilda Pollard amid a crowd of local literati led by Lucius Beebe. Joe was forty-three; Luke, as he called her, was thirty-nine.

It must have been a good party, in the phony, old-West, Comstock-lode ghost-town atmosphere of Virginia City. In short order, though, the honeymoon was over. Joe and Luke and Susie settled for the school year in an apartment at 1209 Astor Street on the Near North Side of Chicago. In a matter of weeks, Liebling and *Collier's* soured on each other. Their deal feel apart, and Liebling found himself stuck in Chicago with no job and a wife whose major act for the fall seems to have been to order a fur coat. In his letter to Harold Rosenwald at New Year's, Liebling said that Lucille was "slinking around the Gold Coast like a Nordic Mata Hari, impressing all the tradesmen into raising their prices." He added, "But I love her." He was, however, even more in love with his stepdaughter. "Susan," he told Rosenwald, "is getting so grownup that I feel self-conscious about goosing her. I think I will follow railroad precedent and treat her as a child until she is 12 (May 2) but she is already bigger (and prettier) than most women."

By December, Liebling had reinstated himself as a *New Yorker* writer, selling Ross two pieces, but he was still bitter and somewhat shaken by his treatment at the hands of *Collier's* management. The only account of this imbroglio is in a letter Liebling wrote to his lawyer, Bill Welling, at the end of the debacle, on November 27, 1949:

Dear Bill,

Re what I told you Friday. When Ruppel and Anthony hired me to do the Time and Tribune series last April, they were lionlike in courage. They were going to do a job on Time, let the chips fall where they may, etc. The whole idea was theirs. Ruppel had his then managing editor Oscar Dystel (since fired by him) call me at the New Yorker and ask me to come to Collier's and talk to Ruppel. Ruppel then broached the Time project. I agreed to do three, or four (if that seemed best as the thing developed) stories on Time, at $2500 each. They were to be my kind of stories. The Time stories were to be done before I left for Europe in the Fall, my then intention.

Two days later Ruppel called and asked me to come up and meet him and Ed Anthony, the publisher of Collier's and an old acquaintance of mine, at the Hotel Winthrop, or Winslow,° at Lexington Avenue and 47th Street. Ed said that he thought I should crown my career as a critic of the press by doing a definitive series on the Chicago Tribune, which after publication in the new Collier's, would make a great book. He wanted at least six installments and thought I might need a full year for the job. (Note on what has happened since: Collier's has been losing money as fast as before Ed took over, and if I turned in a series of six pieces next September 1, the magazine might have no use for them, since it might a. have folded; b. have a new publisher and policy. This is one reason why they want out, I think.)

They pressed me strongly, talked big, poured a lot of drinks. I told them I would give them a decision in a couple of days; we made an appointment for two nights later at the Villa Pensa, an Italian restaurant. At the Pensa I agreed to do the Tribune thing. The agreement we reached is embodied in the contract you drew. As a consequence I gave up my plan for a trip to Europe as correspondent for the New Yorker (last time I did that I made $15,000 in three months).†

I had told Ruppel I could not start on work for Collier's until

° Winslow.

† In the subsequent letter to Harold Rosenwald, Liebling indicates that he had received $18,000 in advance from *Collier's* and would have received another $18,000, for an annual retainer of $36,000, if the deal had not fallen through.

June, and that I would do a couple of stories for the New Yorker during the year to keep on good terms. He agreed, as did Anthony. I went to work on the Time series in June, interviewing around 15 Time and ex-Time men. In July, as you know, I went out to Reno. While out there I saw that I would not be able to get the Time pieces done before Sept. 1, so I wrote to Anthony, saying that the Time project was fully as extensive as the one on the Tribune and would take much more time than we had anticipated.

When Lucille and I came back to New York on Sept. 7, all was still sweetness and light. Ruppel was going to Chicago on a business trip and he found this apartment for us and engaged it on Oct. 8. This should be an indication that they didn't consider the contract breached by my failure to report in Chicago Sept. 1.

I worked on the Time pieces through September and early October, interviewing and researching. By October, there were already hints that they were frightened. Ed said he wanted a funny piece with a light touch. I had announced I wanted to do a whole installment on the way Time contradicted its own correspondents' despatches on China, and generally worked against official American policy there. John Denson, the new managing editor, (an old Ruppel henchman who follows him from job to job) said he didn't think much of that. Ed also said that if we were too hard on Time it would look like sour grapes as we (Collier's) were losing dough, and Time was making it. Said the advertisers would take a poor view of this. (The first time anybody had ever mentioned advertisers in discussing a story with me.)

In the spring, Anthony had told me that Roy Larsen, President of Time, Inc., had twice telephoned to old Winger, President of Crowell-Collier, raising hell about the contemplated series. At the time poor old Ed, still full of bounce, told me that we would go right ahead anyway, not to bother about it. By now the heat was apparently beginning to get through.

I took Luke and Susie to Chicago and established them in the apartment here, then returned for an interview with Luce Oct. 20. After that I holed up in the Hotel Seville and began frantically pounding out copy which it was growing plainer by the minute Collier's didn't really want. . . .

I turned in the first piece Nov. 7, which they considered too hard on Luce. Ruppel said Fortune had written a nice piece about Collier's, so why should we even mention Fortune (Time's running-mate). I asked if he had hired me for a social secretary. They also said I had made too much of Time's unfairness in news stories to Roosevelt. . . . I said I'd try to rewrite the story. . . . Two weeks later I handed in a new version of the first part, in which I relied almost entirely on quotes from Luce and his magazine to make my points. I also turned in a second part. This was on Monday the 21st. Ruppel said he would read them that night.

On Tuesday I could not reach Ruppel; I finally got a message to call him the next day. By that time I had a clear feeling the enterprise was shot. Wednesday I called him and he said to come in. I did and he and Denson met me in his office. He told me they had decided to call the whole thing off, because I hadn't written the kind of story they expected, and had wasted a lot of time (this was not for them to decide, of course) and I had written a book review for the New Yorker!—no reason why I shouldn't have, of course. Ruppel also said he heard I had been talking to Harold Ross on the Pacific Coast (as if I didn't have a right to talk to anybody I pleased) and he could go into the pieces in detail but it would take too much time—so the deal was off. . . .

I wish you'd have a couple of copies made of this curious document, as I may want to read it for amusement some day in the future.

Cordially,

Joe (A. J. Liebling)

Liebling kept what *Collier's* had paid him and returned to the *New Yorker* fold. The Luce/Time, Inc., manuscript must have remained the property of *Collier's*. Liebling did not, at any rate, publish it in any form elsewhere. And over the years, the piece has become a legend, a literary phantom, like one of the unrecorded Sherlock Holmes cases Watson mentions in passing.

In the summer of 1976, a typescript of several fragmentary versions of the so-called "time piece" turned up among Liebling's papers. These shards seem to be various states of the major revision Liebling undertook to mollify *Collier's*. Page after page is filled with barbarous examples of Timeprose, especially the hyphenated epithets the magazine employed to pigeonhole its subjects and to attack people it did not like, people such as Mayor Fiorello La Guardia of New York, who, Liebling showed, was at different moments in 1941 described by *Time* as hen-shaped, bustle-bottomed, duck-bottomed, emitting Donald Duck squawks, steatopygous, rump-sprung, Punchinello, little, bounding and baggy.

During his interview with "Presbyterian-missionary's son, Confucian-minded, didactic," "narrow-eyed" Henry Luce, Liebling "twitted" the "Timogul" about his magazine's epithet tic:

> "There isn't any more of it," said Luce. "I bet you won't find an example of it in the current issue." First thing read aloud by him on picking up Time was "In Bogota's plush-and-gold Colon theatre, 500 blue-ribboned Conservative delegates last week nominated pouchy-eyed Laureano Gomez.
> "Gee," said Luce, "he must be a bad guy."

Among the other passages from *Time* that Liebling selected for his lethal anthology was one that had caught Luce's eye in 1940 and particularly pleased him. It came from a review of the film of John Steinbeck's novel *The Grapes of Wrath*:

> Pinkos who did not bat an eye when the Soviet Government exterminated three million peasants by famine, will go for a good cry over the hardships of the Okies. . . . It is no more important that California deputies kill strikers than that Tom Joad, who is a killer before the picture begins, kills again at the end.

The reviewer was Whittaker Chambers, a leading figure at *Time* until he began his second career, as an ex-communist informer, in early 1949. Liebling dismissed Chambers and his imitators as "windy" mystics in love with "verbal claptrap." In general, Liebling's attack on *Time* was fierce, but the ferocity was tempered with irony. The assault, moreover, was almost entirely a matter of rhetorical criticism, of showing how a corrupt style corrupted the news.

In short, the "time piece" was a longish, seventeen page exercise in technical press criticism, precisely the sort of extended left-liberal argument grounded in the analysis of journalistic minutiae that the *Collier's* editors should have expected from Liebling.

At *The New Yorker*, he received far better treatment. Ross published almost everything Liebling wrote, and he did not change his copy significantly. For example, Liebling's cabled manuscript dated May 4, 1950, for a piece about Las Vegas titled "Action in the Desert" went to press almost word for word as Liebling gave it to Western Union in Chicago.

Aside from some trivial changes in wording and some other adjustments in Liebling's text that appear to have been made to appease *The New Yorker*'s legendary fact checkers, there are only two places where the cable text differs from the published article. One sentence, expanding on the notion that Las Vegas depended on California visitors, was dropped. Liebling had written: "A California license plate is not an object of derision as in northern Nevada, but is noted with the tenderness a rancher reserves for a gravid cow." Did Ross find the comparison far-fetched or possibly too biological? It hardly matters. It could not have mattered much to Liebling at the time, any more than he is likely to have minded losing a dangling and mannered paragraph on the special gambling odds a new casino would give to other casino proprietors on opening day.

Ross generally seems to have treated Liebling's copy with respect. Liebling, for his part, returned the compliment backhandedly in an obituary for Ross. He called Ross a "great editor" because "he knew when to back down." Ross did, however, play an active role in every sentence that went into his magazine. Liebling recalled:

> His great demand was clarity. This is a fine and necessary quality, but you can go just so far with it. You cannot make subtlety or complexity clear to an extraordinarily dull reader, but Ross in editing would make himself *advocatus asinorum*. He would ask scores of marginal questions, including many to which he full well knew the answers, on the off chance that unless all were pre-explained in the text some particularly stupid woman might pick up a *New Yorker* in a dentist's waiting room and be puzzled. Out of the swarm of questions there were always a few that improved the piece—on an average, I should say, about 2¾ per cent, and none that did any harm, because you could ignore the silliest and leave Shawn to talk him out of the rest.

By a lucky chance, all Ross's swarms of questions for all his writers from the spring of 1949 until the spring of 1950 have been preserved, by Miss Eleanor Gould, *The New Yorker*'s redoubtable guardian of diction. These so-called Ross notes do indeed make a fetish of clarity, as collating them with Liebling's pieces amply demonstrates.

In the late winter of 1950, Liebling attended a cockfight in Connecticut (he had evidently absented himself briefly from his exile in Chicago to visit his mother and sister in Norwalk and slipped out of the house to see the fight) with a local doctor and his old crony Fred Schwed, who lived nearby. "Dead Game," though never reprinted, is one of Liebling's outstanding achievements, a cool, precise account of an outlawed, violent sport, probably modeled on Hazlitt's classic personal report of an illegal boxing match, "The Fight." Ross thought the piece was "very interesting and good." But he had more than four pages of single-spaced questions to ask about it (the piece itself ran only to thirteen columns).

He wanted to know:

> Does a cock never quit? Is one cock always killed, i.e., is the fight always to the death? (There is talk of a draw in the fight L. describes in detail, but I don't know whether that was serious or not.) Does a cock ever escape so whole that he lives to fight again?

Liebling had not given his cockfight companions full names in the piece because, he wrote, "it is not very neighborly to use anybody's right name in writing about cockfighting." Ross queried his usage:

> *Neighborly* is a resourceful word, and I hate to have to say think it not very good, because earlier Liebling has indicated he in Conn., only for the weekend, thus pointing he not a neighbor of these people. *prudent, judicious?* Maybe *politic* better than those.

Ross had his way; the final text substituted "politic" for "neighborly." Liebling seems, however, to have won other skirmishes. Ross let him refer to Thucydides (from whom he paraphrased an anecdote about cockfighting repeated in Pierce Egan's *Boxiana*) as "major general, retired," instead of revising the reference to conform with modern military usage: Major General Thucydides (retired). Ross, sensing, for once, the absurdity of the quibble, wrote: "I guess better left as is. for, for one thing, a first name and middle initial would go in there, too; and for another thing, what the hell?"

"Dead Game" may have been improved by Ross's scrutiny, but its basic merits sprang from Liebling's own, Hazlittian flair for reproducing the colloquial, rough good nature of the cockpit. Like Hazlitt in "The Fight," he began his account with a leisurely prologue. He explained how he got to the fight, who was there, packed into the frigid farmhouse cellar, where they came from, what they could expect to win, how they attached the razor-sharp gaffs to the "chickens." Hazlitt's buildup comes to a bloody but clinically observed blow-by-blow finale: "Neate seemed like a lifeless lump of flesh and bone, round which the Gas-man's blows played with the rapidity of electricity or lightning . . . the other returned it with his left at full swing, planted a tremendous blow on his cheek-bone and eyebrow, and made a red ruin of that side of his face."

Liebling, undoubtedly aware of his eminent predecessor in sportswriting (and that "The Fight" had generally been considered to set the standard, since it appeared in 1822, for writing about sporting violence), must have had "The Fight" in his mind as he wrote. At least, it is tempting to speculate that Liebling was "fighting" with Hazlitt, copying his structure, his interest in vernacular speech, and most of all, competing with Hazlitt's famous description of a bloody fight.

After several slashing encounters interrupted by brief periods of respite called "handles," the gray cock Liebling had bet on was blind in both eyes, or as the men in the crowd put it, the animal was doubly "blinked" and had to fight "on the feel." Somehow the gray managed to draw blood:

> The red was blinked now himself; the two cocks had one eye between them. Still, every time they were placed upon their marks after a handle, the blind gray stumbled forward and the one-eyed red sidled up to him and struck, although by now his blows were hardly more than pushes. The gray, sensing the direction from which the hurt came "on the feel," tried to grab the red with his bill, to fix

his target. "Fights smarter than when he had two good eyes," Jimmy
said. Sometimes the gray would get on the red's blind side, and the
obsessed creatures would flutter about, unable to find each other, until one owner called for a count. That meant that the referee would
count to ten while both men picked up their birds and brought them
back to their scratchmarks. Then the referee would count another
ten, during which Coveralls would blow on the back of his bird's
head and massage its thighs, and Budlong would hold a licorice stick
in the red cock's open bill for a second (licorice is supposed to clear a
cock's windpipe), and then blow down his throat. Once, during a
handle, Budlong got a gaff through the ball of his thumb, and his
blood spurted out to mingle with his bird's. After he had set the cock
down for the next go, he backed to the side of the pit and held his
hand out behind him, and a friend spat tobacco juice on the wound,
as a form of antisepsis. Budlong didn't take his eyes off the birds.
Both cocks were now making a rattling noise as they breathed.

"They're dying," my friend Fred said in a tone of astonishment.

"Looks like a good draw," one of the old Irishmen said during a
count. . . . They set the cocks down again right after that—it must
have been for the fortieth or fiftieth time—and the birds tottered out
as usual. Something the red bird did touched off a dormant reserve
of pained energy in the gray. They went at each other as strongly as
they had two-thirds of the way through the fight, when each had
been only two-thirds dead. They fought each other around, without
ever losing contact, until they were up against one of the sideboards.
Then the tormented gray got a billhold, a deadlock on the red's lower mandible, and hit him a great lick, which I didn't see, but which
must have been with his right leg, for the red fell to the gray's left,
with the gray on top of him.

There is a cold, choreographic feeling to "Dead Game," but the
piece forecast warmer work to come, when Liebling would turn to
regular reporting from the prize ring. "Dead Game" was like a brilliant bit of shadow boxing, practice for the real fights, for the live
game of pugilism. Meanwhile, back in Chicago, Liebling was mark-
ing time and getting out of town whenever he could.

He visited Springfield, Illinois, the state capital, to poke about in
the remnants of the Lincoln legend, and produced a mostly forget-
table piece called "Abe Lincoln in Springfield," whose high point is

an anecdote about an old black man who claimed to have slept in a former Lincoln bed. Liebling also traveled to Columbus, Ohio, in May 1950, to watch a group of men prepare a diesel car for the Indianapolis 500 race. Apart from his jaunt to Las Vegas for "Action in the Desert," and the Connecticut trip that led to "Dead Game," these were his only respites from Chicago until the end of Susan Spectorsky's school year allowed him to return with his new wife and stepdaughter to the wonted comforts of Riverside Drive.

While he waited, Liebling wrote several mocking "Wayward Press" articles on Colonel McCormick of the Chicago *Tribune*. This series, which began appearing in *The New Yorker* in January 1950, was, on a smaller scale, the equivalent of the McCormick series Liebling had come to Chicago to write for *Collier's*. It was, if anything, more acerb and damaging than the Luce article that *Collier's* had rejected. Drenched in the bilious sarcasm that Liebling reserved for the subjects he detested most, "Cassandra on Lake Michigan" begins:

> Colonel Robert Rutherford McCormick, crouching behind the Business Gothic battlements of his Tribune Tower, in Chicago, as he awaits an atomic-bomb attack, daily assures Chicagoans that personal violence, national bankruptcy, and extinction by guided missiles are the normal expectation of man in Chicagoland. Chicagoland is the term the *Tribune* uses for most of Illinois and extensive adjoining areas in Indiana and Michigan, to the east; Wisconsin, to the north; and Iowa, to the west. In compensation for the grim fate in store for them, the Colonel offers Chicagolanders a guarantee that life everywhere else is much worse.

It was this boosterism, this Babbittry writ large in banner headlines, that repelled Liebling as he read the insular Chicago press and tried to lead his life as an unhappily transplanted New Yorker. Eventually, back in Manhattan, the boil continued to fester. And with the publication of the three-part series "Second City" in early 1952, Liebling's discontent, which had built up during the 1949–50 exile, poured out in one vindictive spurt. Fair or not, "Second City" is now the fullest record of Liebling's state of mind during his sojourn in the Midwest.

"The Loop," Liebling wrote,

> with its lakeside screen, forms a unit like the Kremlin as described by
> Richard Harding Davis when he attended the coronation of Nicholas
> II, in 1896—a small city surrounded by a boundless agglutination of
> streets, dramshops and low buildings without urban character. The
> Loop is like Times Square and Radio City set down in the middle of
> a vast Canarsie.

Liebling's scorn for Chicago's ugliness, for its provinciality and its
overdeveloped sense of its own inferiority, spilled out in richly
mocking sentences stuffed with eclectic references plucked from
the heights of literature and the depths of popular culture. Colloquial and Latinate at the same time, Liebling growled about Colonel
McCormick's pessimism ("It is a miasmic influence, discernible in
the conviction of every Chicagoan that he is being done") or compared himself, settling down in Chicago with wife and stepdaughter, to "various of Hakluyt's venturers" who arrived in a remote
place, "with women, hens, and demi-culverins, only to perish of
shipwreck, arrows, or malaria."

The Lieblings did not perish; they languished. They lived across
the hall from a chummy woman who suggested they leave the latch
open "so we could wander in and out like one big family." They declined. They also did not much like the Chicago press ("The reader
who stays on Chicago newspapers exclusively for a month [I made
the experiment] feels, on seeing his first *New York Times* or *Herald
Tribune* after the ordeal, like a diver returning to the light"), deplored the city's skimpy literary life ("At every party my wife and I
went to in Chicago, we met Nelson Algren. . . . For a city where, I
am credibly informed, you couldn't throw an egg in 1925 without
braining a great poet, Chicago is hard up for writers") and mar-
veled at Chicagoans' warm nostalgia for the St. Valentine's Day
Massacre of 1929, in which seven gangsters were lined up and shot
by another mob in a garage ("Citizens of a city celebrated in the
movies, [Chicago children] are little Scarfaces as they sit with their
molls in the darkened cinemas and identify themselves with the glo-
rious past"). By the time of Liebling's sojourn there, Chicago no
longer had gang fights. "Chicagoans," he wrote, "are left in the

plight of the Greeks at the beginning of history, when the gods commenced ceasing to manifest themselves."

The Chicago series provoked bags of angry mail. Close readers of Liebling without distracting loyalties to Chicago will, however, detect in the pages of this genial diatribe the first full-scale appearance of the mature Liebling style. The man who had always been a kind of cultural jitney service, bringing together, in his life and his articles, disparate regions of life—boxers and existentialists, con men and cooks and generals—now had begun to write in the same way. His syntax shifted nonchalantly from Augustan to breezy. His allusions ranged from street talk to the classics. It was an aggressively classless, democratic style that preened itself on its lack of respect for distinctions of high and low. Liebling had assimilated the Shakespearean sonorities of Philadelphia Jack O'Brien and the bluff slanginess of that muscular aristocrat Anthony J. Drexel Biddle, Jr. Mark Twain had done something like this, mixing sophisticated thoughts and skills with a wisecracking country manner. The newspaper columnists Liebling had read all his life—F.P.A., Ernie Pyle, Ring Lardner—had also cultivated an informal, purposely jumbled style. Their basic mode was unabashed bathos.

In traditional rhetoric, with its clearly demarcated categories of high and low, bathos is always an asethetic failure. Bathos, according to J. A. Cuddon's *A Dictionary of Literary Terms*, "is achieved when a writer, striving at the sublime, overreaches himself and topples into the absurd." Cuddon quotes Pope's mockingly bathetic passage:

> Ye Gods! annihilate but Space and Time
> And make two lovers happy.

Bathos in American hands was not a mistake but an expression of the national personality. Thoreau could delineate his household accounts in full-throated Latinity. Twain couched a great social novel in the illiterate parlance of a country boy. Liebling, in Chicago, exploited the same freedom, but he was Twain's mirror image. He was a city slicker plunked down in the boondocks, and, within that role, he was an educated middle-class writer-artist who affected the speech and outlook of an urban street person, a telephone booth Indian. Liebling described his report from Chicago in a slangy boast that embodied bathos, in its style and its claim:

> So this isn't a between-trains job. I gathered a lot of material which I discarded; the report is packed down rather than built up, and I think it is exact, in the same sense as El Greco's picture of Toledo, not the one in Ohio. The suppressed detail would, if retained, merely have messed things up.

No one can say whether or not the flowering of Liebling's mature style owed its appearance in the early fifties to specific events and changes in his personal life. It is, however, reasonable to speculate that in those early, happy days of his second marriage, Liebling found the support that gave him the confidence to speak in his own voice. This is particularly a speculation for the Chicago year, since there is only one surviving witness of consequence and she was, then, only a girl.

Susan Spectorsky was, by her own account, a "serious, quiet and worried" child. Joe Liebling adored her and treated her as if she had been his own daughter. He was her sole support, paid her tuition at the liberal, exclusive Francis Parker School in Chicago, and doted on her faithfully.

> I never doubted for a moment [Miss Spectorsky recalls] that I was fantastically important or that he would do anything I asked for. I was his child. He had odd hours and was home a lot. We took long walks together; he would talk to me about New York City. He told me about Stanford White and the girl in the red velvet swing. We laughed together at the newspaper society pages. He was physically affectionate. I would sit on his lap and punch him. He was good at a German-Jewish accent and used to imitate the kind of person who touches you for punctuation. I was tall enough to kiss him on the cheek, but he used to throw his stomach out so I couldn't reach.
>
> When I was sick with pneumonia in Chicago, he read me all of Sherlock Holmes in an English accent.

Liebling fell easily and often into fond, avuncular relationships with other people's children, buying them gifts, introducing them to his own favorite boyhood writers, telling them stories, roughhousing with them and, in the case of his nephews, showing them a bit of the sporting world and the urban demimonde he knew so well. But Susan was his favorite. Their love survived Liebling's divorce from Lucille, and already in Chicago they had become inseparable. His short story "The Bank Across the Street" is about a former war correspondent and his tall twelve-year-old daughter in Chicago. Little more than an anecdote about cashing a check in a bank where the father wasn't personally known, this story is a tribute to the smiling, innocent daughter, and it idealizes the father's affection for her.

Lucille, on the other hand, crops up in Liebling's Chicago pieces rather neutrally, referred to as "my wife" and functioning only as a kind of faceless companion. Once, he quoted her as an expert on the state of fashion and women's apparel retailing in Chicago. Smart Chicago women insisted they could only dress themselves in New York, which was yet another example of Chicagoans' insecurity about their city. Lucille found plenty of dresses in Chicago, despite her years of residence in New York and her background in modeling.

Together, Liebling and Lucille hit the literary cocktail circuit with regularity, attended various public events and pined for New York. By midsummer, they got their wish. They resettled at 131 Riverside Drive and prepared to make the best out of what the First City and *The New Yorker* might offer.

ten

Sweet Scientist

"Liebling's back, eating crow," said Harold Ross, plainly delighted to have his prodigal son return, but killing no fatted calves to show it.

Liebling had lumbered back to *The New Yorker* resignedly, on the edge of fifty, a failure as a free lance, in debt as always, battling gout with painful regularity. He had wanted to go to Korea to cover the war, but Lucille told him he "had responsibilities." And, he implies in an apparently autobiographical passage in "The Bank Across the Street," Ross thought he was too old to be a war correspondent and wouldn't send him.

Without much real choice, then, Liebling returned to his old job and set out to make the best he could of a familiar predicament.

In the Guys-and-Dolls district of midtown Manhattan, Liebling was a landmark. Disheveled, his navel showing through perpetually unbuttoned shirts, in hand-tailored suits badly cut by a tailor he had "discovered" in the *New Yorker* building, pockets overflowing with clips from the day's papers, Liebling perambulated into lunch at the

Red Devil on Forty-eighth Street like Haroun al-Rashid among the fellahin.

Liebling at lunch was a monument, a local institution. Young journalists would look on from neighboring tables as he indulged his legendary appetite in a series of martinis, in piles of oysters and double portions of lobster fra diavolo and osso buco. Waiters loved him; he tipped with a gambler's largesse. His cronies from *The New Yorker* all remember Liebling's gluttonous performances at various Times Square restaurants of dubious hygiene.

Berton Roueché recalls watching in awe as Liebling ate an entire broiled chicken at the Red Devil. "There weren't any bones left," says Roueché.

When Liebling invited a *New Yorker* writer to lunch, it was a great honor. But there was no snobbishness on Liebling's side. Indeed, he was quicker to invite new people out than many other veteran writers. Ved Mehta remembers that after he had been ignored by everyone else at the magazine ("They probably thought it would be awkward to lunch with a blind person"), Liebling took him to The Lobster. "He was so large it was impossible to walk next to him on the sidewalk. At the restaurant, four men rushed over to lead us to a table. Then I heard him talk about getting five dozen oysters. I was alarmed. I thought he wanted them for us, but he was ordering them for a party. He read me the entire menu. I ordered a hamburger."

As with any heroic encounter, lunch with Liebling was a risk. Often he fell into glum silences or muttered unintelligibly to himself or hummed. Friends bore with these bouts of depression; most of them knew about Ann, and close friends like Joe Mitchell also knew that Liebling had taken his troubles to Leo Stone and various psychotherapists over the years. They were willing to bear with Liebling's silences out of friendship and because they knew that he might just as easily burst into a lunch-long stream of anecdotes and imitations. The greater risk for the more fastidious of Liebling's friends was his affection for greasy spoons. "He loved to go to dumps," says Philip Hamburger, "the greasier the better. There was an awful clam store near the subway at Sixth Avenue and Forty-second Street. Something beckoned him there. I belong to a club called

The Coffee House that has the best home cooking in New York. I took Joe once. He got so outraged at the discreet bourgeois surroundings that he carried it over to the food. 'My God, this is a tearoom,' he told me. 'I'm eating lobsters in a tearoom.'"

Liebling simply refused to join a crowd of *New Yorker* writers at a nearby Stouffer's. He was most at home eating with Joe Mitchell, who understood the complicated importance of gutbucket gluttony in Liebling's life. The two Joes had been stopping at crummy basement Italian restaurants together since the Depression, eating sheeps' heads, down to the eyes. "They were served as a split skull," Mitchell says, "and they were the cheapest thing you could get in those days. It made me think of the scene with the lamb in *Sea and Sardinia*. We felt we were in touch with the preliminaries of eating. Joe ate a lot, but that wasn't his concern with food. He learned about other people by eating their food. He saw the poetry of food and how eating ties together so much meaning."

Food, for Liebling, had, like everything else, a literary significance. It connected him with other bibulous gourmands, such as Rabelais and Stendhal. And gluttony was a consolation for the normal domesticity he'd missed. Mitchell says: "I think if he'd been anchored with a family of his own, with a child, he might have taken care of himself, wouldn't have eaten and drunk so much."

Eventually Liebling was to refine his neo-Rabelaisian zest for heroic dining and heroic diners into a literary gem. *Between Meals* celebrated *gourmandise* as an art and as an attitude toward life, an attitude of rebellion and hedonism. *Between Meals* is Liebling's *apologia pro gula sua,* an apology in Cardinal Newman's and Philip Sidney's sense, not an excuse but a confident defense. But by 1962, when *Between Meals* was published, Liebling had, in effect, destroyed himself with food and drink. Ten years earlier, as he ordered his second brace of pigeons at the Du Midi, the process of gastronomic suicide was still reversible, although the danger was clear.

Dr. Louis Soffer treated Liebling from 1946 until he died. Over the years he watched Liebling's weight go up from 225 to 246, saw his gout advance, treated him for kidney stones, warned him as signs of systemic kidney and heart trouble showed up. Overeating was behind all these problems.

Liebling cheered himself, pulled himself out of his chronic depressions, by eating and drinking and generally plunging himself into the life of a *bon vivant* and sportsman. Crowds, especially at public entertainments of a disreputable cast, exhilarated him. Mitchell recalls that "at the tracks, particularly at Belmont, he would have an extraordinarily good time. He loved the milling around. He would disregard the pain of his feet and go down before every race to look at the horses. He never sat in the grandstand. Crowds at the beach and at boxing matches affected him the same way."

From such heights of good cheer, Liebling could tumble into stony sadness. "He could be so austere and withdrawn, for days," says Mitchell. Food and drink helped him out of these black moods. At the track with the Mitchells, he went through abstruse calculations on oversize paper, picked only losers and spent the ride home sunk in gloom. "He drank an amazing amount of Scotch whisky, leaving the water untouched. Eventually, he began singing 'As I Go Rolling Rolling Home.' At first, he was miserable, but he came through it into jollity."

Whether or not Mitchell is right that Liebling might have escaped such unhappiness and avoided excessive eating and drinking if he had had a child of his own, children did bring out the best in him. Certainly, his longest, best relationship with a woman was the stepfather's role he played with Susan Spectorsky. Liebling's friends' children also received memorable amounts of affectionate attention from him. To Nora Mitchell he was like a friendly uncle who gave her Babar books and rode her around on his bald head. Before she could speak, he tried to teach her her first words, repeating again and again, with a mischievous glint, "Lots and lots of money. Lots and lots of money."

His nephew John Stonehill idolized him. Uncle Abbott took him to the Copa when he was quite young, bought him his first drink and interested him in going to Dartmouth. John's brother, Arthur, was also a Liebling favorite. Uncle Abbott brought him comical but educational Christmas gifts: white mice that danced, when he was four or five; later, he gave him an ant colony housed in a glass case so that the boy could observe the insect community at work and play. When little Art was just beginning to read, Uncle Abbott showered him with books, books Stonehill remembers as too advanced for him. In fourth grade, he was given Du Chaillu's *Country of the Dwarfs* and had to put it aside. His uncle could hardly wait to introduce the boy to the books and the other sides of life he loved himself.

When John Stonehill was only fourteen, he began spending part of his Andover vacations with Uncle Abbott in places few boys his age ever penetrated. Liebling took him to his favorite saloons: to Bleeck's, the newspaperman's bar near the *Herald Tribune;* to Costello's on Third Avenue, where *New Yorker* people hung out, where James Thurber had decorated the walls with whimsical cartoons.

"My brothers and I were his surrogate sons," Stonehill says. "He took me to the track several times. He invited me to parties at his house, where I met the *New Yorker* crowd, people like John Hersey and Bill Shawn, even Felix Frankfurter."

Liebling's frequent forays into avuncular pseudo parenthood were also performances, as genially subversive in their way as his writing. With Art and John and the others, Liebling was posing as a father, but a peculiar kind of father who really used his gifts and his attentions to undermine conventional values. Just as, in his *New Yorker* pieces, Liebling constructed a raffish, anti-bourgeois image for himself and then led highly bourgeois *New Yorker* readers into the lower depths of urban life and left politics, so in his relations with his "foster children" he was an anti-father, a benign corrupter of youth.

Liebling kept his real domestic life, with Lucille, quite separate from the excursions he took into New York's lower depths. When he went barhopping with that ultimate Times Square aborigine, Colonel John R. Stingo, the pseudonymous racing columnist for the New York *Enquirer*, Lucille did not come along. Stingo was seldom invited to visit Liebling's apartment and was not a favorite guest. Lucille was only exposed to Liebling's more presentable friends. Indeed, the Liebling ménage at 131 Riverside was so respectable and lavish, with a daughter in private school and a black cook, that Ross once observed, "Liebling wants to live like a stockbroker, but he won't be one."

As a result, he was always in debt. He had his personal expenses—from restaurants and bars and cabs to gambling debts and the tab for entertaining friends at home—as well as the regular checks to Ann, and the cost of dressing Lucille in the glamorous style on which she insisted. And so, although Liebling earned impressive amounts, he was constantly in a panic over money.

His income is reliably estimated to have ranged from $25,000 in the forties to around $60,000 a year by 1960. But he invariably ended the year owing thousands in taxes, because he refused to pay an estimated tax.

On several occasions, while it was still legally permissible to do so, *The New Yorker* "excused" the debt he owed on his drawing account. The magazine also helped out by sending him abroad for eighteen-month stints so that he could qualify for the $20,000 deduction then allowed by the Internal Revenue Service to taxpayers resident abroad for at least that length of time. All this notwithstanding, Liebling habitually dunned Ross and Shawn for payment almost as soon as they accepted an article. He was almost pathologically suspicious with publishers, and his correspondence with them is an embarrassing mixture of wheedling and accusations of double-dealing. He made a fairly frequent practice of picking up freelance and royalty checks in person.

It is impossible to draw the line here between the effects of real financial desperation and a neurotic inability either to manage money or to trust others in business dealings. His favorite literary masters—Stendhal and Villon and Defoe and Borrow—had all scraped and grubbed for money. Stendhal, as Liebling wrote in a review shortly after the *Collier's* debacle, had taken a diplomatic job to buy the time to write *Lucien Leuwen,* but then couldn't publish the book because it might have cost him the job. It is no doubt excessive to think that Liebling consciously overspent so as to join his models in their Micawberish misery. Rather, as Saul Steinberg says, "A man picks up a model for good reason." Stendhal and the other proto-Lieblings were unimpeachable forerunners. They helped take the curse off Liebling's kited checks and his constant borrowing from one friend to pay off another.

At the center of Liebling's perpetual panic for funds was Lucille.

She held Liebling in thrall, played on his physical passion for her, milked him for the furs and dresses he, with his compulsion to put women on gilded pedestals, could never refuse her. She also milked him for all his growing fame as a *New Yorker* writer was worth. Because of him, her life turned into a literary salon. But then she tired of him.

It is a simple thing to collect low opinions of Lucille Liebling among Joe Liebling's surviving friends. Her swirling entrances must, however, have been memorable, because so many people have remembered them. Tall, dark, "Egyptian," "a narcissist," Lucille played to the tatty clique of *New Yorker* writers and other Liebling friends as if they had been a chic pack of first nighters whom she was compelled to dazzle, but whom, with perverse pride, she also had to snub. Lucille was inevitably, mechanically late. She would sweep into a party an hour after everyone else had arrived. And the act did not end there.

To some extent, Lucille's manner was a pathetic attempt to hold her own in a world where she was intellectually outclassed. Liebling would shower her with gifts, but she didn't want to be treated that way. Instead, she tried to learn French. He would laugh at her mispronunciations, and she countered by making a show of correcting him.

"She would hear Joe talking about books," Mitchell recalls, "and then she would try to convince him that Taylor Caldwell was really a good writer. The poor woman was trying to be a member of the wedding. She had no business giving her opinion, but she couldn't help it. She had to put up with a lot from Joe. Lucille was a kind of victim."

Liebling's patience with such antics eventually wore thin. Mitchell says:

> Lucille identified with Mary Todd Lincoln, who she thought of as a sinned-against woman, a feminist heroine. That drove Joe into paroxysms of rage. "God damn Mary Todd Lincoln," he would say. "Fuck Mary Todd Lincoln." He used to fantasize that Mary Todd Lincoln had run up huge debts, like Lucille, and that if Lincoln hadn't been assassinated, he would have gone to debtor's prison. One night in Costello's, furious at his ragging, she said, "If you mention Mary.

Todd Lincoln again, I'll scream. Please don't." He knew she would. Later they were in a cab, going home; he hopped out of the cab and came back to Costello's, saying that she had enough money to get home and after that he didn't care.

Lucille also did her best to hurt Joe through his widowed mother. Anna Liebling was living in her daughter Norma's house in Norwalk. Lucille couldn't stand her. When she visited her mother-in-law, she managed to be even later than usual to spite the old lady. Worse still, she liked to compare her unfavorably to the mother of her first husband, Stephen Barr. She had Mrs. Barr to dinner, called her "Mummy" and rubbed it in by saying how much more a lady she was than Mrs. Liebling.

As a counterpoise to this indictment of Lucille, there is the friendly testimony of Pierre and Charlotte Guedenet. The two couples became very close and shared restaurant meals once a week, often in the company of Jean Riboud. The Guedenets profess to remember nothing unpleasant or even anecdotal about those constant and apparently banal encounters. A correct diplomatic family, the Guedenets were at the extreme conservative end of Liebling's acquaintance. He introduced them to his other conservative French friend, Riboud, and they, in turn, became good friends. What is particularly interesting about this network of friendships is its relative normality. Two couples and a French businessman met regularly in mediocre restaurants, mostly French, in the theater district. These unremarkable get-togethers were, moreover, the Lieblings' most important joint social activity.

Lucille seems, at least before 1953, to have been quite amenable to spending time with her husband's old and unglamorous friends. She was so pleased with a weekend they spent with Arthur and Ruth Jacobs at their weekend place on the north shore of Long Island that she went right out and located a country house for herself and told Joe to buy it. He himself had toyed with the notion of a country place, because he had enjoyed the fishing and swimming in the Sound at the Jacobses'. But the property Lucille found, in a rural hinterland of East Hampton called The Springs, was really an estate, stretching back a mile from Fireplace Road in a narrow parcel of some thirty acres of meadowland. The main house (there were several buildings) was a smallish white clapboard gem. It came furnished. The price was $16,500. Liebling did not have the money.

He told Berton Rouché about the house, at the Du Midi in early 1952. Rouché said, "I don't think you ought to buy that house."

"I don't think we should either," Liebling agreed. Rouché felt Lucille kicking him under the table.

Ultimately she had her way. Arthur Jacobs was able to arrange a mortgage, for $10,000. He lent Liebling part of the balance, and Harriet Schwed was good for the rest. When closing day rolled around, Joe and Lucille were off on a Caribbean cruise; so Jacobs acted for them, putting the title in Lucille's name but the financial obligation in Joe's.

Liebling soon came to love The Springs. He was awed and just plain pleased to be a man of property. Although he never spent extensive periods of time at the house—Lucille frequently went out by herself, leaving Joe and Susan in the city—he loved to show visitors around the land. He liked to lie on his back in the middle of the fields, relishing his acres. He mowed his lawn and gardened with a little tractor, producing various crops, including okra. His other Springs pastime was cooking lobsters in a big pot. He couldn't stand the idea of plunging them live into boiling water. Instead, he would submerge them in a gallon of white wine at room temperature. He would leave them there long enough for them to get drunk; then he would boil them in the wine. "They died happy," he would say.

The house was several miles out of town. To get there, Liebling, who never learned to drive, made heavy use of the local cab company and became friends with the drivers. From time to time, he even returned to New York City by cab, more than a hundred miles, paying roughly fifty dollars to avoid the slow, jostling Long Island Rail Road. One driver recalls that they always stopped halfway for a feed at a roadside restaurant.

Liebling's appetite and his habitual verve did not flag during the post-Chicago year, even though his marriage to Lucille was in increasingly rocky shape. Susan Spectorsky said: "Things went badly between them all through my high school years. Mother drank too much. She would scream a lot. He didn't scream much. But nobody stood much of a chance against Mother. Vivien Leigh in the movie of *A Streetcar Named Desire* was a replica of her. She was unstable. With someone like that who needs a constant stream of goodies, no one treat, no one person, is ever enough. Eventually, everything palls."

Liebling, for his part, did not give up on the marriage. He wanted it to work, right up to the end. He and Lucille continued to throw big parties, over the Christmas holidays, on Susan's birthdays, and on election day, 1952, when Adlai Stevenson, whom they had met in Illinois and greatly admired, lost to Eisenhower.

Liebling's behavior at these parties ran the gamut from taciturn to uproarious. Sometimes the alcohol completely preempted any kind of dialogue. One night, Liebling started making toasts with akvavit every ten minutes, as if he were a Norwegian laborer. He fell down drunk in the bathroom and was wedged tight between the tub and the toilet. Guests struggled to pry his 250 pounds of dead weight loose and put him to bed.

For the most part, the pressures and pains of his private life did not disrupt Liebling's work at *The New Yorker*. He wrote profusely and better than ever. His spirits were definitely raised in 1952 when he was awarded the Legion of Honor at a ceremony in New York attended by the Guedenets and his family. He wore the rosette proudly from then on, although it seems to have slightly embarrassed him. Several years later, he wrote: "I got a French decoration for the most disappointing of reasons: being a writer—I sometimes take it surreptitiously from its case and stare at it, pretending that I won it by jumping a horse over the bayonets of a British square at Waterloo and, once in, decapitating a Colonel the Honorable Something-or-Other, a Tory back-bencher in the House of Commons."

Still, anyone who knew him well could not fail to notice the unhappiness that enshrouded him, the moodiness, the hilarity that covered desperate feelings.

It was in the early fifties, too, that Liebling and Mitchell went to Providence together to see Ann Liebling. Mitchell recalls:

> She was living in a furnished rooming house. I had come along, because she was paranoid about Joe. She thought he would recommit

her. Anyway, she wouldn't answer the bell. There was no one we could call, because by then she was on the outs with her family. We stopped for a drink and passed through the Weybosset Market, an old-fashioned covered iron arcade. Joe saw a sign for rare ripes. He began to cry. "Rare ripes" is an expression for scallions. It reminded him of the thirties, when restaurants in New York had served radishes and scallions in oval glass bowls. We drank all the way back. He was quite boozed, not maudlin, but he would sob wordlessly.

He never saw Ann again or tried to see her, but she continued to preoccupy him. He always sent her money. She responded with occasional cards, at Christmas usually. Once she sent him a gift, a small piece of jewelry. The day it came, he went to lunch and left it on his desk at *The New Yorker*. When he got back, it was gone. "I don't think I ever saw Joe so disturbed," says Philip Hamburger. "He was absolutely furious with himself."

Mostly, though, what Hamburger and Brendan Gill and other office neighbors of Liebling's saw was a writer enormously delighted with the work that rolled out of his typewriter. Hamburger, for instance, says: "I've never known anyone so pleased with himself as a writer. Most of them here are close to self-extinction. With him, you could tell he was coming to show you a piece because you could hear him chuckle or hum off key. Then he would read something, immobile with self-esteem."

His editor from about 1948 on, Gardner Botsford, also found Liebling to be self-confident and virtually untemperamental:

> He was an absolute professional. I learned the device of editing Joe very quickly. When you had one of his manuscripts, you would never go to Joe and say, "I think it would be better to move paragraph nine higher." He would say, "No, no. It's perfect." Once, I made a change without asking. He didn't say a word. In fact, he generally liked the final result. Often my editorial fiddling around would show him where a hole was and I'd get a couple of extra pages from him.
>
> He was a very fast writer and very untidy. He made corrections on manuscripts with a pencil so blunt it left an illegible half-inch swath. But he was very easy to work with. Once, after I had reduced a "Notes and Comment" piece of his from three pages to twenty

lines, he sent me a note in his terrible handwriting that said: "Thanks for making me sound like a writer."

The New Yorker offered Liebling the consolations of craft, fellowship and even domesticity. His office, more than any of his apartments or the house in The Springs, was his true home. It was an untidy burrow littered with the sources and emblems of his protean concerns. The best description of Liebling's office was put together for his *New Yorker* obituary, in 1963, but that catalogue of clutter he kept around him then gives a roughly accurate sense of what his office must have looked like at any time after the war:

> . . . unsorted, unfiled, within reach, scattered and heaped on his desk, tables, chairs, shelves, and air-conditioner, and, in some cases, hanging at odd angles on his walls, were such items as the latest *Annual Report of the New York Historical Society*, a 1927 biography of Boss Tweed, two lithographs of jockeys, a drawing of Bob Fitzsimmons just after he defeated Jack (Nonpareil) Dempsey for the middleweight championship in 1891, Robert Aron's "Histoire de la Libération de la France," the *American Racing Manual*, a volume on "The Theory and Practice of the Preparation of Malt and Fabrication of Beer," Harold Nicolson's "The Congress of Vienna," a month of issues of the Las Vegas *Sun*, General Freiherr von Bernhardi's "Cavalry in War and Peace," three volumes of Pierce Egan's "Boxiana," the 1955 edition of the *Guide Bleu Algérie-Tunisie*, a Christmas card from "The Officers and Men of the First Infantry Division," the third volume of Stendhal's "Journal," the November 28th edition of the Miami *Labor Tribune* and the collected works of Albert Camus.

All these interests cropped up from year to year in Liebling's *New Yorker* work. But in 1951 he eased off on "The Wayward Press" and turned his mind with special concentration to boxing. Why this shift of focus? Liebling himself wasn't sure. Reflecting on the decision that gave him the chance to be the most literate and analytic ring writer of the century, he wrote:

> It was in June of 1951 that it occurred to me to resume writing boxing pieces. . . . There was no particular reason that I came back to

boxing—"Suddenly it came to me," like the idea to the man in the song who was drinking gin-and-water. It was the way you take a notion that you would like to see an old sweetheart, which is not always the kind of notion to act on.

He may be referring here to the abortive visit to see Ann in Providence. Perhaps, by some complex process of thought, one failed nostalgic impulse inspired another? His actual account was more matter-of-fact:

> I had written a number of long boxing pieces for the *New Yorker* before 1939, but I dropped them, along with the rest of what Harold Ross used to call "low-life," in order to become a war correspondent. Low-life was Ross's word for the kind of subject I did best.
>
> When I came back from the war in 1945 I wasn't ready to write about the Sweet Science, although I continued to see fights and to talk with friends in Scientific circles. I became a critic of the American press, and had quite a lot of fun out of it, but it is a pastime less intellectually rewarding than the study of "milling," because the press is less competitive than the ring. Faced with a rival, an American newspaper will usually offer to buy it. This is sometimes done in Scientific circles, but it is not considered ethical. Besides, the longer I criticized the press, the more it disimproved, as Arthur MacWeeney of the *Irish Independent* would put it.

Liebling did not abandon the press. Actually, he kept up a steady flow of "Wayward Press" pieces until his death, but not so many after 1951 as before. This may help to explain his eccentric view, expressed somewhat later, that "The Rubber-type Army," a gleefully wicked debunking of comically inaccurate newspaper estimates of the size of the Chinese Nationalist Army, was "the apogee of my career as the unheeded Whitey Bimstein of the American press."

The piece came out in April 1951. Two months later, Liebling was sitting at ringside as a fight writer. How fitting, then, if this farewell press piece, or at least the last one published during his main phase of press criticism, had been his best. It wasn't. Although "The Rubber-type Army" is in Liebling's characteristic style—he compares various statements and stories and discovers that the estimates for Chiang Kai-shek's army ran from 800,000 to 15,000—he had done many better pieces for the "Wayward Press" column in the six years since he had ambled into the assignment. Just as casually, now, in the spring of 1951, he jumped from the press back to the prize ring.

Liebling had continued to box, with determination and some alleged skill, until 1946, when his physique no longer could sustain his will to spar. At some point before his retirement from the ring, Liebling put on the gloves with that other literary pugilist, Ernest Hemingway. Or at least that is what Liebling told the trainer Freddie Brown. Brown thinks the two writers did little more than jab at each other for a round or two. Liebling never told him where or when the match took place.

Brown was one of the many "friends in Scientific circles" Liebling had kept up with in the late forties and early fifties. Whitey Bimstein was also one of his mentors. The trainer Ray Arcel was another. After fights, Liebling would go out with them to discuss what had happened, to get the insider's point of view. He was also a regular at the Neutral Corner bar at Fifty-fifth Street and Eighth Avenue, near the old Madison Square Garden. And he spent many an afternoon at Stillman's gym in the same neighborhood, watching the young hopefuls spar and imbibing the atmosphere of the fight world.

Liebling went even further in his informal research into boxing lore and history. He spent time with boxing lowlifes and pugs, with whoever could put him in touch with the dying art of what Pierce Egan had called "milling."

Another *New Yorker* writer, Ed Newhouse, recalls accompanying Liebling on one such "interview":

> After the fight, we took Sam Langford out to eat. He was a black middleweight who had been so good in his day that he fought only heavies. That was before the First World War. We found him in front of the Garden. He was blind and used to stand there with a tin cup. God only knows where he slept, but it was in his clothes. He was so fragrant we had to take him to some dismal place. Joe drew him out about boxing. Langford said, in his addled way: "You got to make him lead. You got to make him lead."
> Joe asked: "What if he won't?"

"You got to run 'im out of the ring."

"What if you can't?"

"You gotta."

"All right, you gotta, but what happens if you try and you can't?"

"Then, it's back to the A & P."

"Why the A & P?"

"You can always get a job loading. The boxes come open. At least you're eating."

Afterward, Liebling said to Newhouse: "Well, we're all pitiful. He's a little more pitiful than you or I. But he's not as pitiful as some of our friends."

With Langford and some of his other Scientific acquaintances, Liebling had dug down as low in the urban status heap as he could. But such "pitiful" derelicts gave him serious matter to report, "intellectually rewarding" information. They gave him the same kind of authority as a ring writer in 1951 that Pierce Egan, another explorer of the fistic underworld, had had in 1812. And Egan was Liebling's model as a boxing writer and man about town. In the introduction to *The Sweet Science,* the collection of his own boxing pieces published in 1956, Liebling wrote:

Egan . . . was the greatest writer about the ring who ever lived. Hazlitt was a dilettante who wrote one fight story. Egan was born probably in 1772, and died, certainly, in 1849. He belonged to London, and no man has ever presented a more enthusiastic picture of all aspects of life except the genteel. He was a hack journalist, a song writer, a conductor of puff-sheets and, I am inclined to suspect, a shakedown man. His work affords internal evidence that he was self-educated; if he wasn't he had certainly found a funny schoolmaster. In 1812 he got out the first paperbound installment of *Boxiana; or Sketches of Ancient and Modern Pugilism; from the days of Broughton and Slack to the Heroes of the Present Milling Era. . . .*

A great charm of *Boxiana* is that it is no mere compilation of synopses of fights. Egan's round-by-round stories, with ringside sidelights and betting fluctuations, are masterpieces of technical reportage, but he also saw the ring as a juicy chunk of English life, in no way separable from the rest. His accounts of the extra-annular lives of the Heroes, coal-heavers, watermen and butchers' boys, are a panorama of low, dirty, happy, brutal, sentimental Regency England that you'll never get from Jane Austen.

Egan suited Liebling perfectly, right down to the fact of his almost total obscurity in modern times. Egan's books are exceedingly rare. He was entirely out of print in Liebling's day and had been for decades, because, as the editor of a selection from *Boxiana* published in 1976 states, "Egan enjoyed a large public in his own day, but with the advent of narrow, mid-Victorian ideas of respectability, his works vanished almost without trace."

To quote Egan thus not only established a precedent for Liebling in his ambition to make literature out of the world of boxing, but it also allowed him to indulge in ironic learned references to a forgotten classic. The mere mention of Egan was a succinct "scholarly" attack on official, scholarly notions of literary value.

Liebling went further. He wrote in a style that was a pastiche of Egan's arch, slangy, orotund prose. This mixture of high and low styles was Egan's trademark, and it became Liebling's. Egan's rhythms and phrases were echoed quite deliberately by Liebling in his boxing columns in *The New Yorker*.

Here is part of Pierce Egan's account of that same historic fight between Tom Hickman, the Gas-light Man, and Bill Neate of Bristol which Hazlitt reported on in his famous "The Fight":

> If the backers of the Gas could not see the improvement of the Bristol hero, Hickman was satisfied that he had a dangerous customer before him, and found that the length of arm possessed by his opponent rendered it highly necessary for him to act with great caution and steadiness, and determined to wait for his opponent; the Gas, in consequence, was compelled to make play, and he planted a sharp hit on Neate's head, and laughing, nodded at him. Encouraged by this success, he was about furiously to repeat the dose, when Neat caught him with his left hand on his nob, which sent the Gas down on his knee; but his courage was so high and good, that he jumped up and renewed the fight like a gamecock, till he was hit down by another tremendous blow. The Bristolians now took a turn with their Chaffers, and the shouting was loud in the extreme. The partisans of the

Gas-light Man were rather on the fret, and several of them had got the uneasiness.

It was that sort of tone that Liebling copied and improved on when he wrote: "Moore, jabbing now with dazing snap, had got Johnson's nose bleeding. It was a wide, flat nose, which bled reluctantly. . . ."

These unstated connections with the rhetoric of Pierce Egan were often accompanied by direct quotations from *Boxiana*. And he completed his *hommage* to the master by treating *New Yorker* readers to long passages of dialogue and narrative drawn from the extra-annular world of Stillman's and the Neutral Corner, in much the same way as Egan had filled his Scientific sketches* with "pageant scenes of trulls and lushes, toffs and toddlers, all setting off for some great public, illegal prizefight." It was this London-life side of Egan's work—his "cockney characters, and his direct quotes of how they talked"—that especially delighted and inspired Liebling. This bawdy, sly demimonde of sluiceries (bars), flash Mollishers (low prostitutes) and blue ruin (gin) was, as Liebling put it, "a gift to Dickens." It was also a gift to Liebling, who found similarly colorful talk in the Neutral Corner.

Liebling also went to Whitey Bimstein, Freddie Brown and the saloon's other ring personalities, looking for general insights, not just guidance about individual fights. Part of the task of being the new Egan was to chronicle the large trends, the grand historical movements in boxing. Liebling used Bimstein's apparently trivial position on the dangers of women for young boxers as, in fact, an overture to a full discussion of the difficulties of training fighters, of seasoning their skills properly in an era of prosperity, compulsory education and television. Liebling's "instructive conversations" with the Scientists at the Neutral taught him that fewer youngsters were any longer hungry enough to start boxing early enough to learn the skills that a great boxer needs. Television undercut the social process of pugilistic education still further. Regular telecasts of important fights distracted fans and dried up their interest in local club fights

* "The Sweet Science" was originally Egan's phrase.

of an inferior technical quality. As the clubs declined and closed, because of this competition from television, boxing's "farm system" began to collapse.

There were also fights to cover. Liebling reported on many, many matches, with a skill at describing the blow-by-blow that has never been surpassed. It would be tedious to synopsize the eighteen chapters of *The Sweet Science*, and it would distort Liebling's purpose to treat these collected articles as if they were simply well-written rundowns on what happened when Rocky Marciano fought Joe Louis or Joey Maxim floored Sugar Ray Robinson. You could find that kind of thing in your daily paper. Liebling, ever the Thucydidean, looked for the motives behind the punches, for the strategies that failed or succeeded; he probed for the fighter's point of view.

Habitually, he began his search for these covert explanations before the fight, in the training camps where the future antagonists were available for inspection. For example, at Pompton Lakes, New Jersey, in 1952, Liebling came upon Sugar Ray playing hearts with his campmates: "He was wearing a green-and-white straw cap and a red-and-white Basque shirt and cinnamon slacks, and he looked as relaxed and confident as a large Siamese tomcat." This composure boded ill for a middleweight about to go against a light heavyweight packing fifteen and a half more pounds of fighting muscle. The painless sparring that Robinson waltzed through that day also helped to explain why he collapsed from exhaustion in the tropical heat that blanketed the ring on the night of the actual fight, and why he could not make a dent in his bulkier opponent's plodding defenses.

Liebling's special brilliance as a boxing writer was his ability to speculate, from the limited evidence at the camps and from his knowledge of the fighters' past performances, on how the fight would go. Even if his guesses were wrong, they gave him a basis, a theory for watching the bout and understanding it. This habit of intellectual prognostication reached its height before the Marciano–Archie Moore fight in 1955. In this instance, Liebling could not visit the training camps, because he was abroad until just before the

fight, but, he wrote, "I knew all the members of both factions." On
the plane home, he tried to "envision the rival patterns of ratiocination":

> I could be sure that Marciano, a kind, quiet, imperturbable fellow,
> would plan to go after Moore and make him fight continuously until
> he tired enough to become an accessible target. After that he would
> expect concussion to accentuate exhaustion and exhaustion to facili-
> tate concussion, until Moore came away from his consciousness, like
> everybody else Rocky had ever fought. He would try to remember to
> minimize damage to himself in the beginning, while there was still
> snap in Moore's arms, because Moore is a sharp puncher. (Like Bill
> Neate of old, Marciano hits at his opponents' arms when he cannot
> hit past them. "In one instance, the arm of Oliver [a Neate adversary]
> received so paralyzing a shock in stopping the blow that it appeared
> almost useless," Egan once wrote.) Charlie Goldman would have in-
> structed Marciano in some rudimentary maneuver to throw Moore's
> first shots off, I felt sure, but after a few minutes Rocky would forget
> it, or Archie would figure it out. But there would always be Freddie
> Brown, the "cut man," in the champion's corner to repair superficial
> damage. One reason Goldman is a great teacher is that he doesn't try
> to teach a boxer more than he can learn. What he had taught Rocky
> in the four years since I had first seen him fight was to shorten the
> arc of most of his blows without losing power thereby, and always to
> follow one hard blow with another—"for insurance"—delivered
> with the other hand, instead of recoiling to watch the victim fall. The
> champion had also gained confidence and presence of mind; he has a
> good fighting head, which is not the same as being a good mechani-
> cal practitioner. "A *boxer* requires a *nob* as well as a statesman does a
> HEAD, coolness and calculation being essential to *second* his efforts,"
> Egan wrote, and the old historiographer was never more correct.
> Rocky was thirty-one, not in the first flush of youth for a boxer, but
> Moore was only a few days short of thirty-nine, so age promised to be
> in the champion's favor if he kept pressing.
>   Moore's strategic problem, I reflected on the plane, offered more
> choices and, as a corollary, infinitely more chances for error. It was
> possible, but not probable, that jabbing and defensive skill would car-
> ry him through fifteen rounds, even on those old legs, but I knew
> that the mere notion of such a *gambade* would revolt Moore. He is

not what Egan would have called a shy fighter. Besides, would Ahab
have been content merely to go the distance with the White Whale?
I felt sure that Archie planned to knock the champion out, so that he
could sign his next batch of letters "The most appreciated and deeply
opulent fighter in the world." I surmised that this project would
prove a mistake, like Mr. Churchill's attempt to take Gallipoli in
1915, but it would be the kind of mistake that would look good in his
memoirs. The basis of what I rightly anticipated would prove a mis-
calculation went back to Archie's academic background. As a young
fighter of conventional tutelage, he must have heard his preceptors
say hundreds of times, "They will all go if you hit them right." If a
fighter did not believe that, he would be in the position of a Euclid-
ian without faith in the hundred-and-eighty-degree triangle. Moore's
strategy, therefore, would be based on working Marciano into a position where he could hit him right. He would not go in and slug with
him, because that would be wasteful, distasteful, and injudicious, but
he might try to cut him up, in an effort to slow him down so he could
hit him right, or else try to hit him right and then cut him up. The
puzzle he reserved for me—and for Marciano—was the tactic by
which he would attempt to attain his strategic objective. In the formation of his views, I believed, Moore would be handicapped, rather
than aided, by his active, skeptical mind. One of the odd things
about Marciano is that he isn't terribly big. It is hard for a man like
Moore, just under six feet tall and weighing about a hundred and
eighty pounds, to imagine that a man approximately the same size
can be immeasurably stronger than he is. This is particularly true
when, like the light-heavyweight champion, he has spent his whole
professional life contending with boxers—some of them considerably
bigger—whose strength has proved so near his own that he could
move their arms and bodies by cunning pressures. The old classicist
would consequently refuse to believe what he was up against.

And so it went. Moore swayed and feinted, even knocked Marciano down once, through superior craft, but the old man was not
strong enough to withstand the champion's hail of punches. He was
knocked out. Liebling's ratiocination had proved more accurate
than Moore's. Liebling had, moreover, entered so completely into
the thoughts and movements of the boxers that, in a sense, he had
made their fight his.

It was almost always Liebling's purpose to play a role of some sort in his pieces, if only as the genially intruding narrative sensibility. But the boxing articles marked a new advance in his steady progress toward the limelight in his own work. He was physically and mentally present at ringside, personally obtrusive as a handicapper but also as a fan who waited for beer or was trampled by hordes of Marciano followers. He made himself into a fixture, a *genius loci*, in the Garden. One read him in *The New Yorker* to share *his* experience of a fight, to savor *his* re-creation of *Boxiana*. None of this "personal journalism" was, however, truly autobiographical. As with his war reportage, Liebling kept his boxing pieces well within the bounds of journalism. They were filled with astute judgments, commentary, personal asides—the author never hides himself—but he is using "Liebling"only as a device.° He is only along for the ride, as a professional observer, not as the reason for the exercise. He tells only enough about himself to carry the boxing commentary forward. Sometimes this self-restraint is obvious and even obtrusive.

For example, in his first year as a ring writer, in early 1952, Liebling wrote a feature about a bantamweight fighter who couldn't find work because of the general decline of the lower weight divisions. The article was not collected for *The Sweet Science*, doubtless because it does not deal with an actual fight. It is also an unremarkable piece, except for its opening two columns, which discuss the phenomenon of Jews in boxing. In Egan's time, there had been only one Jewish boxer, Abraham Belasco. And in the postwar period, when Liebling started writing about boxing in earnest, there were no Jewish fighters at all. This amounted to a notable change in the

° There is an exception to this, one that in fact "proves" or tests the rule. After the Marciano-Moore fight, Liebling stopped for a cup of tea and a sandwich at the 167th Street Cafeteria, near Yankee Stadium, where the match had been. With Proustian care, he records what the place looked like, what he ate, and then tells how an article in the official program, which he read while he "munched" his salmon sandwich on a soft onion roll, reminded him that he had attended the first boxing "show" ever held at Yankee Stadium, in 1923, just after he had been expelled from Dartmouth the second time. He could recall each bout with exactness. He compared it in his mind with the fight he had just seen and concluded that Moore could have beaten any of the big names he had seen as a young man in the same place. This reminiscent and highly personal passage is certainly very close to straightforward autobiography, and its Proustian manner forecasts the full-blown effort at recapturing the past that Liebling had already begun to produce in that same year, *Normandy Revisited*. In the 167th Street Cafeteria digression, he was still, however, nominally responding to a public event.

sociology of the modern prize ring. "There were good Jewish fighters right up through the nineteen-thirties," Liebling wrote, "and in
cities like New York, Philadelphia and Chicago they were among
the best drawing cards." So, too, in late eighteenth-century England, there had been many important Jewish fighters. But "the
first period of Jewish prize-ring glory," Liebling observed, had
come to an abrupt and mysterious end by 1821. By contrast, the
more recent disappearance of Jews from boxing was a simple matter
of economics. Freddie Brown, who was Jewish and had been a boxer before he went into partnership with Whitey Bimstein, also a
Jewish ex-fighter, told Liebling one day at Stillman's: "When the
kids didn't have what to eat, they were glad to fight. Now that any
kid can get a job, they got no ambition."

Prosperity had spoiled Jewish boxing. Jews had abandoned the
ring for jobs, for respectable employment. Liebling did not draw
the parallel, but it must have struck him that in much the same way
his own father had deserted the brawling, gritty life of the Lower
East Side for bourgeois Far Rockaway after he had made a success
in the fur business. By coming back to the city, and to one of its'
least respectable corners, the world of the prize ring, Liebling had
found a symbolic way of bringing his father back to town and of
making amends for his ill-considered departure a half century before. Indeed, all of Joe Liebling's activities as a reporter on the
seamy side of New York can be seen as versions of the life his father
might have lived if he hadn't gone proper. Of all these alternatives,
on Broadway or in the world of sport, boxing was the ideal anti-
bourgeois subculture. It was shrouded in illegality; it was violent in
its essence; all Jews had forsaken it; it recruited only from the desperate poor. But the discerning man saw that, far from being the
squalid and brutal sink of crudity that it appeared, pugilism was an
art with a history. It was, in fact, as Liebling's blow-by-blow analyses demonstrated, a science. The boys at the literary quarterlies
could brandish their dichotomies, but the man of Science understood that meatier intellectual questions lay hidden in the biceps
and brains of "milling coves." To miss or reject the importance of
boxing and newspapers and the other arts and pleasures of the poor
was narrow and wrong-headed. It was as if a doctor confined his at-

tentions to the obvious and superficial circulation of the blood and completely ignored the esoteric and purulent but no less vital meanderings of the lymphatic system.

Because he felt this way, Liebling admired and strove to imitate earlier writers who had also identified with the underside of life. More and more, as time went on, Liebling's sense of himself as the modern Egan or Stendhal grew. He was playing a literary role. Gradually, but unmistakably, his reportage turned into an indirect form of autobiography. His articles became character studies of himself, a writer at work in the demimonde.

Liebling nevertheless hesitated to cross the line into true autobiography. But there came a time, in 1952, when he discovered a way to infuse himself into another man's nature in such a manner that he created an ostensibly real portrait that was in one sense fictional, in another, a retouched composite of two flesh-and-blood men.

The result of this complicated blurring process was the profile of Colonel John R. Stingo, alias James A. Macdonald, as it appeared in various *New Yorker* pieces and, finally, as *The Honest Rainmaker*, a book published in 1953. The real Stingo did write a racing column for the New York *Enquirer*. He did live in the Hotel Dixie, to the west of the *New Yorker* building, down Forty-third Street on the other side of Broadway. And Stingo, by all accounts, did come forth with a fantastically exfoliating sort of speech, when he was "on his magic carpet," floating among the cruddy Times Square bars where Liebling used to meet him. But there was a difference between the natural seediness and extravagance of the real Stingo and the superlatively glib Stingo presented by Liebling.

Stingo died some time ago, but those who are in a position to compare him with his Liebling image all agree that he was mightily improved and inflated with a very special gas in *The Honest Rainmaker*. The jacket blurb concedes that it is difficult to say "how much of the lore recounted in this engaging biography is gospel and how much is unashamedly apocryphal." Perhaps the blurb writer meant to cast doubt only on Stingo's veracity as a source for his own life. But the con game in *The Honest Rainmaker* runs much deeper than that.

Stingo was the last and most elaborately conceived of the many foils Liebling had used over the years to represent himself in print. Like the New York locality mayors, Stingo existed, but Liebling put words and stories in his mouth. Liebling's Stingo was the archetypal lowlife, the chief of the telephone booth Indians. He was the completely unclassifiable, anti-bourgeois hustle artist, sportsman and garrulous, improper denizen of the deepest, darkest recesses of the city's back streets and lowest depths—he was, in short, the converse of all that commanded respect in the suburbs. Stingo was the loose-tongued, swivel-minded, Irish, hard-drinking scapegrace, the omnium-gatherum of all the traits that Liebling admired and aspired to as a writer and a man-in-the-city.

This should not be cause for surprise, since Liebling invented or at least perfected him with all the unscrupulous, joyful mendacity that Stingo himself supposedly applied to his own schemes. Stingo was an early version of the half-fictional picaro so common in the avant-garde fiction of the sixties and seventies. He was also a fantasy self-portrait of Liebling, the complete lowlife, mad carny-barker-cum-prosemaster whom Liebling was in reality too conventional ever to be.

The Honest Rainmaker purports, of course, to be a biography of Colonel Stingo as told to a Boswellian Liebling. The book proceeds or rather it saunters through the man's supposed adventures as a peripatetic journalist and buncombe artist. Laurence Sterne lurks among these meanders, but the tone is all-American. When Stingo describes his life in San Francisco just after the Great Fire, he says:

> It was a life gracious and delightful and not at all sordid. I remember the weekly embarkation of Tessie Wall and her bejeweled girls for the races at Emeryville, across the Bay. It was like a painting by Watteau, or a story by De Mossopont. Tessie had been for years the reigning madame of the city, the arbitrix elegantrium or, as the troubadours would say, the queen of love. She wore so many diamonds she was attractive, in spite of her grenadierian mustachio and not inconsiderable seniority. But the girls were pips.

From Stingo's early days in New Orleans newspapering comes this vignette of that piss-elegant editor Dominick O'Malley:

Mr. O'Malley had abandoned his desk at the usual hour of twelve
and betaken himself for prandial relaxation first to the bar of the St.
Charles Hotel, where he had a threebagger of Sazeracs, then to Hy-
men's bar on Common Street, where he increased his *apéritif* by four
silver gin fizzes and after that over to Farbacher's saloon on Royal
where he had a schooner or two of Boston Club punch. O'Malley was
not of that *sang-pur* elegance which would have got him past the
portal of the august Boston Club, the most revered in New Orleans,
but he had bribed a fancy girl to wheedle the formula from the Boston Club bartender. It consisted of twelve bottles of champagne,
eight bottles of white wine, one and one half bottles raspberry syrup,
one half bottle brandy, one half bottle kirschwasser, one quarter bottle Jamaica rum, one quarter bottle Curacao, two pineapples, two
dozen oranges, two and one half lbs. sugar, seltzer and ice. This was
enough to serve several persons.

When he had finished his preparations bacchanalic he strolled
over to Antoine's, where he had four dozen freshly shucked oysters
without any muck on them, a red snapper flambée in absinthe, a salmis of three woodcock and four snipe, a chateaubriand, *bleu*, six bottles of Bass's ale, and a magnum of La Mission Haut Brion of the
comet year. After that he smoked a made-to-measure cigar, as long
as his arm from the inside of the elbow to the tip of the middle finger, and drank a dipper of Calvados from a cask that had been
brought to Louisiana from Normandy with the first cargo of sparkle-
eyed Cyprians in 1721. Not more than one quart had been drawn
from the cask in any one year since, and it had been carefully replen-
ished each time. Having effectuated the *trou normand*, O'Malley
consumed an *omelette au kirsch* and a small baked Alaska, followed
by a caffé espresso for which he sent the maître d'hôtel to a dive operated by the Maffia. "The hardest thing to get in New Orleans," he
always said, "is a decent cup of coffee." He then started to walk back
toward the office, which was on Camp Street, with some vague notion of pausing on the way to drape a beautiful octoroon's ivory
throat with pearls, and would have arrived at his usual hour, after
half-past four, had he not met with an unforeseen vicissitude.

For all his exuberant ties with Rabelais and the American tall-tale
tellers who were his immediate antecedents, Stingo-Liebling does
not wear well, certainly not at book length. *The Honest Rainmaker*
was, in fact, a popular failure. Stingo has, however, found a circle of

admirers, in excerpt, reprinted in William Cole's anthology, *The Most of A. J. Liebling,* and in a paperback collection of Liebling lowlife pieces called *The Jollity Building.* And in the bathetic sparkle of his gab, his appetites and his manic life, he prefigured Liebling's major works—the gearloose babble of *The Earl of Louisiana,* the gutbusting *haute cuisine* of *Between Meals* and the refracted self-portrait of *Normandy Revisited.*

Stingo-Liebling pointed the way to these later works, but Stingo himself also filled a real niche in Liebling's life, as a crony, someone Liebling authentically liked and cultivated in his nonworking hours. It was in the same spirit of real friendship and as a *flâneur* on the sidewalks of New York that Liebling fell in with Henry Wittenberg.

The two men met in 1949. Wittenberg had won a gold medal as a wrestler, at 191 pounds, in the 1948 Olympics and then joined the New York Police Department. He was a detective assigned to the main office squad at headquarters. Liebling tried to do a profile of him. He followed him around and even moved into his house for a while, to immerse himself in the routine of this voluble Jewish athlete-cop. The piece never ran, because the Police Department insisted on reviewing the text. Liebling tore it up rather than submit to official censorship, but he and Wittenberg became very good friends.

Wittenberg was the living proof that Jews could match anyone else as fighters and tough customers. He was one of the few men Liebling confided in over the years. Outsiders thought he was a kind of bodyguard, Liebling's bulldog, but he played a most sensitive role in Liebling's life, as his leading nonintellectual friend. In addition to his undoubted physical credentials, he was quite intelligent and even had an artistic side. Once, he found a stone, a pebble really, with a pear shape. It reminded him of Liebling, and he painted his picture on it, with the skill of a born caricaturist.

On one occasion, however, Henry Wittenberg did in fact act as Liebling's protector and private policeman. The episode later became Liebling's short story "The Dog in the Millpond" and appeared in *The New Yorker* in late 1954. As fiction it failed, because of the same pathetic character, Allardyce Meacham the feckless ex-foreign correspondent, who stands, weakly, for Liebling in so many of his stories. But both the story and the real anecdote, as recalled by Wittenberg, show Liebling coming ambivalently to terms with his public image as a celebrity writer and Times Square insider.

One afternoon in early 1954, Liebling received a telephone call from a well-known stripper whom he had never met. She couldn't make their date, she said. Liebling asked her, "Who are you trying to reach?"

"Mr. Arthur Liebling," the stripper replied. Liebling hung up. The stripper called back immediately and insisted that she had made a date with Liebling the *New Yorker* writer.

Liebling told her there must have been a mistake and then called Wittenberg, convinced that someone was impersonating him with stripteasers. This was not the first time he had thought so. During World War II, another burlesque queen had met Harold Ross at a party and claimed that Liebling was at work on a profile of her. Liebling was then in London, but when he returned to New York, Ross asked him if he had come home to interview the stripper.

It was impossible to tell how many other strippers the impostor had contacted between the World War II incident and the phone call in 1954. Wittenberg suggested that Liebling trap the man. He told him to tell the stripper to make a date with pseudo-Liebling. "Then we'll nab him," Wittenberg said. "I'll take care of it."

Liebling went ahead and persuaded the stripper to arrange to meet the man at a bar called La Vie en Rose, where Liebling knew the maître d' and was able to involve him in the scheme. And so Wittenberg and the real Joe Liebling were sitting at the bar at nine-thirty when the stripper came in with a man rigged out as an intellectual writer in a sports jacket, crepe soles and horn-rimmed glasses. The maître d' sat them at a table where they were trapped next to a balcony; then he brought over Wittenberg and Liebling, saying: "I'd like you to meet Mr. A. J. Liebling, the *New Yorker* writer."

"Oh, this is Mr. Liebling of *The New Yorker*," said the stripper, playing her part with visible nervousness.

The impostor got up to flee, but Wittenberg pulled out his police badge and made the man show his wallet. He began to cry. The stripper ran away in tears.

"I've had a good time with the girls and I so admired A. J. Liebling," the impostor said.

"Couldn't you have picked Wolcott Gibbs?" asked Liebling, who by then had begun to feel sorry for his would-be double, and angry with Wittenberg for getting too tough with him. The man was completely humiliated, and he had only done it, as the stripper said, "to gain proximity." Eventually Wittenberg gave up pretending he was going to arrest "Arthur" Liebling and let him slink away. Joe Liebling felt guilty about exposing the poor man's fraud, and when Wittenberg later accused him half seriously of exploiting the episode in his short story, he "protested wildly." After a lifetime of glorifying con men, he could take no pleasure in unmasking a harmless faker whose pose was really a compliment to Liebling's own power to convince readers that he was the king of sports and Broadway's favorite writer.

Nevertheless, Liebling resented the notion that he was the sort who spent all his time in nightclubs and consorted habitually with strippers. His "Broadway" was a wider and harder and more interesting turf than that. It took in all of New York that wasn't reputable. It was really a state of mind, a devious conception of life that could thrive almost anywhere among people whose imaginations were not stifled by regular, middle-class paychecks and middle-class notions of propriety. It was, indeed, the discovery that the Broadway mentality could thrive even in the Nevada desert that took him back to the scene of his divorce on several working trips all through the early fifties.

There was even a newspaper in Nevada that came close to Liebling's idea of what a fighting liberal daily ought to be. The Las Vegas *Sun* was published by a Jewish war hero named Hank Greenspun, who had previously been convicted and fined for running guns to the Israelis, thereby violating the United States Neutrality Act. Greenspun distinguished himself further, as an editorialist, by slinging mud at Senator Joseph McCarthy, whom he could vilify with abandon because McCarthy had libeled Greenspun in public as a "confessed communist" and could not, therefore, effectively sue Greenspun for libel. Greenspun's other chief foe was Nevada's own Senator Pat McCarran, the right-wing author of a repressive immigration law.

McCarran, who was additionally a colorful old pol, became the focus of Liebling's investigative energies during the year and a half, beginning in the fall of 1953, that he spent looking into the senator's efforts to thwart the Pi-Ute Indians' campaign to reestablish control over their ancestral lands around Pyramid Lake, north of Reno.

Liebling had stayed at the Pyramid Lake Guest Ranch while waiting for his divorce in the summer of 1949. It was then that he first learned about the Pi-Ute claims. While he was researching the Pi-Ute affair, Liebling stayed again at the Pyramid Lake Guest Ranch, with Lucille, and there stumbled upon a second malignant manifestation of the American way: the organized hunting of wild horses for sale as pet food. By the time he was finished with Nevada, Liebling had written the equivalent of a book on the state, in which he exposed the covert operation of the two great evil forces of American history—the exploitation of nonwhites and the rape of nature and wildlife—in a desert paradise ostensibly devoted to hedonism.

In March 1954, the prologue to this muckraking report from the last frontier appeared in *The New Yorker* as "Out Among the Lamisters." Lamisters was Hank Greenspun's word for the Nevada immigrants, on the lam from other, more restrictive parts of the country. It sets the scene for the two more ambitious series, on mustangs and Indians.

With a slowness of pace almost unknown in journalism, Liebling spent most of the first part of the mustang piece painstakingly sketching in the fine lines of the ironic setting of his antiheroic tale of the new Old West. There is much unpressured elaboration on the mood of Harry Drackert's dude ranch, set in the middle of a Pi-Ute reservation by a desolate lake, of its bar, where workaday Westerners and divorcing tenderfeet met, and in particular there is a vignette of an Italian journalist blundering about in search of the real West and finding only aviator-cowboys who hunted mustangs with a Piper Cub for the benefit of ravenous citydwelling Great Danes.

"The Mustang Buzzers" is almost over before Liebling witnesses the actual chase, with the little plane harrying the terrified horses down out of the mountains into a corral with no exit. When he arrives at the scene of the hunt, Liebling stops his narrative one last time, for a final freeze frame of anti-pastoral, bleak country apparently untroubled by human interloping.

Liebling saw that the drab and empty ecology of Pyramid Lake was its authentic natural setting, and that the mustangs, descendants of stock horses abandoned by failed ranchers, were intruders upon it almost as much as their hunters. This attitude is only implied, never actually stated. But it is clear enough by the time the chase starts so that Liebling escapes any false sentiment when he recounts the capture of a scarred, half-blind stallion, "wide between the eyes, Roman-nosed, and authoritative."

Lucille Liebling hated the hunt and tried to entice the horse to jump the corral gate. For her, mustang buzzing was just plain cruelty to animals, and she blamed the cowboys. Liebling remained ambivalent. He knew that large economic forces lay behind the roundup of the horses, that the cowboys were only agents of pet owners in big cities. And he had looked too closely at the stallion to think of him as an innocent and blameless creature. "I felt a bit blue," he conceded, "but I can't explain why. There was nothing friendly about the old stud." Liebling considered the hunt part of the fundamental savagery of the natural order, in which man played as brutal a part as any other animal. Still, it bothered him. Passing a poisoned coyote on the way back to the ranch, he shrugged: "Everybody has trouble, even in Nevada."

The Pi-Utes around Pyramid Lake were a more glaring case of trouble brought to this parched paradise by immigrants from the master culture. But their trouble was more easily correctible. It was possible for them to regain their ancestral lands if they won their long-standing battle with local white settlers and if they surmounted various legal and political hurdles.

Liebling bird-dogged this cumbersome legal action as it gradually resolved itself in a settlement mostly favorable to the Indians. His chronicle ran to four parts in *The New Yorker*. They formed, in their encyclopedic way, a diary of Liebling's own involvement. "The Lake of the Cui-ui Eaters" was an unusual effort for Liebling. It was egregiously serious and solid. Without being dull, the piece did not cloak its mission in a humorous and genial manner. With the exception of a vignette of the cheerfully villainous Senator McCarran, the piece did not deal with antic con men. The Pi-Utes were real, not telephone booth Indians.

In this mammoth article, Liebling reached out for significance and found it. He continued to write in Shandean digressions and to toy with autobiography, but he held his normal dandyism almost completely in check. This restraint deprives his prose of its customary twinkle. But with "The Mustang Buzzers" and "The Lake of the Cui-ui Eaters" Liebling may have been proving to himself that he could take on subjects of real substance and carry them off without tricks or swagger. Or it may simply be that the seriousness of the material itself overwhelmed his natural impulse to emphasize the raffish side of things. Perhaps, too, the looking-glass world of Nevada, where lowlife was high life, turned Liebling upside down, worked on his perverse nature and spurred him into a rare and uncharacteristic experiment in straightforward reportage. Liebling knew that his Nevada reporting was special. He thought of it as the fulfillment of a pledge to Harold Ross, who had encouraged him to write about the state but had only lived to see Liebling's earlier, slighter pieces out of Reno and Las Vegas in 1950. Ross had, as usual, been right about Liebling. Nevada had brought out the best in him.

Still, as Liebling said, in Nevada everybody has trouble. It was at Pyramid Lake during the mustang hunt that Liebling's marriage to Lucille, a stale business at best by early 1954, started to fall irrevocably apart.

Perhaps Liebling had an inkling of what was to come when he wrote:

" 'And what will happen when the horses are *all* gone?' my wife asked the partners. She thinks Hugh and Bill are darlings, but she wishes they would find a nicer way of making a living, like being outriders at a race track."

Lucille was definitely interested in those cowboys. How far her fascination had taken her at that point is impossible to say, but she was interested. And by the end of the year she knew she didn't want to stay with Joe Liebling anymore. Her daughter Susan was about to go off to Radcliffe in the fall of 1955. For his part, Liebling had agreed, under pressure from taxes and with Lucille's encouragement, to move that spring to Europe, where, the plan was, he would file to *The New Yorker* and simultaneously write a column in London for *The Observer*, then at its zenith under David Astor.

Lucille had no intention of going along. She saw her chance to be free of both her daughter and her husband; and she seized it, surreptitiously. During all the preparations for the move to England, she pretended that she was going. By one account, she did not reveal her true plan until the very last moment, packing her things and Joe's, as if they were going together, but packing them in entirely separate groups of bags, so that when the men came to take the luggage for shipment to Europe, she pointed to her bags and reportedly said, "Don't take those. They stay here."

Even if Lucille showed her hand somewhat earlier, the effect was the same. Lucille stayed in the United States and eventually resettled with one of the mustang buzzers in Nevada. Susan went to Radcliffe. And Joe Liebling flew to England via Glasgow, arriving on April 16, battered and alone.

eleven

Far-Flung Corre- spondent

Below the stinging pain of his involuntary solitude, Liebling felt another ache deep within him as he touched down on a bright April Saturday at Glasgow's Prestwick Airport. Having reached the ambiguous age of fifty, successful but unfulfilled, he had come far enough in his life to see its shape behind him and its impending end ahead. The vision, common to many men in middle age, might not have been sufficiently sobering in itself to have focused his mind on mortality. But Liebling's body had been giving off unmistakable signs of danger.

It did not require a battery of medical tests to suggest that decades of epicurean self-abuse had led to some 250 pounds of lethal obesity, to gout, and to insidious problems with his kidneys, his liver and his heart. But there had been tests, and the results confirmed the worst forebodings of common sense. Joe Liebling, if he was to remain the same Joe Liebling, stuffing himself daily like a Strasbourg goose, was shortening his life with each bite and gulp.

Despite palliative treatment with colchicine, cortisone and Bene-mid, the basic gout problem persisted. By 1953, tophi, the solid concretions of urate of sodium associated with advanced gout, had begun to appear.

"I tried to get him to diet," says his doctor, Louis Soffer, "but he couldn't do it. He was so unhappy with himself and the way he looked. He thought he had so few pleasures in life. He knew he was shortening his life, but had no compelling reason to diet."

Having elected, then, to curtail his days in unrepentant *gourmandise*, Liebling, with a logic both desperate and exultant, turned his mind to his past and became a tourist revisiting the crucial scenes of his own life.

Autobiography had always been his natural mode, but autobiography costumed in irony, disguised as reportage or hinted at in his rummage through history and literature for precursors of himself. From time to time, he did step forth as himself, in the early years, but his major forays into true autobiography then were written as prefaces, to the two collections *Back Where I Came From* and *The Wayward Pressman*, not as journalism for *The New Yorker*. Perhaps he felt freer to show himself when he was the author of a book published wholly under his name, freer than he did when contributing a piece to an inherently collaborative magazine. But the difference of genre can only be a small part of the reason for Liebling's dramatic transition into uncloaked autobiography during the last eight years of his life. Although he continued to write articles in his former manner—"Wayward Press" commentary, boxing reports and several dozen anonymous "Notes and Comment" for "The Talk of the Town"—he gave his major energies, while he still had major energies, which is to say until around 1961, to work that told about himself, openly and, when it was best, in a reminiscent vein, mixed the present with vignettes from his past. Such Proustian attempts to recapture time were a natural extension of similar, if more guarded, previous work, but in those late triumphs of nostalgic self-observation, *Normandy Revisited* and *Between Meals*, Liebling, while never lapsing into blatant confession, did make himself the subject of his journalism more completely than ever before. And in so doing he incidentally justified more than at any other time his tacit claim to be a writer of lasting significance who worked within the confines of factual reportage.

The earliest sign that this new turn had been taken appeared in

The New Yorker of June 18, 1955. The headline read: "REVISITED.
GLASGOW: PEACE HAS DESCENDED." Liebling had returned to Glasgow for the first time since the troop build-up for D-day. He had
first flown into the local airport, Prestwick, two years before that, in
July 1941, on a lend-lease Liberator, protected from the chill of the
unheated bomber by a flying suit that did its job but left him feeling as if he were "traveling inside a mobile cold snap." He recalled,
in the opening to his 1955 piece, that "the food provided for us
froze, and I had to work a ham sandwich inside my flying suit and
thaw it out against my skin before I could bite into it."

Upon landing, as he remembered with great warmth, he felt the
"excitement of transition from a fat, peaceful land to a country ex-
periencing the stimulation of war." The dramatic memory contrast-
ed sadly with the feel of his return to Scotland. Comfort had replaced privation; the thrill was gone, replaced only by the cheap
thrills of an aging, lonely tourist:

> One Saturday morning a few weeks ago, I arrived back at Prestwick
> in weather that reminded me of that long-ago day in July. This time,
> however, I had had a rather different crossing. I had boarded a Scan-
> dinavian airliner at Idlewild at six o'clock the evening before, and
> spent four enjoyable hours over apéritifs and dinner. Alternate
> courses were served by one of the prettiest girls I've ever seen (the
> apéritifs, chiefly champagne, sharpened my perception of this truth),
> and since I had the good fortune to occupy one of the two hindmost
> seats in the plane I could watch her slow and graceful progress down
> the aisle from the forward compartment: soup and a smile to her
> right, left profile and dimple to me; soup and a smile to her left,
> right profile and dimple to me; the uniform taut over one breast and
> then the other as she extended alternate arms with the *consommé
> double*. She was what my friend Colonel John R. Stingo calls a Lis-
> some—remarkably symmetrical. The sunset came up through the
> clouds, giving the impression that we were flying across a brazier.
> We were several miles higher than the Liberator of 1941, but the
> sensation of flight was gone.

Peace had long since descended on Glasgow. Liebling tramped
about the city, but never was able to recapture the bracing gloom he
remembered. Instead, he found full employment and a thriving me-

tropolis. This made him morose. In his hotel, he could have a drink at any hour, and even this normally welcome opportunity—which had not been available in wartime—was cause for melancholy. He wrote: "Imbibition, I discovered, no longer seemed a privilege, and I soon went on up to bed, suspecting that I was growing old."

Entraining for London, cast down but full of plans, Liebling rapidly established himself in the capital in a style most especially his own. He settled into a brick pile of a Victorian hotel called Duke's, which had not yet achieved its present renown as one of the best middle-size hotels in London. Its location, however, on a tiny dead-end street off St. James's, could not have been more swank. He was a short stroll from Piccadilly and an even shorter one from the best and most expensive British restaurant in Britain, Wilton's. But as Michael Davie, Liebling's editor at *The Observer*, has said, Liebling liked the area "not because he thought it a smart quarter but because he thought it was raffish. He believed he could detect, under the surface, the old tradition of gamblers and cock-fighting layabouts."

To some extent, he was able to recreate his life at Fleming's during the blitz. He was thick as thieves with the Duke's staff. When he was writing, he would hole himself up in his room and subsist on his own larder, which in peacetime consisted of canned turtle soup instead of the gulls' eggs of the old days. In place of the blacked-out, black-market eating clubs of the early forties, which had gone the way of New York's speakeasies, Liebling would meet his cronies at a legal but unassuming club called Jack's on Orange Street off the Haymarket. At Jack's he held court among old friends such as St. Clair McKelway and suffered with a somewhat ill grace the adulation of younger journalists like Sheward Hagerty, then a reporter in *Newsweek*'s London bureau.

His old friends also helped him connect with postwar London. The Paniguians offered warm hospitality in town. Mollie Panter-Downes and her husband did their best to interest him in country life at their place in Surrey. Through David Astor, Liebling met the Austrian refugee sculptor Siegfried Charoux and his wife, Margaret, and took to dropping in at their small Kensington flat for one of the extraordinary meals that Siegfried Charoux would cook.

As time went on, Liebling also acquired his own London lowlife coterie. There was a cockney driver who conveyed him to the track in his role as sports analyst for *The Observer*. There were jockeys and messengers and bookies. It was as if he had turned London into a version of that seamy side of New York where he had previously felt most at home. And just as his travels in New York's lower depths had been a complex exercise in filial piety, there was in his London life of the late fifties yet another unavowed attempt to enact the existence his father might have led had he stayed on the Lower East Side of Manhattan. Even Liebling's outwardly most British act carried with it a buried but quite conscious allusion to his father's early business life in New York.

On one of his promenades up St. James's, Liebling bought a bowler hat at Lock's, London's most tradition-encrusted hatter. He perched the stiff black derby on his massive pate and strode off to pick up Mollie Panter-Downes for lunch. "We should never have given up India," he said. Panter-Downes thought the hat (and a black umbrella Liebling had bought at the same time) was just some kind of joke about British dress. But Liebling continued to wear the hat regularly. He even took it with him when he returned to New York and wore it there, drawing stares in the street, which he attributed with a straight face and perhaps even with sincerity to his growing popular fame, not the peculiarity of his headgear. His New York friends dismissed the bowler as a piece of eccentricity and left it at that. But they were wrong. Liebling eventually explained what he was up to in an autobiographical sketch called "A Stranger in New York" which ran in *The New Yorker* in late 1956:

> Not long ago, when I was in London, I bought myself a derby or dicer, a bowler or titfer or *chapeau melon*—in other words, a billy-cock or hard hat, although the shop where I bought it prefers to call it a coke. It was the first I had ever owned, and made me feel full grown for the first time in fifty-one years, because my father, like every other New Yorker of his day, always wore one when I was a boy. All I have to do now is learn to shave with a straight razor on a moving railroad train and I will satisfy my time-obscured image of adulthood.

All this personal hat history notwithstanding, Liebling did undoubtedly also intend to lampoon upper-class British mannerisms when he put a bowler on his lordly dome. He declared himself quite openly as an ironic chronicler of the English upper crust's modes and manners in his very first *Observer* piece, an account of Derby Day at Epsom, in which New York and British racing customs, French and British food, top hats, English prejudice against French horses and Liebling's own previous experiences with all these matters were woven together into a genial, cosmopolitan and apparently haphazard marvel of controlled audacity. "A New Yorker's Derby" was certainly Liebling's best effort for *The Observer*, saying in capsule form all that he thought in essence about the differences between the three countries he knew best and rendering the flavor of the Derby with spectacular concision.° Liebling wrote several more sports pieces for *The Observer* over the next two years, but never with such panache. Even so, British readers must have taken uncommon delight in coming upon daffy Liebling leads like this in their most literate Sunday paper:

> For a number of years now I have been acquainted with an Italian-American linguist and economist, five feet three inches tall, named Bobby Gleason, who manages a Cuban heavyweight boxer, six feet three inches tall, called Nino Valdes, who wears a nineteen collar.

Adequate as such stuff may have been for an audience unaccustomed to vintage Liebling fizz, it was clear even to Michael Davie, whose job it was to go round to Duke's and pull Liebling's copy out of his typewriter, that *The Observer*'s resident American had other, more important things on his mind. "I think," Davie says, "he started writing for us because he thought he could get tickets and access to sporting events that he couldn't get as a *New Yorker* writer."

Liebling was fundamentally distracted by his marital situation. No letters survive from this period, but it is clear from subsequent events and correspondence that he must have been trying to patch things up with Lucille. And at the same time he did his share of

---

°The joy of this piece is in the discovery that all its elements fit together. No excerpt can show this well, and the full text remains in print, in the Cole anthology, pp. 240–243.

pursuing women in London, quite younger women, without, apparently, any success.

Nora Sayre, the daughter of Joel Sayre, a *New Yorker* writer whom Liebling had known, was in London, teaching herself to write, and was amazed to find the proverbially taciturn Liebling eager to expatiate about their craft over heavy French meals:

> "Eat more," he used to croak, beaming across the table. "Have more," as I dove into huge platters of cold salmon or *tournedos* or skate in black butter. He deplored the popular fiction that the young don't need to eat—later, he would be horrified to hear that Jean Stafford sometimes fed herself mustard sandwiches when dining alone—and he used to send me cans of Swiss fondue and lush soups from Fortnum and Mason's: grouse and cockaleekie, lobster bisque and sorrel soup, which arrived like CARE packages in the small dark basement that cost 5 pounds a week and where I first began to write. . . . One day at lunch, while I was examining the earrings and necklace which he had pushed across the table with one finger, he produced a delicate 18th Century enamel brooch: on its painted oval, Jacob was wrestling with the angel. I handed it back to him, but the finger slowly worked it across the table again, and he muttered that it was for me. He'd decided that the angel was a writer and that Jacob was an editor: in this tiny version, the angel was sure to win the struggle. He advised me to always give editors a hard time: "And never spoil them!"

Such encounters over lunch often led to more than avuncular gift-giving and professional advice. As Sayre recalls:

> Lonely in London until he encountered Jean Stafford, Liebling hurled himself impulsively at a number of women: the suddenness of the onslaught in the taxi or on the banquette caught most by surprise. Yet he also hoped for a renewal of his marriage. He told me that his wife had asked for a six months' separation to "think about" resuming their life together. . . . He tried to make a joke of all this, but as he talked, it wasn't funny at all. So he continued to pursue others with a mingling of recklessness and reserve: the abrupt lunge of a man who rather expects to be rejected. Once he made a pass at a

very young Englishwoman whose parents were his close friends. She recoiled with some amazement, since she had known him all her life and had always thought of him as a venerable, cozy uncle. . . . Fearing that she had hurt his feelings, she began to apologize for her involuntary squawk, explaining that to her he seemed like a relative, when he cut her short with a jovial pat on the back and rumbled, "Well, as they say in racing, they can't roll you off the track for trying."

The six months of trial separation passed quickly enough. In addition to the probably minimal amount of time devoted to the half-hearted seduction of girl chums, Liebling made several trips to France, gathering material for *Normandy Revisited*, and writing segments of it which began appearing in *The New Yorker* that fall and continued to come out sporadically over the next two years. The excitement of the project must have been great, but Liebling dropped everything in mid September and flew back to New York on schedule to see Lucille. She had the good grace to meet him at the airport, but she did not want him back. "Let's try another six months apart," she said. And he agreed; it is not recorded with what language or in what temper, but it is obvious that he could no longer have believed too hopefully in the likelihood of a reconciliation. Lucille kept her own course, but it is hard to resist the conclusion, based on her subsequent actions, her dilatory and evasive attitude toward discussing divorce and her pleas for money which plagued Liebling long after their marriage did officially end, that in 1955 Lucille was stringing Liebling along, dangling in front of him the dim prospect of their getting back together so that she could retain a wife's claim on the income he was earning in London while at the same time holding on to her freedom, at a comfortable distance of several thousand miles from the conjugal bed.

Liebling stayed in New York less than two months, during which time he returned to ringside for the Moore-Marciano fight and produced his finest boxing chronicle just in time to include it in his forthcoming collection, *The Sweet Science*. He also published a very long and now largely uninteresting historical reconstruction of a nineteenth-century crime, "The Case of the Scattered Dutchman." And he sold to *Sports Illustrated* a two-part series on Still-man's gym, which he called "The University of Eighth Avenue." In it, he roamed over familiar and delightful territory, revisiting the Neutral Corner and quoting the fistic observations of Whitey Bim-stein, Sam Langford and Pierce Egan. The series is an excellent in-troduction to Liebling's ring writing, but even though it contains fresh material (notably a disquisition on the historical and current role of monkeys as fighters' companions), "The University of Eighth Avenue" recycled and repeated old pieces of business; it was like a survey course of Lieblingisms calculated to popularize a manner al-ready well known to specialists.

Still, it is fine stuff, written while Liebling was under consider-able stress, and it was the last thing he produced before returning to Europe in November on a ship that docked at Le Havre. "The Uni-versity of Eighth Avenue," which ran in *Sports Illustrated* in early December, was, moreover, the last piece Liebling published for four months, an unheard of interval of silence.

He was probably spending his time on *Normandy Revisited*. And he flew back to New York at Christmas for a month. He also spent significant amounts of time traveling with two old buddies, Hracia Paniguian and Jean Riboud.

The trip with Pan was a comic odyssey. The two former journal-ism students had turned into very fat men, and in a foredoomed mood of eagerness to slim themselves, they set out together in mid-winter 1956 for the famous Bircher-Benner fat farm in Switzerland. The scheme was a hilarious failure. Reflecting on it a few years lat-er, Liebling wrote, "No sane man can afford to dispense with debili-tating pleasures." Ascetics, like Hitler, could not be considered sane. The Bircher-Benner, he said, was

> like a mental hospital where, as a result of a mutiny, the inmates had
> taken over from the staff, and now addressed one another as "Doc-
> tor." All the kind, fat, sensible people like me, who longed for some-
> thing decent to eat, were under restraining orders, while the *soi-dis-
> ant* doctors, who were free to eat normally, chose to drink rosehip tea
> and eat muck made of apple cores and wheat germ. They permitted
> us to eat only minuscular quantities of that. The nurses and therapists
> ate in the same ironically denominated *Speise-sal,* and except that

they had larger portions than we, appeared to slop in identical slop. (Once, as a special reward for fortitude, I got three peeled hazel-nuts.)

Sometimes in the evening, Paniguian and Liebling would sneak out of the "ruinously expensive para-Buchenwald" to bolt down a real meal in a restaurant. After two weeks, Liebling fled to France. From Zurich, he called ahead to Suzette Namin, who lived with her husband at the border in Pontarlier. Suzette and Liebling had not seen each other since the liberation, when he had surprised her by coming to her house unannounced in the middle of a blackout. On February 16, 1956, when he came through customs at the Pontarlier railroad station, he tottered into her arms, shaking with flu.

As Mme. Namin remembers it:

"He had a *grippe épouvantable*. I treated him like a little child. I gave him a heating pad for his chills. But then he woke us up in the middle of the night wrapped in another blanket. He had burned up his bedroom with a short circuit—sheets, pillows, and the electric blanket."

The local doctor was appalled at Liebling's condition and con-cluded that he had been starved. He prescribed guinea hen and brook trout and no more than two liters of wine a day until he had begun to mend. Then heavy (!) food would be safe. As a result of this regimen, Liebling left Pontarlier heavier than when he had ar-rived in Switzerland for his *cure*. He got on the train with a crowd of students carrying skis. "He was in his huge derby," said Mme. Namin. "It was the last time I ever saw him."

He seems to have stayed in France for the next month and a half. Probably he returned again to Normandy for more research. He may also have taken some time to review Graham Greene's pre-scient Vietnam novel, *The Quiet American*. At any rate, the review of the book ran in *The New Yorker* on April 7, and was an oddly mistaken critique, full of roundhouse punches at Greene, most of which missed. Liebling had picked up the British edition of the book in the London Airport waiting room and read it on his flight to New York in December 1955. He didn't like it much. He accused Greene of contriving to "make his Quiet American, Pyle, a perfect specimen of a French author's idea of an Englishman," that is, "a naïve chap who speaks bad French, eats tasteless food and is only accidentally and episodically heterosexual." Liebling called Greene a "whodunist." His character, Pyle, was "not a Hemingway hero," but "nearer the grade of Hemingway hero that occurs in unsolicited manuscripts." Behind these ill-tempered snipes was Liebling's outrage, absurdly innocent in retrospect, over the key incident in the plot, when Pyle, an *agent provocateur* attached to the American legation in Saigon, arranges for a bomb to explode on a crowded street during business hours. Liebling refused to believe that the State Department was involved in cloak-and-dagger work. None of the revelations about CIA undercover work in foreign countries had been made in early 1956, and Liebling, still an unreconstructed patriot whose mind was at that time saturated with memories of the holy war he had seen in Normandy, thought Greene had concocted an irresponsible and weightless indictment against the United States. The book was a case of sour grapes. A British author apparently resented passing on world leadership to the Americans. The ill will was understandable. It was "part of the ritual of handing over." But, Liebling concluded, there was a difference "between calling your oversuccessful offshoot a silly ass and accusing him of murder."

Graham Greene was not amused. Several months after the review came out, Nora Sayre was dining at Wilton's with the photographer Walker Evans and witnessed this comic confrontation between author and critic:

> . . . Liebling [seated at a nearby table, alone] sailed blithely into his dinner, unaware that Greene and his companion had frozen on his entrance; they stared furiously at him while whispering with their heads close together. It really did look as though a gangland execution was being planned. (Obviously, Liebling didn't know Greene by sight.) The charade of deathly enmity persisted through several courses, then Liebling joined our table for raspberries and coffee. Then the lethal glares included all three of us. Crowned with the little derby hat he usually wore, Liebling left . . . still innocent of the lurid glances directed at him. . . . As Walker and I strolled up St. James, laughing about the extraordinary pantomime we'd seen, we

suddenly heard heels hitting the pavement hard behind us. Greene and his sinister friend passed us swiftly, then wheeled around to glower at us. All the way up that long street, they followed or flanked us: one would appear scowling in a lighted doorway, then the other would dart ahead of us, then their footsteps would echo loudly at our backs again. . . . When I told Liebling about it the next day, the bulging eyes widened in mild astonishment, then the fat shoulders shook.

In relatively high spirits that spring, Liebling flew, on April 5, from Orly Airport, outside Paris, to Tunisia as the guest of Jean Riboud. Riboud was by then an important figure in the oil business in France. He was making a tour of the newly discovered Saharan oil fields, and he took Liebling along in a chartered plane. The two men stayed together for two weeks and then Liebling remained in Tunisia for another week on his own, immersing himself in the foamy fields and other desert scenery that he had not looked at since the early days of World War II.

Liebling wrote only one piece as a result of this trip, an account of a fight night including a bout between one Bill-Jo Cohen and Emmanuel Martinheira. The piece is full of Liebling touches. He captured the atmosphere of Tunis with quotations from the local press and with bits and pieces of patois and ringside crowd noises. But the high point of this forgotten article was its beginning, an unlikely application of fistic wisdom to the understanding of an art object from antiquity:

> On the floor of the Bardo Museum in Tunis, there is a mosaic picture of a knockdown that took place about 200 A.D. Nat Fleischer's *Ring Record Book* does not go back that far, so it has been impossible for me to date the bout more exactly. The fighter who has been knocked down wears a beard, like Archie Moore, but it is improbable that even Moore was boxing that long ago. The mosaic came from the ruins of Thuburbo Majus, a Roman colony forty miles south of the Carthage-Tunis urban complex. The bearded fellow looks like a smart city fighter who was brought to Thuburbo for a soft touch and then encountered unexpected opposition. No Thuburban sport would have paid for a mosaic of a Thuburban boxer being jolted; the sport was going to look at that mosaic every time he lay down to eat, and he would want it to remind him of a happy occasion. I imagine he

won a bundle of sesterces on the match and commissioned the mosaic to celebrate the coup.

The fellow on the receiving end has an experienced, disillusioned look, like that of a boy who has fought out of town before. The humiliation he has just undergone is the kind of thing that could happen to a visiting boxer in what Whitey Bimstein, a trainer friend of mine, refers to as the State of Cleveland, Ohio. He is older than his beardless opponent, who has nailed him with a right swing to the left temple. Blood is spurting from the point of impact in a long arc of separate drops, represented by red stones, and the swing has carried the local slugger part way around, so that he is looking over his left shoulder. The older fighter is squatting on his hunkers, neither knee quite touching the ground. The punch has dazed him; he has his elbows pulled in tight to his body and his fists in front of him, ready to hit as soon as he can bounce up. There was no count in those days, and it was up to him to resume fighting as soon as possible. It must be difficult to give the effect of motion in a mosaic; in any case, the fight scene has the implausibly static appearance of a picture taken with a high-speed camera.

The mosaic is like some prephotographic press shot taken from ringside. In admiring its accuracy, Liebling pays respect to yet another precursor. And in describing it so well himself, he tacitly competes with the artist in reproducing the knockdown. The piece as a whole is also characteristic of Liebling's manner because it is about lower-class Jews: Whitey Bimstein, Bill-Jo Cohen and Liebling's Tunisian Sancho Panza taxi driver, a young Jew from Nefta who chimes in with his own quite definite opinions as they stand there in the Bardo by the mosaic.

Among Jews who boxed or drove taxis Liebling was in his element, and by this point in his career, he felt free to identify such Jewish subjects explicitly as Jews. His confidence about discussing Jews was growing and would reach its height when he traveled to Jordan the following winter. But the expansive, self-gratifying effect of having written most of his masterpiece—*Normandy Revisited* must almost have been finished by that spring—shows itself in the benign assurance of this throwaway dispatch from Tunisia. At last he was writing the way he had always hoped he would, and it spilled over even into the least significant of his works.

On this same wave of what he might have ironically called *bien-être*, Liebling returned to London and fell deeply in love.

They met in late June or early July on a sort of blind date arranged indirectly by Katharine White. The writer Jean Stafford had come to London for the summer, planning to stay in a service flat in a Belgravia manse at 20 Chesham Place. It looked, she recalled, "like a great big respectable brown German bordello. I'd hired the flat sight unseen. There was a bombsite just behind the building, and the day after I got off the ship, they began working on it with pneumatic drills."

Next Stafford fell ill and didn't think she would get galley corrections on a short story back on time to Mrs. White, her editor at *The New Yorker*. She wrote to explain and also, because she thought she might move out of Chesham Place at the first opportunity, she began using *The New Yorker*'s little London office as a mail drop.

Meanwhile, Katharine White, mother superior to her writers and an exaggeratedly solicitous friend of the sick, wrote Liebling to tell him to look up the ailing Miss Stafford, and when, consequently, Stafford was in the *New Yorker* office picking up letters on a summer day and Liebling phoned from Duke's to check on a piece, he learned that Stafford was there and invited her to tea.

Perhaps Liebling had more than mercy and a favor to Katharine White in mind when he made the invitation. He had been lunging at almost every woman who crossed his path that spring, and this one was being sent along in a weakened state, needing manly support. It is possible also that having read some of Stafford's work, Liebling was curious to meet her, just as he would have been curious to meet any well-known colleague. For her part, Stafford knew quite well whom she was going to meet in the tiny lobby of Duke's:

> I was awfully, awfully timid about it. I'd been reading him for years. We had some booze in the lobby. I was so impressed; he was wonderfully amiable. Mostly we made jokes about the Whites, about her obsession with illness, how people would say Andy had come down with something: "he had a paper clip on his tongue."

If Liebling hadn't known at first (and he must have had at least an inkling), he rapidly understood that the acerb and stunningly lo-

quacious golden girl knocking them back with him in the fastidious
foyer at Duke's was a writer of primary consequence and a woman
who had, at forty-one, escaped, seriously scathed but in one leathery
piece, from exactly those upper reaches of American literary life
which Joe Liebling usually sneered at and claimed to abhor.

Jean Stafford happened to have come from solid western stock.
Her father, John Stafford, happened to have written western novels
under the names Jack Wonder and Ben Delight. But neither her
birth in Los Angeles County, nor her girlhood spent in Colorado,
nor her two degrees from its university in Boulder, could change the
fact that she had gone directly from the Rockies into the arms of
Liebling's *bêtes noires*, the boys from the literary quarterlies. She
had not only written fiction on numerous occasions; she had published it in little magazines. She had even worked for one, *The
Southern Review*. She had consorted freely with New Critics. She
had won two Guggenheim fellowships. And both her former husbands were full-time literary men. But while Liebling might easily
have dismissed Stafford's second spouse, Oliver Jensen, as a writer
and an editor of the second *cru*, and a passing fancy whom she had
divorced after a brief connubial interlude in 1953, he could by no
means so easily overlook her eight years of marriage, from 1940 to
1948, to Robert Lowell.

Lowell was not only a poet but the most celebrated young American poet of the time. He was, in other words, the leading youthful
figure in that corner of the writing world that lay farthest from
Liebling's own turf. The two men could not have been more different. Lowell was a neurasthenic poet; Liebling was a robust reporter
with deep mistrust for aesthetes. Lowell was a Boston Brahmin.
Liebling was the son of a Jewish immigrant. While Liebling was
eating fire patriotically with the First Division, Robert Lowell had
sat in jail as a conscientious objector.

We will never know what Liebling said to himself that summer
on those numerous expeditions he and Stafford made by hired Rolls
to country race tracks—to Lewes and Brighton and Doncaster and
York. Perhaps Jean Stafford had lost some of the ferocity of her
youthful bookish brilliance, which Lowell remembered even twenty
years afterward:

how quivering and fierce we were,
there snowbound together,
simmering like wasps
in our tent of books!

Poor ghost, old love, speak
with your old voice
of flaming insight
that kept us awake all night

Gone, too, were the "Heidelberry braids and Bavarian peasant aprons" Stafford had worn in her artsiest phase, after her year of study in Heidelberg at twenty-one. By 1956, she was drinking too much, much too much, and she was not any longer writing at the peak of her form. She had, in other words, the taint of waif's vulnerability upon her. She needed a friend. She needed money. Liebling had adoration and found the cash, the time and the will to drink with her. She had the spirit to like the scruffy bars and sportsmen he liked. And best of all, she could rant with the moxiest of his lowlife chums. From her ancestors on the Isle of Arran off Scotland she had inherited the wild speech of the Celtic fringe. Jean Stafford fitted into the bluff and gabby cast of Liebling molls and mugs. She had her fancy, Jamesian side, but for Liebling she could whistle a more popular tune, with a rougher tongue. In any case, Stafford had run from Lowell filled with enough revulsion for decayed complexity to last a lifetime. Remembering with vengeful zest Lowell's sad, mad fixation on a distant Jewish forebear, Stafford liked to call Liebling her "first completely Jewish husband."

Liebling could take the joke. He was also confident enough of his own achievement and literary powers that he could fall in love with a woman writer he considered (and was not at all shy about touting to friends as) the best living writer of English. She returned the compliment, accepting him wholeheartedly, and on his own terms, as an important writer whose talents had gone unfairly unnoticed.

Stafford and Liebling were, in short, a match. She was, moreover, tickled to be put on a pedestal, courted with lavish meals and gifts. She liked his old-fashioned style. And for the rest of the summer, this odd but loving middle-aged couple carried on a classic romance. Jean had long since moved into her own room at Duke's, where the staff, dizzily loyal to Liebling, accorded her regal treatment. Still, despite the exhilaration of their fling, Liebling and Stafford reached no understanding and made only jocular plans for the future. Liebling had not yet come to an agreement with Lucille; even at that late date, Stafford recalls, he hoped that Lucille would live with him in England. And, eventually, the summer came to an end. Stafford went home to Westport, Connecticut, wearing suits Liebling had had made for her and full of glamorous memories. Toward the end of the month, Liebling flew to Algeria to cover the guerrilla war of independence, armed with a new portable typewriter, which he used to compose one dispatch to *The New Yorker* and three letters to "Blessed Jean" and "Very nice Jean" from Dwight Eisenhower's old room at the Hotel Saint George in Algiers. They were light, newsy notes, packed with funny vignettes of local folk, like the Dutch geologist he had run across at an oil-drilling camp in the Sahara compiling a dictionary of colloquial French synonyms ("Joyeuses was one of the six he had listed for couilles, and I think it is the nuts"). Once, on September 22, Liebling dropped this breezy, palsy tone, confiding to Stafford at the end of his letter:

> We had a hell of a time at the races and in places, and I'd love to have you in an air-conditioned cabin where we could work out the form together.

Returning to London through Paris, he wrote Stafford again on October 16, this time with open admiration throughout:

> I seem to have held a very great lady in my arms at all those race meetings. It was a very great honor! I've been reading "Children Are Bored on Sundays," and really you are a better writer than almost anybody I know.

He was altogether exultant, having won the equivalent of $175 during three days of "hilarious and successful" racing in Paris. Even a "feverish chill" that had put him to bed just after his arrival in London had not dampened his spirits. He bubbled with plans to frame the racing prints she had left for him, with the desk at Duke's, and reminded her to convey gratitude to Katharine White for bringing them together. After all that, Stafford must have wondered why no more letters came to her from Liebling for almost a month. When he did write, on November 13, it was an odd mixture of *billet-doux* and political infuriation:

Jean Darling,

The Charoux, who have named their kitten Jeanie, for you, are now about to adopt a poodle puppy, which they will name Joe. When I called them on their return to town, a fortnight ago, and was invited for dinner, Charoux demanded: "Is Cheanie in town? We could squeeze her good in." I could squeeze you good in, too.

I haven't written in a while because from October 22, when the French kidnapped those five Algerians, until the evening of Election Day, when Eden called off the Suez thing, I was in a continuous rage. Nobody else here was in a rage about the Arabs, but after the Suez ultimatum on Oct. 31, everybody was fighting mad, on one side or the other. Our kindly placid friends, the Brit people, were split as never since the Spanish War and Munich. The atmosphere twanged like a bowstring and our side won. The Liberal papers and the Observer slugged harder than the official Labour press. David Astor wrote an editorial calling Eden "crooked." Four of the directors of the Observer Trust resigned their well-paid sinecures in protest, and 823 subscribers canceled. But more amazing, Jakey Astor, the M.P. who asked me if I would mind sitting in the same car with a socialist, stood up in the House and defied the Government. After that he returned to White's Club and was called a coward. It had never before occurred to him that he might be, and he was quite put out. I cabled a piece to the New Yorker ending: "M. Lacoste has kidnaped M. Eden." So emotional that I cabled again the next day and told them to spike it and charge it off to therapy. What they thought of that I don't know—it must have cost several hundred dollars. Basically I was right, but the piece as worded would have ended forever the public image of the calm reporter Liebling. It read like a vibraphone. That was before Sir Anthony reneged, and now we must gather the errant sister to our bosoms and pretend it never happened.

And now I am bound to Naples to join up with the U.N. Army,

which sounds like a Children's Crusade. It's the first time there has been an international peace army, though, and I cabled to Bill, along with a message about a piece I had written, that we ought to cover this story unique in history. I got a cable right back saying he thought it was "the story we have been waiting for." And now I'm stuck with it. I don't mind the Naples part, and even going to Port Said with one of the contingents, but I'm *not* going into the Sinai Desert until they build a hotel there. It is my earnest intention to return from this assignment within ten days. I'll miss Pan's return to London, but I'll catch him later, and hear all the news of Tim's and the Cathedral of Advertising. And you. I hear a lot about you in the interim, from Mrs. Charoux, who says she is sure that you and I have gained a great deal from knowing each other and it will some day come out in two great works of art. She is the only German I ever liked for being so German. Also I have commissioned a bookshop Johnny to get me your out-of-print works, and I have read the Catherine Wheel and am now in the Adventure. I like you better and better. How can you stand anybody but me? *Please* write about the London literati and Lewes. Like the girls in your stories, you overrate anybody you are taken with, as for instance me. But I do not overrate people I am taken with, as for instance you. I lean backward, like the Observer, which published a review by Toynbee knocking my book. And I tell you that you're a great woman, and much more of a writer than I am. And don't contradict me, or I'll call you a silly woman.

Love, Joe

The letter brushes over much of what had been disturbing Liebling that November. Soviet troops had just entered Budapest to crush the revolution. Adlai Stevenson had lost the election. Worst of all, *The New Yorker* had refused to send Liebling to Suez. In reply to his cabled request to cover the hostilities, he was told, by return wire, that he must continue his reportage on the Crazy Gang, a four-man team of British music hall comics. Janet Flanner and Mollie Panter-Downes would handle Suez from their respective coigns of vantage in Paris and London.

In a matter of days, however, Liebling was able to escape the frustrating, epicentric political quarreling of London. As a "peace" correspondent, he followed the United Nations peace-keeping force to Naples, its jumping off place for Egypt. Bureaucrats had kept the press off the military transport planes, which Liebling, in a dispatch from Naples filed on November 17, deplored hyperbolically: "This expedition with greater implications than the Trojan War or the Normandy landing carried no Homer or Ernie Pyle. . . ." He did his best to infiltrate the international operation temporarily stalled in crowded barracks at the Naples airport and also managed to get an Egyptian visa for himself. Thinly disguising the fact that he was the Jewish correspondent benefited by this act of pan-Semitic good will, he wrote:

> The good feeling surrounding this operation in Naples has extended at least as far as the Egyptian consulate, where three correspondents applying for visas were required to state their religions. One of the correspondents is a Jew and wrote the fact out, in large, indignant letters, just where he was asked to. The consul gave him his visa anyway. "There are a hundred thousand Jews in Egypt," he said. "Live and let live." It is an unimpeachable sentiment.

On November 18, he wrote to Stafford:

> I wanted very much not to miss the story. The only other time I ever felt myself in a similar jam was when they asked what to put on my dogtags during the war—C, P, or H, for Protestant, Catholic or *Hebrew*, the most insulting word for Jew. If they had had a fourth category, for don't-give-a-damn, 64% of the Army would have chosen it and we wouldn't have had the biggest cemetery in France. But that would have led to an agonizing reappraisal of religion in America. No matter what letter you chose, some brand of eunuch would have the last say over you. It says H on the dogtag, but there was a bitter struggle, because actually I loathe rabbis more than either of the other brands, just as Joe Mitchell loathes preachers the worst, and my wife Ann loathed priests. I wonder how many cross-filings were made on those grounds? Anyway I cheated the unctuous bastards and lived to win the price of three bottles of champagne.
>
> Love,
> Joe

During the next six months, Liebling traveled all over the Middle East, from Cairo to Tel Aviv to Damascus, and finally to Jordan. Reading straight through the ten articles these Levantine wanderings produced, it is not hard to notice that he gradually became more explicit about his personal predicament, as a Jewish journalist covering the Arab-Jewish conflict, often on hostile Arab territory. Indeed, by the time he had returned to London in the summer of 1957, Liebling had decided that his own Judeo-reportorial difficulties were, as one says, the news. This was a radical conclusion toward which he had long been moving. It was radical in the general professional sense; modern American reporters, even Liebling in his most self-observant manner, avoided focusing as exclusively on their routine problems of access to sources and material as Liebling focused on his dogged campaign to gain entry to Jordan in "Along the Visa Via."

Liebling's decision was also radical in the personal sense, because he had never before (except in one sidelong and jocular reference in *The Wayward Pressman*) revealed in print that he was Jewish. He would have defended this, it is certain, by saying that he was Jewish only in the most trivial way, by heredity, not by conviction or practice or training. This attitude definitely lay behind everything he wrote about the Middle East, and it was strengthened by his belief that his role there, more crucially perhaps than in other places he had covered, was to apply objective scrutiny to both sides of a question. Liebling wanted to perform in the classic manner of reporters, to look dispassionately and closely at the sharply polarized claims of Arabs and Israelis, to sift out the cant from both in order to arrive at a working version of the truth.

Liebling's report on Egyptian Jews was, in fact, sympathetic to the deportees and properly skeptical of Egyptian claims that their property would eventually be restored. But he was also very even-handed and betrayed no special bias, except perhaps a predisposition to investigate the "Jewish problem" in Egypt as carefully as possible, without hysterically crying "holocaust" where the term was plainly unjustified. Perhaps seeing dozens of uprooted Jews, in a place where his Jewishness put him at official disadvantage, also had some intangible effect on Liebling's visceral feelings of Jewish identification. But he would probably have denied it. He does not, indeed, seem to have been profoundly affected by Egypt.

After he left Cairo in December, his letters to Stafford from Rome and then London, where he spent the holidays with the Charoux and other old friends, are full of news, but they do not touch on any of Liebling's feelings, except his feelings for Stafford. He missed her enormously and was disturbed to learn from her that she had not been able to work in his absence:

> I want you to write because you're a great woman, and I love what you write, and because you'll never be happy—for more than one afternoon or one night at a time—unless you do yourself justice. I'll not give you up, and I'll combine things to have you together with me as soon as possible, and I'll make love to you as much as I want, which is certainly as much as you'll want, and we'll see wonderful things together and mortise our minds like the rest of us.

He was also concerned about the lapsed marriage he had left behind in New York, and explained to Stafford:

> My own conjugal status is a mystery. Lucille and I are out of touch altogether. She was in Nevada a month ago. Whether she still is I don't know. So I don't write. I haven't anything to say anyway. I suppose she feels the same way.

Loneliness and curiosity quickly persuaded Liebling to make a quick trip back to New York in mid January 1957. He couldn't stay long, because that would have imperiled his twenty-thousand-dollar income tax deduction for residing abroad, but he did manage two weeks. Stafford moved in from Westport and stayed in a sublet apartment in the East Eighties. Liebling maintained himself discreetly at the Fifth Avenue Hotel. Despite such chaste precautions, it was clear to everyone that Stafford was Liebling's "official girl." They were inseparable, and he gave her a Victorian pin of a horse, a memento of their racing days the previous summer.

Nothing marred this Arcadian interlude except one *memento mori* in the form of renal colic. Stafford recalled: "We were drinking brandy Alexanders, when an expression of unbearable pain came over him." He was about to pass a stone. Morphine was administered. It was the first of several such incidents that Stafford would witness. "He would roar like a bull through the house," she said, "and drink quarts and quarts of water to help things along."

Recovered, restored and refinanced (with a contract from Simon & Schuster for *Normandy Revisited*), Liebling flew to London at the beginning of February 1957, stopping only long enough to throw off the effects of jet lag and to "feast discreetly with my friends." By February 10, he was at the Louvois in Paris, looking up people "who told me useful things" and paying homage to the great trotting mare Gélinotte at the Vincennes track. But this was only another short stopover on the way back to the Middle East, where he stayed until summer.

He began his pilgrimage in Israel, arriving on February 14 in Tel Aviv, which he found, "from its navel north like the more respectable reaches of Coney Island. South Tel Aviv and Jaffa, the old Arab city, from which all Arabs have fled, are one reeking ruin. . . . " Jerusalem he liked although he did not feel "the magical mystical mumbojumbolical sensation that the more compulsive Zionists say is in the air there." He was especially put off by the official Saturday sabbath and told Stafford in a letter dated February 23 that it was "more abominable encore than a Philadelphia Sunday." Overall, Liebling's first impression of Israel was negative. "This is an extremely *dull* place," he wrote in a postscript to the same letter (which was signed, "I love you, Poodle," in a playful reference to his canine namesake at the Charoux's in London), "full of earnest, intelligent people acting on premises I rejected when 7½ years old."

The tedium of urban Israel was far surpassed, however, by the enforced monotony he saw the following week during the six days he spent in the internment camps of the Gaza Strip. There, he circulated among 200,000 Palestinian refugees who had been "stranded for eight years, without the slightest idea of how they'll be refloated, without much hope either, I'm afraid," he wrote Stafford on March 5. In the same letter he vented his contempt and anger at the suburban smugness of the Israeli administration that ran the refugee camps:

> Over on the other side of the demarcation line the Jews beetle
> about adjuring the visitor to contemplate the marvels of civiliza-
> tion—real Levittowns and nylon-footed sox knitted in Israel. They
> are just too fucking stupid to understand that their conduct ain't
> kosher.

Writing to Stafford, Liebling could safely let off his rancor against the Israelis, knowing as he did it that his tone and diction were irresponsible and unprintable. Two sentences earlier in the same letter, he warned himself: "It isn't a concentration camp, because there are no tortures, no gas chambers, no true starvation, and I must carefully refrain from saying that it is worse, because that is just rhetoric. I suppose it is like Yaddo° with no release ever."

Liebling followed his own advice. His two pieces on Gaza, both published in March in *The New Yorker*, were sober and factual and even prophetic. He portrayed the desolation and ennui of life in the camps. And he argued that the fate of the Gaza Palestinians was "a possible key to the whole refugee problem of the Middle East" which in turn was the key to the Arab-Israeli struggle. Liebling called for authentic resettlement of refugees in Egypt and Israel. This position was perfectly fair; it called upon each side to open its end of the Gaza Strip and to end its intransigence. But Liebling's unvarnished guide to the Gaza camps won him no friends among dogmatic Zionists. It did, nevertheless, give him a vested interest in the closed borders of the Middle East and the hardships they worked on individuals as well as nations.

Later that month, in his room in the King David Hotel in Jerusalem, Liebling looked out on the old walled city, which was then part of Jordan and completely cut off from Israel. Occasionally, when the wind brought the sound of electronically amplified muezzins from beyond the wall or of antiaircraft fire from the frontier, he mused about this most flagrantly artificial of all Middle Eastern

° The writers' colony at Saratoga Springs, New York.

borders. In his last piece about Israel, he wrote wistfully of the "other" Jerusalem:

> . . . I felt as I used to feel when I inhabited an apartment on Riverside Drive and, from my bed every morning, shot my first look of the day at the houses atop the New Jersey Palisades, across the Hudson. The people who lived in them were abstractions, because there was no way of approaching them more closely without making a ridiculously long detour by way of the George Washington Bridge, a distance of at least ten miles. Between the Old City and me was a barrier three furlongs wide that was more formidable than the Hudson . . . My shortest practicable route to the other side of the garden wall would have led from Jerusalem, Israel, to Cyprus; from Cyprus to Beirut, in Lebanon; from Beirut to Amman, the capital of the Hashemite Kingdom of Jordan; and from Amman to six hundred yards from my bedside—provided I could have got the three sets of visas involved.

"Along the Visa Via" is the story of how Liebling finally did get to the other side of that garden wall. It is also a study in the art of delay, official and personal.

To begin with, Liebling could have got to Jordan faster if he had not lingered for days in Athens, racing and dabbling in local politics, before and after he got his Lebanese visa. But he was in no hurry to get to Beirut (the best place for him to get a Jordanian visa without returning to the United States). And he was in no hurry to come to the ostensible point of his article, which was the rigmarole of equivocation and string-pulling it took for a Jew to get a visa to Jordan. Almost the entire first part of the series elapses before he finally bestirs himself to apply for a visa at the Lebanese consulate in Athens. It could not have been plain laziness that kept him hanging back. He obviously did not like wrestling with the problem of his religious/ethnic identity for the benefit of some hostile functionary.

Still, he put down "Juif" on the application form. It was better than pretending he was Christian, and he wanted the story. But he needn't have bothered. The consul rejected the application. No Jews could travel to Lebanon.

Over coffee, the day after he got the bad news by phone, Liebling tried to think of a persuasive argument that would make the consul change his mind:

> . . . I was an American journalist—not a Catholic, Druse, Jewish, Protestant or Sunni journalist—and had covered a lot of stories of various kinds without giving them a Catholic, Druse, Jewish, Protestant, or Sunni slant.

At the consulate, they were not impressed. They would not let him substitute "American Journalist" for "Juif." But a sympathetic woman clerk came up with the solution. "If you don't believe," she said, "then you have no religion. Put down 'Sans Religion.'"

It worked, and he sailed to Beirut a few days later, passing customs his way, as an agnostic.

Unfortunately, the Jordanians were not as complaisant as the Lebanese. One of them eventually told Liebling: "We are what we are born." He finally conceded, on the first page of the second installment of "Along the Visa Via," that "in that sense I am a Jew." He was willing, under pressure, to acknowledge his heredity, but he would not swear falsely that he was a Christian, and Jordan required an affidavit of membership from a church. For a moment, he wavered:

> I was beginning to think that I was making too much of an issue of the whole thing—after all, a wiser man than I had found Paris worth a Mass—and that I might as well swear to being a cross between a Mormon and a Brahma rooster. . . .

But by that point, Liebling had virtually the entire English-speaking diplomatic community in Beirut working on his behalf. Cables were sent. Ambassadors made phone calls. He sat around his hotel pool imbibing local rumors and waiting. Later, he would describe the Kafkaesque process in dozens of good-natured pages. It was a solid month of hope deferred, of time-marking trips to Damascus and Tripoli. Finally, after interventions at the highest level, the visa came through, with no false claim on it. He had everything his way in the end. He entered Jordan not as a Jew but, following the suggestion of a friendly diplomat, as a "Humanitarian":

> At about four the next afternoon, with the consent of Allah—or, at least, of the government of King Hussein, the direct descendant of His Prophet—I arrived at the airport of Amman, without having had to make oath that I was anything I wasn't.

On June 4, he stood on the Jordanian side of the frontier he had last looked upon two months before from the King David Hotel. But after all the trouble it had taken him to get there, Liebling did not, apparently, find very much to write about in Jordan. The one piece he produced is a somber and unexciting account of a brief visit to a border village, which was mainly enlivened by quotations culled from Herman Melville's Holy Land reportage. Liebling's real energies had been focused so totally on gaining access to Jordan that he seemed to have no vitality left for the actual assignment. On the other hand, his time in Jordan was brief and his mission had never, in itself, been an earth-shaking affair. Only the entrance requirements had turned it into a grand opera and a personal achievement.

Liebling had managed to disclose his Jewishness, and to define it for what it was and wasn't, entirely as part of legitimate journalism that also illuminated both his personal views and the racial politics of the Middle East. By practicing his craft with creative obstinacy, Liebling had triumphed over Arab parochialism and his own reticence. All his cards were on the table. He could go home now, see his girlfriend the writer and get on with the books he had always meant to write.

twelve

Twilight Landscapes

True love does not always move with the speed of romance in novels. Liebling languished for Stafford for several months at Duke's, writing playful letters, working, trying to cajole Lucille into taking the final action that would divorce them in Nevada, where she was a resident. A legal separation had by then been hammered out, in which Lucille agreed to sell back the East Hampton house to Liebling, in effect allowing him to buy it for a second time. He continued to pay for Susan's Radcliffe education, and that summer he got her a job at *The New Yorker*.

He was, in other words, carrying on all the crucial parts of his life, except his work, at long distance, a tax exile winding up his eighteen months of penance in the lonely luxury of St. James's.

Finally, on September 6, 1957, Stafford disembarked at Southampton. Liebling hired his favorite chauffeur and met her at the docks. They spent the fall together in separate rooms at Duke's, passing the time as before with racing and at dinner with the Charoux, the Paniguians and other friends. And when they were ready to

sail home on the *America* in mid November, they knew they would
be staying together permanently in New York. Nevertheless, Liebling continued to put a discreet face on their affair, and in the letter
he wrote the Mitchells on the eve of their departure, he announced
circumspectly: "Jean Stafford is traveling by the same boat—a good
companion."

Even in New York, they maintained a thin fiction of chastity, settling into separate rooms on separate floors of the Fifth Avenue Hotel. Liebling engaged a suite on the sixteenth floor; Stafford took up
nominal residence in a room on the sixth. And there they stayed for
more than a year, while Lucille refused to be divorced. Even after
the decree finally came through, it took them, Joe and Jean, a while
to get around to making their match official. "We kept getting too
busy to get married," said Stafford.

They were busy, yes, with plenty of dining out and meeting each
other's friends. Their work, on the other hand, dwindled to almost
nothing. Liebling worried when he saw Stafford withdraw into domesticity. He, meanwhile, published nothing in *The New Yorker*
between his arrival on November 20, 1957, and March 8, 1958,
when he reviewed Jean-Jacques Servan-Schreiber's book about his
military experiences in Algeria. For the next thirteen months, Liebling's output consisted of two more book reviews, thirty-nine "Notes
and Comment" pieces, five articles (of which only one, the "Visa
Via" series, was of any real importance, and it was a holdover from
work done a year earlier) and an obituary for Harold Ross written
in 1959.

In other words, Liebling filled more than a year with a string of
anonymous editorials and little else. His "Notes and Comment"
pieces were by no means despicable efforts. They ranged from the
(supposed) upswing in public kissing to Mideast politics to the in-
congruous rectilinearity of some new carpentry that had been added to his otherwise sagging house in The Springs. He quoted Siegfried Charoux *in extenso* on the philistine reaction to his statue of
Richard Strauss when it was installed in Vienna. Sometimes Liebling transformed "The Talk of the Town" into a forum for press
criticism. On July 5, 1958, he spoke out against the "long, Snopesian
wrangle" over the secondary-school careers of seven Negro adoles-

cents in Little Rock, and joined Harry Ashmore, the executive editor of the *Arkansas Gazette*, in deploring the press's neglect of the Little Rock desegregation story after "federal troops restored a surface order to the troubled city." The *Gazette* had won two Pulitzers for its courageous coverage of the original confrontation between the black students and Arkansas segregationist governor Orval Faubus. It had continued the struggle, but the courts and the federal government seemed to have lost interest in it. "On May 7," Liebling wrote, "the school board petitioned the United States District Court to let it not obey the law for a couple of years, and last week the District Court acceded to the request, leaving the *Gazette* lonely with its honors."

Later that summer, Liebling aimed his old Wayward Pressman's irony at some absurdities of language in the *Herald Tribune*. The style of his unsigned "Notes and Comment" critique was unmistakably Liebling's:

> Spring is for poets. Autumn is for editorial writers—when the nomination pokes its head up through the first ground cover of falling leaves, like *Crocus sativus* (saffron). The editorialist receiving its scent, like a cat sniffing *Nepeta cataria* (catnip), flings himself flat on his back and begins to roll, clawing ecstatically at the surrounding humus. When this happens, the city husbandman needs nor calendar nor almanac to advise him to free his woollen clothes from the cleaner's clinging cellophane casings. We got the message last Tuesday, when we read in the *Herald Tribune* about a great cleansing wind that swept through the Republican convention as it nominated Rockefeller for Governor. "It was the spirit of an army girding for victory," the *Herald Tribune* said. "This groundswell at the grass roots had carried something more than Rockefeller along with it." The description of a barely subcutaneous invasion of land by an oceanic phenomenon disconcerted us at first reading, but then we decided that the leader writer might be from upstate, and might think a ground swell was a variety of earthquake.

If these charming squibs had been the sum total of Liebling's work in the year after his repatriation, they would have been a sign of trouble in a writer previously so prolific, who had just prior to his return looked ready to come forth with some major and very personal work of the highest quality. But this spate of "Notes and Comment" pieces was only an apparent lapse into anonymity and lassitude. Liebling turned to them because they brought quick cash, did not take him away from New York and Jean Stafford, and kept him active while he was plotting and achieving bigger things.

Journalism per se had never been enough for him; he had always pushed against its confinements. In the last six years of his life, he ceased all real pretense at limiting himself to the reporter's genre, to the short article meant primarily for instant publication. He published three books that had originally been conceived as books. Each was serialized in *The New Yorker* before it came out as a book between hard covers, but for the first time in Liebling's career, his work had been planned in book-length units and then cut up into installments for the magazine. He was stepping out on his own at last, making a serious bid for fame and independence.

Unfortunately, Liebling did not become a household word, although he did what he could to gain notoriety. He appeared on television, on news commentary shows that investigated the state of the American press. But Joe Liebling did not have star quality. He tended to mumble. His looks were all wrong for a mass visual medium. His manner was sheepish and bashful.

He did not perform with any greater dash on the lecture platform. On December 11, 1957, he delivered the first of his many campus lectures, at Vassar.

Lamely, lengthily, he rambled on about his inexperience as a public speaker and lecturer. He had tried, he said, to write his speech on the boat from Europe and on the train to Poughkeepsie. "Panic spread" and reminded him of another "Dartmouth nongraduate," who had made a career delivering sermons written by his father. "I had no sermons," Liebling explained. But he did have his favorite books, his own five-foot shelf written by his scapegrace favorites: Borrow, Defoe, Cobbett. So he read from them and from that early nonfiction novel, Joseph Fielding's *Jonathan Wild*.

In print, Liebling was able to speak with far greater assurance, in a voice of his own, which he had developed over many years as a personal variant of the same literary-journalistic models he proposed to his audience at Vassar. The culmination of all this creative imitation and of an entire career of self-conscious literary practice appeared in the fall of 1958. *Normandy Revisited: A Sentimental Journey* was Liebling's masterpiece. The subtitle appears only on the dust cover and may not, therefore, be from Liebling's hand. It does, nevertheless, fittingly allude to Laurence Sterne's *A Sentimental Journey Through France and Italy*, which was one of Liebling's favorite works. Sterne's book covered the same Norman ground and moved with the same maddening slowness that Liebling himself cultivated in *Normandy Revisited*. The perversely digressionary pace was, in any case, a tribute to Sterne's manner and, more generally, it reproduced the feel of all the early books of literary reportage Liebling admired, books in which the difficulty of travel and its slowness created a leisurely setting and a justification for extended authorial observations about the passing scene. Cobbett on horseback, Stendhal and Borrow on foot or in coaches, were forced to move deliberately through exotic countrysides, and as Liebling said in his Vassar lecture, they imparted a similarly deliberate and ruminative "movement" to their narratives and to their prose. Liebling had previously adapted the slow-motion travel adventure to his own purposes, most recently in "Along the Visa Via." For him, it offered the extra advantage of putting the traveler-reporter in the foreground without making him abandon his formal objectivity. If "Liebling" was the subject of the reportage, then Liebling the author could write about "his" perambulations and "his" reactions to "his" new surroundings just as he might discourse objectively on the adventures of any third party he might have encountered on a normal journalistic assignment.

In *Normandy Revisited*, Liebling carried this approach as far as it could go, for he was writing about the phenomenon of "Liebling" in the middle fifties traveling in Normandy in order to compare what he saw then with what he had seen and experienced and been on previous visits, as a student and as a war correspondent. Liebling the author of *Normandy Revisited* was reporting on "Liebling" the aging writer, who in turn was reporting on two earlier "Lieblings."

These epistemological complexities never intrude on the actual experience of reading *Normandy Revisited*, which is so skillfully constructed that Liebling passes from one time frame to another,

and back again, as easily as he makes the round trip between
Bayeux and Port-en-Bessin in a chauffeured Ford Versailles in
1955. Some people have compared this elaborate structure of reminiscence to Marcel Proust's *Remembrance of Things Past*. The intended compliment gives a false sense of the scale and the ambition
of *Normandy Revisited*. Although its subject—the passage of time
filtered through the author's memory and through his changing sensibility—is, in a general sense, the same as Proust's, Liebling's book
confines itself to a limited part of its author's life.

Because of its narrative intricacy, *Normandy Revisited* is not easy
to summarize or to quote from briefly. Its general plan retraces Liebling's progress from Weymouth pier in England just before he
sailed with the invading Allied forces until the liberation of Paris
nearly three months later.

At Weymouth, he looks for the berth of the landing craft that had
taken him to France on D-day. The nostalgia is so strong it makes
Liebling feel frivolous to be retracing his footsteps as a tourist in
happy times:

> . . . If the quay had been rebuilt, as the ganger said, it wouldn't look
> the same anyway. And what was I going to do if I didn't find the
> berth? I asked myself. Put a plaque there like the one on Norfolk
> House? "At this point in space and history 177 (approx. fig.) men
> (among many thousands of others) sweated out the invasion of *Fes-
> tung Europa*, telling what jokes they could think of and playing pok-
> er badly for small sums"; or "Sacred to the memories of Moran,
> Frere, and Simone, whose first names I have forgotten. Moran was
> going to write a book, and Frere had a girl named Hazel." They
> hoisted Frere and Simone, dead, aboard a hospital ship, and when I
> reached up to steady one of the wire baskets, blood poured down in
> my face. I was soaked in blood, and when I washed it off my glasses I
> looked down and saw the stuff on the deck. The soldiers, who messed
> on deck, had left a case of canned milk, and a piece of our shell had
> opened the cans. We walked down to the tomato boat just the same,
> and I said it looked like the place all right, but of course it didn't.

In Normandy, he had himself driven around by a White Russian
chauffeur, Michel, who kept grousing in bad French when Liebling

insisted on leaving the high road of *luxe* tourism to head off into odd corners of the countryside where he had stopped during the invasion. Like his hero Cobbett, Liebling includes enough detail of his itinerary so that a reader could retrace the path of his rural ride through the *bocage normand.* The absurd squabbling between Liebling and Michel fits into the classic tradition of picaresque fiction, of Don Quixote, the wise fool, and his simpler, more mundane attendant, Sancho Panza. Their debates about where to go are not just comic relief but a device for getting the feeling of movement, of covering ground, into the story. When they finally reach a little place like Vouilly, Liebling has spent ten pages creating a geographical mystery about this former site of Allied press operations. The denouement begins with a nostalgic vignette of the town and its surrounding landscape, painted in quietly heroic shades:

> Vouilly is less than a dozen miles inland, but when you get there the sea is forgotten. Bayeux, with its ten thousand inhabitants, seems an incredibly large city in retrospect, and its cathedral, embodying renovations right up through the fifteenth century, is Saarinen compared to the small, unornamented Romanesque church of Vouilly, with its front and rear elevations like equilateral triangles on squares and its tower no higher in proportion than a peaked helmet on a Norman swordsman. The Vouilly church hasn't been changed since the eleventh century. The tower is off to one side of the peaked roof, like a fighter's head tucked in behind his shoulder. It surveys a countryside where the fields are surrounded by ditches and banks of earth, with trees, all ensnarled with vines and bushes, growing out of the tops of the banks—the most ancient of cattle fences. The rain falls most days, the grass grows all through the year, and the cattle turn it into milk. During the fighting in Normandy, the Army Civil Affairs branch tried to evacuate peasants from farms that became battlefields, but they wouldn't go. They said the cows had to be milked. The cattle, in the open all year round, but never out of call of the milkmaid, develop a character that is neither wild, like that of range cattle, nor passive, like the milk factories that spend most of their lives in front of a manger. They are, like the Normans, independent, gluttonous, and indomitable. The Germans defended the hedged fields as fortresses, and the cattle remained in them as audience, chewing the rich grass as the shells burst among them and falling on

their sides like vast milk cans. In the immediate vicinity of Vouilly, however, there had been no fighting.

The description itself was a constant movement—first inland from Bayeux, then up to the Vouilly church steeple, then out over the fields, and in, close enough to the ground to see grass and ditches. The constantly interspersed similes contrast this rural scene with urban settings far away, with Finnish modern architecture and boxers, and with distant rural habitats of other cattle on ranges and in barns. Then the imagery turns local: the Norman cows are like the Norman people. They stood their ground under fire and waited for it to move on. Some died. But none turned into inanimate milk cans at Vouilly, a charmed spot. Liebling, too, had been there, and now he has returned, infused with a complex historical and personal nostalgia:

> We drove between the hedged fields, over the bridge and into the farmyard. Mme. Hamel and her son were sitting under an apple tree, shelling peas. They were surrounded by fat, sleepy hens, among whom walked peacefully a fat, sleepy tomcat. When Michel stopped the Versailles, Madame looked at us, shading her eyes with one strong hand, and called out to her son, "It's he!" She rose—a trifle heavier but even more impressive than I had remembered her—like a great, noble Percheron mare, white with age, getting up in a field, and walked over to the car as I got out. Her son came with her, and as they reached the car, she said to him, "I knew he would come back some day."

Now the memories flow unimpeded, memories of how he and the other war correspondents covering the recapture of of Saint-Lô had bivouacked in the pastoral calm of Mme. Hamel's farm in the summer of 1944. Liebling's slow, meandering progress to this point has invested it with special importance. Unobtrusively, he has *placed* his own unheroic, rear-guard adventures so profoundly in their setting—the bull that charged a jeep, the pigs that ate leftover pancakes and syrup from the correspondents' mess—that they ring, quietly, but with the same vivid sound that Stendhal and Waugh caused to ring in their accounts of war.

Liebling, of course, had seen his war as a reporter, and it is from this special viewpoint that he wrote *Normandy Revisited*, moving with the troops but not, except by tragicomic accident during the helter-skelter race to Paris, at their head, where the shots rang loudly and he turned tail, as discreet as Falstaff, as valorous as Fabrice.

Normandy Revisited sold only 3,500 copies, although the reviews, as usual with Liebling's books, were good. The book also brought him back in touch with Ann. He had mailed her what must have been a set of proofs around Labor Day. She wrote him a ten-page letter, rambling on about best-selling books she had read recently, about the evils of psychiatry, about Liebling's latest articles in *The New Yorker*, and, finally, on page eight, she came to the point:

> I came home the other day after seeing "Cat on a Hot Tin Roof."
> Don't go to many movies but it was good & interesting drama. As I
> came into the hallway I saw a package from the New Yorker up
> over the mail boxes. I wear reading glasses now, and I couldn't
> make the address out. I always get my weekly one from the neigh-
> borhood drugstore & from different news stands so I thought how
> nice, some other tenant besides myself in the Bldg. reads it. As I
> told you I stay pretty much alone and don't know anyone to talk to
> altho I've been here a few years. The package was there a couple
> of days & my curiosity got the better of me & I looked at the ad-
> dress. When I saw it was addressed to me I took it & ran up the
> stairs to what I call my reading room, since I won't allow a T.V. or
> radio in it & opened it, and oh Joe my heart was in my mouth,
> and I was very close to tears in fact the tears came but I pushed
> them back. I have finished it Joe, and its deep sensitivity, and hu-
> mor you must know, struck just the right chord with me. I appreci-
> ate so much Joe you sending it to me, you were always thoughtful.
> Anyway, I guess living alone with much loneliness has its compen-
> sations, because it made me very happy. I used to feel that you
> really didn't want me & in a way didn't need me, some years ago
> & I was always trying to find a way to step aside & become just a
> nonentity or something. I was always proud of you, would fight to
> the death for you and wanted you to become the biggest & the
> bestest writer also a happy one & my wanting you to be happy was

important & I knew a woman like my own sickness & sadness
would have been only a hindrance. The separation has been like
one long ache. Stay tender and lovable Joe & yes when necessary
sassy and all my love—

Ann Liebling

Thanks lots & lots & lots.

From this time on, at widely spaced intervals, Ann and Joe Liebling exchanged letters and greeting cards and gifts. Only her letters
survive, pathetic, saddening reminders of a love that could no longer be. Meanwhile Liebling also continued to hear from Lucille, who
was never ashamed to wheedle some money out of him. She would
call him at the office, even after their divorce and after the March
1959 closing on the Springs house she had sold back to him had severed all their official connections. Once, on a trip back to New York
from Nevada, Lucille cornered Liebling at his favorite bar, Costello's. He continued to send her and Ann money until the end of his
days.

Undaunted by these lingering obligations, Liebling went ahead
and married Jean Stafford on April 3, 1959, in a civil ceremony at
New York's City Hall. Joe and Therese Mitchell were the witnesses.
Afterward they went uptown to Costello's to celebrate, holding a
sort of open house in the saloon's upstairs room. Various *New Yorker*
cronies dropped in; so did Colonel Stingo. "We all got absolutely
stoned," Stafford recalled.

The wedding was merely a formality. Mr. and Mrs. Liebling had
already moved into a spacious apartment at 43 Fifth Avenue, on the
northeast corner of Eleventh Street. The building was a distinguished structure put up in 1904, the year of Liebling's birth. He
and Stafford thought it had been designed by Stanford White (the
actual architect was Henry Anderson), and it made Liebling feel
grand. He used to tell Stafford that he often had the urge to stand
on the balcony and review imaginary troops coming back from the
Civil War. The very idea of doing it made him think he owned
New York.

They entertained frequently, in a lavish, heavy style. His good

New Yorker friend and neighbor at the east end of Long Island, Berton Roueché, remembers a dinner party right after the Lieblings' marriage that began with crab meat and went on to zampone, a kind of rich, fatty Italian sausage.

Stafford, who rarely ate or cooked anything of substance, did not suffer at all in her epicurean household. Everyone had asked her how she dared to marry such a gourmand. But the Lieblings seldom ate at home, and the cooking there was done by a faithful black maid called Madella, whose repertoire was composed mainly of "finger-lickin'-good" dishes. Madella also served Liebling his breakfast when he got up, around nine.

On a typical day, he would work at home until noon and then go off to lunch with Mitchell or McKelway or other cronies at the Red Devil and other favorite haunts near the office. At the end of the day he would call Stafford, and they would meet friends for dinner.

In the summer, they spent large patches of time at the Springs house. Liebling had to keep coming back to town, because he could only work well in the bustle of the city and with other people around him in the *New Yorker* office. "It was a hangover from his newspaper days," Stafford said. "He could only last in The Springs for three weeks at a time. But he rejoiced in owning the land and in gardening. He particularly liked the daisies that used to grow in the third pasture and was very reluctant to let the neighbor farmers plant feed corn there. He agreed because he didn't want to object and sound effete. He loved to lie in those daisies."

In the first summer of his third marriage, Liebling still had his daisies; his career was at its height; his health was stable; he was living in the flamboyant, urbane manner he craved, in an apartment that suited his Balzacian fantasies of success, and he was with a woman who was on his own intellectual level. It was undoubtedly a happy time. Only one thing bothered him. He had married a writer, partly because he admired her work, but she wasn't writing. As Stafford put it: "During our marriage, which was short, I was *extremely* unproductive. It was a source of woe to Joe. I could never figure out why it happened. Perhaps it's too simple an explanation, but I was happy for the first time in my life. He thought that if I wasn't writing, it meant I was unhappy with him." It wasn't so, of course. Stafford was delighted when Liebling dragged her out of her "self-protective and self-destructive shell." He had introduced her to racing and fancy food and taught her to enjoy travel. He got her to dress up for the Metropolitan Opera, where they had a subscription, because, he said, it would make them feel grown up. "His pleasure in everything," she said, "was so contagious you couldn't help having a good time."

And if Stafford did not get much of her own writing done in the midst of so much unaccustomed worldly pleasure, she did lead Liebling to one of his very best subjects. She told him about Earl Long.

"It came about in an interesting way," Stafford recalled many years later, sipping bourbon and milk in the memento-filled parlor of the Springs house. Liebling had once again been squabbling with *The New Yorker* about finances. But this time the quarrel turned serious. Liebling talked to Philip Graham, who had just bought *Newsweek* for the Washington Post Company, and Graham offered him a job. News of the offer got out, and William Shawn decided to try to hold on to his wayward pressman. Stafford explained: "Mr. and Mrs. Shawn came to our house for coffee after dinner. They wouldn't come for a meal, because Shawn was afraid we'd serve sauces or meat, things like that. It was just at that point that Long had begun to get interesting, buying all those canned goods at supermarkets for no reason at all and generally behaving erratically. I started to talk about his high jinks. I'd known about Louisiana politics ever since I'd lived down there. Shawn was interested. He put Joe on the story."

Earl Long was then governor of Louisiana. He had even more peckerwood charisma than his older brother, Huey, whom Liebling had interviewed twice in the thirties (both times the colorful demagogue had received him while reclining in green pajamas in his New York hotel room), before he was assassinated in 1935. But Earl was a survivor, less blatantly corrupt than his brother. And he had not aroused the kind of hate and outrage locally and nationally that would incite the Baton Rouge legislators to think about impeaching him, as many of them had wanted to impeach Huey. Earl's problems were less extreme, but they were real problems. In a segregationist state, he was a sort of liberal who believed in black voting rights. Or at least, that was one way to interpret some of his public statements. More gravely, Earl was crazy. That, at any rate, was how it looked to a serious reader of the northern press. Liebling wrote:

> Dispatches in the New York papers had left small doubt that he had gone off his rocker during the May session of the Legislature, and I wanted to see what happens to a state when its chief executive is in that sort of fix. The papers reported that he had cursed and hollered at the legislators, saying things that so embarrassed his wife, Miz Blanche, and his relatives that they had packed him off to Texas in a National Guard plane to get his brains repaired in an asylum.
>
> By late July [1959], when I arrived in Louisiana, he had heaved himself back into power by arguing his way out of the Texas sanitarium, touching base at a New Orleans private hospital and legalizing his way out of the Southeast Louisiana State Hospital, at Mandeville.

The Democratic primary elections, tantamount to election in overwhelmingly Democratic Louisiana, were scheduled for December 5, four months away. Long was about to go into zany high gear on the campaign trail when the Lieblings came to see him in Baton Rouge. Long kept them waiting for three hours. When he finally greeted them, he was suspicious. "All right, you set there," he said warily.

Liebling broke the ice immediately. "I'm not so interested in politics," he said. "But I do want to know how you pass the time. How do you play the horses? Do you use speed rating?"

Long began talking a blue streak, and kept on ranting for most of the three weeks that Liebling stuck with him up and down the state. Taking no notes as usual, Liebling came away with a headful of ranting Longisms and a large case of admiration for the governor, who was a spectacular southern edition of the fast-talking, loony con man that Liebling had previously met in New York, Las Vegas and Tunisia. Liebling spent more time on Long, because he was writing a book, and for that reason *The Earl of Louisiana* is the greatest of all his lowlife portraits, the climax of all those hundreds of squibs and sketches and features Liebling had been writing since his first days with the *World-Telegram*.

Even before he left for Louisiana the first time, Liebling had known that Earl Long was his kind of character. He had just bought forty-four cases of cantaloupes and seven hundred dollars' worth of cowboy boots; he had bet frenetically on horse races, made endless phone calls in the middle of the night and fought with his friends. Off the rails, apparently, Earl was really under control, but in an original way. His mouth was his fortune.

In a newsreel made that May during the fracas in the legislature, the camera had caught him grabbing the microphone from the hands of opposition speakers. As Liebling described the scene:

> He would shake his finger in his subjects' faces or grab the lectern with both hands and wag his bottom from side to side. He interrupted one astonished fellow to ask, "What's your name?"
>
> "John Waggoner, from Plain Dealing." (This is the name of a town.)
>
> "Well, well, you look like a fine man. Don't let nothing run over you."

In an impromptu debate with a segregationist from Summerfield, Louisiana, named Willie Rainach, Long ad-libbed wildly but lethally, like a buzz bomb that bobbled erratically before plopping down right on its intended target:

> "I think there's such a thing as being over-educated. Scientists tell me there's enough wrinkles up there to take care of all kinds of stuff. Maybe I'm getting old—losing some of mine. I hope that don't happen to Rainach. After all this is over, he'll probably go up there to Summerfield, get up on his front porch, take off his shoes, wash his feet, look at the moon and get close to God. And when you *do*, you got to *recognize* that *niggers* is human beings."

Liebling did more than quote Long's genial bombast. He used his candidacy as a focus for explaining the Gothic complexities of Louisiana politics, its satrapies and leading personalities.

His main guide and source for local anecdotes about New Orleans Mayor "Dellasoups" Morrison and the other Louisiana muck-a-mucks was a native-born reporter who had tasted the liberal air at

Harvard as a Nieman fellow and in Washington as an editor of the *New Republic*, Tom Sancton. After Liebling flew back north, Sancton kept him posted on later events in a stream of letters. Liebling returned to Louisiana at least twice more, for the two primaries. Earl Long was knocked out in the first, but the book inevitably took the shape of a report on an election; so Liebling had to wait for the runoff, which Morrison won, before he could finish it.

Undoubtedly, *The Earl of Louisiana* would have been a better book if Long had won. His defeat destroyed the symmetry of Liebling's profile, turning the last sixty pages of it into epilogue. Liebling was furious with the *Times-Picayune*, the major New Orleans paper, for opposing "Longism" and helping thereby to eliminate the one liberal force in the field. The result reminded Liebling of "one of those automobile accidents in which a driver, swatting at a wasp, loses control of his car and runs it into a bayou full of alligators."

The epilogue had a tragic coda. Long ran for Congress in 1960, won, and then died of a heart attack almost immediately after his victory.

By the time Liebling's book came out, in 1961, Long was also dead as a subject for political reportage. The old codger had pulled Liebling down with him. The book did not sell. But it has acquired the status of a minor classic of journalism about the South.

During the year and a half that elapsed between his first visit to Baton Rouge and the publication of *The Earl*, Liebling had curtailed his usual schedule of piecework for *The New Yorker*. The book took up his time, and by the summer of 1959 he had definitely entered a new stage of life. Aside from his new domestic arrangements, his stepdaughter had graduated from college and was about to move abroad for an extended period. Harold Ross had died and been replaced by William Shawn. And although Liebling had worked closely with Shawn for almost his whole career at *The New Yorker*, this shift of leadership, coinciding as it did with so many other major changes in Liebling's life situation, may have helped to liberate him from his dependence on the magazine and to confirm his commitment to write books. Just before he was researching *The Earl*, he had also finished work on another series of pieces that would become still another book. The four articles that ran in *The New Yorker* as "Memoirs of a Feeder in France" eventually appeared in 1962 in expanded form, with other chapters, as *Between Meals: An Appetite for Paris*.

Formally speaking, *Between Meals* is Liebling's last book, since one of its chapters was completed in 1962, but almost all of it had already been published in *The New Yorker* in 1959. The impulse that made Liebling write nostalgically about his life as a glutton therefore dates primarily to early 1959. And it is as a product of this last truly creative period of his life that *Between Meals* should be considered.

More even than *Normandy Revisited, Between Meals* is a work of nostalgia for vanished youth, unrecapturable delights, innocence and appetite undarkened by a fat man's guilt. In 1959, Liebling tipped Dr. Soffer's scales at 243 pounds. He was as obese as ever, and degenerating fast from constant overeating, without any serious intention of calling a halt to the gorge that he knew was killing him. But none of the somber side of his life's feast darkens the sparkling memories of *Between Meals*.

The book opens with a celebration of Yves Mirande, "one of the last of the great around-the-clock gastronomes of France." Mirande was a popular playwright who, in his prime, would

> dazzle his juniors, French and American, by dispatching a lunch of raw Bayonne ham and fresh figs, a hot sausage in crust, spindles of filleted pike in a rich rose *sauce Nantua,* a leg of lamb larded with anchovies, artichokes on a pedestal of *foie gras,* and four or five kinds of cheese, with a good bottle of Bordeaux and one of champagne, after which he would call for the Armagnac and remind Madame to have ready for dinner the larks and ortolans she had promised him, with a few *langoustes* and a turbot—and, of course, a fine *civet* made from the *marcassin,* or young wild boar, that the lover of the leading lady in his current production had sent up from his estate in the Sologne. "And while I think of it," I once heard him say, "we haven't had any woodcock for days, or truffles baked in the ashes, and the cellar is becoming a disgrace—no more '34s and hardly any '37s."

Toward the end of his life, Mirande fell ill and limited himself to healthy food cooked at home. This regimen, Liebling insisted, did him in. Moderation "began its fatal inroads on his resistance." He fell into the "trap of abstinence" and died.

Liebling's own history as an eater was less perfectly heroic than Mirande's. He had not yet died for his palate, and he had never reached the heights of *gourmandise* attained by his model. Indeed, the point of his account was to show how an innocent from America had groped his way from crude cravings for sweets as a child, held in control by a joyless German governess, to a comparatively exalted level of taste and sheer abdominal capacity. He describes the salutary effect that a limited allowance had on his powers of discrimination in the restaurants he could afford during his student year at the Sorbonne, wallowing in memories of his first tripe sausage and the other poor man's dishes he would never have learned to love if he had started his adventures *à table* with money enough for caviar and the better cuts of meat. He learned other lessons from his teammates in the rowing crew he practiced with on the Marne. They didn't do much rowing, as it turned out, but they knew how to eat such fare as muzzle of beef and crocks of hare pâté at their frequent training meals. Later, toward the end of his year in France, Liebling drank himself into acute oenophilia, sampling the better bottles of wine merchants he visited on a slow trip through Burgundy, drinking for free at local *caves.*

As a correspondent, he had more to spend and moved up to better but still authentic restaurants. On the Rue Sainte-Anne, in 1939, he stumbled into the place of his dreams, an unassuming bistro run by a great cook named Louis Bouillon. Liebling went there often, and even made the early morning rounds of Les Halles with Bouillon, whose "limp, drooping mustache . . . looked as if it had been steamed over cook pots until it was permanently of the consistency of spinach."

Bouillon and another favorite restaurateur, named Pierre, both taught Liebling what great food was. And then they stopped making it. By the time Liebling returned to Paris in 1956, Bouillon was no longer in business and Pierre had cut out the heavy, elaborate dishes of the prewar glory days. But the memory of their menus, laden with salmis of woodcocks and intricate versions of boiled beef, gave Liebling a standard for judging food for the rest of his life. And in *Between Meals* he was able to pass on this notion of the high value of rib-sticking, carefully tended cuisine to a new generation of Americans. But like his favorite restaurants, his ideas about food were too old-fashioned to make a dent in the trend toward faster, leaner foods that swept America and later France. And his enthusiasm for finding earthy magnificence in humble and unfashionable locations—which paralleled similar enthusiasms for the high-flown rhetoric of lowlifes and the esoteric art of boxers—did little to temper the aspirations of the new breed of American gourmets, who sped from three-star restaurant to three-star restaurant up and down France all through the sixties. Those who did appreciate Liebling's message, like him, could find few remannts of the trencherman tradition whose last days he had hymned.

Between Meals is not, however, a jeremiad. It has the wistful, bittersweet tone of any memoir written by an old man about the juices of his youth. But the balance of the book is a celebration of Liebling's growth into knowing hedonism. This is why a book explicitly devoted to memories of food ends with a warm portrait of a woman, the Left Bank tart who lived with Liebling in his student digs. She helped him believe in his fantasy of himself as a man about Paris who could wine and dine and wench just like his heroes Villon and Stendhal.

For the next thirty years, Liebling had lived his real life by the standards of that pleasure-worshiping, reckless fantasy of the writer's life. At the center of this vision of ideal manhood was the refusal to obey the bourgeois principle of delayed gratification. In other words, Liebling had raised self-indulgence (as he defined self-indulgence) to the level of a first principle. To eat and overeat was, for Liebling, more than a crude gorge; gluttony was a badge of freedom. His belly was the outward and visible sign of an inward and manly grace.

And so it is altogether fitting that Liebling's last book should be about food. It stood for all his appetites and values. Soon, and he must have known it in 1959, his passion for food would kill him. Perhaps he wanted it that way. But it is more likely that until death was inescapably upon him, Liebling managed to con himself into believing what he had written about the epicure Mirande. To gorge was like "the indispensable roadwork of the prizefighter." Once a man cut back on exercising his system with daily bouts of rich food, rot set in.

Certainly, in that summer of 1959, Liebling acted as if he were convinced of his own immortality. With the Earl Long book still to write, he sailed to Europe in late August with Jean Stafford and Susan Spectorsky, brimming with projects and a sense that the highest of times and his best work lay just ahead.

The official reason for the trip was an *Observer* assignment, to cover the impending British general election. Liebling had expected Prime Minister Harold Macmillan to schedule the vote for October 22, which would have given Joe and Jean and Susan time to tour in Greece beforehand. But Macmillan moved the date up, so that Liebling had to write his pieces during September.

Settled in at Duke's, the Lieblings had returned to the scene of their courtship days. Susan Spectorsky had a chance to see her stepfather's London and patch up the trouble that had arisen between them. Susan had hurt Joe deeply by not inviting him to her Radcliffe graduation. She had not originally intended to go to the graduation exercises. But then her father had invited himself, and Lucille wheedled and shouted on the phone, insisting that she and Spectorsky must both attend the ceremony. Susan wearily acceded to her mother. Liebling, who had paid Susan's tuition, spent the day in New York.

Dismayed but still devoted, Liebling gave his stepdaughter a very special graduation present. He offered her a year of study abroad, just as his own father had paid for him to spend a year at the Sorbonne. "Go wherever you want," Liebling said.

Susan Spectorsky chose Cairo. She had decided, after taking a few Harvard courses on the Middle East (her actual field of concentration as an undergraduate had been modern European history), to do graduate work in Arabic. This pleased Liebling, who had set an example of Islamophilia during most of her life.

Susan left for Egypt after two weeks in London. She spent three years in Cairo and eventually became a professor of Arabic at

Queens College of the City University of New York. Some of Liebling's favorite Arabs, Ibn Khaldun and a few Tunisian boxers among
them, had played a benign role behind the scenes in the making of
an American Arabist.

Liebling meanwhile spent five weeks "running through the country Tuesdays, Wednesdays and Thursdays and writing like hell Friday mornings for a two o'clock deadline (not inflexible, but so far
I've been able to meet it every time). I do a 2,500 word story for
each Sunday's paper."

Jean Stafford took the opportunity to visit the Scottish island of
Arran, off the Firth of Clyde, where three of her grandparents had
been born. She made two trips in search of her roots and discovered
that everybody up there looked exactly like her. Liebling wrote
Mitchell that "when she got off the boat, they thought she had just
been shopping in Glasgow—they hadn't noticed that she was
away."

Once the *Observer* work was finished, the Lieblings flew to Athens and traveled to Samothrace, the Aegean island. They returned
to Athens, and before sailing home on the *Exeter*, Liebling wrote a
long letter, on October 30, to his new literary agent, James Oliver
Brown, recapitulating the depressing details of his career as an author of non-best-selling books. The letter is a remarkable document.
Liebling wrote it in the Hotel Grande Bretagne, without any of his
personal records to hand, but he was able to remember the exact
amount of the advance on his first book ($200) and the number of
copies sold of *Chicago: The Second City* (about 3,500). Nor had he
forgotten any of the details of his dispute with Doubleday over se-
rial rights to *The Honest Rainmaker*.

Liebling had always been obsessed with the business aspects of his
work. And Brown's files would soon be full of querulous notes from
him pressing for payment from publishers. He was unreasonably
nervous about receiving his royalties and frustrated at his publishers' inability to sell his books. In the letter to Brown, he complained
ironically about the "Liebling Phenomenon": "While my books always got good reviews, stirred up controversy, were remembered
and maintained their prices remarkably well on Fourth Avenue—I
have had to pay as much as $6 for a copy of the *Telephone Booth*

Indian, when I was out of them—they simply didn't sell."

Brown had his work cut out for him. And so did Liebling. After a leisurely cruise, making landfalls at Naples, Marseilles, Genoa, Leghorn and Barcelona, he and Jean returned home on November 25, both resolved to do the best writing of their lives.

It was not to be. Stafford remained blocked. Liebling finished his work on *The Earl*, but in the last three years of his life he wrote only sixty-two articles, and of those roughly half were "Notes and Comment" items or book reviews. Without perhaps realizing it himself, Liebling had slowed down.

Even so, it would be misleading to call Liebling's output in the sixties a decline. He continued to write brilliantly about the press and the ring. He produced enough writing to satisfy any reasonable standard of fertility. And he remained as variously alert to the world as ever.

In a January 1960 "Talk of the Town" obituary, he memorialized his favorite reporter, Albert Camus:

> When we last met Camus—in Paris, in November, 1955—he was getting ready to go to Algiers to bring the millionaires and the Moslems together. He felt the world as close as water on his skin, and never grew the scales appropriate to a Big Fish. He was without insulation—the antithesis of the detached Stranger with whom his name will eternally be associated.

In May, he anatomized the tortuous squirming of the press as it struggled to come up with the right reaction to the U-2 scandal. Was Francis Gary Powers an airborne official spy? Had President Eisenhower known that he was flying on a reconnaissance mission over the Soviet Union when Power haplessly crashed? Liebling wrote:

> This story, as you remember, went on and on, becoming progressively more disconcerting each time the newspapers, like an old-fashioned German band chased by a cop, tried to resume the concert. When they rallied round the piccolo tootling, "Ike didn't know," the bass drum boomed, "He *did* too know, he *did* too know," and Ike was playing it.

After denying we did it, admitting we did it, denying Ike knew we did it, admitting Ike knew we did it, saying we had a right to do it and denying we were still doing it, we dropped the subject.

In June, Liebling went to the Polo Grounds to watch a rematch between the high-living heavyweight champion Ingemar Johansson and Floyd Patterson. He had not lost his Eganesque flair:

> Patterson had no time to think about the rewards of virtue—he was too busy reaping them. He hit the hedonist with a left hook to the body and then switched it to the head. The Swede was in the same place when the punch landed as when it started. He went down like a double portion of Swedish pancakes with lingonberries and sour cream. He got up, though. There was no quit in him; he was still, in spirit, disputatious. Patterson swung his left again, like a man with a brush hook clearing briars. It hit the champion's chin, his head went back on a loose neck, and he struck the mat with a crash that I swear I heard at a distance of at least three hundred yards.

In July, he moved out to The Springs, by himself. Jean Stafford had gone on a trip out West. In a sense, the separation was a symbol of their relationship, which was a union of two very distinct people. As time went on, their lives ran increasingly on separate tracks. Jean was not eager to see many of Joe's old friends. Certainly, she could not endure Colonel Stingo. She tired of racing. And she began to really herself with some of the literary figures she had known before her marriage to Liebling.

For his part, Liebling abhorred the bookish salons of Manhattan's Upper West Side. He used to do a malicious imitation of Philip Rahv, then coeditor of the *Partisan Review*. And when Stafford told him she had accepted an invitation for the two of them for an evening at the home of the literary critic Alfred Kazin, Liebling objected: "Sheenies who are meanies will be there."

Then there was the matter of the Ouija board. Jean would drink too much, put the board on the floor and start to consult it. Liebling would try to get her to put it away. He hated it. It made him think of Ann's madness. But his interfering made Jean cranky. She didn't like it either when he encouraged her to write humorously. She wanted to get back to her Jamesian mode, which Liebling did not admire.

Still they got on well enough, and when Jean went to California, Liebling missed her. He wrote the Guedenets that he was bored to distraction, unable to get any work done on the last chapters of *Between Meals*. Cars had run over two of the Lieblings' cats on Fireplace Road. And even a bumper crop of peppers and cucumbers in the garden was not enough to console him for the inconvenience of the Long Island Rail Road strike then in course. He solved the commutation problem with cabs, paying fifty dollars per trip, sharing the ride with his maid, Madella, who had children to visit in the city.

As a result, Liebling cast a cold eye on bromidic newspaper reports he read that claimed Long Island commuters were having an easy time during the strike. He looked closer and found that coverage of the strike was full of holes and unanswered questions. He then wrote a sharp "Wayward Press" critique, concluding that "what newspapers called pigheaded in a railroad conductor is what they call devotion to principle in a railroad president."

On August 20, Liebling flew to Rome for three weeks, to cover the Olympics. He filed three times, reporting gracefully on the highlights of the games but without his customary force. An attack of gout undoubtedly cut into his energies. From time to time, nevertheless, Liebling's prose regained its usual spirit, as in this description of the Via Veneto:

> Tables set out on the sidewalks by hotels and cafés have multiplied, converging from curb and wall until the path between is hard to discern and impossible to turn around in. A fair-sized man vainly trying to thread his way from the Hotel Excelsior as far as the Flora has to reverse engines and back out, like a steamship on the upper reaches of a tropical river. The tables are occupied by visitors to the games, gasping like stranded sea robins and staring at one another in search of the stigmata of celebrity. This human edema is confined to the four blocks where it is impossible to buy an Italian newspaper, although girls in blue uniforms sell every other kind in the world, including Japanese. Once seated at a table, the unwary celebrity-starer is likely to be stuck there. Waiters fit other tables in and people fit

themselves in about him as if he were one bit in a jigsaw puzzle, and when he tries to rise, he finds that he has become a permanent part of a *galantine d'hommes*. Once in a while, the vast mass stirs gelatinously; a rumor runs from table to table that Elizabeth Taylor, or someone who looks like her, is getting out of a taxi. The pieces of the jigsaw puzzle try to hoist themselves out of their frames of reference to look. Elbows accumulate melted ice cream. Too late—she is gone. None of the human mixed fruits in the jello will ever know if it was she.

The heat and general confusion of Rome wore him down further. Fortunately, his nephew John Stonehill was on hand (he had a Prix de Rome as an architect that year) and he arranged for a doctor when the renal colic struck, and also persuaded Liebling to take a day off to rest in bed.

Liebling's recovery was rapid and sufficient enough to permit him and Stonehill to go restaurant-hopping together. And by the end of the three weeks, Liebling wrote Stafford that the last week of the games had been exciting. But he was eager to return home (after a stop for a meal with Pan and Jean Riboud in Paris), on a plane that would arrive in New York on September 14. The only really notable result of this Roman expedition was that it brought Liebling and Cassius Clay (later Muhammad Ali) together.

Back in New York, the rest of 1960 and most of 1961 were essentially a fallow time for Liebling. He covered the third Patterson-Johansson fight in Miami in the spring of 1961. He also made fun of the sniping in the American press when jingoist reporters tried to belittle the achievement of the pioneer Soviet astronaut Yuri Gagarin. David Lawrence, in his syndicated column, had challenged Gagarin's claim that he had seen meadows and fields two hundred miles away through the portholes in his spacecraft. Liebling countered:

I would remind Mr. Lawrence, first, that the glass in the portholes may have been ground to a prescription, like a Texas windshield, and, second, that last year, during the fuss over the U-2 reconnaissance flight, he himself said that the Air Force had a camera that could take a photograph of a golf ball from a height of six miles, which I said was a long way to go for the purpose. You can get roughly forty-nine golf balls into a square foot. A one-acre plowed (or unplowed) field has 43,560 square feet. It is therefore 2,134,440 times as visible as a golf ball, while the major was a mere 31.17 times as far away as the golf ball photographers.

In June, Liebling returned to ringside to venerate Archie Moore. In July, he wrote a "Notes and Comments" obituary for another hero, Ernest Hemingway. If Liebling had ever felt scorn or envy for Hemingway, it had burned away with his death. The obituary is a model of sympathy for a writer who, Liebling said, had "exhausted his past" and "wandered about the world of the thirties for embers of what he needed to warm himself, shooting poor beasts and chronicling the death of bulls." Hemingway's failure as correspondent was no more surprising than the failure of Tolstoy would have been if he "had been engaged by a weekly in St. Petersburg to cover Plevna and was expected to write the equivalent of 'War and Peace' every week against a deadline." Hemingway's real downfall was his own success. He was "an irrevocably public personage, exposed to incessant social interruption, which, being a gregarious man, he did not sufficiently repel."

Hemingway's failure to write the big novel he had been hoping to bring off ever since the war was a failure Liebling understood completely, a failure he could project himself into with the pure generosity of someone who has tried the same thing, come even less close to the goal, and still has the largeness of spirit to praise the more successful man's attempt in an anonymous (and therefore ideally selfless) eulogy.

Very likely, thoughts of mortality and the writer's life were much on Liebling's mind that summer. He could not fail to have been struck by the phenomenon of his own sapped fecundity. His finances were as Micawberish as ever. And he had been reading two books on another tragically strapped, doomed writer and personal hero, Stephen Crane.

In August, Liebling published a long, impassioned review of *Stephen Crane: Letters*, edited by R. W. Stallman and Lillian Gilkes, and of *Cora Crane* by Miss Gilkes.

"The letters clearly show us," Liebling wrote, "that Crane was the victim not of self-indulgence or a death wish, as it has been popular among critics to assume, but of his situation, which was banal. He died, unwillingly, of the cause most common among American middle-class males—anxiety about money."

As a man who was up against it constantly on an income of sixty thousand dollars a year, Liebling was a vehement sympathizer of poor Crane, who had survived wretchedly on much less and prostituted his talents to pay off earlier debts run up with publishers. Crane's letters document his feverish struggle to turn a dollar with his stories. They made Liebling rage against the unfairness of the marketplace to writers. "At the top of his fame," Liebling noted, "Crane got three hundred dollars for 'The Blue Hotel,' and as the market went, that was a good price, while my own father, a furrier in New York, could get five hundred dollars for an Alaska-seal coat."

Melville couldn't earn a living either, Liebling noted. He had stopped writing altogether and made ends meet at the New York Custom House. Dostoevsky, Liebling went on, had told his publisher in 1849, "'I struggle with my small creditors like Laocoön with the serpent.'"

At this very moment, Liebling himself was almost overwhelmed with money problems and the need to squeeze work from his typewriter. His rapacious Fifth Avenue landlord raised the rent so high he forced the Lieblings to move to a boxy apartment in a new building at 45 West 10th Street. They took up residence in the fall of 1961, somewhat consoled by the location, which was across the street from Joe and Therese Mitchell. Meanwhile, to help pay pressing bills, he free-lanced a trivial piece in the September 1 *Vogue*. The editor's note preceding the article said: "A. J. Liebling, the sudden object of a national crush, pays no attention to it. The crush has been partly the result of several television appearances, especially on the WCBS-TV program, 'The Press.'"

The "national crush" was short-lived at best. But Liebling had begun to believe, hoping against hope, that he had finally broken into the big money. His agent's files are full of letters about movie and magazine deals. He signed a contract to do a book on the horse and New York City, a nostalgic history of the old days before the automobile, when the city's population had included three million people and three million horses.

Thomas Meehan, then a young "Talk of the Town" writer, spent six months doing legwork for Liebling and handed him 450 pages of double-spaced typed notes. The book was never written, but Liebling was under terrific pressure to get to work on it.

During most of 1962, he was still able to write at the old pace when he had to. Meehan recalls that he could stay up all night and produce five thousand polished words, on "the messiest manuscript you ever saw."

"I went into the *New Yorker* men's room at 1 A.M. once," Meehan said, "and saw Liebling naked to the waist. He was washing himself after a night of writing."

Meehan was in a sense Liebling's protégé. They went to fights together, barhopped afterward looking for Colonel Stingo, even went out reporting together once. Meehan had located an ancient stableman for the horse book. But he had trouble talking to the man. He took Liebling out to the stable in Long Island City. "Liebling drew the stableman out immediately. He used silences. He radiated warmth," Meehan recalls.

On the surface, Liebling was as strong and capable as he had ever been. And his career seemed to blossom. Ballantine brought out his collected press pieces in a paperback titled *The Press*. It first appeared in September 1961 and went into a second printing in July 1962. During the same period, *The Earl of Louisiana* and *Between Meals* also came out. And then Ballantine published a collection of lowlife pieces called *The Jollity Building*. And while this boomlet in Liebling was at its peak, William Cole set to work on a Liebling anthology, *The Most of A. J. Liebling*, for Simon & Schuster.

All five of his last books represented long since finished work. Three were anthologies. None sold very well.

Meanwhile Liebling was actually treading water, writing very little, breaking no new ground. The horse book never got farther than Meehan's notes.

In March 1962, he visited Cassius Clay on the eve of his first professional bout. He found the poet-pugilist at the gym doing sit-ups
but not too winded to recite his newest ode:

> You may talk about Sweden
> [down and up again],
> You may talk about Rome
> [down and up again],
> But Rockville Centre is
> Floyd Patterson's home
> [down].

Clay's poetry, Liebling said, was in an old tradition of fistic verse
dating to Bob Gregson, a fighter whose doggerel had been quoted
by Pierce Egan ("The British lads that's here/Quite strangers are to
fear"). Clay was also the last in a line of loquacious ring figures
whom Liebling had written about, from Philadelphia Jack O'Brien
to Whitey Bimstein.

Liebling covered five more prize fights before his death. Every
one of the accounts can still be reread with pleasure for the prose
and the analysis of human motives and movements. He never lost
his touch, only his momentum.

He wrote four "Wayward Press" pieces in 1963, at the time of
the 114-day New York newspaper strike. In them, Liebling hit his
old stride, mixing humorous and incisive quotations and analyses of
such papers as the Las Vegas *Sun* and the *National Enquirer* with
dour commentaries on inadequate coverage of the strike printed in
more serious places. Liebling concluded, as he had on many previous occasions, that newspaper coverage of labor problems, particularly journalistic labor problems, was slanted heavily against labor.

He made this point again that spring in a speech delivered at a
Harvard *Crimson* dinner. But after the strike ended, Liebling read
A. H. Raskin's step-by-step history of the event in *The New York
Times* and was forced to admit that it was fair and full. He summarized Raskin's twenty-thousand-word article in detail and then, still
incredulous that the *Times* had set Raskin free to tell the unvarnished truth about them in its own columns, he saluted the paper. In

what was to be his valedictory as a newspaper critic, Liebling concluded: "I doff my bowler."

Only three other Liebling pieces deserve special note. In October 1962, he wrote a splendidly unclassifiable essay on the *rascasse*, a spiny fish which gastronomers, including Waverley Root, all insisted was absolutely essential to the preparation of an authentic bouillabaisse, but unavailable in America. Liebling mentioned this to his friend the zoologist Samuel B. McDowell, over lunch at The Lobster. McDowell pursued the matter and discovered that *rascasses* were abundant in local waters. He reported his research in detail to Liebling, who wove long quotations from McDowell's letters into a hilarious piece of ichthyogastronomic scholarship.

The other two articles appeared posthumously in *The New Yorker* in early 1964. *"Paysage de Crépuscule"* is a paean to Times Square and the Manhattan lowlife milieu, as viewed from the window of Liebling's office, looking west down Forty-third Street at twilight. It was Liebling's farewell to Colonel Stingo, who was living in the Hotel Dixie, and to the ex-fighter Jack Willis, "the astrologo-nutritionist, yogist and poet," who stayed off and on at the Hotel Woodstock, and to the Paramount Building, where Liebling had interviewed Pola Negri in 1931 in a state of utter infatuation. The piece centers on Stingo, who was nearing the end of his mendacious days. It reminisces about the old Stingo, before he had retired from writing his column, when he had sailed through the neighborhood, getting "stiff as a board." But times had changed. Stingo had told Liebling over the phone: "Now, when I hear the city calling, I just turn over on the other ear and go to sleep again."

Liebling had also ceased to prowl along the streets that run into Times Square. He must have known he was dying when he wrote those words. Stingo had always been his foil, and he used the old man's decline as a metaphor for his own twilight days.

Still, he was able to face death with gallows humor. From time to time, he would pull out the stenographer's tray from his desk and laugh at the letter he had taped on it. A reader from Hico, Texas, had sent it to him at the time of Wolcott Gibbs's death. It said: "Well, Gibbs is dead and soon the whole damn lot of you will be."

Liebling's last piece was a review of Camus's *Notebooks* (the first installment, covering the years 1935–1942). It took him months to finish, longer probably than any short article he ever wrote. But by the summer of 1963, Liebling was profoundly tired and blocked. For the first time in his life, he had lost the flow of words on which everything depended.

He carried Camus's posthumous book with him wherever he went, worrying over it, until he finally got the judgments and the tribute to his brother in spirit right. Camus was the writer Liebling yearned to be. Born poor in Algeria, he had not forsaken his neighbors in the Bab-el-Oued district of Algiers, but had incorporated into his "remarkably pure, poetic French style . . . a command of the street language of Algiers, learned in the street. That gave him an arresting change of pace." He had been a heroic newspaperman during the war, had written great fiction and plays, had done all the things Liebling thought worth doing in a style and with a courage Liebling admired as one admires the perfection in another of his own highest aims.

More a eulogy than a book review, Liebling's assessment of Camus, like his defense of Stephen Crane and his obituary of Ernest Hemingway, sprang from fraternal feeling. But his sympathy for these three writers and the tragic cutting off of their careers before they could pull together the books that would have crowned their lives signified more than one author's generalized admiration for other men who had worked some of the same literary terrain. Crane's fatal illness, Hemingway's suicide, Camus's crash, all forced Liebling to think about the shape of his own life. Liebling did not push his despair upon his readers, but his growing sense of the short time left to him rings like a muffled tattoo in the background of these three literary tributes. By the spring of 1963, Liebling had fallen into a deep depression. With Camus's notebooks always beside him as a measure of how far he had fallen short of his goals, he traveled wretchedly through the places he had loved, his spirit eroded by illness and melancholy.

Advanced gout made every step torture. His toes, fingers, elbows, knees and ears were disfigured by deposits of urate of sodium. Diverticulitis, paratyphoid and recurring flu kept him weak and unable to enjoy food. Worst of all, Liebling still couldn't write.

"For the first time in his life," Jean Stafford recalls, "he developed a real block. Depression was new to him. Looking back on it, I wasn't sufficiently sympathetic because I had always had depression with me."

He tried to ignore the trouble. In the early spring, he insisted on visiting fight training camps when he should have stayed in bed. In May, he flew to Algeria for three weeks, hoping for inspiration with the Camus piece and gathering material for a sort of "North Africa Revisited," which he never completed. Returning to New York via Paris on June 3, Liebling got off the plane in an exuberant mood, which lasted until the next morning.

Paratyphoid from the trip aggravated the relapse into depression. When he had lunch with Susan Spectorsky in July, he fell into a five-minute silence, looking at his lap. Finally, looking up again, puzzled, he said, "Oh, you're here."

Desperately scraping together his last nickels, he took Jean Stafford to Europe at the end of the month. They spent most of August in France, retracing old steps in Normandy, chauffeured from Paris to Bayeux and Mont-Saint-Michel, with Henry Adams at the ready. They turned south through the Loire country, stopped for two weeks at Jean Riboud's chateau, La Carelle, in the department of the Rhône and then went back to Paris, where local life had virtually stopped, because of the *grandes vacances*. Liebling's depression got worse. "My surmise," said Jean Stafford, "is that he knew he would never see France again."

In London, Liebling was no better. After dinner at the Charoux's, he fell asleep in his chair. "The whole of him seemed tired and spent," Margaret Charoux remembers.

On September 7, the Lieblings flew back to New York. Superficially, they resumed their old life. He went to the *New Yorker* office and eked out a few pages. William Cole's anthology of his work was published. After the Kennedy assassination, which upset Liebling deeply, he began assembling clippings for a "Wayward Press" piece, which he never wrote.

One day that last November, he went to lunch, as he so often had before, with his office neighbor and old friend Philip Hamburger. The two men passed the Hippodrome Garage on Forty-fourth

Street, just down the block from the *New Yorker* building. Hamburger recalls: "One of those New York grotesques appeared, half-crippled, half spastic. Joe took one look and began to cry. I could see something was wrong. He was on the edge."

Death is always tragic, never more so than when it carries off a person of talent who still has things to do. Joe Liebling had just turned fifty-nine when he died. If he had lasted ten more years, he could have written press criticism about Vietnam and Watergate. When the Six-Day War broke out, he might have dusted off his First Division fatigues and revisited Egypt and Israel. He did not make it to ringside for the antic championship defenses of Cassius Clay after he turned Muslim and called himself Ali. Liebling missed out on dozens of big stories, stories he would have written better than anyone else could or did. No one has replaced him at *The New Yorker* or elsewhere as a press critic, ring writer or guide to telephone booth Indians.

The work Liebling left behind is an awesome corpus, learned without heaviness, funny, stylish, verbose, rebellious and, finally, heroic. Liebling's journalism is the cheerful and defiant, confident monument of a troubled, pained, diffident man. At the typewriter, he could shake off his sadness and blarney himself into high spirits. When the knack left him, he had no protection against his fundamental melancholy.

On December 21, 1963, Abbott Joseph Liebling was admitted to Doctors Hospital with a bad case of viral pneumonia. He did not improve. Six days later complications set in, serious complications, congestive heart failure and renal collapse. An ambulance rushed him, comatose, to the intensive care unit at Mount Sinai Hospital, where he died the next day, December 28, Saturday. His last words were not set down or even precisely understood. They were in French. Jean Stafford, who was with him in the ambulance, thought that in his delirium he was having an imaginary, impassioned conversation with Camus. It must have been the kind of talk he had had in mind when, in the very last sentence he ever wrote, he said that reading Camus's notebooks was "intensely enjoyable for its own sake—a long conversation with a companion who does not pall."

thirteen

Postscript

On December 30, 1963, funeral services were held for A. J. Liebling at 1 P.M. at the Frank E. Campbell Funeral Chapel, Madison Avenue at Eighty-first Street, New York. Joseph Mitchell read this eulogy:

> As I am sure all of us know, Joe had no religious convictions, and I have been chosen, as one of his oldest friends, to say a few words. Over the years, Joe and I attended a number of funerals together, and it so happened, we attended three together in this room. One was the funeral of a newspaper reporter, an old colleague of ours, at which, in accordance with the man's own request, no words were said. Everybody sat for a while with his own thoughts, some music was played, and then it was over. I was shocked by this, and, as Joe and I walked up the street afterwards, I said so, but Joe said that he wasn't. I have forgotten his exact words, but he said something to the effect that it was the only funeral he had ever attended that he completely approved of. Remembering this, I am going to be brief.
>
> Shortly after I heard that Joe was dead, I went over and looked at

his books in a bookcase at home. There were fifteen of them. I looked through *The Road Back to Paris* and reread "Westbound Tanker," which is one of my favorite stories of his, and when I finished it I suddenly recalled, with great pleasure, a conversation I had had some years ago with the proprietor of one of the biggest and oldest stores in the Fourth Avenue secondhand bookstore district. I had been going to this store for years and occasionally talked to the proprietor, who is a very widely read man. One day I mentioned I worked for *The New Yorker,* and he asked me if I knew A. J. Liebling. I said that I did, and he said that every few days all through the year someone, sometimes a woman, sometimes a young person, sometimes an old person, came in and asked if he had *Back Where I Came From* or *The Telephone Booth Indian* or some other book by A. J. Liebling. At that time, all of Joe's early books were out of print. "The moment one of his books turns up," the man said, "it goes out immediately to someone on my waiting list." The man went on and said that he and other veteran secondhand bookstore dealers felt that this was a sure and certain sign that a book would endure. "Literary critics don't know which books will last," he said, "and literary historians don't know, and those nine-day immortals up at the Institute of Arts and Letters don't know. *We* are the ones who know. We know which books can be read only once, if that, and we know the ones that can be read and reread and reread."

In other words, what I am getting at, Joe is dead, but he really isn't. He is dead, but he will live again. Every time anyone anywhere in all the years to come takes down one of his books and reads or re-reads one of his wonderful stories, he will live again.

Tim Costello once referred to Joe as "that good, kind, brave, decent man." In the last two days, I have recalled a multitude of examples of Joe's goodness. I will refer to only one, and to that only because for some reason that I don't understand it haunts me. We had been up to the Red Devil restaurant for lunch. It was one of those times when he was in bad shape physically. His right hand was red and swollen from gout, his feet were giving him trouble, he was apprehensive about an income tax matter, before long he had to raise a cruelly large sum of money and didn't know where to turn, and he was having doubts about something he was writing. At lunch, he had been talking about Stephen Crane, and evidently this put something in his mind. All of a sudden, as we were walking back to the office, he asked me to go with him over to a flower store on Madison Avenue. Joe had an amazing variety of friends, and one of them was an elderly woman who was living in a nursing home in the Bronx. Joe liked her for two reasons. As a young woman, she had been a friend of Stephen Crane. Also, though she was crippled and couldn't get around and had outlived all of her old friends and was pretty much alone in the world, she still had a great appetite for life and could find pleasure and delight in things as commonplace as a cup of tea. We went into the flower store and Joe ordered a dozen roses to be sent to her. We started out of the store. The woman had lived in France for many years long ago and loved France, and Joe must have thought of that. He went back and asked the man to put six blue irises in among the roses. Then we went on down to the office, and walking beside him I thought of a line in Yeats. I felt that he "was blessèd and could bless."

As I said before, Joe had no religious convictions. However, he certainly never scoffed at those who had. On at least two occasions that I know of, he had masses said for friends of his. He had sympathy for friends who suffered from religious turmoil of one sort or another. And now I know it would be proper if we all stood up, and then those who wish to can say, each in his or her own way, a silent prayer for Joe.

In the pews at Campbell's sat Liebling's assembled family, friends and colleagues. Ann Liebling did not attend. She had come down from Providence briefly and gone back again by train, greatly moved. She wrote this letter to Therese Mitchell, who had kept in touch with her over the years:

> Monday night
> December 30, 1963

Dear Therese,

I know I promised not to write until after the New Year, but I just feel like it now & I hope you don't mind.

I got to Grand Central & did not have to wait for the Prov. train on track 34. When it was a few minutes to one I took out Joe's letter & read it to try and console me because I could not hold the tears back any longer. My head was near bursting from trying to for so long. I folded it and put it in my purse & went in & took a seat. There was plenty of seats and I was glad of that.

I looked out the window & up at the blue sky and thought of him. Then I would look at a lake all cold & frozen with ice. Once I spotted one solitary little white duck gliding along on a strip of water & wondered where the others were & why he was so alone & so far away from them. It must have been his own shore because a few mins. later I did see many more ducks in a kind of formation— The few boats were blanketed with snow. I knew it must be very cold outside & inside the coach & no one could have been colder than I felt. In the distance & quite far away from the ducks I saw one lone figure on horse back in the snow. Sometimes it was hard for me to see at all because the tears were blinding my vision & scalding—I still had to use control because deep sobs would try and push their way up from deep inside of me. I also saw some children ice skating & they looked happy & I was so glad for them. I heard a man call out milk & ice cream & decided I would like a small container of milk—I don't care very much for milk—perhaps because I just never had very much of it & as is usual with orphans learned to go without. I started to drink it & suddenly Jesus I'm crying like hell can't help it & drinking milk to boot—I'd better get back on the ball—I didn't have anything to read since I had left my book & the mg. I had bought to read in the hotel.

The ride didn't seem to take too long but by the time the train reached Union Station in Prov. I had become violently sick. I never was so cold & I was shivering. I ran into the ladies room where the matron helped me & I thought I would never stop vomiting—I finally did tho rested for a few mins. & went on home—I tried to lie down & rest but certain sentences in Joe's letter kept ringing in my head. "The city was dead for four days." & then my next thought would be and now my Joe is dead. then his "and I will always love you" as tho he was telling me on Nov 26 that he was going away somewhere. Then the thought flashed in my head that I had been selfish because it was people of all faiths, creeds, colors & all social levels that he loved. It had to be that "people" not just me, because [illegible] that would be me or was me until I became frightened of them and ran away— Does any thing of this make sense at all? in other words there was a finality in his words, as tho he wouldn't be with us much longer—

My room was dark when I got here the bulb had gone out—but I happened to have had a small candle globe by which I'm trying to write & can barely see what I'm writing & furthermore have not been able to find my glasses to write by—

There was a knock at my door for a telephone call & it was a woman friend calling to say she was sorry about Joe. She said the paper said it was pneumonia & I said yes, but you know me well enough that had I known Joe was ill & in the hospital, *no one on the face of this earth* could have kept me from his bedside. & I know hospitals from A to Z so well that no doctors, nurses, cops, no one would have kept me from him. She said she had seen me pull many a patient out of a much more severe illness than pneumonia even when doctors had given up— In my opinion too many people are killed off in those frigging hosps with their unhealthy heat & nutty regulated thermostats. It was only about three weeks ago that this patient I was taking care of kept telling me I'm so cold, so cold—I asked the nurse for a blanket & she said it's not cold in here & started to look at the thermostat. I said I don't give a damn what you think or your reading of the thermostat. The patient had only been down from OR a few hours. She got a blanket because [illegible] or no [illegible] I would have gone in & got 4 blankets or five if she needed them. I hate the AMA profession & for good reasons—& how.

I am out of paper Therese have 4 doz envelopes tho, so used this [a printed sheet in memory of John F. Kennedy] Joe Liebling certainly did [illegible] for his country. I still am & always was very fond of him—

Love Ann

On May 14, 1964, Ann Liebling's body was recovered from the Providence River. Police had been dragging the area for several days, because a woman's handbag and a partially filled bottle of wine had been found on a nearby dock.

Notes

Where there is a possible choice, page references are given to Liebling's work as it appears in book form, always to the most recent American edition, except as specified otherwise. Where relevant, the original date of newspaper or periodical publication, usually in *The New Yorker*, is given.

Book names are abbreviated as indicated in the concise Liebling bibliography below.

References to *The New Yorker* are specified only as to issue date and pages; any article citation for which no magazine name is given refers to the appropriate number of *The New Yorker*.

All Liebling's papers and letters, including letters written to him by Ann Liebling and other people, are or will soon be at the Cornell University Library, Ithaca, New York, filed among the E. B. White papers. In certain instances, the dates I give for letters is the result of my own deduction.

All direct statements in the text which are not attributed in these notes to a printed source have come to me in the form of personal communications.

Bibliography

BM   *Between Meals: An Appetite for Paris*. New York: Simon & Schuster, 1962.

BWICF *Back Where I Came From*. New York: Sheridan House, 1938.

Cole   *The Most of A. J. Liebling*. Edited by William Cole. New York: Simon & Schuster, 1963.

EL   *The Earl of Louisiana.* New York: Simon & Schuster, 1961.
HR   *The Honest Rainmaker: The Life and Times of Colonel John R. Stingo.* Garden City, N.Y.: Doubleday, 1953.
JB   *The Jollity Building.* New York: Ballantine (paper), 1962.
Mollie   *Mollie and Other War Pieces.* New York: Ballantine (paper), 1964.
MRH   *Mink and Red Herring: The Wayward Pressman's Casebook.* Garden City, N.Y.: Doubleday, 1949. (Reprinted 1972, by Greenwood Press, Westport, Conn.)
NR   *Normandy Revisited.* New York: Simon & Schuster, 1958.
RBTP   *The Road Back to Paris.* Garden City, N.Y.: Doubleday, Doran, 1944.
RSI   *La République du Silence.* Edited by A. J. Liebling and Eugene Jay Sheffer. New York: Harcourt, Brace, 1946.
RS2   *The Republic of Silence.* Edited by A. J. Liebling and Eugene Jay Sheffer. New York: Harcourt, Brace, 1947.
SC   *Chicago: The Second City.* New York: Knopf, 1952. (Reprinted 1974, by Greenwood Press, Westport, Conn.)
SS   *The Sweet Science.* New York: Viking, 1956. (Reprinted 1973, by Greenwood Press, Westport, Conn.)
TAS   *They All Sang: From Tony Pastor to Rudy Vallée.* By Edward B. Marks, As Told to Abbott J. Liebling. New York: Viking, 1934.
TBI   *The Telephone Booth Indian.* Garden City, N.Y.: Doubleday, Doran, 1944.
TP   *The Press.* New York: Ballantine (paper), 1961. Revised edition, 1964. Second revised edition, with introduction by Jean Stafford, 1975.
WP   *The Wayward Pressman.* Garden City, N.Y.: Doubleday, 1947. (Reprinted 1972, by Greenwood Press, Westport, Conn.)

ACKNOWLEDGMENTS

Page
xiii   "wrote between seven": WP, p. 103.

WHAT IS A LIEBLING?

2   "American cities": TP, p. 28.
3   "Within a week": Ibid., p. 331.
4   "A couple of Negroes": Mollie, p. 185f.
4   "It seemed more reserved": Ibid., p. 186n.

4   "For the first time": Ibid., p. 235.

5   "A dozen Gardiners Island oysters": BM, p. 10.

6   "Most of [Izzy's] evening guests": JB, p. 8.

7   "Jack O'Brien": SS, p. 1.

7   "Both came out": Ibid., p. 301.

BACK WHERE HE CAME FROM

13   "People I know": BWICF, p. 13.

14   "the weight-lifters": Ibid., p. 14.

14   "the carters left": Ibid., p. 16.

14   "the gay life": Ibid., p. 17.

15   "made a substantial gift": Ibid., p. 15.

15   "a dependent skirt": "To Him She Clung," 10/12/63, p. 145.

16   "Father": Ibid., p. 150.

16   "My route": Ibid., p. 156.

16   "faced with white stone": Ibid., p. 157.

16   "What they taught me": Ibid.

16   "As a pre-literate": Ibid., pp. 157–158.

18   "at unforgettable speed . . . simultaneously": BM, pp. 42–43.

18   "chocolate filling": Ibid., p. 55.

18   "Europe proper": Ibid., p. 42.

18   "The language": Ibid., pp. 44–45.

18   "some uninspiring dish . . . soda": Ibid., pp. 52–53.

19   "Boys liked their sodas . . . collateral": Ibid., p. 54.

19   "*vespasiennes* . . . knife": Ibid., p. 55.

19   "Where the gold light": Ibid., p. 46.

19   "Their smell": WP, p. 17, p. 16.

20   "My mother": Ibid., p. 16.

20   "would monopolize": Ibid., p. 17.

20   "It is impossible": p. 18.

21   "embodied a style": BM, p. 48.

21   "Irene Castle": Ibid., p. 50.

22   "Her father": "To Him She Clung," p. 163.

22   "been a high school valedictorian . . . dodge off": Ibid.

22   "among middle-class enterprisers": BWICF, p. 16.

OYSTERS AND DOLPHINS

24   "The years from 1911": BM, p. 56.

24   "tall, gaunt house": Ibid., p. 58.

26   "Liebling's feet": Far Rockaway H. S. *Dolphin*, 2/20, p. 16.

27   "a German-American kind": BM, pp. 56–57.
27   "theater people . . . milieu" WP, p. 20.
28   "To Margaret": Unpublished ms., Cornell Library.
29   "Princess, You": Ibid.
29   "I'd like to sit": Ibid.
31   "began to feel": BM, p. 59.
31   "on several fronts . . . pillow": Ibid., p. 60.
32   "a great success . . . way": p. 4.
32   "(Boyibus Printi . . .")": p. 13.
32   "The Field of Glory": pp. 4–5.
33   "Poor Barrett": pp. 6–7.
33   "Pals": pp. 6–9.

RENEGADE "INDIAN"

35   "The college": WP, p. 21.
42   "I could not believe": Ibid., p. 26.
46   "Above all avoid affictation": The original of this letter remains in the possession of Mrs. Stonehill, who graciously provided me with a photocopy for use here.
47   "Interviewing the Commissioner": p. 221.
48   "The one I selected: 12/8/56, p. 165.
49   "because nobody I knew . . . stories": Ibid., p. 166.
49   "a kind, vague man . . . Boulevardier": Ibid.
49   "I wanted to be . . . women": Ibid., p. 170.
50   "I have been noticing": Ibid., pp. 171–172.
51   "I'm sorry": Ibid., p. 175.
52   "waffles-and-coffee": Ibid.
52   "some kind of career": Personal communication from Norma Stonehill.
52   "In deciding to go": WP, p. 27.
52   "conquer journalism": Ibid..
53   "My queerest disillusion": Ibid., p. 28.
54   "colorless, odorless . . . A&P": Ibid.
54   "thought journalism sounded fascinating": Ibid., pp. 27–28.
55   "The newspaper world": Ibid., p. 26.
55   "cold as a glacial crevasse . . . summer": Ibid., p. 34.
55   "a plump, gray man . . . issue": Ibid.
56   "I liked even the sociable smells": Ibid., p. 41.
56   "Max knew the East Side": Ibid., p. 34.

57   "He was only five years older": Ibid., pp. 36–37.
57   "murders by perverts": Ibid., p. 37.
57   "the old raspberry-sherbert-faced biographer": Ibid., p. 40.
57   "I liked to pound up": Ibid.
57   "There was a police slip": Ibid., pp. 41–42.
58   "different colonies": Ibid., p. 42.
58   "As a maraschino cherry": Ibid., p. 43.

THE ROAD BACK TO NEW YORK

59   "By this": WP, p. 44.
59   "use my legs . . . tastes": Ibid.
60   "adequate . . . interest": Ibid., p. 45.
60   "cursory look . . . effort": Ibid., p. 46.
60   "there was, for a man of twenty-one . . . element": Ibid., pp. 47–48.
60   "acknowledged a profound dislike": Ibid., p. 51.
61   "some boy with pimples": Ibid., pp. 51–52.
63   "a department-store owner": Ibid., p. 53.
63   "irresponsibility": Ibid., p. 54.
63   "It's a dirty trick": Ibid.
63   "if I had not had my experience": Ibid., p. 59.
64   "Providence": Ibid., p. 57.
64   "but he was no George Washington": Ibid., p. 60.
64   "there was more space": Ibid.
64   "oozed prose": Ibid.
64   "I decided to take . . . story": Ibid., p. 61.
65   "King horse": 5/23/26, p. 1.
66   "Although her horses": Ibid.
66   "Miss Ann Kenyon": Ibid.
67   "This is the kind": WP, pp. 61–62.
67   "having a fine time": Ibid., p. 62.
67   "The taint was on me": Ibid., p. 63.
68   "As a matter of fact": Ibid., pp. 62–63.
68   "the girl is ten years older": BM, p. 74.
69   "he had a very good idea": Ibid., p. 77.
69   "I had two months": NR, p. 29.
69   "a dozen *huitres*": Ibid., p. 31.
70   "the hotel on top . . . wheels": Ibid., pp. 153–154.
70   "like a partridge": Ibid., p. 132.

71   "Dear Folks": Undated.
72   "The consistently rich man": BM, p. 69.
73   "The girls were like": Ibid., pp. 174–176.
73   "idealized notion": Ibid., p. 180.
73   "Her neck": Ibid., p. 179.
74   "*passable* . . . fees": Ibid., p. 177.
74   "monkeys on a raft . . . what I was": Ibid., p. 185.
74   "coming around as often": Undated letter to parents, late October 1926.
75   "The blood ran": BM, p. 94.
75   "instrument like a stapler": Ibid.
76   "The skin in time": Ibid., pp. 94–95.
76   "where literary figures": Ibid., p. 96.
76   "Raspail": Ibid.
76   "a grace unequaled . . . wrote about them": Ibid., p. 102.
77   "In a sixth-floor room . . . feature stories": SP, p. 63.
78   "rowdy nest": Ibid., p. 80.
78   "three great rooms . . . building": Ibid.
78   "When I resumed": Ibid., p. 65.
79   " ' Wallah' ": p. 3.
80   "Spry as a lad": p. 1.
80   "the seasonal repetitiousness": WP., p. 82.
80   "I got mad as hell": Ibid., p. 81.

HIRE LIEBLING

82   "You have been misinformed": WP. p. 82.
82   "It had more talented writers": Ibid.
83   "Hire Joe Liebling": Ibid., p. 84.
83   "story of the misadventure": Ibid., p. 86.
83   "a tall young man": Ibid., p. 89.
84   "That's the way it goes sometimes": Ibid., p. 91.
84   "The period that always": New York *World* Sunday Magazine, 1/18/31, p. 2, "When Knights Were Bowled Over."
85   "Dynasties is the word": 2/15/31, "The Air Is Full of Wrestlers."
85   "They battled": WP, p. 95.
85   "Pompeian lapidaries": Ibid., p. 96.
85   "as limited as an account": Ibid., p. 97.
85   "The pattern": Ibid.
86   "hermaphrodite-rigged": Ibid., p. 103.

86   "a punch-drunk enterprise": Ibid., p. 99.

86   "a ludicrous rag": Ibid., p. 102.

86   "crazy old building": Ibid.

86   "between seven hundred": Ibid., p. 103.

87   "some of them were good . . . writing": Ibid.

88   "The Marx Brothers": 8/17/32, p. 6.

89   December 14, 1931: p. 10.

90   Liebling's seven stories: 1/12/32, p. 3; 1/14/32, p. 6; 1/15/32, p. 11; 1/16/32, p. 4; 1/19/32, p. 12; 1/20/32, p. 14; 1/22/32, p. 6.

93   Comedians: 3/21/32, p. 21; 3/22/32, p. 21; 3/23/32, p. 21; 3/24/32, p. 23; 3/25/32, p. 21; 3/26/32. p. 15.

93   Weber and Fields: 9/6/32, p. 21; 9/7/32, p. 19; 9/8/32, p. 21; 9/9/32, p. 21; 9/10/32, p. 15.

93   old-time performers: 11/7/32, p. 27; 11/8/32, p. 13; 11/9/32, p. 21; 11/10/32, p. 21; 11/11/32, p. 25; 11/12/32, p. 15.

93   jongleur: 9/27/32, p. 14.

93   cockroaches: 5/25/34, p. 2.

93   Casey Stengel: 10/2/34, p. 9.

93   Jack O'Brien: 2/20/35, p. 2.

93   "suit": 9/17/31, p. 27.

93   fish: 7/12/32, p. 16.

93   Thomas Mann: 5/29/34, p. 2.

93   Bankheads: 10/5/34, p. 9.

93   Paderewskis: 5/23/31, p. 26.

93   "It is easy for a Céline reader": "Notes from the Kidnap House," III, 5/6/44, pp. 58–59.

96   "Very early in my *World-Telegram* life": WP, P. 103.

97   "I did not belong": Ibid., pp. 103–104.

99   group of straightforward political articles: 11/12, p. 17; 11/13, p. 21; 11/14, p. 23; 11/15, p. 25.

100   piece for Groundhog Day: 2/2/34, p. 1.

101   "a due bill": WP, p. 107.

101   "Or maybe it was": Ibid., pp. 110–111.

THERE AT THE NEW YORKER

103   "All moveables of wonder": Max Byrd, formerly of the Harvard *Crimson*, called my attention to this passage.

104   "I might as well admit": *The Years with Ross* (Boston: Atlantic-Little, Brown, 1959), p. 92.

105   "was as great as anybody": April, p. 14.
105   "never let his notion": Ibid., p. 15.
105   "I think that all the reporters": Ibid., p. 16.
105   "Personally": Ibid., p. 17.
106   "rescued": Ibid.
106   "a million-word book": WP, p. 116.
106   "Divine had been aided": Ibid., p. 115.
108   "Verinda is a very tall": 6/20/36, p. 23.
109   "acts of skill": 9/26, p. 18.
109   "He has to make sure": Ibid.
110   " 'Hymie is a tummeler' ": JB, p. 16.
110   "Hymie has been around": Ibid., p. 17.
110   "This is the really critical phase": Ibid., p. 18.
111   "best-known prizefight second": BWICF, p. 95.
112   "a bundle . . . wax": Ibid., p. 94.
112   "I like the country . . . spot": Ibid., p. 104.
112   "Being associated . . . hoodlum": Ibid., p. 103.
112   "a passion for frankfurters": Ibid., p. 102.
112   "Shortly after Whitey's graduation": Ibid.
113   "Louis trained": TBI, p. 28.
113   "high-toned language": BWICF, p. 113.
113   "I have always loved": Ibid., pp. 113–114.
113   Shuberts: TBI, pp. 126–167.
113   "spectacular pseudo-Gallic": 5/15/37, p. 27.
114   "a rehearsal": Ibid.
114   " 'Get out of here' ": Ibid.
114   "the profession": 7/24, p. 20.
114   "The average bookmaker": Ibid.
115   Tim Mara: TBI, pp. 99–112.
115   "from an artistic": TBI, p. 254.
115   "It is as hard": 4/15/39, p. 25.
116   "It seemed to me": BWICF, pp. 56–57.
116   "rather good": Ibid., p. 60.
117   "There never were": Ibid., pp. 60–61.
117   "The restaurant": Ibid., p. 62.
118   "What do you expect": Ibid., p. 63.
118   "The cook": Ibid.
120   "Defoe did not achieve": Foreward to *A Journal of the Plague Year* (New York: New American Library, Signet [paper], 1960), p. viii.

121   "Crash Bernstein": 12/26, p. 7.
122   "Although she was angry": Ms., p. 21.
126   "I attracted the assignment": *Nieman Reports*, April 1959, p. 16.

LIEBLING AT WAR

127   "Sucking back four bloody oaths": RBTP, p. 20.
127   "From the manner": Ibid., p. 22.
128   "national lupanar": Ibid., pp. 23–24.
129   "I knew very little": Ibid., p. 18.
129   "Letter from Paris": 11/4/39, pp. 38–39.
129   "They circulate": Ibid., p. 39.
130   profile of General Gamelin: 5/11/40, pp. 24–27; 5/18/40, pp. 22–26.
134   "One Sunday": pp. 36–37.
135   "I don't want": pp. 37–38.
136   "Frau Weinmann and the Third Reich": BWICF, pp. 161–172.
137   "The new phase": 5/18/40, pp. 36–40.
139   "From a military standpoint": RBTP, p. 91.
139   "His dispatches": Ibid., p. 96.
140   "There was a climate . . . catastrophe": Ibid., p. 99.
140   "Getting off the plane": Ibid., p. 112.
141   "I don't feel": Ibid., p. 115.
141   "You forget": Ibid., p. 114.
141   "The Jollity Building": TBI, pp. 40–86.
141   "What was perhaps": Ibid., p. 85.
142   profile of Roy Howard: Ibid., pp. 184–252.
142   "Right from the start": Ibid., p. 206.
142   "was losing a million": Ibid., p. 217.
143   "I am not sure": RBTP, p. 119.
143   "PROPAGANDA": May 1941.
145   *New Yorker* piece: "Due Credit to Hull," 2/14/42, pp. 38–48.
145   "V for Victory" campaign: "Colonel Britton and the Rhythm," 10/4/41, pp. 40–51.
146   "The Colonel of the Ship": 5/2/42, pp. 38–49.
146   "with a blarneying facility": "The Omnibus Diplomat," 6/6/42, p. 23.
146   "the best leg man": Ibid., p. 22.
146   "The eight governments": Ibid.
147   "You know, old sport": Ibid., p. 25.

148   "I turned in early": RBTP, pp. 182–183.
148   "to feel more curious . . . Atlantic": Ibid., p. 165.
148   "Pearl Harbor had left": Ibid., p. 205.
149   "The Rolling Umpty-Seventh": 12/5/42, pp. 52–66; 12/12/42, pp. 50–64.
150   "getting the feel": RBTP, p. 214.
150   "Letter from Oran": 12/19/42, pp. 38–40.
150   "Letter from Algiers": 1/16/43, pp. 49–50.
150   "reactionary to an extent": RBTP, p. 218.
150   "There was in truth": Ibid., p. 219.
151   "examples of Jewish bad taste": Ibid., p. 225.
151   "didn't know what to make": Ibid.
151   *New Yorker* "letter": pp. 49–50.
151   "Probably no one": p. 50.
152   "Up to here": RBTP, p. 238.
152   "I hope you don't mind": Ibid., p. 239.
153   "I never heard any more": Ibid., p. 250.
154   "I took the lid off": Ibid., pp. 262–263.
155   "sensing when to hop": "Guerrilla from Erie, Pa.," 2/13/43, p. 22.
155   "The situation": Ibid., p. 26.
155   "shrewdness and dash": "Find 'Em, Fix 'Em and Fight 'Em," I, 4/24/43, p. 24.
155   "throw himself into": Ibid., p. 22.
155n   "They advance hesitatingly": Ibid., II, 5/1/43, p. 27.
157   "The Foamy Fields": RBTP, pp. 239–278.
158   "When I walk": Mollie, pp. 40–41.
158   "Suppose . . . that the corpse": Ibid., p. 41.
159   "out of an old-fashioned boy's book": Ibid., p. 42.
160   "My notion": Ibid., p. 135.
160   "sordid guerrilla": Ibid.
161   "I am still waiting": 3/5/44.
161   "not as exciting": Ibid.
161   "Run, Run, Run, Run": Mollie, pp. 136–152.
162   "time-killing expedient": Ibid., p. 152.
162   "Notes from the Kidnap House": Ibid., p. 153–162.
163   It "made me feel . . . vessel": Ibid., p. 179.
163   "Cross-Channel Trip": Ibid., pp. 165–203.
163   "Just about then": Ibid., pp. 182–184.
166   "Everybody . . . examined": Ibid., p. 165.

167   "brothel called La Feria: Ibid., p. 209.
168   "street fighting": NR, pp. 108–109.
169   "In my mind": Ibid., p. 178.
169   "I was consequently": Ibid., p. 180.
170   "an Old Black Jove": Ibid., p. 183..
170   "our 1937-or-so Chevrolet": Ibid., pp. 186–187.
170   "in a mood of modified rapture": Ibid., p. 187.
171   "dashing cortege": Ibid., p. 237.
172   "as big as an eiderdown": Ibid., p. 241.
172   "It was the only trophy": Ibid., pp. 241–242.
172   "Mlle. Yvonne": Ibid., p. 243.
173   He visited a village: "The Events at Comblanchien—November, 1944," Ibid., pp. 257–285.
173   "I know that it is socially acceptable": p. ix.

WAYWARD PRESSMAN

177   "foreign news": WP, p. 116.
177   "mosaic of what life must be": Mollie, p. 152.
177   "Some of my reactions": WP, p. 117.
177   "some pretty hard socks": Ibid.
177   Liebling did his first column: 5/19; WP, pp. 119–129.
178   "a chronic, incurable": TP, p. 120.
178   "There are three kinds": Ibid., p. 317.
179   "The M.B.I.": 1/3/48; TP, pp. 178–186.
179   "A couple of months ago": Ibid., p. 178.
179   " 'Over some protests' ": Ibid., p. 180.
179   "The story of the M.B.I.'s creation": Ibid., p. 186.
179   "fine-mesh news net": Ibid.
180   a second column: 2/7/48.
180   "What impresses": TP, p. 192.
181   "The Great Gouamba": 12/7/46.
181   "the inordinate longing": TP, p. 141.
181   "QUEENS . . . HOURLY": Ibid., pp. 142–143, 147.
183   "newspaper strike: "No Papers," WP, pp. 134–149.
183   "the effect was the same": WP, p. 136.
183   "Sometimes news disappears": Ibid., note 2.
183   "supplementing them": Ibid., p. 137.
183   "Obits": 1/19.
183   "to indicate that Dreisers": WP, p. 146.

183   "papers within papers": 3/30/46; WP, pp. 155–166.

184   In one column: "Mayor into Columnist," 2/23/46; WP, pp. 147–154.

184   "The Talk of the Town": 40/20/46, pp. 22–23.

187   "Department of Amplification": 5/4, p. 99.

187   *Top Secret:* 4/20/46, pp. 101–105.

187   Harry Butcher: *My Three Years with Eisenhower*, 4/27/46, pp. 80–86.

187   "landlocked naval officer . . . title page": Ibid., p. 80.

188   effect of war stress: *Men Under Stress*, by Roy R. Grinker and John R. Spiegel, 5/18/46, pp. 100–106.

188   Matthew Josephson: *Stendhal: A Biography*, 10/19/46. pp. 126–132.

188   Joseph Medill Patterson: "Mamie and Mr. O'Donnell Carry On," 6/8/46; WP, pp. 167–174.

188   cross-country drive: "And the Sun Stood Still," 8/3/46; WP, pp. 175–182.

188   "Potomac city": Ibid., p. 176.

188   "the doughty little coupe": Ibid., p. 177.

188   "How wet was that?": Ibid.

188   "Antepenultimatum": 7/7/46; WP, pp. 191–196.

188   "conspicuously civilized": Ibid., p. 191.

188   "we had left": Ibid., pp. 191–192.

189   "The Scribes of Destiny": 9/28/46; WP, pp. 197–205.

189   "Newspaper people": Ibid., p. 197.

189   "Not since Ellsworth Vines": Ibid., p. 202.

190   he hopped to the theater: 12/46, pp. 136, 201–202, 204, 209.

190   *All the King's Men:* 1/47, pp. 68, 205–210.

190   *American Racing Manual:* 8/47, pp. 40, 100.

190   *An Ernie Pyle Album:* 5/47, pp. 50, 164–168.

190   "The Superfluous Obbligato": 3/47, pp. 48, 139–140.

190   "A belief": Ibid., p. 139.

190   "Once, while I was at Dartmouth": Ibid., p. 140.

191   "Mr. Existential Brooks": pp. 48–49.

191   "Sartre's existentialism": Ibid., p. 48

192   "stubby, applecheeked little man": Ibid.

192   "friend and sparring partner . . . way": Ibid.

192   "father, or at least the foster-father": Ibid.

192   "I think of a clean-shaven American": Ibid., p. 49.

193   "Camus and I agree": Ibid.

193   "Brooks": Ibid.

196   In August: 8/16/47; MRH, pp. 19–27.

197   "the newspapers": Ibid., p. 22.

197   A month later: 9/6/47; MRH, pp. 29–38.

197   "that primarily express . . . TITO": Ibid., p. 29.

197   "PR FIGHT": Ibid., p. 30.

197   "GREEN": Ibid., p. 32.

197   "how anybody could slug": Ibid., p. 33.

198   "ATOM ROLE": Ibid., p. 34.

198   cold war restrictions: MRH, pp. 39–46.

199   press bias: 10/18/47; TP, pp. 147–156.

199   anti-labor bias: MRH, pp. 57–63.

199   press reaction: Ibid., pp. 65–73.

199   "one of those cascades": Ibid., pp. 70–71.

200   "Horsefeathers": 11/22/47: TP, pp. 127–138.

200   "there is no concept": Ibid., p. 127.

200   Princess Elizabeth: 12/6/47; MRH, pp. 85–91.

200   two indulgent looks: 4/10/48; MRH, pp. 109–116.

200   resistance press: 3/19/49; MRH, pp. 145–157.

200   "made me feel": p. 225.

200   "Wayward Press" piece: 10/4/47; MRH, pp. 129–143.

200   Oslo: 5/22/48, pp. 63–75.

201   three-part article: "Reunion with a Tanker," I, 1/22/49, pp. 30–43; II, 1/29/49, pp. 29–41; III, 2/5/49, pp. 35–51.

201   "Wayward Press" column: MRH, pp. 172–179.

201   "long, dreary exhibition . . . deteckative": Ibid., pp. 175–176.

201   "character murder": Ibid., p. 178.

201   "If it should be argued": Ibid., p. 179.

205   The next week: 9/4/48; MRH, pp. 183–190.

205   October 23, 1948: Ibid., pp. 199–207.

205   November 13, 1948: Ibid., pp. 217–227.

205   "the tangled story": Ibid., p. 222.

205   "For a person": Ibid., p. 225.

206   July 23, 1949: TP, pp. 197–208.

206   "This sort of thing": Ibid., p. 208.

207   retrospective amplifications: Ibid., pp. 208–217.

208   "newspapers": Ibid., p. 212.

209   "Toward a One-Paper Town": 2/18/49; TP, pp. 45–54.

209   "I think the *Star*": Ibid., p. 50.

209   "coverage": 6/11/49, pp. 86–93.

209   *La Nausée:* 4/30/49, pp. 102–106.
209   "100,000—Count 'Em—1,000": pp. 64–70.
209   "Calmly handled": Ibid., p. 64.
209   "alarmed . . . excited": Ibid., p. 67.
210   "The *Times* report": Ibid., p. 70.
210   In late February: *New York Times Book Review,* 2/27/49, p. 7.
210   "This is an angry piece": 3/6/49, p. 2.
210   "The one portion": p. 21.
212   "You wouldn't like it": TP, p. 525.

By Way of Chicago

214   "lingering . . . little": 4/29/50, p. 86.
215   "Slot Machines and Repose": Ibid., pp. 86–95.
215   "Once, walking": Ibid., p. 86.
215   "all froth": Ibid.
215   "It was at the Toscano": Ibid., pp. 90–91.
221   "Action in the Desert": 5/13/50, pp. 106–113.
221   "great editor": p. 17.
221   "His great demand": p. 16.
222   "Dead Game": 4/1/50, pp. 35–45.
222   "very interesting": A copy of Ross's notes on Liebling's copy for 1949–50 has been added to the Liebling papers at Cornell.
222   the final text: 4/1/50, p. 35.
222   "major general, retired": Ibid.
223   "Neate seemed": William Hazlitt, *Collected Works.*
223   "the red was blinked": pp. 42–43.
224   "Abe Lincoln in Springfield": 6/24/50, pp. 29–48.
225   Indianapolis 500: 6/10/50, pp. 52–69.
225   This series: 1/7/50; TP, pp. 234–243. 1/14/50, pp. 68–74. 1/21/50, pp. 54–65. 3/25/50; TP, pp. 223–233.
225   "Colonel Robert Rutherford McCormick": 1/14/50, p. 68.
226   "The Loop": p. 8.
226   "It is a miasmic influence": p. 59.
226   "various . . . malaria": p. 32.
226   "so we could wander": p. 33.
226   "The reader who stays"; p. 71.
226   "At every party": p. 81.
226   "Citizens": p. 138.
226   "Chicagoans": p. 143.

228   "So this isn't": SC, p. ix.

229   "The Bank Across the Street": 12/23/50, pp. 47–50.

229   Once, he quoted her: SC, pp. 63–64.

SWEET SCIENTIST

230   "The Bank Across the Street": 12/23/50, p. 47.

235   Stendhal: 7/22/50, p. 64.

239   "I got a French decoration": BM, p. 61.

241   "unsorted, unfiled": 1/11/64, p. 107.

241   "It was in June": SS, p. 6.

242   "I had written": Ibid.

242   "the apogee": TP. p. 287.

242   April 1951: 4/7/51; TP, pp. 272–277.

243   "friends in Scientific circles": Ibid., p. 6.

244   "pitiful . . . rewarding": Ibid.

244   "Egan": Ibid., pp. 8–9, 10.

245   "Egan enjoyed": John Ford, in the introduction to his Folio Society *Boxiana* (London).

245   "The Fight": Ibid.

246   "Moore, jabbing": SS, p. 212.

246   "pageant scenes"; Ibid., p. 11.

246   "Cockney characters": Ibid.

246   "a gift to Dickens": Ibid.

246   "instructive conversations": Ibid., p. 183.

247   "He was wearing": Ibid.

248   "I knew all the members": Ibid., p. 292.

248   "I could be sure": Ibid., p. 71.

250n   With Proustian care, he records: Ibid., p. 304.

250   a bantamweight fighter" 2/9/52, pp. 65–75.

251   "When the kids": Ibid., p. 65.

252   various *New Yorker* pieces: "Yea Verily," I, 9/13/52; II, 9/20/52; III, 9/27/52.

253   "It was a life": HR, p. 221.

254   "Mr. O'Malley": Ibid., pp. 54–56.

255   "The Dog in the Millpond": 10/9, pp. 117–125.

258   "Out Among the Lamisters": 3/27/54, pp. 71–86.

258   most of the first part: 4/3/54, pp. 35–53.

259   "wide between the eyes": 4/10/54, p. 82.

259   "I felt a bit blue": Ibid.

259   "Everybody has trouble": Ibid., p. 86.
259   His chronicle ran: I, 1/1/55, pp. 25–41; II, 1/8/55, pp. 33–61; III, 1/15/55, pp. 32–69; IV, 1/22/55, pp. 37–73.
260   " 'And what will happen' ": 4/10/54, p. 86.

FAR-FLUNG CORRESPONDENT

264   June 18, 1955: pp. 66–79.
264   "traveling inside . . . war": Ibid., p. 66.
264   "One Saturday morning": Ibid., pp. 66–67.
265   "Imbibition": Ibid., p. 75.
265   "not because he thought": Preface to *The Best of A. J. Liebling,* edited by William Cole (London: Methuen, 1965), p. 13.
266   "A Stranger in New York": 12/8/56, pp. 165–175. The passage quoted appears on p. 165.
267   "A New Yorker's Derby"; 5/29/55.
267   "For a number of years now": 9/4/55.
268   " 'Eat more' ": *Nation.* 10/7/78, p. 349.
268   "Lonely in London": Ibid., p. 351.
269   *The Sweet Science:* pp. 287–306.
269   "The Case of the Scattered Dutchman": 9/24/55, pp. 50–111.
270   "The University of Eighth Avenue": I, 12/5/55, pp. 32–42; II, 12/12/55, pp. 33–34, 46–52.
270   "No sane man": BM, p. 87.
270   "like a mental hospital": Ibid., pp. 88–89.
271   "ruinously expensive": Ibid., p. 89.
271   *The Quiet American:* Cole, pp. 307–313.
271   "make his quiet American . . . heterosexual": Ibid., p. 307.
272   "not a Hemingway hero . . . manuscripts": Ibid., p. 308.
272   "part of the ritual": Ibid.
272   "between calling": Ibid., p. 313.
272   "Liebling sailed blithely": *Nation,* 10/7/78, p. 351.
273   account of a fight night: 6/9/56, pp. 56–87.
273   "On the floor": Ibid., p. 56.
277   "The Old Flame," lines 32–39, in *For the Union Dead* (New York: Farrar, Straus & Giroux, 1964), p. 6.
277   "Heidelberry braids": Robert Lowell, "Jean Stafford, A Letter," lines 4–5, from *Day by Day* (New York: Farrar, Straus & Giroux, 1977), p. 29.
278   one dispatch to *The New Yorker:* 11/3/56, pp. 156–173.

278   "Joyeuses": 9/22/56.
278   "We had a hell of a time": Ibid.
281   dispatch from Naples: 12/1/56, pp. 210–216; the passage quoted is on p. 210.
281   "The good feeling": Ibid., p. 216.
283   "I want you to write": 12/13/56.
283   "My own conjugal status": 12/27/56.
284   "feast discreetly": 2/10/57.
284   "from its navel . . . there": Letter to Stafford, 2/23/57.
285   two pieces on Gaza: 3/16/57, pp. 128–134; 3/30/57, pp. 115–127.
285   "a possible key": 3/30/57, p. 117.
286   "I felt as I used to feel": 8/3/57, p. 33.
286   "Along the Visa Via": I, 8/9/58, pp. 30–57; II, 8/16/58, pp. 30–67; III, 8/23/58, pp. 28–65.
287   "I was an American journalist": Ibid., I, p. 56.
287   "If you don't believe": Ibid., p. 57.
287   "in that sense": Ibid., II, p. 30.
287   "I was beginning to think": Ibid., p. 66.
288   "At about four": Ibid., III, p. 65.
288   "The one piece he produced": 9/14/57, pp. 100–121.

TWILIGHT LANDSCAPES

290   "Jean Stafford is traveling": 11/12/57.
290   March 8, 1958: pp. 134–139.
290   public kissing: 3/28/58, p. 23.
290   Mideast politics: 7/26/58, p. 15.
290   new carpentry: 5/10/58, p. 29.
290   statue of Richard Strauss: 6/14/58, p. 23.
290   July 5, 1958: pp. 13–14.
291   "federal troops": Ibid., p. 13.
291   "On May 7": Ibid., p. 14.
291   "Spring is for poets": 7/6/58, p. 21.
292   Vassar: A tape of the lecture is with the Liebling papers at Cornell.
294   "If the quay": NR, p. 21.
295   "Vouilly": NR, pp. 81–82.
296   "We drove": NR, pp. 82–83.
297   ten-page letter: 9/11/58.
301   "Dispatches": EL, pp. 16–17 (pages from British edition).

302   "He would shake": Ibid., p. 25.

302   " 'I think there's such a thing' ": Ibid., pp. 29–30.

303   "one of those automobile accidents": Ibid., p. 199.

304   "Memoirs of a Feeder in France": I, 4/11/59; II, 4/18/59; III, 4/25/59; IV, 5/2/59. Also see *Vogue*, 9/15/62.

304   "one of the last": BM, p. 11.

304   "dazzle his juniors": Ibid., p. 12.

305   "began . . . abstinence": Ibid., p. 34.

305   "limp, drooping mustache": Ibid., p. 152.

307   "the indispensable roadwork": Ibid., p. 34.

308   "running through the country": Letter to Joe and Therese Mitchell, 10/1/59.

308   "when she got off": Ibid.

308   *Observer* work: Four articles: 9/13/59, p. 1; 9/20/59, p. 6; 9/27/59, pp. 10–11; 10/4/59, p. 8.

309   obituary: 1/16/60, pp. 23–24.

309   U-2 scandal: 5/21/60; TP, pp. 379–387.

309   "This story": Comment appended to the Powers piece when it was reprinted in TP, p. 388.

310   Eganesque flair: 7/9/60, pp. 66–80. The passage quoted is on p. 79.

311   wrote the Guedenets: 7/27/60.

311   "what newspapers called pigheaded": 8/20/60; TP, pp. 157–169.

311   He filed three times: 9/10/60, pp. 85–98; 9/17/60, pp. 186–196; 9/24/60, pp. 152–161.

311   "Tables set out": 9/10/60, pp. 94–95.

312   wrote Stafford: 9/10/60, pp. 92, 95.

312   Patterson-Johansson fight: 3/25/61, pp. 147–160.

312   Gagarin: 4/29/61; TP, pp. 401–407.

312   "I would remind": Ibid., pp. 406–407.

313   Archie Moore: 6/24/61, pp. 33–51.

313   Hemingway: 7/15/61, p. 18.

313   *Stephen Crane: Letters:* 8/5/61, pp. 48–72.

314   "The letters clearly show us": Ibid., p. 48.

314   "At the top of his fame": Ibid., p. 53.

314   " 'I struggle' ": Ibid., p. 72.

314   *Vogue:* "What Is Fascination?" pp. 206–207.

316   Cassius Clay: 3/3/62, pp. 104–117. Quoted passage is on p. 104.

316   five more prize fights: 7/7/62; Cole, pp. 279–284. 10/6/62, pp. 103–110. 11/10/62, pp. 211–233. 3/30/63, pp. 122–142. 8/10/63, pp. 62–69.

316   newspaper strike: 1/12/63; 1/26/63; 3/16/63; 4/13/63; all in TP, pp. 75–116.

316   He summarized: TP, pp. 104–116.

317   "I doff my bowler": Ibid., p. 116.

317   *rascasse:* 10/27/62, pp. 189–202.

317   *"Paysage de Crépuscule":* 1/11/64, pp. 95–106.

317   "the astrologo-nutritionist": Ibid., p. 95.

317   "stiff as a board": Ibid., p. 106.

317   "Now, when I hear": Ibid.

317   *Notebooks:* 2/8/64, pp. 128–138.

318   "remarkably pure": Ibid., p. 134.

Index